explorer

CHINA

Christopher Knowles

AA Publishing

Essential

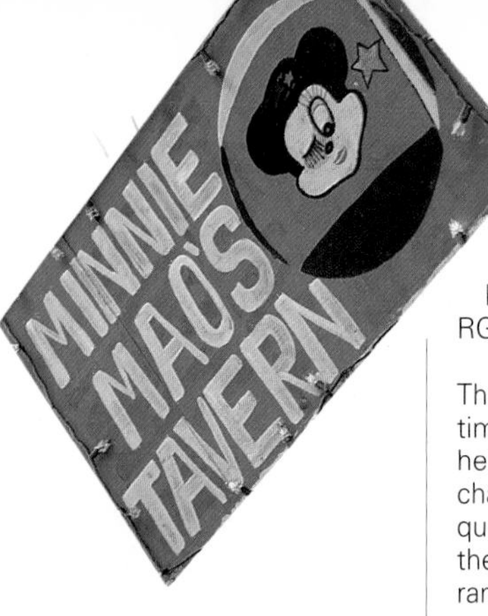

Written by Christopher Knowles
Original photography by Ingrid Morejohn
Edited, designed and produced by AA Publishing
Maps © The Automobile Association 1995
Distributed in the United Kingdom by AA Publishing, Norfolk House, Priestley Road, Basingstoke, Hampshire, RG24 9 NY

A CIP catalogue record for this book is available from the British Library.

ISBN 0 7495 1025 0

Published by AA Publishing (a trading name of Automobile Association Developments Limited, whose registered office is Norfolk House, Priestley Road, Basingstoke, Hampshire RG24 9NY. Registered number 1878835).

Origination by Fotographics Ltd
Printed and bound in Italy by Printers SRL, Trento

Cover picture: Detail, Forbidden City, Beijing
Page 3: Detail, Imperial Wall, Beijing
Page 4: Detail, Forbidden City, Beijing
Page 5: Nine Dragon Screen, Beihai Park
Pages 6–7 (top): Cheung Chau Bun Festival, Hong Kong
Page 6 (bottom): Autumn harvesting in the Datong area
Page 7 (bottom): Beijing traffic
Page 9: Sanya Harbour, Hainan Island
Page 29: Terracotta Army, Xi'an
Pages 128–9: Jiayuguan Fort
Page 166: Nanjing Road, Shanghai
Page 255: Rickshaw drivers
Page 273: Fragrant Hills Hotel, Beijing

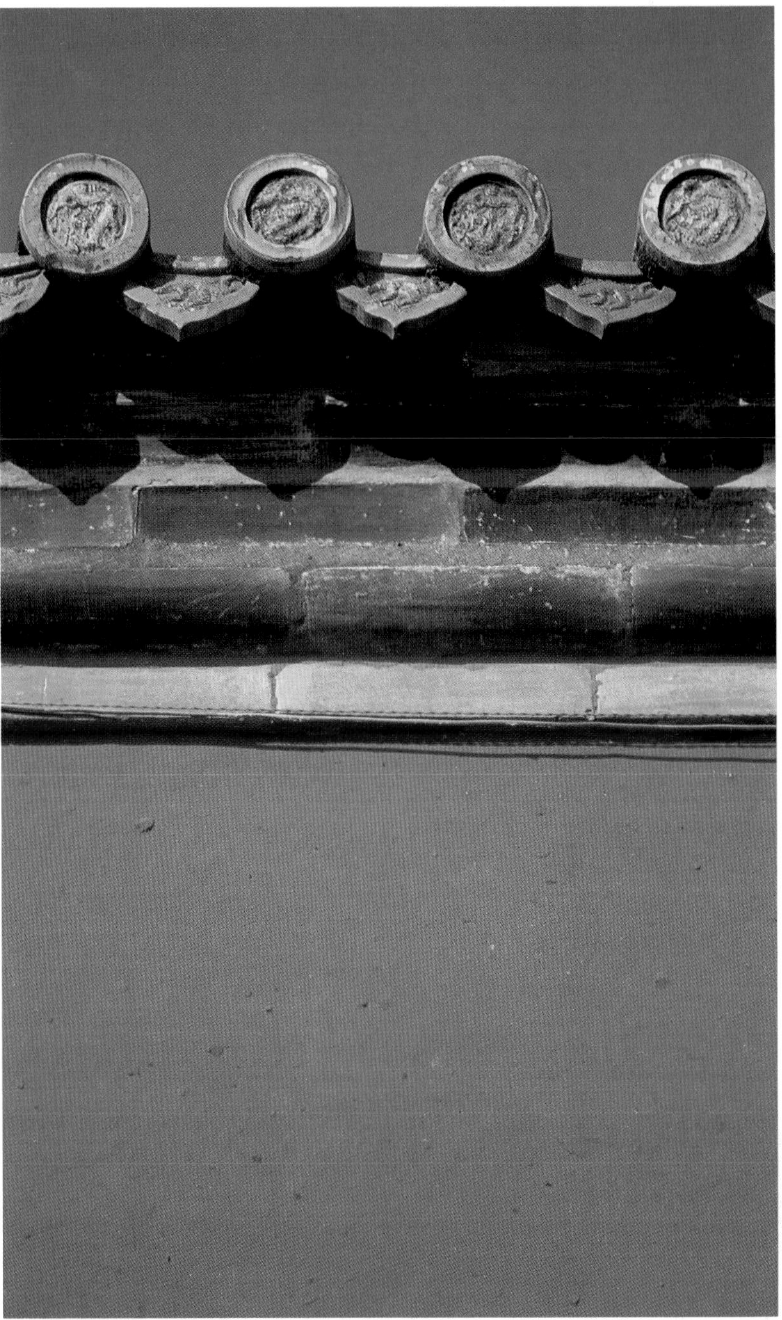

Christopher Knowles has led dozens of tours in China, and since his first visit in 1981 has witnessed many changes there. His travels have taken him all over the world and he has written guide books on Shanghai, Moscow & St Petersburg and Tuscany.

How to use this book

This book is divided into five main sections:

- ❑ Section 1:
  China Is
  discusses aspects of life and living today, from communism to streetlife

- ❑ Section 2:
  China Was
  places the country in its historical context and explores those past events whose influences are felt to this day

- ❑ Section 3:
  A to Z Section
  covers places to visit, with suggested walks. Within this section fall the Focus-on articles, which consider a variety of topics in greater detail

- ❑ Section 4:
  Travel Facts
  contains the strictly practical information that is vital for a successful trip

- ❑ Section 5:
  Hotels and Restaurants
  lists recommended establishments in China, giving a brief description of what they offer

How to use the star rating
Most places described in this book have been given a separate rating:

▶▶▶ **Do not miss**

▶▶ **Highly recommended**

▶ **Worth seeing**

Not essential viewing

Map references
To make the location of a particular place easier to find, every main entry in this book is given a map reference, such as 176B3. The first number (176) indicates the page on which the map can be found; the letter (B) and the second number (3) pinpoint the square in which the main entry is located. The maps on the inside front cover and inside back cover are referred to as IFC and IBC respectively.

Note on spellings
As a general rule, the official romanisation system, *pinyin* (see page 271), has been used in this book. However, a few exceptions have been made where alternative, more familiar names have been adopted. In such cases both forms are given in the Index.
The geographic legend on page 271 gives the English translations for terms used on the maps.

Contents

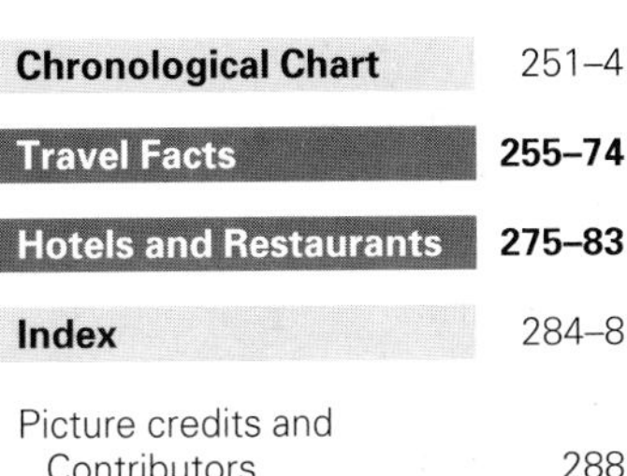

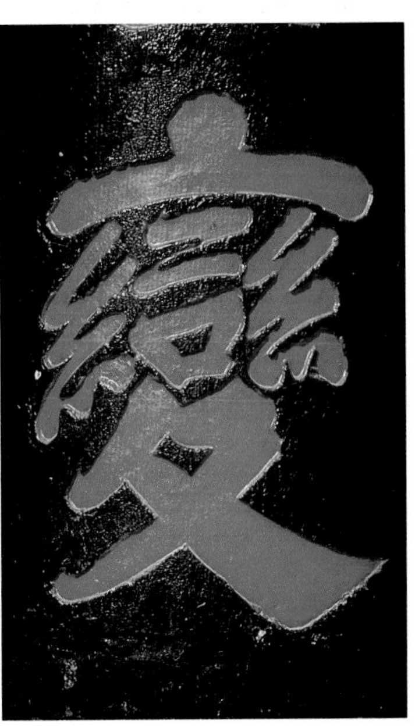

Quick reference

This quick-reference guide highlights the elements of the book you will use most often: the maps; the introductory features; the Focus-on articles; the walks.

Maps and plans

China Is

China Was

Focus on

Walks

Cycle rides

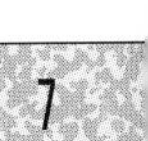

River cruise

Travel Facts

Zhu Xiao Ming
Zhu Xiao Ming was born in Beijing in 1956, the daughter of a high-ranking military officer. Although she spent some time herself in the People's Liberation Army (teaching tank technology), she eventually became an interpreter and tour guide. She is currently working in tourism in Britain.

My China

by Zhu Xiao Ming

I grew up in Beijing. When I go back there now, it is hard to believe that this is the same city that I knew as a child, growing up in the years of the Cultural Revolution. Then, political propaganda predominated and everybody was thrown into the political movement regardless of background or age. Not quite understanding, at the age of ten, what the purpose of the movement was, I felt it was all-powerful, and that Mao was such a hero (at least, everyone said he was) that no one could possibly be excluded from it. Ideologically, we were taught to defend the motherland against revisionism and capitalist corruption, and to regard the outside world as alien and undesirable. Some of my childish memories are not pleasant.

Although politically China is still very far from being a free country (Westerners have to understand that in a country as old as China change takes time), it is fascinating to see the progress that has been made. But some things stay reassuringly the same. Going home to China still means, above all, constant noise and movement in the streets and in the home. The family, too – and the enjoyment of good food – remain central to Chinese life; the Chinese, as visitors will find, show their hospitality by giving their guests feasts, offering them the best food in the house. Such simple homeliness is, in spite of all, the best of my China.

Hua Lei
Born in Shanghai and brought up in Beijing, Hua Lei studied architecture at Tianjin University and taught at Tongji University, Shanghai, for five years before going to Cambridge, England. He studied and worked as an architect for four years in England before returning to Shanghai to set up his own architects firm in 1993.

My China

by Hua Lei

I was born in Shanghai, but my soul belongs to Beijing. My Beijing is in the densely populated alleyways that form an intricate lace between the city's main roads. Here the close-knit lifestyle has not changed for centuries. A winter backdrop suits those alleyways best, cold grey walls against a clear blue sky, the pale sunlight shining thinly through; in the early morning, bundled in many layers, neighbours chat over fried dough-sticks, and in the evening their courtyard homes are steamy and warm, heated by a central stove. In the rush of modernisation, many alleyways have been destroyed, but the character of Beijing, cold and harsh on the outside yet warm and friendly inside, is perpetuated in the simple, honest natures of its people.

Shanghai is *yang* to Beijing's *yin*, a bustling town of merchants, businessmen and indefatigable shoppers, whose mercantile natures have not been repressed by 40 years of socialism. I like to think of the city in summer, when the characteristic tree-lined boulevards offer shade against the insufferable heat and humidity. Neglected by the central government since liberation, the imposing colonial architecture has gone to seed, but the elegance and sophistication lives on in the people of Shanghai. Quick to take their chances in the economic reforms, they are restoring old buildings to their former glory and putting up new ones in every available space. Now Europeans, Americans, and emigré Chinese like myself are arriving in droves to explore Shanghai's newly released riches, and make it once more the attractive, cosmopolitan city it originally was.

CHINA IS

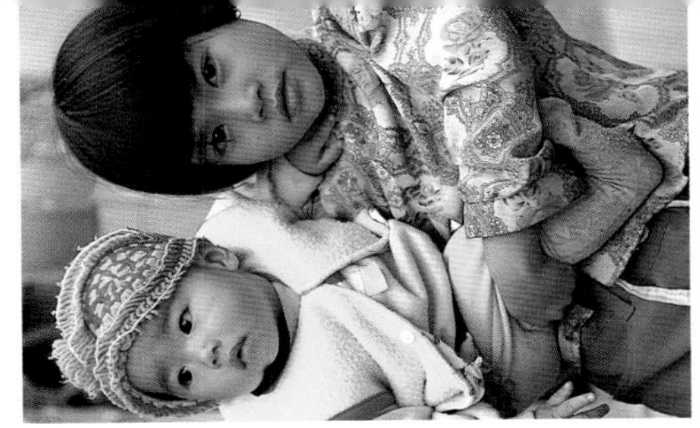

CHINA IS *The past*

■ Nowhere in the world is the past more woven into the present than in China and no other country can boast the sense of continuity that has been bred into the Chinese people over at least three thousand years of continuous civilisation.....■

Pressure of history Chinese history has been a source of great strength and resilience in difficult times. Perhaps no other country could have survived such a cataclysmic event as the Cultural Revolution only to become one of the world's fastest growing economies a mere 20 years on. In few other countries, on the other hand, would the Cultural Revolution have occurred in the first place. The pressure to do as your forefathers have done and conform to ancient (and frequently outmoded) ideas, is very great indeed in China. Occasionally it becomes too much for some parts of society to bear. The stranglehold exerted by the past so frustrated the young people of China in the 1960s that they were easily mobilised by Mao, assisting in his radical but ultimately futile attempt to sweep away all reminders of the past and start all over again. Ironically, the communism that Mao espoused has proved to be little more than the former imperial system under a new name.

Inflexibility Sometimes it seems that age-old habits are actually fused into the genes of the Chinese, so automatic are they, and so widespread. One example of this is always giving the answer that the listener wants to hear. For more worldly Chinese this is frustrating, because these habits seem almost impossible to break.

At its best Chinese conservatism, a determination not to change merely for change's sake, combined with a belief in the overriding power of precedent, is admirable; at other times it is tiresome, as when agreement is reached to do something in one way only to find that ultimately the old way prevails.

Outside influence In most civilised societies the past is manifested in tangible remains, and, where they survive, this is also true of China – for even in the case of contemporary art and architecture the tendency is always to evoke the past. Yet the material residue from Chinese history is less important than the impact that the past has had on the Chinese mind. Chinese history is remarkable for the fact that outside influences have had almost no effect on the national psyche. Without an appreciation of this fundamental fact, it is impossible for the visitor to understand modern China.

❑ 'Our nation has a great responsibility...to enrich our culture with Western culture, and to enrich Western culture with our culture, so that they may fuse into a new culture.' – Liang Qichao, *Impressions From My European Journey*, 1919 ❑

Of the many issues facing the Chinese today, the most contentious is the battle between old and new: progress, in the modern Western understanding of the word, is seen in some quarters as an admission of defeat. The encroachment of Western values, for so long resisted, is considered as a worrying phenomenon: for old communists, veterans of the Long March (a few of whom are still involved in the running of the country) it must sometimes seem that the values they fought for are being replaced by the free-for-all capitalist values that they had sought so hard to suppress.

Traditional courtyard houses in Beijing, backed by high-rise flats

The tiger awakes On several occasions this century, when it seemed China was about to alter course, she was in fact merely retrimming her sails. Now, change seems more certain; the challenge is to recover the best of the past and marry it to the realities of the modern world.

Opposite (top) and below: villagers in Yunnan air their effigies of local gods at Chinese New Year

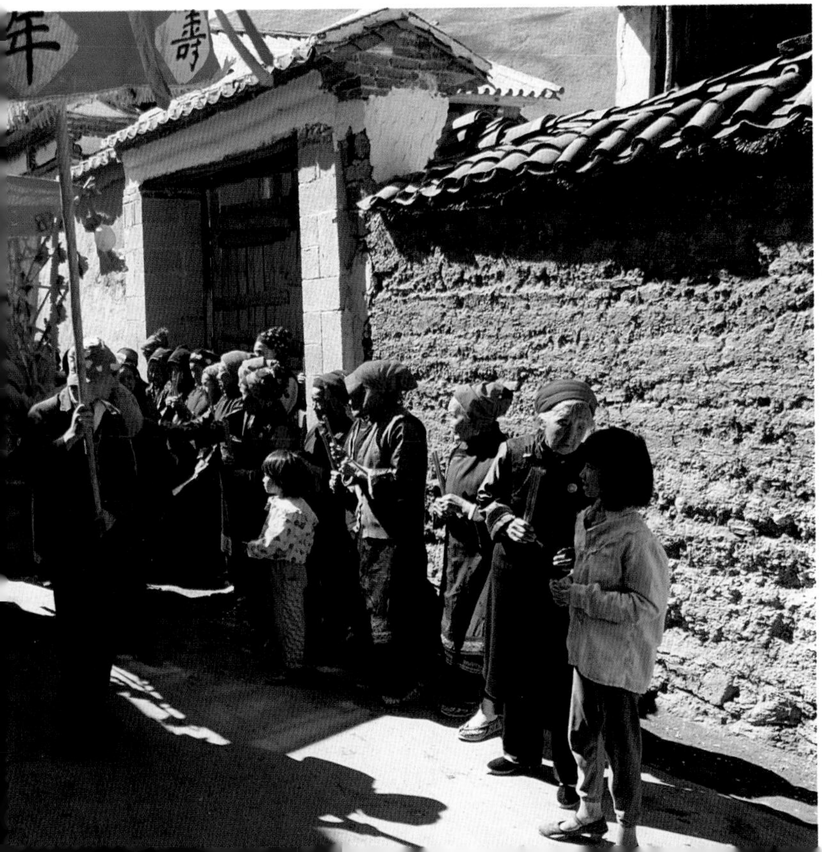

The Chinese way of life is distinctive in many subtle ways. Western notions of the centrality of the self are alien to many Chinese, who see themselves in relation to family, community and the past, rather than as entirely free agents.....

Family The most important ingredient in Chinese society is the family, an institution whose strength has been sorely tested by events in recent decades when, under Mao, children were encouraged to report the 'misdemeanours' of their parents and close relatives. Yet it was not long ago that most marriages were arranged by parents or by a professional matchmaker, and in remoter areas these practices have continued unchecked; even in major cities the matchmaker has recently made an unexpected comeback. Weddings are big affairs and huge sums, out of all proportion to income, are spent on the celebrations. Once married, the bride customarily moves in with her parents-in-law, at least until the new couple can secure their own flat.

The idea of bachelorhood is practically unknown among the Chinese

A member of the matriarchal Naxi people sits holding his grandson

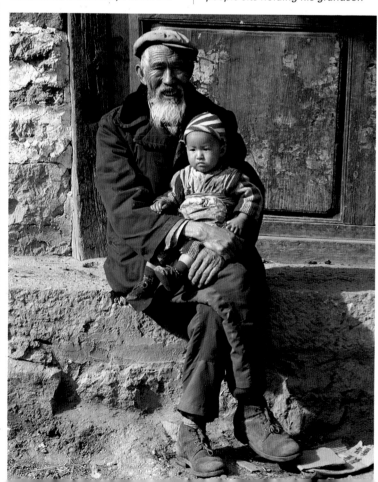

because children are considered essential to continuing the family line and for providing a means of support in old age. In this respect, the Cultural Revolution's emphasis on the enforced denunciation of relatives has only led to a subsequent resurgence of family loyalty, as well as to the pain of collective guilt.

❑ The Chinese have traditionally deferred to the elderly because, it is thought, old age brings wisdom. For this reason, the government has, until recently, consisted largely of old men. This is another frustration for many Chinese, for youth is admired, but only in the most patronising way. ❑

The government's policy of one child per family (designed to alleviate the population problem) has led to the rise of a generation of 'little emperors', for whom the absence of siblings has meant unbridled adulation. It has also brought a certain lack of confidence because a large family meant security and influence. In the past you could count on *guanxi*, that is, obtaining favours, jobs, contracts or gifts from your relatives – an essential feature of Chinese life that might perhaps be thought of, by the purer mind, as corruption.

Losing face Romantic love is not a Chinese notion. Pragmatism is the order of the day though the younger, more independent-minded Chinese are demanding the right to make their own decisions. As a result, divorce, traditionally unutterably shameful, is becoming more widespread.

Indeed, the idea of shame, usually expressed as 'losing face' (*diulian*), is integral to the Chinese attitude to life. Losing face is more than just shame, however, for shame implies a subjective feeling of guilt whereas loss of face is something more – it is a slight, a missed opportunity, family shame, regional shame, a failure to perform a duty according to the expectation and judgement of one's peers, particularly in front of foreigners. It can be any one of these things, or a little of all of them.

Privacy The obsession with face creates all sorts of social tensions, especially in a highly controlled society. For this reason the Chinese traditionally avoid situations where face may be lost, preferring anonymity to exposure. Contact with the outside world is making this more difficult – Western business investors in China often express frustration with Chinese lack of initiative, not recognising that to many Chinese, being a faceless member of a crowd is the norm, and individual self-expression therefore an unsought luxury.

Lack of privacy also means lack of space. Flats in the cities are generally small and everyone has to be able to tolerate the goings-on of everyone else, which explains the Chinese ability to concentrate amid cacophany, and to sleep at will. What seems intolerable to Westerners is in fact the essence of the Chinese way of life.

Newlyweds: today, for those who can afford it, Western dress and a video recording are common

■ China continues to be ruled by the Communist Party, though since the early 1980s and the beginning of the 'open door' policy, the country has demonstrated a willingness to adopt foreign trade investment and new ideas.....■

Communism? In 1993 Ferrari made the first delivery of one of its luxury cars to a Chinese entrepreneur in China (despite the fact that there are few enough roads where such a car could be used). Shanghai now has a thriving stock exchange. In these and in countless other ways the traditional picture of Chinese life under communism is rapidly changing. Even so, all the Party maxims, slogans, shibboleths, dictums and homilies traditional to communism are still trotted out by the Chinese government whenever the occasion seems to demand them. Nor is the government afraid to act with undemocratic severity, as the massacre of students and citizens in and around Tiananmen Square in June 1989 amply demonstrated, not to mention the continuing suppression of Tibet and the detention without trial of numerous dissidents, kept in conditions not far removed from the death camps of Hitler and Stalin. Of course, by comparison with the years of the Cultural Revolution, to name just the most brutal of the various repressive movements presided over by Chairman Mao, life in China today is a haven of tranquillity. But persecution continues (Qinghai province is known as China's gulag) and the average Chinese has no legal means of avoiding the heavy hand of the state, should he wish to.

Below: a face cream advertisement – economic reality is eroding communism. Top: Mao memorabilia

The truth is that the Party still wields enormous influence; real freedom – to travel as one wishes, to read what one chooses, even to talk in an uninhibited way – remains an elusive goal. If physical persecution is more of a rarity, deviation from accepted social norms still incurs the wrath of local committees who have the power to take away your job, your home, your very right to exist as a citizen. The Party also dictates where you work: for example, bright and able graduates have to work at repetitive jobs, such as sewing buttons, as 'payment' for their education. Outspoken criticism of the government, associating with foreigners (especially journalists) and evangelical Christianity (as opposed to passive worship) are all offences liable to lead to arrest and imprisonment.

Understanding Considering Chinese history, the size of the population and its accompanying social problems, and the vastness of the country with its variety of geography and peoples – then the current system, though still undesirable, is at least comprehensible. Autocratic government is all that most Chinese have ever known – and the history of intrusive government is almost as old as Chinese history itself. Thus for many Chinese, the years since the end of the Cultural Revolution in 1976 are a golden era, Mao Zedong himself remains a hero to a large number of people, and those observers who thought they were witnessing the crumbling of the communist grip in the 1980s have been proved wrong several times over. None the less, things are much improved – peasant farmers are now allowed to keep and sell the surplus produce they grow, and married couples are no longer liable to be separated and sent to work in different parts of the country at the whim of some malicious bureaucrat.

Future Perhaps the most telling achievement of Chinese communism is the way it has been able to bring some semblance of organisation to what was a chaotic country, where the gap between rich and poor was seemingly unbridgeable and where there was no sense of nationhood. The time is fast approaching, however, when the issue of democracy has to be addressed, for prosperity, based on 'communism with Chinese characteristics', looks increasingly like capitalism with universal characteristics.

A Confucian ideal in communist clothing: posters asking for respect for authority are a common sight

Making money

■ Though China remains a communist country in formal political terms, informally ideological rectitude is the farthest thing from most people's minds. To make money has become the overriding ambition of a large number of people for whom the strictures of Marx, Lenin and Mao are mostly irrelevant.....■

Competition The Chinese have always enjoyed a reputation for business acumen and it is certainly possible to become rich in modern China. A visit to any of the major cities will quickly establish that – wealthy Chinese driving Mercedes Benz cars and frequenting luxury hotels happily spend in a day what the average Chinese could not earn in a lifetime. The competition is as fierce and as cut-throat as in any established capitalist society, and although a lack of sophistication in business matters still shows through from time to time (in the form of overweening salesmanship, or a disregard for the ethical implications of contracts) the Chinese have learnt remarkably quickly how to package what they have to offer in an attractive and winning way.

In the blood Making money, like the traditional love of gambling, seems to be a compulsion in China. The appeal seems to be that money brings power and it is power, more than wealth, that is seductive. Perhaps power is particularly attractive in China because it is almost the only significant way of rising above the common herd. Until recently individuals achieved power by rising through the ranks of the Communist Party; whilst that remains the case to a certain extent, there is an alternative route to power and influence outside politics through money. Capitalism, albeit in diluted form, is now an accepted part of Chinese life and although it has its theoretical limits,

A stretch limo at the five-star International Hotel, Beijing

the general feeling is that this strange mixture of communist ideology and hard-faced business attitudes is here to stay.

Salaries Only a few years ago it was impossible even to think of earning anything other than a pitiful state salary. Private enterprise was not just frowned upon, it was simply out of the question. The state would provide everything that the Chinese citizen could or, more correctly, should, desire. Everybody was on a salary scale which corresponded precisely to their social rank and whilst the salary of officials tended to be higher than most, it had a defined limit – even the Chairman of the Party, the top man in China, received a salary in line with this. Corruption was the more or less inevitable result, as officials extracted what price they could in compensation for low salaries.

❑ The colloquial Chinese euphemism for leaping into the rising tide of private business is *xiahai* or 'going down to the sea'. But some take it seriously. In an interview with a Western journalist, one of the new entrepreneurs said, 'We just feel very happy when we see the company succeed.' ❑

government bureaucracies for a meagre state salary. This, too, has changed and in the major cities there are few who do not have a finger in some enterprise, however humble. This period of transition is bringing immense social change, especially for the coastal Special Economic Zones, which are clones of Hong Kong, involved in low-wage mass production of low-technology

A newly purchased portrait of Sophia Loren is carted home on that other status symbol, the motorbike

Social change When economic reforms were first introduced in the 1980s ambitious city-dwellers were disgruntled to see the peasants becoming rich whilst they slogged in

products. Even so, these Zones have contributed to China's record-breaking economic growth, attracting a steady stream of country people looking for work. Exploitation, low wages, and unhealthy working conditions are the result. For those Chinese unmoved by the entrepreneurial spirit, life must seem devalued – but such is modern China.

■ Over a thousand million people, about one-fifth of the world's population, live in China, geographically the third largest country in the world, and the forecasts are that this figure will reach 2,000 million by AD2000. The number of cities bearing unfamiliar names, yet with populations as great as those of London, New York or Tokyo, is astonishing.....■

Humankind In China there are people everywhere – you are never alone and every pavement is crowded. The roads between them, previously the preserve of a few trolley-buses, lorries, donkeys and bicycles, are rapidly becoming filled with cars. Even the landscape has been shaped by man, for every patch of fertile land, no matter how small, is under cultivation. Wilderness is rare, and magnificent works of nature, such as the Stone Forest near Kunming, are not left to stand for themselves but are 'enhanced' by the addition of man-made art.

Similarities Considering the size of the country, there are remarkably few regional differences north to south or east to west. A Chinese, it is true, is more likely to tell you the name of his town or province before his country, since for him the differences are great. But for the outsider the homogeneity of Chinese culture is astonishing. This is largely due to China's history for, despite the presence of 56 different nationalities within her borders, 92 per cent of the population is Han Chinese – that is to say people with the basic physical characteristics of slim build, black hair and almond eyes, whose first language is Chinese, or a variant of it, and who loyally regard Beijing as the national centre of power. Traditional Han China is everywhere except Xinjiang, large parts of Yunnan, Tibet, Qinghai, Inner Mongolia and parts of Manchuria, and has been so for some 2,000 years.

Top: market day, northern Sichuan
Below: a Tibetan woman and child

❑ Although most members of the minority peoples of China speak and write Chinese, there are in fact more than 30 scripts still in use throughout the country, about 20 of which, including Mongolian, Tibetan, Dai, Yi, Uygur, Korean, Russian and Manchurian, have been in use for many hundreds of years. Others – for example, that of the Zhuang who had no script of their own – were artificially created in the 1950s on the basis of the Latin alphabet. ❑

Nationalities The other 55 nationalities, the remaining five per cent of the population, none the less comprise an element of Chinese life that cannot be ignored. Three nationalities, the Tibetans, the Mongolians and the Uygurs, whilst comparatively few in number, occupy homelands which

make up a large geographical proportion of the country – Tibet and Qinghai, Inner Mongolia and Xinjiang. In at least two of the cases, Tibet, and to a lesser extent Xinjiang, local opposition to Han rule has manifested itself in violently rebellious outbursts which have occasionally caught the imagination of the outside world. The Chinese government, which finds it hard to conceal its disgust with troublesome minorities, deals with the problem by filling minority areas with Han Chinese, who them- selves are sent either under duress or through financial inducement. The result is that indigenous peoples then become minorities in their own lands.

Diversity In Han China proper there is considerable cultural and linguistic diversity. There are the Hakka, for example, who were driven south during the Song dynasty and wear distinctive fringed hats. There are the dark-skinned Tujias scattered among the mountains of Hunan, Hubei and Sichuan. Even the Cantonese, who are not a minority, differ physically from northerners and speak a dialect that has almost nothing in common with the dialects of Shanghai or Beijing.

Numerically, the largest minority is the Zhuang, numbering well over 15 million according to the 1990 Census, most of whom live quietly in the Guangxi Zhuang Autonomous Region of southern China. Almost indistinguishable from the Han, they may be related to the Vietnamese. Most of the minorities have become absorbed into mainstream Chinese life, which is to say (quoting the author David Bonavia) 'they are admirable, infuriating, humorous, priggish, modest, overweening, mendacious, loyal, mercenary, ethereal, sadistic, and tender. They are quite unlike anybody else. They are the Chinese.'

The Hani minority people of Yunnan cling to their ancient ways

■ **In China, nobody wants to be a peasant farmer, and yet that is the fate of three out of four Chinese. City-dwellers have traditionally looked down upon their country cousins, yet recent economic reforms have radically improved the farmers' lot (at least in the fertile areas of the country) and they are now among the richer members of Chinese society.....■**

Rural character China remains predominantly rural despite attempts since 1949 to industrialise the country. Even in the major cities open markets – and bicycles, lorries and beasts of burden loaded down with fresh produce to sell there – are still part of urban life. The fact that China is almost self-sufficient in food is remarkable when you remember the size of the population and that, with most of the country either mountain or desert, only a small percentage of land is fit for cultivation.

The wiliness and perseverance of the Chinese peasant are legendary, hence Mao Zedong's dictum, in his misguided attempts to reform China, to 'learn from the peasant'. This did not stop him, unfortunately, from trying to impose ideological ideas on these same farmers that led to the death by starvation of millions during the Great Leap Forward of 1958–9.

Autumn harvesting in northern China's loess area, in the Hengshan Mountains

Land sculpture Such is the longstanding relationship between the Chinese farmer and his land that the very landscape is often defined by human activity. The most obvious example of this is terracing, a technique developed to make the most of undulating or hilly countryside. Taking the train from Changsha to Canton in high summer, as it picks its way around the curving contours of tiers of land densely planted with yellowy green, or driving from Chongqing to Dazu when the rice is

❑ You glorify Nature and meditate on her;
Why not domesticate and regulate her?
You follow Nature and sing her praise:
Why not control her course and use it?
– Xunzi, philosopher, 3rd century BC ❑

Market day, Yunnan province: fast food has reached China, but out of town it's still the fresher the better

still under water, glazed by a broiling sun, you cannot but admire the industry, ingenuity and regard for nature that has gone into the working of Chinese farmland.

Land management The fact that there are so few roads in China (and those that exist are very narrow) is because every piece of land is precious. Water is precious, too, and a single canal will provide irrigation for a succession of fields, whilst mud from its bed will be used, along with animal dung and human waste (still collected from cities), as manure.

Fuel, too, must be managed with care. Thus in the north houses are traditionally built facing the south and the sun, away from the harsh desert winds from the northwest. In poorer areas a large portion of the interior of the house is given over to the *kang*, a raised brick platform heated by the stove or by straw fires from outside and which may serve as a bed. Such arrangements are becoming rarer as farmers prosper, buy lorries and build houses according to their own taste, fitting them with modern conveniences. Yet the same prosperity is bringing a new set of dilemmas, not just for farmers but for the whole of China – how to modernise without throwing half a billion people out of work. Since the demise in the 1980s of the commune system, farmers have been responsible for providing quotas of staple crops to the government, in return for which they are allowed to rent a limited amount of land from the government on a 15-year lease and earn what they can from it. So long as farming remains largely manual, the rural population remains employed. But as entrepreneurial farmers, earning a private income from their leased plots, increasingly turn to mechanisation, encouraged by Western agronomists, the stability of the countryside does not look likely to last.

■ China might be an essentially rural country, but it boasts some of the largest cities in the world. In parts of those cities people still carry on their lives on the streets much as they have done for centuries.....■

Public face The reasons for this public existence are not hard to fathom – poverty and a large population have meant simple and confined living space. In some parts of China, therefore, the street becomes a kitchen, a sitting-room, even in summer a bedroom. The street is where everyone meets in the course of the day so that allotted tasks are accompanied by opportunities for constant conversation. Shelling prawns, doing the washing, pumping up a bicycle tyre, playing cards may all take place simultaneously within the space of a few square metres, accompanied by exchanges of views and a general commentary on life. Nobody appears to be taking much notice of traffic or passers-by but in fact nothing escapes the locals' eagle eyes.

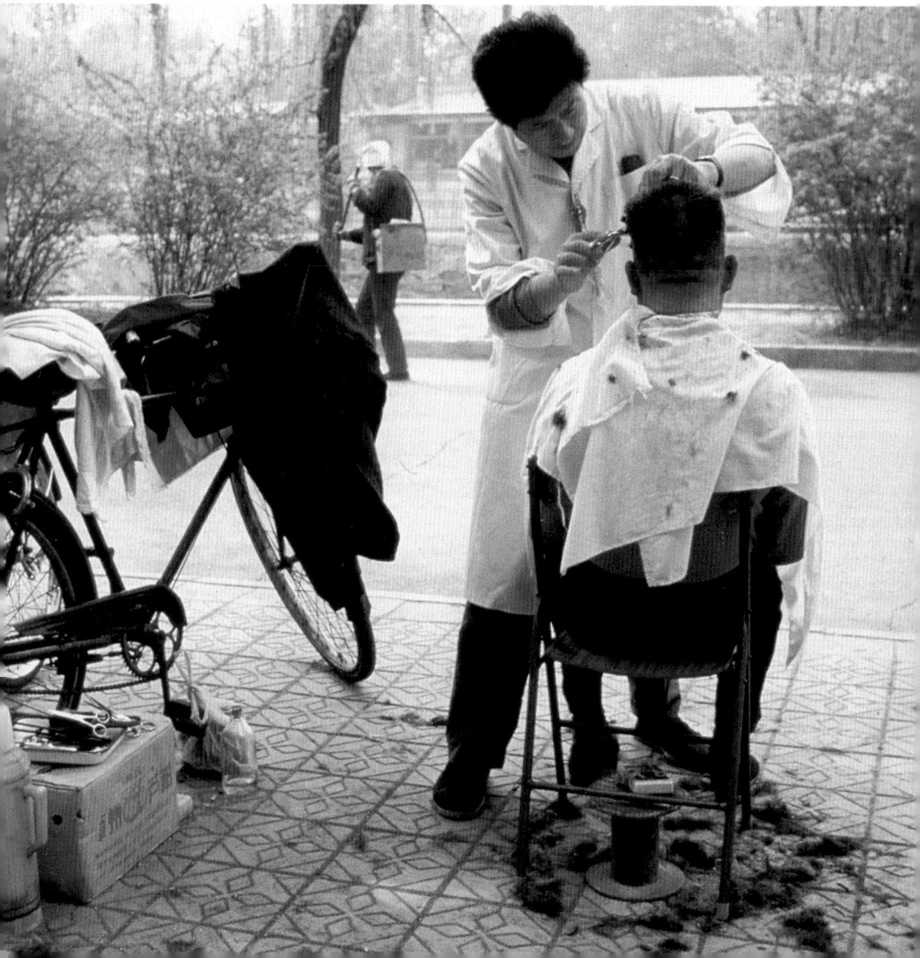

The street, the open-air office of the self-employed businessman

The streets In the wider world (just beyond the front door), lies the commercial hub of the average small

Free-style disco dancing in the public park area of Tiantan, Beijing

town. The open-air market is the liveliest area but elsewhere on the streets there are barbers busy with their scissors and dentists advertising their skills with lurid paintings of a set of clackers. Passers-by are invited to step on to scales to have their weight told. Noodles and beancurd are being made on the spot, and dough sticks sizzle in blackened woks. Tables and chairs are set up, and customers served; at night tables may be illuminated with festoons of electric lights. In summer people gather under street lamps to play cards or chess.

Movement Most striking is the restless movement that accompanies all of this. Despite the surface equanimity which appears as a glaze on Chinese daily life, there is a burning energy beneath. Watch people eating or talking – even if the upper body is at rest the leg pounds a beat on the floor and the eyes are constantly darting. Sometimes this latent energy can be frightening. Considering the crowded conditions, street brawls are a comparative rarity but when they do occur it is with a ferocity blind to all plea or blandishment.

From the street it is but a short step to the public parks where, for the same reasons of lack of space and privacy, local people gather to do those things impossible at home or which are preferred as group activities. The commonest of these activities is *taiji*, the slow, graceful exercise routines performed by squads of usually elderly people. In recent years some older residents have forsaken traditional *taiji* in favour of open-air disco dancing. In the same park groups of equally elderly residents are likely to be enacting favourite scenes from Chinese opera.

Entertainment The streets of the newly prosperous cities have changed considerably and, superficially at least, are becoming similar to modern streets all over the world. In front of the karaoke bars and skyscrapers, however, farmers from the countryside and members of ethnic minorities plod by in bewildered fascination, whilst pedlars and street performers are making a welcome return. Less welcome is the increasing number of beggars in the cities but this seems to be an unavoidable part of the construction of a new China.

■ ***Chi fan le ma?* (Have you eaten yet?) is a form of greeting as unconscious (though not quite as meaningless) as 'How are you?' in English. It demonstrates, however, where traditional priorities lie.....■**

Variety In China eating is the psychological motor for everything. It has been said: 'The thought of omitting a meal from the day is only fractionally more unthinkable than omitting rice from the meal. The Chinese possess enormous powers of concentration for as long as the stomach is full; but come the moment when the digestive process has done its work, then physical discomfort sets in and all ability to concentrate disappears.'

The variety of styles and ingredients involved in Chinese cooking is a marvel. The three principal regional

Top: candied haw berries, a winter treat. Below: Sichuan delicacies in traditional steamer baskets

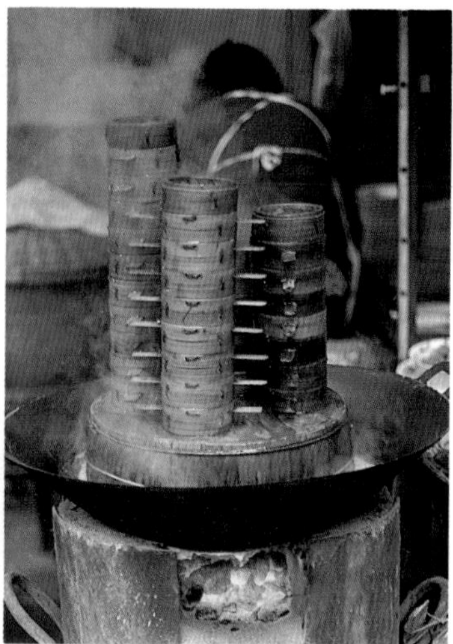

cuisines are familiar to many visitors with experience of restaurants in the West – hot and spicy dishes made with chilli from Sichuan; northern-style cuisine using steamed bread and pancakes instead of rice and preserved vegetables, such as salted and pickled cabbage, because of the freezing winters when nothing grows; and southern style, involving light stir-fried dishes made from a vast array of ingredients, such as seafood, chicken and pork.

❑ Soy sauce, the principal accompaniment to Chinese cooking, is perhaps the oldest condiment known to man. Made from the soya bean, its origins go back to sauces made from fish and game. When soya, or meat or fish are mixed with salt and water or rice wine the protein is broken down into amino acids which stimulate taste. ❑

Freshness It is essential for all styles that when fresh food is used, it is as fresh as it possibly could be – and it is a testimony to Chinese genius that they have developed a style of cooking that obviates refrigeration, despite the rigours of the climate. Blessed with an abundance of good ingredients in the most fertile areas of the country, the Chinese have become expert at extracting the essence of flavour.

History A gourmet appreciation of food can be traced back to several centuries BC, as poetry of the period, listing dishes to tempt the departing soul back to the body, testifies: 'O soul, come back! Why should you go far away? All your household have come to do you honour; all kinds of good food are ready.' By the Han dynasty a scientific approach had been formulated for cooking and a basic rule was that the 'five flavours' (sweetness, sourness, hotness, bitterness and saltiness) should be combined in a meal to achieve balance and harmony. Mincing and the thin slicing of meat and fish were

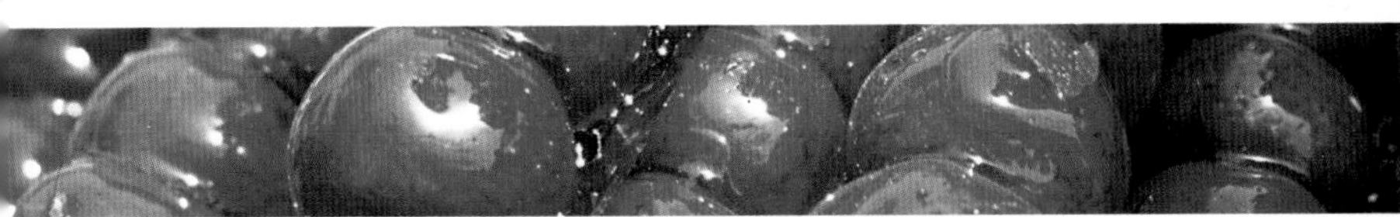

also considered essential for releasing the full flavour. Later, as China expanded her frontiers southwards and westwards, discovering new ingredients in the process, true Chinese cooking developed, although the basic tenets still held. The five-flavours cooking vocabulary is still used, even if it is quite inadequate to describe the full kaleidoscope of Chinese cuisine – as anyone who has experienced the true 'sweet and sour' pork will readily acknowledge.

Methods Cooking methods are vital to the craft of the Chinese master chef. The best results depend on the precise control of heat and this is a skill which is considered crucial. Whilst all methods of cooking are used, from braising and baking to boiling, steaming and roasting over a spit, there is one that is native to China: *chao*, or stir-frying, involves cutting the ingredients finely and rapidly cooking them in a small amount of oil in a pre-heated wok so that they are quickly and evenly cooked. Such dishes must be eaten immediately to benefit from their *huoqi* (vital essence).

As the 14th-century imperial dietitian Hu Sihui put it – 'after a full meal do not wash your hair, avoid sex like an arrow, avoid wine like an enemy'. If the letter of this dictum is no longer heeded, the spirit certainly is.

The proprietor of an outdoor restaurant hands out the food

Its music

■ Chinese music is unique, beautiful and instantly recognisable. Like many things in China it is based on theories conceived at least 2,000 years ago, theories which also influenced the music of Japan, Vietnam, Mongolia and Korea. Its distinctive qualities are dependent on two things – the instruments used and a chromatic scale which differs from that of the West.....■

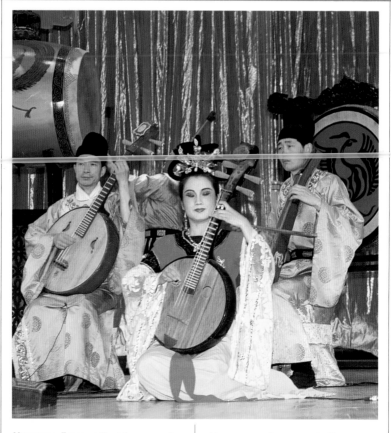

Above: a performance in Tang costume; the instrument is the yueqin
Top: façade of a Beijing music shop

Harmony From earliest times music in China was held in the highest esteem and was an integral part of three important aspects of Chinese life: the festivals of the agricultural year, ceremonies linked to the imperial court and religious rites. It was believed that the function of music was to enhance the harmony between heaven and earth which itself was the fruit of the male principle of *yang* and the female principle of *yin*. The music was based on a dozen notes from which were selected the basic notes of a series of five-note scales (corresponding to the five elements of earth, water, fire, metal and wood). The 12 notes arose from calculations based on the interval of the fourth and fifth, starting from a foundation note known as the 'yellow bell' (*huang zhong*) which was thought to be imbued with a mystical power, considered one of the eternal principles of the universe and the foundation of the well-being of the state. Each dynasty, in fact, had its foundation note, arrived at after only the most careful calculations. Absolute pitch, therefore, was a vital ingredient

❑ A man was going to play a Chinese lute in the street, and many people gathered around to listen. But when the musician began to play, the crowd thought the music too insipid and soon dispersed, except for one man who appeared to remain standing in rapt attention. The musician exclaimed: 'There is still one who can appreciate fine music!' But the man replied: 'If I hadn't lent you that table to use as a stand for your instrument, I'd have gone as well!' ❑

of Chinese music, so vital that as early as the 1st century BC, during the Han dynasty, an imperial office had been established, one of the duties of which was to standardise pitch.

Melody Despite these potentially inhibiting rules, traditional Chinese music is far from dull. Its two principal elements are melody and timbre. Traditional Chinese orchestras are extremely large, their component parts collectively producing a sound that is euphonious and rich; some orchestras employed at imperial temples in Beijing consisted of 150 musicians.

Instruments Traditional music is still widely played, and remains quite distinctive, on account of the instruments, which both look and sound substantially different from their Western counterparts, even when they share some broad similarities. The most typical instrument is the *zheng*, a long, narrow stringed instrument plucked as it rests across the player's lap. This was the instrument of philosophers. Its main rival, an instrument that belongs more to the realm of traditional popular song, is the *pipa*, something like a lute, which became fashionable in the 7th century to accompany Tang dynasty songs.

Both these instruments simply sound solemn to Western ears but the Chinese originally classified their instruments according to the materials they were made of, which fell into

Flute player, Iron Pagoda, Kaifeng

eight categories – instruments with the qualities of stone, metal, silk, bamboo, wood, skin, gourd and clay. Music remains an ubiquitous feature of Chinese life. Although there are great differences between Chinese and European musical traditions, a little practice can allow anyone to acquire the Chinese taste.

In modern China, the principal spoken language is Modern Standard Chinese, based on the dialects of north China, especially Mandarin (from Portuguese 'mandar', to rule). It (and all China's many other dialects) is distinctive by virtue of its tones. The Chinese script goes back to 4000 or 5000BC, justifiably claimed to be the world's oldest written language, and has a staggering 50,000 characters.....

Pictographs Chinese script has evolved from comparatively straightforward, miniature representations of the object in question, to highly stylised designs which need to be unravelled in order to understand them. It is thought that the original pictographs became more sophisticated as attempts were made to convey a meaning that could not be drawn. So, for example, the character for 'to arrive at' (*zhi*) derives from a picture of an arrow hitting a target. The next stage was to convey abstract concepts by combining two (or more) characters: thus the characters for sun and moon placed together became the character *ming*, meaning 'bright' or 'brightness'.

Pronunciation By the Han dynasty the written language had evolved to the point that a modern Chinese would be able to read it aloud, although the meaning might be obscure. Chinese characters convey little clue to their pronunciation, so the advantage of the script is that it is the same throughout the country and thus permits written communication between speakers of different dialects. There is almost nothing in common between spoken Cantonese, for example, thought by some to have preserved Tang dynasty pronunciation, and Mandarin. The government has promoted a simplified version of Mandarin, *putonghua*, with some success, as official Chinese, and in efforts to improve literacy introduced both a common system for writing the language with a Latin alphabet (romanisation), known as *pinyin*, and a system for simplifying the most commonly used characters (in their traditional form they are too complex and numerous for the majority of people to learn), now the norm in mainland China.

Massive characters on a column in the Forbidden City, Beijing

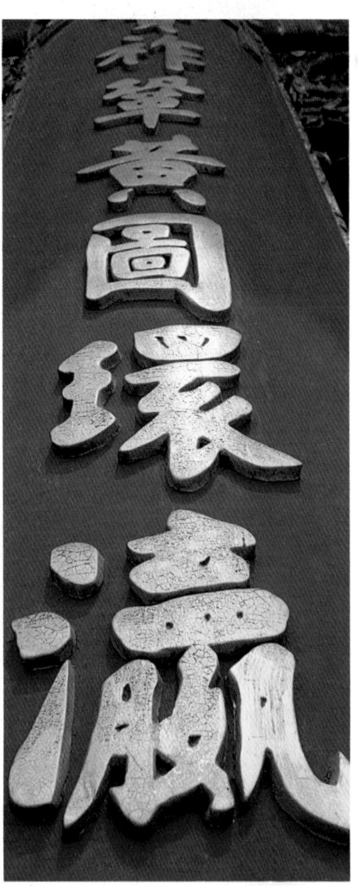

CHINA WAS

■ Although China can boast the longest continuous civilisation in history, it was nevertheless a relatively late starter. Current evidence suggests that the first organised Chinese state did not appear until several dynasties had already come and gone in ancient Egypt. Once underway, however, Chinese civilisation has proved durable and although it has occasionally been bruised and battered over the centuries, its basic foundations have proved rock-like.....■

Prehistory Little is yet known of Chinese prehistory. About 40,000 years ago it seems that the area was populated by people of the Mongoloidal type, and that a recognisably Chinese type with flatter features and particular eyelid shape appeared 20,000 years later, perhaps in response to the freezing conditions of the era. However, it is only from 7,000 years ago that it is possible to trace the origins of the Chinese we know today.

Chinese civilisation Although it was once thought that Chinese civilisation was founded on influences from the Mediterranean, the spontaneous development of a separate culture is now accepted.

The first dynasty of which there is any concrete evidence is the Shang (there still exists considerable doubt about the legendary Xia, supposedly overthrown by the Shang in 1750BC), who probably ruled the areas of the North China plain around the Yellow river in the modern provinces of Shandong, Henan and Hebei and parts of the provinces of Shanxi and Shaanxi. They were skilled and well organised – excavated remains of a Shang city at Zhengzhou show walls 10m in height extending around an area of some 3km – and used bronze, worked not with hammer and anvil, but cast in pottery moulds. Crucially, Shang architecture and family values

❑ Traditional accounts of the origins of Chinese civilisation talk of various figures from whom all Chinese claim descent. The Yellow Emperor is the father of the Chinese but others include Yu the Great, said to have created China's waterways and Shen Nong, the Divine Husbandman. ❑

Bronze Shang ritual wine vessel

were to influence Chinese civilisation to our own times.

There is no doubt that Shang influence spilled across its borders, but there was as yet no sense of Chinese statehood, and other states of varying degrees of power and cultural development operated around the Shang borders, sharing much of its culture but remaining politically independent. One such was the Zhou, who ruled an area not far to the west of Xi'an and who eventually overthrew the Shang in about 1050BC and extended the area of a cultural influence that was becoming recognisably Chinese.

The Zhou dynasty The Zhou (1050–256BC) solved the problem of ruling what was now an extensive domain by establishing a feudal system in which relatives of the Zhou ruler were empowered to govern the various Zhou states. As for the Zhou ruler himself, he was seen as a Son of Heaven and the supernatural influence he wielded (largely founded on the relationship to illustrious ancestors) was sufficiently powerful to linger even after the fall of the dynasty. Just how great was the extent of the Zhou realm is hard to gauge – it seems to have extended through much of Shaanxi, Shanxi and Hebei, reaching the Gansu border in the west and Shandong in the east, and possibly the Yangtze valley. It was sufficiently large to warrant the construction of a secondary capital at Luoyang.

In 771BC, however, the Western Zhou rulers met defeat at the hands of a mixture of barbarian invaders and disgruntled subjects, displaced by the Eastern Zhou rulers. They moved east to Luoyang, but their vitality had been sapped.

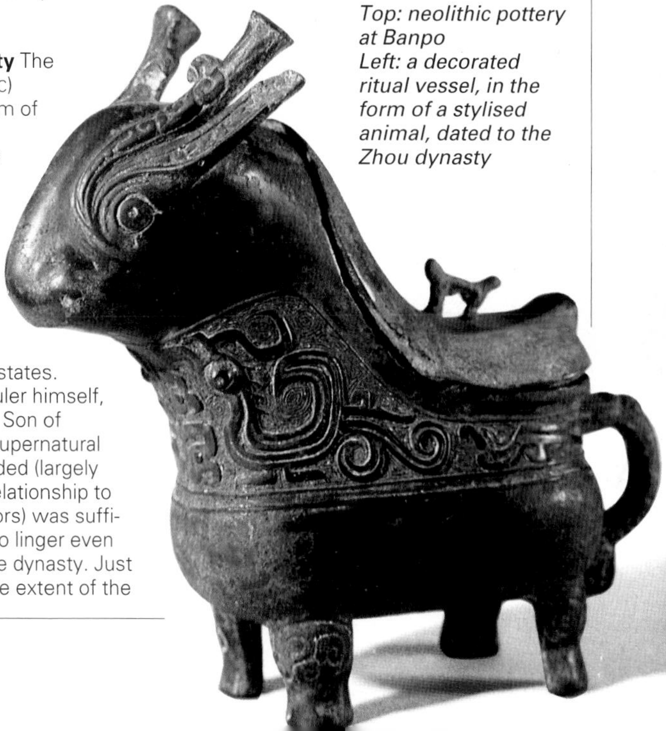

Top: neolithic pottery at Banpo
Left: a decorated ritual vessel, in the form of a stylised animal, dated to the Zhou dynasty

■ Although the Zhou lasted 800 years, its rule was largely nominal. Effective power lay with the nobles in far-flung regions of the kingdom, who frequently fought among themselves, whilst continuing to defer to the Zhou king at Luoyang. Eventually, a newer, stronger state was to exploit this weakness.....■

The famous 'Flying Horse of Gansu', Eastern Han dynasty

Fall of Eastern Zhou Echoes of the ritualistic deference shown to the Zhou king exist even today in public life, for some of the Zhou's administrative features lasted into the 20th century. The Eastern Zhou, the second period of Zhou rule, is subdivided into two, both named after the principal historical source-books – the Spring and Autumn period (during which Confucius) lived and the Warring States period, characterised by internecine warfare among the various states, any one of which might finally have toppled the Zhou. But it was the Qin, occupying the area around the original western capital, that was to prove strongest,

❑ The First Emperor believed his empire would last for 10,000 generations – in fact his own dynasty outlived him by only a few years, although the imperial structure he built lasted for 2,133 years.

The emperor died in 210BC on a trip away from the capital. His chief advisor, Li Ssu, returned the body in a sealed carriage to pre-empt revolt and changed the wording of the emperor's will in favour of a younger, weaker, son. The true heir committed suicide and the new emperor was murdered by Li Ssu, himself killed in the ensuing chaos. ❑

using its favoured position on the fringes of the Chinese and barbarian worlds to expand to a point where it was able to defeat the Zhou in 256BC and the other states in 221BC.

The mighty Qin The Qin dynasty (221–206BC), although one of the shortest in Chinese history, was to prove one of the most influential. Its founder – Qin Shihuangdi, 'the First Emperor of China'– brought to fruition an incipient sense of Chinese statehood. Qin thought was not very innovative, but the adoption of the authoritarian tenets of Legalist philosophy ensured that the Qin triumphed. The emperor's principal aims were centralisation, standardisation and unification: China was divided into military regions and counties, governed from the centre; weights and measures, and the written script were regularised; and intellectual opposition was ruthlessly suppressed. By 214BC he had extended Chinese domains as far as Vietnam, but with his death in 210BC the dynasty fizzled out. His three short-lived successors were unable to cool the simmering resentments which were consequent upon the severity of the First Emperor's rule.

The Han The Han (206BC–AD220), though founded upon opposition to the Legalist framework that had been the key to Qin success, was left with a base upon which to develop into one of the greatest of Chinese dynasties. Confucianism became the state doctrine, absolute imperial power was enshrined as 'the mandate from heaven', and a rudimentary examination system for selecting officials was introduced. It was a period of cultural, scientific and foreign expansion and of consolidation of the Chinese identity. Many regions previously under nominal Chinese tutelage were better integrated and the way west via the Silk Road, a conduit for Buddhism, was opened.

Although the Han fragmented into warring states, it is interesting that the idea of a united China never died. The demise of the Han can be attributed in part to economic factors: before, the southern states had been no match for the Qin once it had acquired the prosperous northern plains; by the end of the Han, the wealth of the Yangtze valley and the Sichuan Basin was well developed and when rebellions led to the fall of the Han, China split into three.

A 'Fairy Mountain' incense burner, as found in a Western Han tomb, made of bronze inlaid with gold

In China philosophy has played a role not unlike that of a religion. Most of the great Chinese philosophers emerged during a period of unrelenting instability, which was perhaps the inspiration for the quest to find a solution to human ills.....

Confucius If one word only were to characterise Chinese civilisation for the last 2,000 years, it would be the word 'Confucian'. No other individual has so influenced the thoughts and minds of Chinese people, and no other philosophy has become so integral to the Chinese psyche. Earlier Chinese beliefs had been based on mythical figures and ancestor worship. Confucius, facing an unstable and violent world, saw the value of keeping some of the old rituals, perhaps as a way of preserving the structure of society, while stressing a natural order that was also a moral order to achieve stability and peace.

Top: Taoist monks. Below: the pagoda (here, at Tiger Hill, Suzhou) is symbolic of Chinese Buddhism

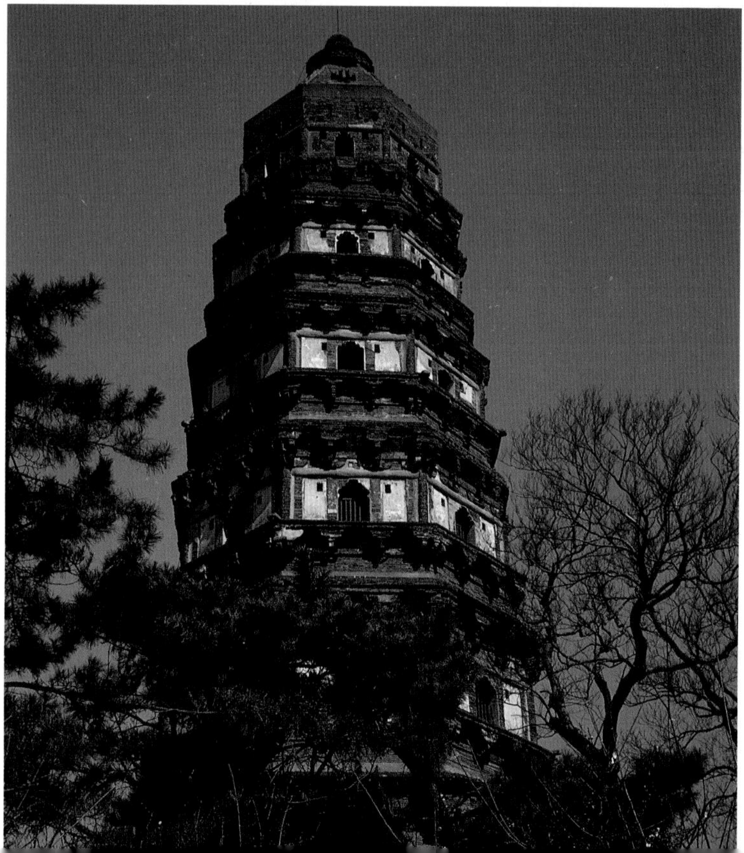

Confucius (Kong Fuzi, *c.*551–479BC) was born in the state of Lu. Though probably of aristocratic stock, he himself had no time for lazy aristocratic rulers: 'Even gamblers do something,' he said. In his thinking he was to emphasise the importance of 'gentlemanly' pursuits, but he rejected the prevailing creed which considered only the arts of war to be worthwhile. He wanted his followers to play an active role in government, and was interested in people of intellect only if

❑ 'One Chuang Chou (Zhuangzi) dreamed he was a butterfly. He did not know he had ever been anything but a butterfly, and was content to hover from flower to flower. Suddenly he woke and found to his astonishment that he was Chuang Chou. But it was hard to be sure whether he really was Chou and had only dreamt that he was a butterfly, or was really a butterfly, and was only dreaming he was Chou.' – Arthur Waley, *Three Ways of Thought in Ancient China*, 1939 ❑

they were interested in bettering themselves through his ideas, and were willing to act on his principles. Confucius saw man as a social being but believed that the conscience of the individual must equally forbid him to withdraw from society or to surrender his moral judgement to it. Intellectual accomplishment was no good without emotional balance.

Although it seems that he did believe in some sort of afterlife, his ideas were based upon the nature of man and society – he did not say that man was good or bad but that he desired happiness, and that essentially all men had the same potential. Thus, if everyone worked for the happiness of all, general happiness would be the result. At least one prince in the state of Lu adopted some of his ideas, which after Confucius's death were to become a recipe for 'good government' (and the theoretical justification for the traditional 'mandate of heaven' granted to rulers), as well as the criteria for selection and entry to the civil service.

Taoism The other major Chinese philosophy was Taoism, in many ways complementing Confucianism. Its first important figure is Laozi (*c.*570–490BC), a near contemporary of Confucius, reputed to have written the *Daodejing*, which translates as 'The way and its power'. The nature of the *dao*, 'way', which is the great underlying principle of human and natural life, is never properly defined, but it might be said to be the bond

Statue of Confucius, Confucian Temple, Beijing

which unites man with nature, with the principle of *wuwei* or 'no action' as its ethos. The second important Taoist figure is Zhuangzi (369–286BC) who wrote a volume of allegorical tales illustrating the tenets of Taoism. Overall, Taoism is a reclusive, contemplative counter to the rigid propriety of Confucianism, and it is still quite possible to see both points of view mirrored in the outlook of the average modern Chinese.

The yin-yang *Taoist symbol*

Tang and Song

After the fall of the Han, China divided into the three states, known as the Wei, Shu and Wu. Constantly at war with each other over the following centuries, the three states eventually fragmented into a jigsaw of small dynasties. Two of China's greatest dynasties were to emerge from the chaos.....

Paradoxically, the era of confusion which followed the disintegration of the Han dynasty was also one of cultural flowering. The Tang dynasty (AD618–907) that followed is often considered the most accomplished of the Chinese dynasties.

The Tang The founder, a general, came from mixed barbarian and Chinese stock. He retained the fundamental Confucian outlook, encouraged education and promoted contact with foreigners. Unusually, he abdicated in favour of his son when he felt China was sufficiently stable.

The good life Life in Tang China was cosmopolitan, vital and stimulating. Chang'an (Xi'an), the capital, had an estimated population of 2 million, probably the largest city in the world at the time. One of the hallmarks of the dynasty was its organisation – elaborate laws were codified throughout the empire, which extended to Korea and Vietnam. On main roads there were post stations every 16km with hostels and restaurants. Confucianist schools were augmented by others specialising in law, mathematics and science. The development of the examination system, which was started in the Han, helped to create the first bureaucracy based on merit. Bills of exchange ('flying money') were introduced. The Tang was also notable for contact with the outside world, as Persians and Jews, for example, found themselves among the traders in Canton and as Chinese influence re-established itself along the Silk Road.

Above: Song dynasty mirror box

Buddhism reached its apogee at this period, before its sudden decline as a result of official attacks on its influence. Painting and music flourished. For the first time central and south China vied in importance with the traditional northern heartland around the Yellow river. Confucian gentry began to earn money from the offices they held, rather than from land, heralding the burgeoning of a 'middle class'. Yet there were no striking political innovations in the period and, ultimately, economic problems – such as the displacement of tax-paying peasants by land-hungry merchants, and the increasing wealth of the aristocracy – led to strife and disintegration.

The Song Five decades of bickering ensued before reunification under the Song (AD960–1279). This was to be another of the great Chinese dynasties, despite barbarian invasions which compelled the court to move south to Hangzhou from its capital in Kaifeng. During this period increasing urbanisation brought about a commercial revolution whilst at the same time education and literacy improved and a cultural renaissance was underway, noted for simple but beautiful glazed porcelain, and the finest painting in Chinese history.

First invasions The first Song emperor decided to centralise the bureaucracy, placing as many ministries under his personal control as possible in order to consolidate reunification. But the threat of invasion was ever present and by 946 the Khitans, of Mongol origin, had reached Kaifeng. Over 3,000 courtiers were captured, and the Song, driven south, were forced to coexist with the barbarians who occupied the north for 300 years.

This was, none the less, a period of progress. Foreign trade prospered and Chinese cities became more sophisticated. The Chinese genius for innovation inspired a series of inventions, including hand-grenades, the compass and inoculations against smallpox, although a less worthy innovation was the fashion for bound feet. It was also an era of decadence and military feebleness which accentuated the Chinese tendency to introspection. As Buddhism continued to atrophy after government suppression during the Tang dynasty, Neo-Confucianism dominated Chinese thought. Thus China remained, more or less, for a further eight centuries.

Buddhist monks at Xi'an's Big Wild Goose Pagoda (left), built AD652

The Mongols

The Yuan was the first foreign dynasty to rule China, and although it was to last little more than a century it was to influence the Chinese outlook for hundreds of years to come.....

The Khans The Mongols' success in taking China can be accredited partly to use of the latest military technology, principally a mobile cavalry; added to this, lack of water in Central Asia finally forced the squabbling Mongol tribes to unite under a single dynamic leader, Ghengis Khan, with the aim of conquering less arid territory. In 1215 Beijing fell but Ghengis did not live to see the full conquest of China; upon his death the Mongol empire was divided into four khanates ruled by three sons and a grandson.

Ghenghis Khan's son, Ogodai, who ruled from the Mongol capital of Karakorum, reinvaded China.

Genghis Khan's mausoleum, Ejin Horo Qi, Inner Mongolia

Although he conquered the Khitan rulers of the North China plain, he met stiffer opposition from the southern Song who resisted all attemps at conquest for half a century. Finally they were overcome by Ghengis Khan's grandson, Kublai, in 1279.

Now ruler of all China Kublai Khan took the Chinese name Yuan ('First Beginning') for his dynasty. The Mongols also pushed into Indochina and briefly reached Java, provoking huge migrations and indirectly contributing to political changes in neighbouring lands as they did so. In 1260 the Mongol capital was moved from Karakorum to Beijing, with Xanadu (now Dolon Nor, in Inner Mongolia) retained as a summer residence for the imperial family.

Above: lions on the Beijing bridge mentioned by Marco Polo. Top, opposite: the Forbidden City or, in Mongol days, the 'Great Within'

Mongol China Kublai Khan employed able men of all nationalities and listened to all philosophies. Dispensing with the civil service examinations, he streamlined the bureaucracy to four ministries – Justice, War, Rites, Finance – and although he hired foreign contingents for Mongol armies, the Chinese were forbidden to carry arms.

Despite the changes, Confucian ideology and bureaucratic political life were maintained. To the disgust of the Chinese, however, Mongolian customs of dress, food, traditions and language were imposed. The Mongols did not use surnames, for example, a barbarian custom to the family-conscious Chinese. Yet cultural and literary activity flourished – with the abolition of the examinations frustrated scholars had to find other uses for their literary skills. Popular drama also developed fast.

Foreign links Furthermore, expeditions were sent to find the source of the Yellow river, whilst links with the Muslim world inspired the introduction of Persian design elements in Chinese art and architecture. China and Europe entered a new era of cultural exchange. Europeans, most famously Marco Polo in 1271, began to arrive as adventurers or as representatives of European nation states, sent to export Christianity, and perhaps find a powerful new ally against the Muslims. There was even a Mongolian counterpart to Marco Polo, a certain Rabban Sauma, a Nestorian monk, who travelled to Rome to meet the Pope. With the collapse of the Yuan, however, and the re-establishment of native rule under the Ming, the Catholic church lost the ground it had made in China, at least for the time being.

Eventually the Mongols lost their grip on their huge and unwieldy empire. None of Kublai's successors matched his ability. Distance and cultural divide wore down the conquerors. As the Mongols began to lose their cultural identity, the familiar symptoms of dynastic decline appeared: famines, uncontrolled floods, excessive taxation, and revolts. As always the rebellious chiefs were not able to unite and it took a single strong Chinese general to seize control.

Ming and Qing

■ The Ming (meaning 'brilliant') was to become the archetypal Chinese dynasty – peaceful, prosperous and stable, the image of traditional China ruled by the scholar-gentry on Neo-Confucian principles. The Qing, another foreign dynasty, was to bring over 2,000 years of imperial rule to a close.....■

Spirit Way, Nanjing, leads to the tomb of the first Ming emperor
Top: detail, Qing palace, Shenyang

The Ming Zhu Yuanzhang, the founder of the Ming dynasty (AD1368–1644), rose from a peasant background to become a general and then an emperor, driving out the Mongols and establishing the first Ming capital in Nanjing. Although Confucianism was revitalised, the emperor became increasingly autocratic. After his death, civil war broke out: his grandson and heir was usurped by his son who had been ruling Beijing as Prince of Yan. He became the Yongle Emperor, the greatest of the Ming emperors.

Great works Yongle relocated the capital to Beijing, as his own power base, close to the Mongol border. He oversaw the beginning of great public works, such as the reconstruction of the Great Wall, the mass movement of populations for colonisation, and the reclamation of areas laid waste by war. This was an era of seaborne expeditions, led by a eunuch admiral, hoping to promote Chinese prestige along new trade routes; at one stage 16 states, including Aden, were paying tribute to China and its emperor.

When these expeditions came to a sudden end – due to resentment against the eunuch leaders and fear of the Mongol menace – foreign relations went downhill. Pirate raids intensified on the coast and along the Yangtze. Chinese citizens were forbidden to travel abroad, and China turned in on itself. Despite this, Jesuit scientists were still tolerated and cultural life flourished, albeit in a scarcely innovative way. Widespread printing allowed the dissemination of encyclopaedias and treatises. Surprisingly, given the inhibiting effects of Confucianism, the novel flourished and several classics were published at this time.

Last years After 300 years the Ming was in its death throes. The state eunuchs, employed in important ministerial positions at the palace, had become too powerful. Court favourites and their families built up great estates and dispossessed peasants joined together to form rebel bands which marched on Beijing. In response, the last Ming emperor committed suicide on Coal Hill, just behind the Forbidden City, but the peasant army did not enjoy the victory for long – taking advantage of the civil strife, a Manchu army swept down from the northeast, to capture Beijing in 1644.

The last dynasty The Manchus were a confederation of Jurchen tribes from central and southern Manchuria. Their leader was Nurhaci, who founded the Manchu state in 1616. He established his capital at Shenyang, and by adopting Confucianism won the support of the 3 million Chinese who lived in Manchuria. His son Abahai proclaimed the new Qing dynasty in 1636, captured Beijing in 1644, and over the next several decades established control over the whole of China. Unlike the Mongols before them, the Manchus decided to preserve the Chinese government structure while simultaneously enforcing some of their own traditions on the Chinese.

Manchu China Internal peace was maintained by military might but the dynasty produced two notable emperors. The Kangxi Emperor (1654–1722) completed the agricultural reforms started under the Ming, initiated attempts to tame the Yellow river, supported scholarship and encouraged artistic endeavour. His grandson, the Qianlong Emperor (1711–99), extended the empire's boundaries, despite several unsuccessful military campaigns which were to leave the country defenceless. But by 1800 there were already signs of cyclical decline, whilst peasant revolts and the spectre of Western influence, taking hold in Canton despite disapproval in Beijing, could no longer be ignored.

Ming vase, with peacock and peony patterns

Foreign influences

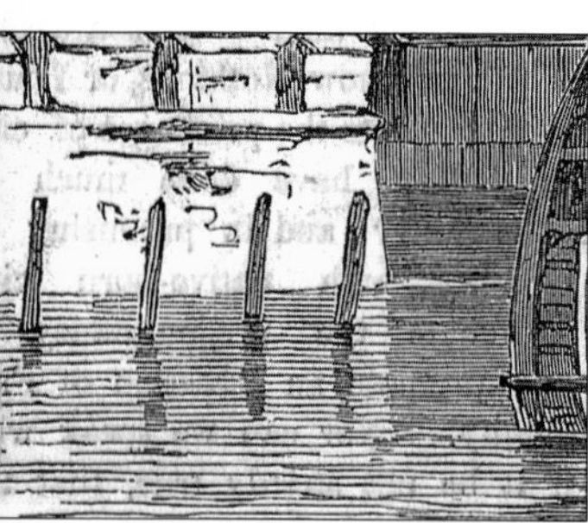

■ The decline and eventual fall of imperial China was a long, painful process. During the final 100 years of the Qing dynasty, influences were at work that traditional resources could not meet. One was the arrival of foreigners in unprecedented numbers, determined to force the Chinese government to enter free trade – a goal that was eventually accomplished through the Treaty of Nanjing which opened certain treaty ports to foreign companies.....■

European barbarians The reactions of Manchu rulers and Chinese intellectuals alike to the presence of foreigners on their soil were mixed: some ignored them while others expressed interest in the new ideas offered by Westerners. Those who favoured Westernisation could not agree on how to proceed. The official line taken by the Manchus was that the foreigners should be ignored; but they were not so easily disposed of and there were in any case other factors to consider. One of these was the Taiping 'Heavenly Peace' Rebellion (1850–64), the gravest of many uprisings at that time.

Sun Yatsen, Father of the Republic

Messiah This rebellion lasted more than 20 years and cost at least 20 million lives. It began when a Hakka peasant, who had failed the official examinations, adopted Christianity, proclaiming himself the head of a new Confucian hierarchy with Christ as the Heavenly Elder Brother. He made considerable headway, taking Nanjing and even enjoying temporary Western support. A typical manifestation of the agrarian unrest of the time, the rebellion, although unsuccessful, showed up how vulnerable the Chinese government really was when faced with a challenge.

❑ The Taiping Rebellion ended in ignominious failure but some of the ideas of its leader, Hong Xiuquan, were remarkable: he believed in state ownership of land, and sharing food, clothing and money. Every 25 households were to be organised as 'comradeships' (*wu*), headed by a comrade leader (*wuzhang*). ❑

Need for change The British and French, in particular, frequently found excuses for acts of aggression. The weak Chinese government seemed powerless to prevent additional treaty ports being added to the list

Port of Shanghai in 1857 (top) and (above) The Shanghai Club – for foreign members only until 1949

originally agreed in 1842 under the Nanjing Treaty, or to halt the ruinous opium trade. Some in the Chinese government saw that reforms were necessary and minor changes were made – land tax was reduced and collected more efficiently, Chinese were sent abroad to learn Western technological skills, an office was established specifically to deal with foreign affairs, and there was some railway and telegraph construction and industrial development.

Dragon empress Predictably there were those who opposed any modernisation. The imperial concubine Cixi (1835–1908), who acted as regent during the minority of her son, the nominated heir, became the *de facto* ruler for the rest of her life when he died in 1875 and was replaced by a four-year-old. She ousted reformers, but in 1898 the young emperor, attracted by foreign ideas, initiated the 'Hundred Days of Reform' movement. Cixi at this point came out of retirement and ruthlessly put an end to it, but none the less foreigners were now permitted to reside in Beijing. All this time, China's foreign residents continued to milk the country for as much as they could.

Last days Tensions finally culminated in the Boxer Rebellion of 1900–1. Initially anti-Manchu, it quickly became anti-foreign. Following its suppression by a powerful Anglo-French army, more humiliating demands were made on the Chinese. Western influence also encouraged the appearance of several revolutionary groups, notably those led by Sun Yatsen (see page 229), who had been exposed to democratic ideals in Japan, America and Britain. But last-minute reforms by the government were too little and too late; in 1912 Sun Yatsen was elected President of the Republic of China after the abdication of the last emperor.

■ **During the 20th century China has been shaken by a series of major upheavals, caused by the struggle to modernise the country after 2,000 years of backward-looking imperial rule. Inevitably the process has been accompanied by ideological battles, notably between the conservative nationalists and the communists who believed in forging a new order based on the common ownership of property and resources.....■**

The First Republic On 12 February 1912, the last Chinese emperor, the six-year-old Puyi (1906–67) was forced to abdicate and the first Chinese Republic was declared in Nanjing. Sun Yatsen, the leader of the reformist movement that opposed imperial rule, was elected Provisional President. His plans to create a truly modern and democratic state were

Top: Chiang Kaishek in Burma, 1942. Below: a statue of Mao (in Shenyang), nowadays a rare sight

thwarted, however, by Yuan Shikai. Yuan was the treacherous head of the imperial army who, despite his duty to protect the boy emperor, had actually orchestrated his abdication.

Yuan regarded Sun Yatsen as a challenge to his own bid for power but, in public at least, supported the republicans. In 1912, however, Sun Yatsen reluctantly agreed to stand aside for Yuan, who was unanimously declared President. Yuan dropped all pretence of republican sentiment in 1915 when he declared himself emperor, but his dictatorial ambitions came to nothing when he died the next year. He did, though, pave the way for a grim period in Chinese history when the various thuggish warlords who controlled sections of the Chinese army battled against each other for supremacy over North China and the possession of Beijing. All Sun Yatsen and his followers could do was work for much-needed reform from the distant southern Chinese capital in Guangzhou (Canton).

Chiang Kaishek At Sun Yatsen's death in 1925, his place as leader of the Nationalist Party (Guomindang) was taken by Chiang Kaishek (1887–1975). The party's main goal was to overthrow the Beijing-based warlords, thus reuniting China through military conquest under its leadership. In preparing for armed rebellion, the nationalists were trained by advisers from the newly created Soviet Union who were working to influence China's political situation. At the same time, Soviet revolutionaries were active in Shanghai where the Chinese Communist Party was formed in 1921.

In 1923 the communists joined forces with the nationalists but strong tensions existed between the two parties, not least because Chiang Kaishek knew that his goals would not be achieved without the support of foreign governments and Chinese industrialists who were implacably opposed to Marxism. Thus when Chiang led his army north in 1927 and declared a new nationalist government in Nanjing, his first act was to ban the Communist Party and to carry out a purge of left-wingers within his own ranks.

Many were killed and many imprisoned during this period, and communists all over China were harried by means of so-called 'encirclement campaigns' whereby the army tried to get rid of the forces in south central China. To escape the nationalists, the communists undertook an arduous 9,000km trek in 1935, heading through China's far west, an expedition that has gone down in history as the Long March (see page 111). Of the nearly 100,000 people who undertook the march, fewer than 10,000 survived. These veterans, including their leader, Mao Zedong, would eventually form an élite within the Communist Party that would come to rule China and force its people into a series of equally heroic, if misguided, campaigns.

Now, however, the bitterest of enemies agreed to cease hostilities and put up a united front against the Japanese, who invaded those areas not already in their control in 1937. Until the surrender of the Japanese at the end of World War II, the communists kept up a constant guerrilla campaign from their bases in the west, while the nationalists, supported by the Western Allies, operated out of bases in the province of Sichuan.

Mao's Red Book, *symbol of oppression*

CHINA WAS *Dominated by Mao*

At the defeat of Japan in 1945, hostilities broke out again between communists and nationalists. US envoys sought to find a compromise and Stalin himself put pressure on the communists to sink their differences with the nationalists, but Mao showed all the stubbornness and determination that was to be his hallmark for the next 30 years.....

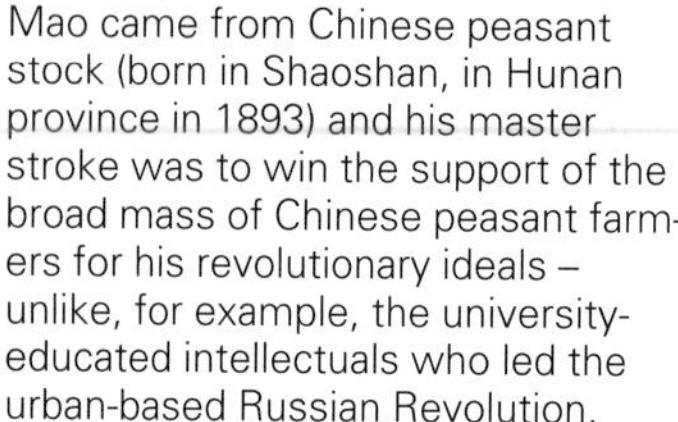

Mao came from Chinese peasant stock (born in Shaoshan, in Hunan province in 1893) and his master stroke was to win the support of the broad mass of Chinese peasant farmers for his revolutionary ideals – unlike, for example, the university-educated intellectuals who led the urban-based Russian Revolution.

The arduous Long March and eight years of war against the Japanese had taught the communists how to survive and win even in the face of extreme hardship. They outclassed and outwitted the nationalists at every stage of the bloody civil war that began in 1946 and ended in October 1949, when Mao finally stood with his supporters at the gates of the Forbidden City in Beijing. Chiang Kaishek packed his bags and fled to Taiwan (having already shipped all the precious Chinese imperial treasures to the island), where he set up a rival government (China still hopes to see Taiwan reunited with the mother country within the foreseeable future).

The People's Republic One of Mao's first acts was to reward his peasant supporters by redistributing all land (former landlords were often beaten up or killed), and by 1956 all industries had been nationalised. The West was prepared to support Mao at first, in the interests of peace and stability, but China was later ostracised for helping Communist North Korea invade the UN-held South in the Korean War of 1950–3.

At first, China turned to the USSR for aid, and in cities such as Beijing and Shanghai the visible symbols of this era are the hotels and tower blocks constructed for and by Russian advisers. Increasingly, however, Mao began to develop his own idiosyncratic brand of communism, launching one mass-action campaign after another and seeming to exercise an extraordinary power to control the collective will of his people. In 1956 his cry was to let 'a hundred flowers blossom, a hundred schools of thought contend'. The aim was apparently to revitalise Chinese culture, but the Party drew the line at overt criticism of its own role and the campaign died in 1957 with the imprisonment of many dissidents.

Next came the Great Leap Forward of 1958–9, intended to mobilise the country into superhuman feats of agricultural and industrial productivity. Instead it resulted in mass starvation, as peasants spent more time in political debate than in physical work, a problem made worse by two years of poor harvests, floods and typhoons. When most in need of help, Mao then quarrelled with the Soviet Union, ostensibly in the name of Chinese 'self-reliance', but really out of pique because the Soviets would not share their nuclear technology with China.

Finally Mao lost all patience with his critics (who were now very numerous) and turned to the young. In 1966 he launched the Cultural Revolution, encouraging armies of young Red Guards to wipe the slate of history clean and build a totally new China. Tragically this resulted in an orgy of iconoclasm, as the Red Guards smashed up historic buildings and museum displays, beat up intellectuals and teachers, turned on their own parents, accusing them of

backward looking 'revisionism', and unleashed three years of terror and anarchy and ten years of repression.

China's travails only came to an end with Mao's death in 1976. Mao's wife, Jiang Qing, tried to seize power but she, and the other members of the so-called 'Gang of Four', were arrested within a month. Deng Xiaoping, Mao's long-time opponent, then emerged as China's new leader. His pragmatic form of communism, and his 'open door policy', to encourage foreign investment, has resulted in a period of calm and the gradual strengthening of the economy. Democracy still remains a distant dream, however, as proved by the massacre of students and citizens in Tiananmen Square in 1989.

Mao (below, as seen on the Tiananmen Gate) is depicted above greeting the People's Army

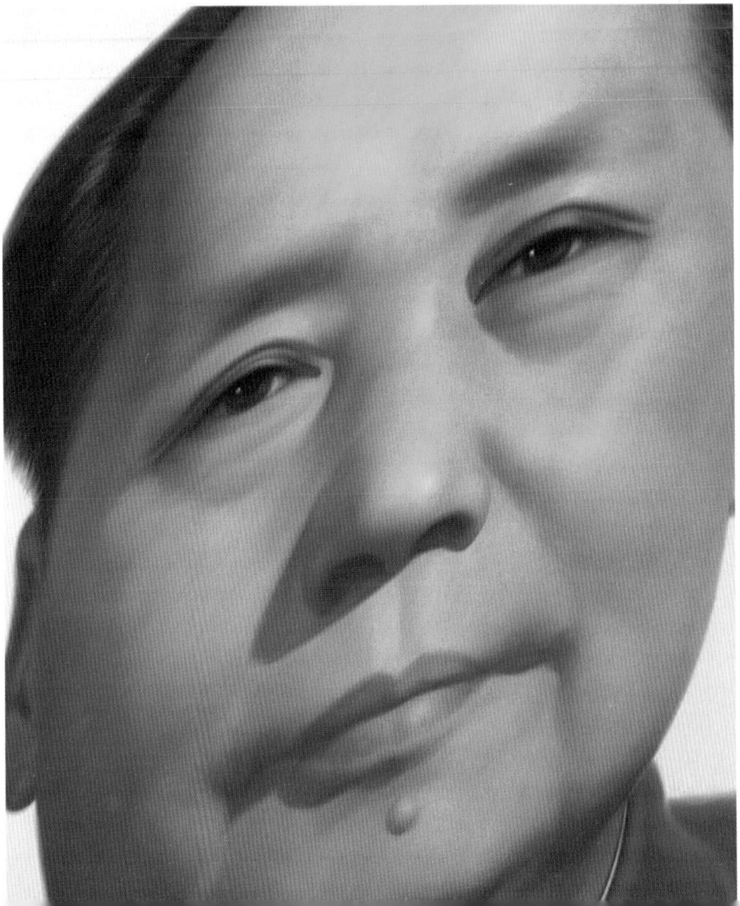

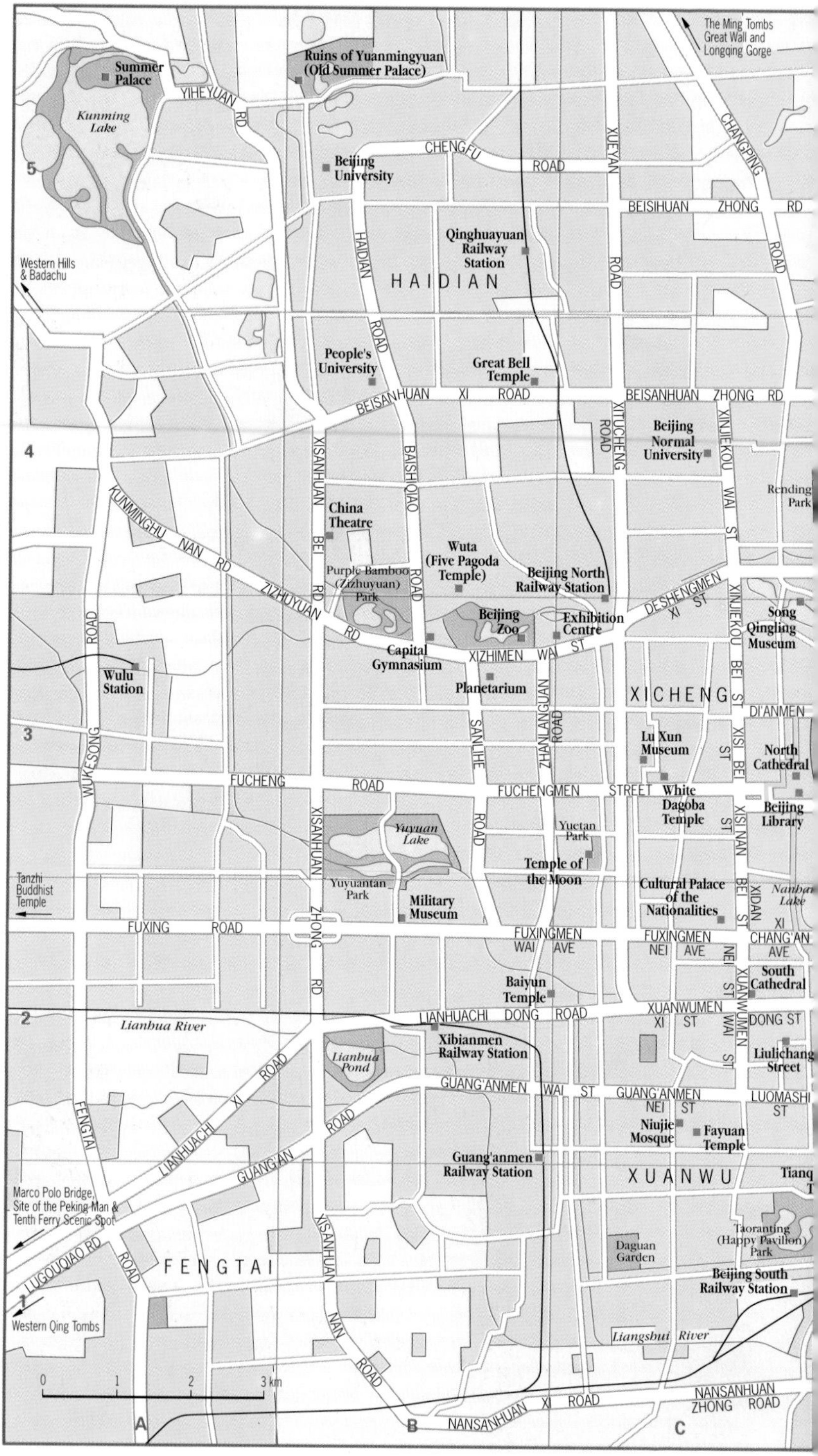

BEIJING

The Ming Tombs
Great Wall and
Longqing Gorge

Summer Palace
Kunming Lake
Ruins of Yuanmingyuan (Old Summer Palace)
YIHEYUAN RD
CHENGFU ROAD
Beijing University
XUEYAN ROAD
CHANGPING ROAD
BEISIHUAN ZHONG RD
HAIDIAN ROAD
Qinghuayuan Railway Station
HAIDIAN
Western Hills & Badachu
People's University
Great Bell Temple
BEISANHUAN XI ROAD
BEISANHUAN ZHONG RD
XITUCHENG ROAD
Beijing Normal University
XINJIEKOU WAI ST
Rending Park
XISANHUAN BEI RD
BAISHIQIAO ROAD
China Theatre
KUNMINGHU NAN RD
ZIZHUYUAN RD
Purple Bamboo (Zizhuyuan) Park
Wuta (Five Pagoda Temple)
Beijing North Railway Station
DESHENGMEN XI ST
XINJIEKOU BEI ST
Song Qingling Museum
Beijing Zoo
Exhibition Centre
Capital Gymnasium
XIZHIMEN WAI ST
Planetarium
Wulu Station
WUKESONG ROAD
XICHENG
DI'ANMEN
SANLIHE ROAD
ZHANLANGUAN ROAD
Lu Xun Museum
XISI BEI ST
North Cathedral
FUCHENG ROAD
FUCHENGMEN STREET
White Dagoba Temple
Beijing Library
Yuyuan Lake
Yuyuantan Park
Yuetan Park
Temple of the Moon
XISI NAN ST
Tanzhi Buddhist Temple
XISANHUAN ZHONG RD
Military Museum
Cultural Palace of the Nationalities
XIDAN BEI ST
Nanhai Lake
FUXING ROAD
FUXINGMEN WAI AVE
FUXINGMEN NEI AVE
XI CHANG'AN AVE
Baiyun Temple
XUANWUMEN NEI ST
South Cathedral
LIANHUACHI DONG ROAD
XUANWUMEN XI ST
XUANWUMEN WAI ST
XUANWUMEN DONG ST
Lianhua River
Xibianmen Railway Station
Lianhua Pond
Liulichang Street
LIANHUACHI XI ROAD
GUANG'ANMEN WAI ST
GUANG'ANMEN NEI ST
LUOMASHI ST
FENGTAI
Niujie Mosque
Fayuan Temple
GUANG'AN ROAD
Guang'anmen Railway Station
XUANWU
Tianq
Marco Polo Bridge, Site of the Peking Man & Tenth Ferry Scenic Spot
Taoranting (Happy Pavilion) Park
Daguan Garden
LUGOUQIAO RD
ROAD
FENGTAI
XISANHUAN NAN ROAD
Beijing South Railway Station
Western Qing Tombs
Liangshui River
NANSANHUAN XI ROAD
NANSANHUAN ZHONG ROAD

0 1 2 3 km

5
4
3
2
1
A B C

BEIJING

White Dragon Pool
ANLI ROAD
BEIYUAN ROAD
BEISIHUAN DONG ROAD
Olympic Village
Beijing Airport
Babe River
BEISANHUAN DONG ROAD
Xihuang Temple
ANDINGMEN WAI ST
Hepingli Railway Station
SHOUDUJICHANG ROAD
China International Exhibition Centre
Qingnian Park
Ditan Park
Temple of the Earth
Bamboo Garden Hotel
ANDINGMEN XI ST
ANDINGMEN DONG ST
Lama Temple
Confucian Temple (Capital Museum)
DONGZHIMEN WAI ST
National Agricultural Exhibition Centre
Houhai Lake
Bell Tower
Drum Tower
Imperial Academy (Guozijian)
DONGCHENG
Qianhai Lake
DI'ANMEN DONG ST
DONGSISHITIAO ST
DONGZHIMEN ST
GONGRENTIYVCHANG RD
Beihai Lake
Workers' Stadium
Jingshan Park
Beihai Park
China Art Gallery
WUSI ST
CHAOYANGMEN NEI ST
CHAOYANGMEN WAI ST
DONGSANHUAN BEI ROAD
Zhonghai Lake
Forbidden City (Palace Museum)
WANGFUJING ST
DONG SI NAN ST
CHAOYANGMEN NAN ST
Ritan Park
CHAOYANG RD
DONGDAN
Temple of the Sun
Zhongshan Park
Monument of the People's Heroes
Museum of the Chinese Revolution
Post Office
Friendship Store
DONG CHANG'AN AVE
JIANGUOMEN WAI AVE
TIANANMEN SQUARE
Ancient Observatory
Eastern Qing Tombs
Great Hall of the People
Museum of Chinese History
Beijing Railway Station
Tonghui River
QIANMEN DONG ST
CHONGWENMEN STREET
Qianmen Gate
Mao's Memorial Hall
Underground City
QIANMEN ST
ZHUSHIKOU DONG STREET
GUANGQUMEN NEI STREET
GUANGQUMEN WAI STREET
DONGSANHUAN NAN ROAD
CHONGWEN
Museum of Natural History
Temple of Heaven (Tiantan) Park
Taoranting Happy Garden
YONDINGMEN NEI ST
Longtan Park
Longtan Lake
YONDINGMEN WAI ST
NANSANHUAN DONG ROAD
D
E

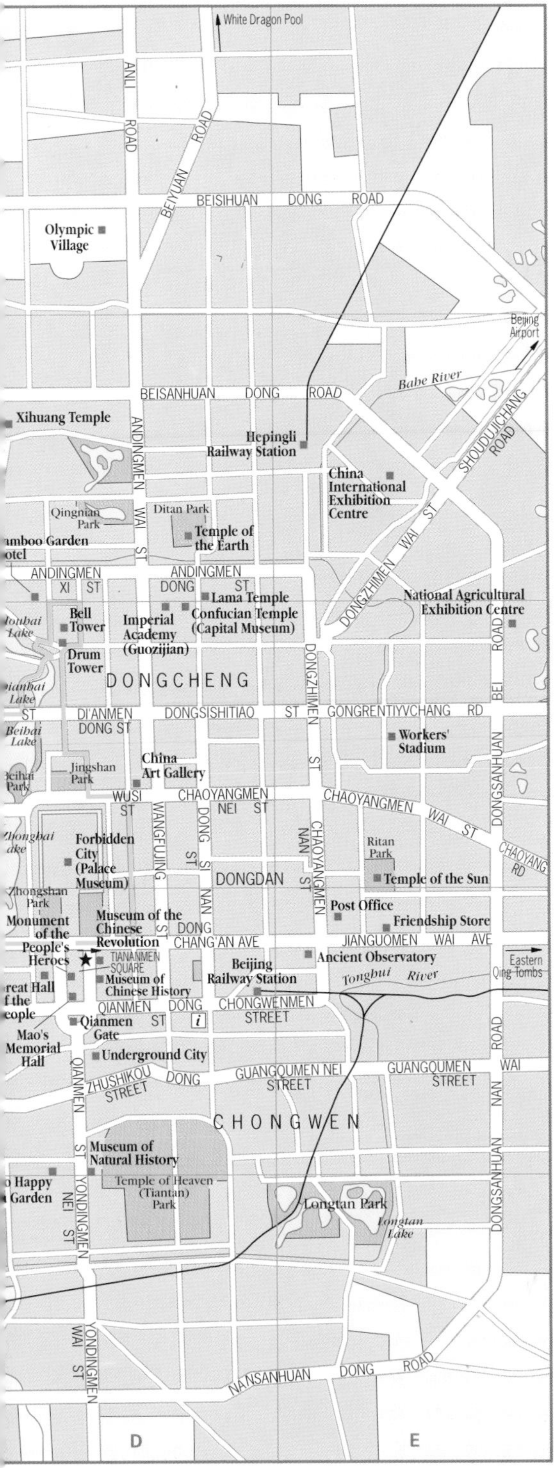

Exclusive Peking
Non cuivis Homini Contingit adire Corinthium. It is the lot of few to go to Pekin.
– John Barrow, Lord Macartney's Private Secretary. *Travels in China*, 1801

The North During China's long history there have been many capital cities. Some were no more than regional capitals for dynasties that did not control the whole of the country. Others, like Xi'an, were state capitals for the earlier dynasties. Beijing was the last of the imperial capitals and has remained capital for most of the 20th century. What is left of its ancient glories derive mostly from the last two dynasties, the Ming and Qing, but it has been a capital on and off for some 3,000 years.

Early days Before the unification of China in 221BC, Beijing was Jicheng or Yanjing, the capital of the Kingdom of Yan, located a few kilometres east of the current site. It remained a provincial town of some significance during the Tang, but became a secondary capital in AD947 under the Liao rulers who controlled the north. The only reminders of this period are the Tianningsi pagoda near Guang'anmen and a stele in the Western Hills. During the 12th century, the Jin rulers named the city Zhongdu and made it their main capital. The most splendid relics from that period are the Marco Polo Bridge and a group of pagodas at Changping.

In its prime position on the corner of Wangfujing and Chang'an Avenue, McDonald's symbolises China's economic liberalisation

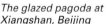

Peking Opera – colourful, noisy, and very Chinese

In 1215 Zhongdu was razed by the Mongols. By 1260, when all of northern China had been conquered, Kublai Khan moved his capital from Karakorum to Zhongdu, rebuilt the city and called it Khanbaliq (Khan's Town), or Dadu in Chinese. It was centred on today's Beihai Park – before that the city's focus had been the area of Guang'anmen. The principal streets ran mostly north–south, the intersecting *hutongs* (from a Chinese word meaning 'barbarian'), or lanes, running east–west. Some of these still exist.

Ming and Qing In 1368, the first Ming Emperor chose to move the capital to Nanjing ('Southern Capital'). One of his sons was made ruler of the principality of Yan, with Dadu, now renamed Beiping, as its capital. In 1403, when the prince became the third Ming emperor, Beiping was called Beijing ('Northern Capital') and became capital of China once again. It was rebuilt mostly on the foundations of Dadu, although it was larger, and the basic dimensions of today's city centre date from this period, as do its principal monuments, the Forbidden City and the Temple of Heaven. During the Qing dynasty the city's layout was altered and additional palaces were built in and around the centre. In the main, however, Beijing retained its Ming flavour. In the first half of the 20th century although several other cities laid claim to the title of Chinese capital, it was from the rostrum above Tiananmen Square in Beijing that Mao Zedong announced the founding of the People's Republic of China in 1949.

Beijing today Modern Beijing is no longer a classically beautiful city – mindless destruction, planned or politically inspired, has seen to that. Yet its extraordinary history has bequeathed to it a certain grandeur and there is no doubt that it impresses. The Forbidden City, one of the most magnificent architectural ensembles in the world, and the other snippets of the past that linger here and there, still make a visit essential.

The glazed pagoda at Xiangshan, Beijing

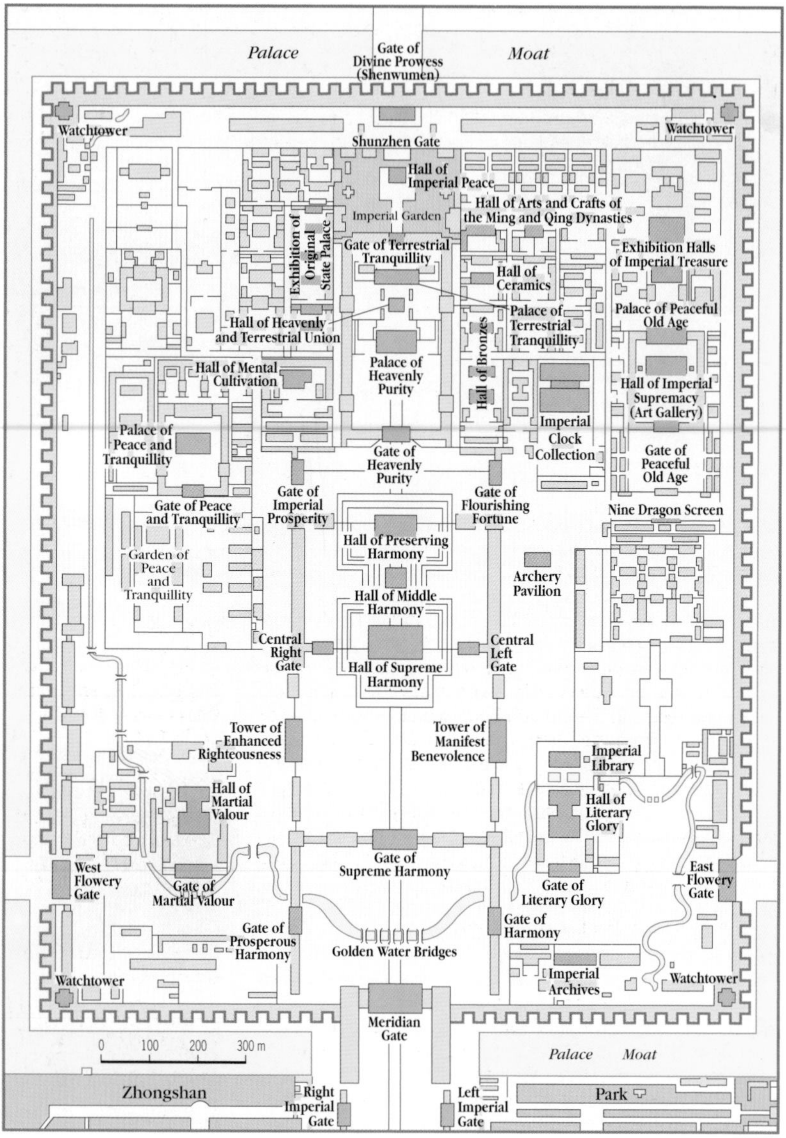

Walk The Forbidden City

The description on pages 53–5 guides you through the Forbidden City, starting at the South (Meridian) Gate and walking along the main central axis to the exit at the Gate of Divine Prowess (Shenwumen). You will pass all the major ceremonial pavilions used by the emperors, the imperial bedrooms and, by taking a couple of diversions, the former residence of the imperial concubines, the imperial treasure exhibition rooms, the painting exhibition and the imperial Clock Collection.

The Hall of Supreme Harmony, in the Forbidden City

▶▶▶ Beihai (North Lake) Park (Beihai Gongyuan) *49D3*

Open 8–4:30, closed Monday.

If you have time, visit this park and classical garden just northwest of the Forbidden City. The heart of the Mongol capital, Dadu, the area retains from the Mongol period only the jade bowl in the **Tuancheng (Round City**, just inside the main entrance on Wenjin Jie) but several buildings in the Tuancheng and the Dragon Screen on the north bank of the lake date from the Ming. The **White Dagoba** was built in 1651 in honour of a visit by the Dalai Lama. Most of the pavilions on the east side were the Qing dynasty pleasure gardens. On Qionghua Island is the **Fangshan Fandian**, which serves dishes favoured by the Dowager Empress Cixi. The park is said to have been a favourite spot of Jiang Qing, wife of Mao and one of the Gang of Four.

Boxer murder
In Zhongshan Park,just outside the Forbidden City, is a memorial to Baron Clement August von Kettler, 19th-century German minister to China. He was murdered by a mob on 20 June 1900 on his way to the Chinese Foreign Office to protest at the violence of the Boxers (an anti-Manchu and anti-foreign sect, see page 43).

▶▶▶ Forbidden City (Zijincheng) *49D3*

Open 8:30–4:30, closed Monday.

The centre of Beijing is dominated by the imperial yellow roofs and vermilion walls of the Forbidden City, sometimes called the Imperial Museum or Palace Museum (Gugong). In Mongol times it was the 'Great Within'. Under the Ming and Qing, Beijing was divided into walled sections or cities – the Forbidden City was the innermost and the most important, for it was the residence of the emperor and the imperial family, the focal point of the empire and the middle of the 'Middle Kingdom' (i.e. China). Entry was strictly forbidden to all but those on imperial business until 1911 when the last emperor, Puyi, was overthrown. It occupies 720,000sq m, there are, allegedly, 9,999 rooms, and it is surrounded by a moat and a 10m high wall with a perimeter of 6km.

You have to visit the Forbidden City on foot and although it is possible to enter it from either the south or north gates, the south (Wumen or Meridian Gate) is preferable. The main ensemble is made up of two groups of three palaces, mostly 18th century, situated one after the other on the central axis called the Meridian Line. Behind them, at the north end, is the Imperial Garden. Alongside the

The White Dagoba in Beihai Park

Birth of an emperor
When Dowager Empress Cixi was a 'virtuous imperial concubine', she became pregnant. Cixi was permitted to select six maids to help her at the birth as well as two midwives and two doctors. As a reward for producing a son, Cixi was promoted and awarded 300 taels of silver and 70 bolts of highest quality fabric.

Hair loom
Preserving the hair of ancestors has long been a sign of respect in China. In the Forbidden City there is a solid gold stupa built by Emperor Qianlong to hold his mother's fallen hair.

Flying cranes on a glazed tile panel in the Imperial Garden

palaces to the northwest are the former apartments of the concubines and to the northeast the palaces of emperor Qianlong and empress Cixi.

The first group of three palaces – the outer court – were for official functions; the second three – the inner court – were for private ones. Before you reach them you pass the towering **Meridian Gate**, reserved for the emperor. Every morning the principal officials would wait atop the gate for the emperor's arrival announced by the drums and bells in the pavilions on either side of the gate. Beyond is a magnificent courtyard across which runs the **Golden Water Stream**, shaped like a Tartar bow, spanned by the five **Inner Golden Water Bridges**. The **Taihemen (Gate of Supreme Harmony)** follows, to the right of which is a group of buildings devoted to Confucian studies and containing the imperial library. To the left is the **Hall of Martial Valour** where the Ming empresses received their female subjects. After Taihemen is another courtyard and the three main palaces of the 'outer court'.

The first of these is the **Taihedian (Hall of Supreme Harmony)**, once the tallest building in Beijing, where the emperor ascended the throne, received high officials and celebrated important festivals. The Taihedian is reckoned to contain 55 rooms, a room being the space between four pillars. No commoner was permitted to build higher than this hall. Roofs were accorded rank, too, and naturally this was of the highest, built in the *wudian* (thatched hall) style with four fully hipped double roofs with curved, overhanging eaves. At each end of the ridge are giant dragon heads (the dragon was the imperial symbol); the mythological figures running down the side ridges ward off calamity, particularly fire. The marble ramp leading up to the terrace, decorated with clouds and a dragon, was for the emperor's sole use. On the terrace are a sundial and grain measure, testifying to the imperial concern for

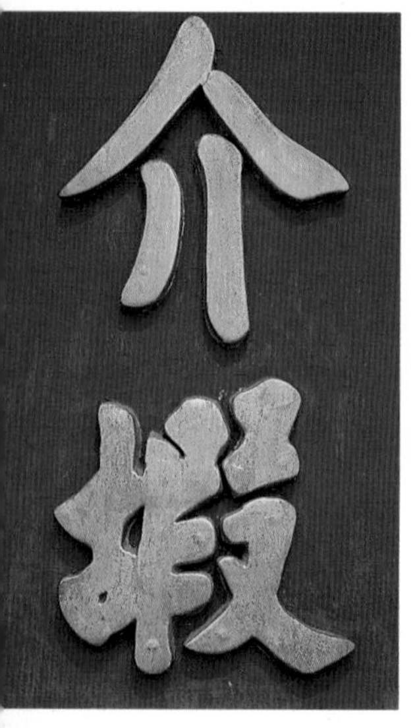

Golden characters on a column in the Forbidden City

the harvest, four incense burners in the form of tortoises and cranes, symbols of longevity, and bronze cauldrons for water in the event of fire.

After Taihedian comes **Zhonghedian (Hall of Middle Harmony)**, venue for rehearsals and receptions for officials from the Ministry of Rites. Then comes the **Baohedian (Hall of Preserving Harmony)**, where the emperor gave banquets to princes from vassal states on Lunar New Year's Eve. Here during the Qing the emperor supervised the final stage of the civil service examinations (see panel, page 67).

As you leave the Baohedian, before you, protected by two gilded lions, is the **Qianqingmen (Gate of Heavenly Purity)**, the gateway to the inner court or residential quarters, in many ways the true seat of power. Proceed through here and come to the **Qianqinggong (Palace of Heavenly Purity)**, the emperor's bedroom and also the office of quotidian administration. Large banquets were given here on festival days. Behind it is the smaller **Jiataidian (Hall of Heavenly and Terrestrial Union)** used for lesser ceremonies. The empress raised silkworms here to demonstrate her industry and it was also used to house the imperial seals. You then come to the **Kunninggong (Palace of Terrestrial Tranquillity**, symbol of the earth), the empress's bedroom and, under the Qing, the emperor's bridal chamber. Behind the palaces is the **Imperial Garden** and the north exit, the Gate of Divine Prowess (Shenwumen).

There are two diversions that also bring you to the Shenwumen. By turning left before the Qianqingmen and then right, and walking along an alley to the left of the Qianqinggong, you reach on your left a gateway which leads to the concubines' quarters. Among them is the **Yangxindian (Hall of Mental Cultivation)**, which became the residence of all the emperors from 1723. Within, to the right, is the **Dongnuange**. Here the boy emperors were told how to conduct affairs of state by the dowager empresses, who sat hidden behind a screen.

Alternatively, turn right before Qianqingmen, pass under a portico, bear diagonally left to a doorway and emerge into a courtyard. On the left is a building housing the **Imperial Clock Collection**. This was where Emperor Qian long lived after his retirement. Return through the doorway, turn left and left again and you come to the **Nine Dragon Screen**. Opposite is a doorway. Go as straight as you can, pass, on the left, the painting exhibition and eventually reach the exhibition halls of imperial treasure. From here you can easily find your way to the exit gate.

The cook and the dragon
In 1803 an unemployed cook, Chen De, tried to assassinate Emperor Jiaqing. As the emperor entered the Forbidden City, a very drunk Chen De slipped through the gates and leapt at him, dagger in hand. The emperor escaped by jumping off his sedan chair. At his trial Chen explained that a dream had shown him that he was destined to be emperor by using his skill in martial arts.

A Forbidden City dragon, symbol of the emperor, chasing the 'flaming pearl'

Impressions of the wall
Not everyone has been moved by the awesome nature of the Great Wall. A British footballer in Beijing to play an exhibition match with his club, West Bromwich Albion, declined to visit it at all on the grounds that 'when you have seen one wall you have seen them all'. President Richard Nixon did go: 'Well, this really is a great wall!', he observed.

Keeping the 'barbarians' out of the Middle Kingdom: a restored section of the Great Wall at Badaling, north of Beijing

▶▶▶ The Great Wall (Changcheng) *49C5*

The Great Wall is a symbol of Chinese genius, a colossal human feat that has captured the European imagination. Although the wall as it now stands dates mainly from the Ming dynasty, at least 20 states and dynasties were involved in its construction over a period of 2,000 years, following different routes or building extensions according to need. Eventually stretching some 6,000km, the wall was garrisoned by up to 1 million soldiers, and was complemented by over 1,000 fortified passes and 10,000 beacon towers. Walls were first built as barriers between states during the Spring and Autumn period – the oldest was built by the Kingdom of Qi in 500BC and extended for 480km. When China was finally united in 221BC under the Qin, the existing walls were linked together to protect the new China from invaders from the north. Different construction materials were used according to the terrain – rammed earth, or stone and brick (as in the Ming wall). Hundreds of thousands of conscripts were involved in the project, many of whom died from exhaustion and malnutrition. The Han emperor extended the wall still further, but it was not until the rise of the Ming dynasty in the 14th century that an imperial regime was to have total control over its entire length again. The early Ming emperors almost entirely rebuilt the wall, extending it westward over 6,400km from Shanhaiguan to Jiayuguan. It was never to play such a significant role in Chinese history again, however – with the advent of the Manchus, who controlled the territory on both sides of it, the wall fell into disrepair, only a few frontier posts being maintained to check travellers going north.

Visitors usually go to the restored section at **Badaling**, 72km northwest of Beijing. You need a ticket to climb on to

the wall; once up, the less crowded (if steeper) side is to the left. Another access point is at **Mutianyu**, which is less crowded but not as well preserved.

▶ The Ming Tombs (Shisanling) *49C5*

The tombs of the Ming emperors are located 25km from the Great Wall, about 50km north of Beijing. Only 13 of the 16 emperors are buried here – the first Ming emperor is buried at Nanjin; the whereabouts of the second emperor is unknown; and the seventh emperor is buried somewhere in Beijing, location unknown. Two tombs are open – **Dingling**, the tomb of the 13th emperor (died 1620), and the only one to have been excavated; and **Changling**, the largest, the tomb of the third emperor (reigned 1403–24).

The search for an auspicious burial site, based on the rules of geomancy (or *fengshui*, wind and water), was started by the third emperor in 1407. Undulating hills form a screen to the north. Dragon Hill and Tiger Hill stand to the south and the Wenyu river provides the water element. The tomb area, once surrounded by a 40km wall, is approached via a sacred way. It begins at a commemorative gateway (perhaps the finest in China) erected in 1541, passes through a vermilion gatehouse and then between 24 stone animals, arranged in pairs, and 12 human figures. At the end is another gatehouse after which the road diverges to the various tombs, each marked with a yellow-roofed 'visible tower'. There is little to see in the vault at Dingling save for some vases, marble thrones and doors, and reconstructed coffins. Some of the treasure is exhibited above ground. Changling, although unexcavated, is grander, housing an exhibition of some of the treasures discovered at Dingling in the magnificent main hall used for sacrifices to the dead emperor.

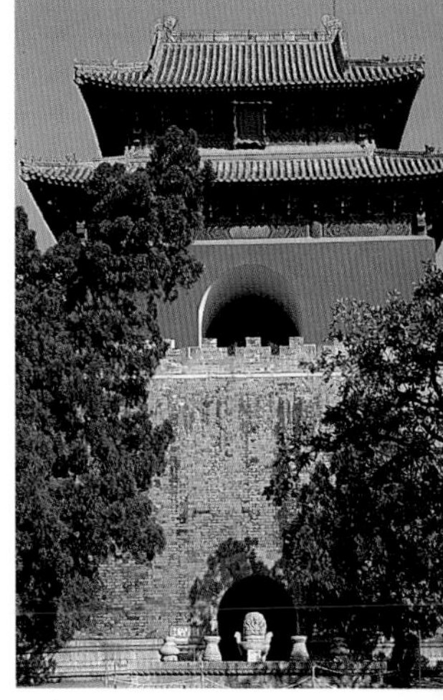

Changling ('Long-lasting Tomb'), one of 13 tombs of the Ming emperors occupying a burial site 55km north of Beijing

Guards in mock Ming period costume stand sentinel on the Great Wall at Badaling

Chinese Nursery Rhyme
The Emperor of Qin
Shi Huang Di
Built a wall
From the hills to the sea.
He built it wide,
He built it stout
To keep his subjects in
And the Tartars out,
The Emperor of Qin.

■ Since 1949 Beijing has run the gamut of destruction, both deliberate (zealous town-planning) and spontaneous (Cultural Revolution). Miraculously, pockets of magnificence survive amid a network of anaemic boulevards.....■

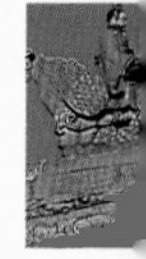

Urban China
The old walled city was considered a perfect example of Chinese town-planning theory, which goes back to the Warring States Period (476–221BC). It is rectangular, surrounded by a wall, and its palace, close to government ministries, is at the centre. It is also excellently situated according to geomantic criteria – open to the south and east, with water at the front and well screened by mountains to the north, to protect the city from evil.

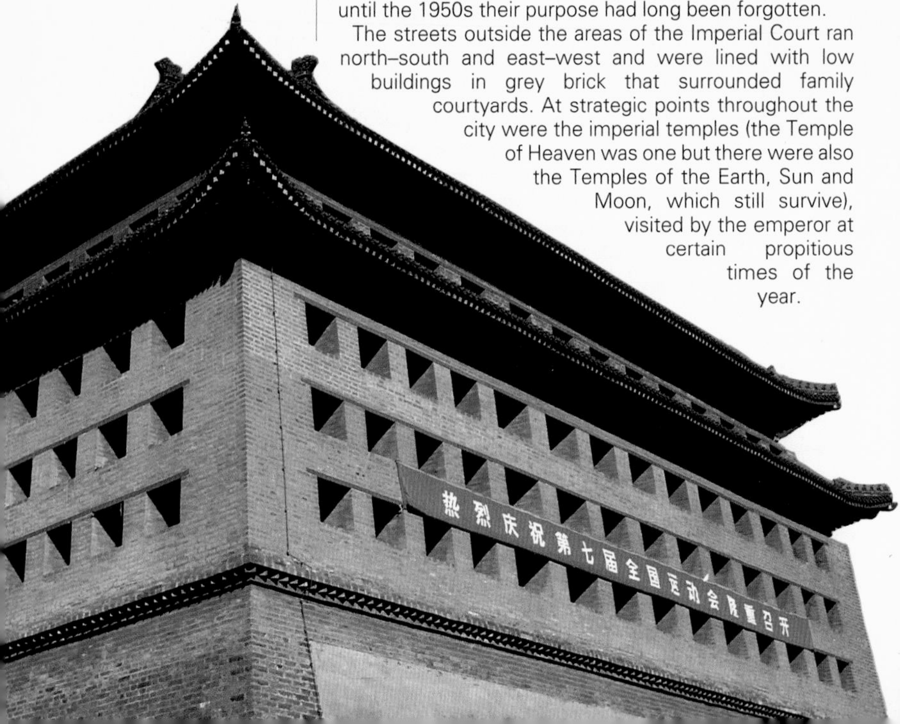

The great tower gate at Dongbianmen, a reminder of the city wall's former grandeur

Imperial cities Beijing still exudes greatness; partly because the street-plan devised under the Ming remains to remind the visitor of its 'celestial geometry'. Yet as recently as the 1950s Beijing would have looked a very different place.

Under the Manchus (the Qing dynasty), Beijing was divided in four. The innermost city was the walled Forbidden City. Outside the Forbidden City lay the Imperial City, where government officials resided. This too lay behind a wall, the remains of which still stand (along the north side of Tiananmen Square) and behind which today's government officials continue their work. The whole was surrounded by the 15th-century city wall proper, from which some of the towers survive. During the Qing this wall enclosed what foreigners called the Tartar City, the northern part of Beijing reserved for Manchus, particularly troops. The southernmost point of the Tartar City wall was the southern margin of Tiananmen Square, today marked by two ancient towers, which conversely were part of the northern wall of the Chinese City. The latter was the quarter where the Chinese were compelled to live; its walls extended south to beyond the Temple Of Heaven (Tiantan) and have completely disappeared. This was the business area of the city. The attempt to separate Manchu and Chinese inevitably failed – although the walls survived until the 1950s their purpose had long been forgotten.

The streets outside the areas of the Imperial Court ran north–south and east–west and were lined with low buildings in grey brick that surrounded family courtyards. At strategic points throughout the city were the imperial temples (the Temple of Heaven was one but there were also the Temples of the Earth, Sun and Moon, which still survive), visited by the emperor at certain propitious times of the year.

The city walls The city walls, of rammed earth with a carapace of grey brick, were thought to be the finest and grandest in the world. They were an astounding 40km in length and between 3m and 4m in height. There were 16 gateways, each surmounted by an imposing tower, and the whole was surrounded by a moat. In winter its frozen water was cut out and preserved underground to be used in the summer. The streets within the walls were a riot of colour and movement – silken pennants hung outside shops and offices and all manner of noises and smells greeted you as you stepped out on the pavement. It is still possible to experience something of this atmosphere by walking through what is left of the old shopping district of Qianmen, just to the south of Tiananmen Square.

Pleasure domes
After the Japanese took control of Beijing in 1937 opium dens were openly allowed in parts of the city. Smokers lolled on benches while attendants brought them opium, a pipe, an oil-lamp and a pin. Addicts speared the opium on the pin and heated it before inhaling the fumes.

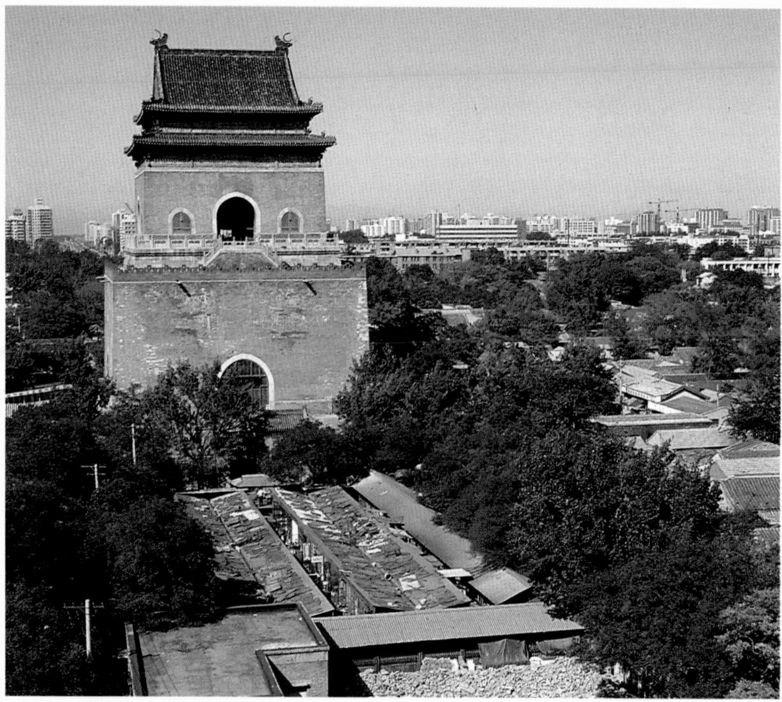

Beijing's Bell Tower

The Legation Oddly enough, one of the areas of the city that still retains the sort of charm that comes with continuity is not really Chinese at all, but European; many of the buildings of the old Legation area east of Tiananmen Square still stand and provide a sort of leafy graciousness absent elsewhere in the city. In the late 19th century the Legation area was less compact, but following the Boxer Rebellion of 1900 it was decided to group the legations together in a compound, with its own crenellated wall.

Beijing was also celebrated for its *hutongs*, the network of alleys and traditional courtyards, most of which have now gone. However, the area between Wangfujing and the east wall of the Forbidden City or Wangfujing and Dongdan still give much of the flávour of old Beijing.

High flyers
In the past kite-flying was a favourite pastime, frequently to be seen all over the city and particularly at New Year, when market stalls were piled high with kites made of bamboo and paper in a variety of shapes, including birds, goldfish and mythical characters. Nowadays kites are still flown in Tiananmen Square, an uplifting sight.

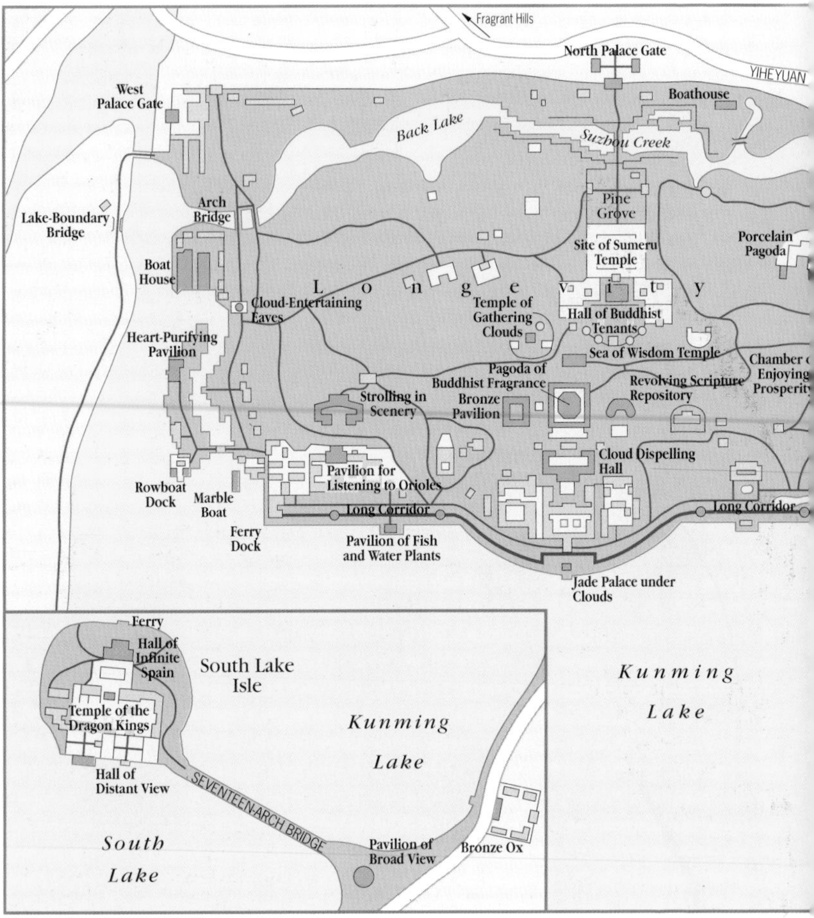

Fragrant Hills
North Palace Gate
YIHEYUAN
West Palace Gate
Boathouse
Back Lake
Suzhou Creek
Lake-Boundary Bridge
Arch Bridge
Pine Grove
Porcelain Pagoda
Site of Sumeru Temple
Boat House
L o n g e v i t y
Cloud-Entertaining Eaves
Temple of Gathering Clouds
Hall of Buddhist Tenants
Heart-Purifying Pavilion
Sea of Wisdom Temple
Chamber of Enjoying Prosperity
Pagoda of Buddhist Fragrance
Revolving Scripture Repository
Strolling in Scenery
Bronze Pavilion
Cloud Dispelling Hall
Pavilion for Listening to Orioles
Rowboat Dock
Marble Boat
Long Corridor
Long Corridor
Ferry Dock
Pavilion of Fish and Water Plants
Jade Palace under Clouds
Ferry
Hall of Infinite Spain
South Lake Isle
Kunming Lake
Temple of the Dragon Kings
Kunming Lake
Hall of Distant View
SEVENTEEN-ARCH BRIDGE
South Lake
Pavilion of Broad View
Bronze Ox

Walk The Summer Palace

The walk through the Summer Palace, described on pages 61–3, is essentially scenic. Enter through the East Palace Gate, bear right, then straighten up to pass near the main halls used by the last emperors. Walk along the Long Corridor on the shore of the lake, visiting more of the pavilions to the right. A diversion at the start will take you to the Garden of Harmonious Interest, whilst the return journey can be effected by taking a ferry from close to the Marble Boat by Kunming Lake.

Taking a rest on the Long Corridor

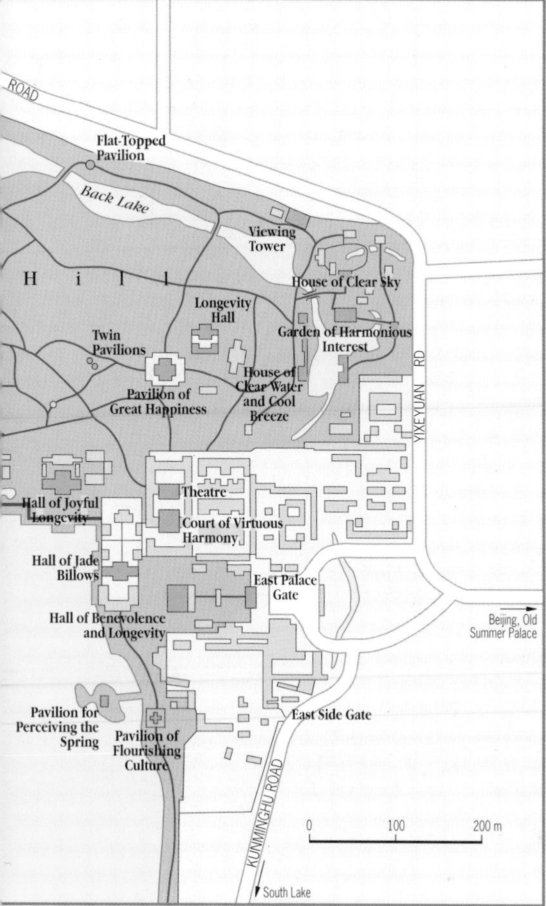

These Chinese beauties in Qing costume are attendants at the theatre museum in the Summer Palace

▶▶▶ Summer Palace (Yiheyuan) *48A5*

Open 6–5:30.

The buildings of the Summer Palace, known as Yiheyuan, date back only to the turn of the century. The site, however, goes back to the 12th century, when the first Jin ruler built his Gold Mountain Travelling Palace on what is now Longevity Hill. The water from the Jade Spring was diverted to form the Gold Sea, an early Kunming Lake. During the Yuan dynasty the Gold Mountain became Jug Mountain and the lake was enlarged. Another palace was built here under the Ming but it was during the reign of the Qianlong Emperor that the area was transformed. Longevity Hill took its name in honour of the 60th birthday of Qianlong's mother and the Kunming Lake in honour of a lake near Xi'an which the Han emperors used for naval manoeuvres.

In 1764 the area became the Park of Pure Ripples (Qingyiyuan), and was part of a grand plan to build a set of pleasure grounds, in the lee of the Western Hills. Apart from Qingyiyuan, there was to be Jingmingyuan at Yuquanshan, Jingyiyuan at Xiangshan, Changchunyuan

Oxbridge

At the mainland end of the Seventeen-Arch bridge in the Summer Palace is the Bronze Ox, which has been guarding Kunming Lake for 200 years. Its presence is based on the legend which said that the Great Yu tamed lakes and rivers by throwing iron oxen into the water.

The Garden of Pure Brightness
Although all that is left of the Yuanmingyuan are romantic ruins, it once included a labyrinth, an aviary, a gazebo, palaces with fountains, and representations of the countryside of Turkestan with moving scenery. Engravings of the pleasure-dome by the Jesuits are to be found in the British Museum, London, and the Bibliothèque Nationale, Paris.

and Yuanmingyuan. The last mentioned, the Park of Perfection and Brightness, was the original Qing dynasty Summer Palace, destroyed in 1860 by the British and French; by 1895 a replacement had been constructed in the Park of Pure Ripples but when the Anglo-French force reinvaded Beijing in 1900 the new Summer Palace was destroyed too. Reconstruction began in 1902, and the result is what we see today – the Summer Palace became a huge classical Chinese garden, the south face of Longevity Hill laid out in vague imitation of Hangzhou's West Lake, the north face following the architectural style of Suzhou. After 1908 the palace was no longer used by the imperial family, and in 1924 it became a public park.

The main entrance is at **Donggongmen** (**East Palace Gate**) which leads to the **Renshoudian** (**Hall of Benevolence and Longevity**, derived from an old saying 'Benevolent people live long lives'), where affairs of state were conducted by Cixi. The grey-roofed buildings between the gate and the hall were the waiting-rooms for officials on duty. The bronze *qilin* (a legendary beast with dragon's head, lion's tail, deer's antlers, ox's hooves and fish-scaled body) in front of the hall was at the original Summer Palace.

To the right of the Renshoudian is the **Deheyuan** (**Court of Virtuous Harmony**) with its theatre, the largest in China, where Cixi watched performances of Peking Opera. Trapdoors in the ceilings and floors of its three storeys were designed as entries and exits for supernatural beings. Beyond the Renshoudian, in the direction of the lake, is the former residential area; here the first and principal building is the **Leshoutang** (**Hall of Joyful Longevity**), the residence of the Dowager Empress between May and November. South of the Leshoutang, at the waterfront and to the rear of the Renshoudian, is the **Yulantang** (**Hall of Jade Billows**, named after a poem by Lu Ji, a third-century poet), the former residence of the Guangxu Emperor. The interiors of the Leshoutang and Yulantang have been preserved as they were left by their last inhabitants. The side halls of the Yulantang were blocked off in 1898 on the instructions of Cixi, thereby confining the Guanxu emperor to house arrest for his involvement in the 1898 'Hundred Days of Reform' movement.

Further west along Kunming Lake is the famous **Long Corridor** (**Changlang**), a covered walkway 728m long, its beams and walkways painted with views of the famous West Lake in Hangzhou and scenes from

A remnant of the south façade of the waterworks at Yuanmingyuan, the Old Summer Palace

Chinese legend, history or literature. It breaks into two halves at the **Paiyundian (Cloud Dispelling Hall**, from a poem by the third-century poet Guo Pu), where Cixi celebrated her birthdays. Built on the site of an earlier Ming temple, the tower above is called the **Foxiangge (Pagoda of Buddhist Fragrance**). Behind the pagoda is the **Zhihuihai (Sea of Wisdom Temple**), covered in religious statues, many disfigured by British and French troops in 1860. To the east of the pagoda is the **Zhuanluncang (Revolving Scripture Repository**) containing a tablet inscribed with an essay on Kunming Lake in the hand of the Qianlong Emperor.

The Long Corridor continues and passes the **Pavilion for Listening to Orioles (Tingliguan**) on the right, the site of a restaurant and shop. The corridor comes to an end at the corner of the lake. In front of you to the right is the **Marble Boat**, an ironic reminder that the funds appropriated by the Dowager Empress to reconstruct the Summer Palace had been earmarked for the Chinese navy. During the summer months pleasure-boats run from here back to the entrance.

The way to the **West Palace Gate** lies beyond the Marble Boat. An old Japanese-built steamboat – part of the old Chinese navy – lies in dry dock, near the old boat-houses. Beyond is a beautiful arched bridge in the south China style.

The north and northeast areas of the palace gardens are in quiet contrast to the showy areas at the lakeside. In the northeast corner is the **Xiequyuan (Garden of Harmonious Interest**), a series of small pavilions around a landscaped miniature lake. Opposite its entrance is a stairway up the hill to **Jinfuge (Tower of Great Fortune**) which offers a fine view to South Lake Isle and the magnificent Seventeen-Arch Bridge. The area of the **North Palace Gate** – the former main entrance – was badly affected by the French and British invasion. Suzhou Creek was once lined with tea-houses and shops and remains a charming area to visit.

Near the Summer Palace, in the northwest suburbs, the remains of the **Old Summer Palace►, Yuanmingyuan**, razed by the British and French in 1860, is a poignant reminder of Chinese decline and European rapaciousness.

An imperial folly: the Marble Boat on Kunming Lake

Lake of poetical inspiration
Kunming Lake in the Summer Palace is as famous as the West Lake in Hangzhou. The Ming poet Wen Zheng wrote: 'The sun sets on blue waters of the spring lake. Sky-high pavilions are reflected down below. The *tenli* green hills are like a scroll painting. Two white birds fly high in a scene of watery land.'

Imperial staff
The Dowager Empress liked to travel with a retinue of at least 1,000. Her arrival at the rebuilt Summer Palace in 1905 was met by 458 eunuchs and her two main meals consisted of 100 dishes.

Mao's Memorial Hall
Mao's resting place was built by 70,000 volunteers in ten months, between October 1976 and August 1977. It is screened by pine trees from Yenan recalling the 13 years Mao spent there. Within is an air-controlled hush, a white statue of a seated Mao gazing prophetically before a giant landscape tapestry based on a design by the contemporary painter Huang Yongyu. Mao himself lies in state in a crystal coffin.

Heroic work
The granite obelisk known as the Monument to the People's Heroes is inscribed with the calligraphy of Chairman Mao. It reads 'The people's heroes are invincible'.

▶▶▶ Temple of Heaven (Tiantan) Park *49D1*

Open 6:30–6.

Built in 1420, Tiantan only became part of the city proper during the Qing, when the Manchus extended the city walls. China's most famous temple, it stands within a 270-hectare park. Entrance, originally at the west gate, is now via the north or south gates.

The whole area is enclosed by a wall the northern portion of which is round (heaven), and the southern half square (earth). The principal buildings are at either end of the Cinnabar Stairway Bridge. **Qiniandian (Hall of Prayer for Good Harvests)**, is to the north, and is an 1890 replica of the building destroyed by lightning the preceding year.

It was here that the emperor came to pray for a good harvest in the first lunar month each year. The day before the main ceremony was devoted to minor rituals after which the emperor fasted in the Hall of Abstinence, west of the causeway. The sacrifice to heaven was made in the Qiniandian. Constructed without nails, this has wooden mortise and tenon joints and wooden brackets on supporting pillars. The 28 pillars (representing the constellations) are made of *nanmu* hardwood. The four large ones represent the seasons, the 12 inner pillars are the months of the lunar calendar and the outer 12 are the two-hour periods into which the day was traditionally divided. Together they become the 24 solar periods of the year.

At the end of the causeway is the **Echo Wall** (see photograph page 68) inside which is the **Huangqiongyu (Imperial Vault of Heaven)**. This was the storehouse for the spirit tablet of the Supreme Ruler of Heaven which, during the ceremony of the winter solstice, was shifted to the vast round Altar of Heaven, to the south.

▶▶▶ Tiananmen (Gate of Heavenly Peace) Square (Guangchang) *49D2*

Today's vast, grandiose space, scene of the student uprising and massacre in 1989, bears little resemblance to its imperial ancestor. During the Ming and Qing it was narrower, and in addition to the Tiananmen Gate to the

Tiananmen Square, backed by the Gate of Heavenly Peace

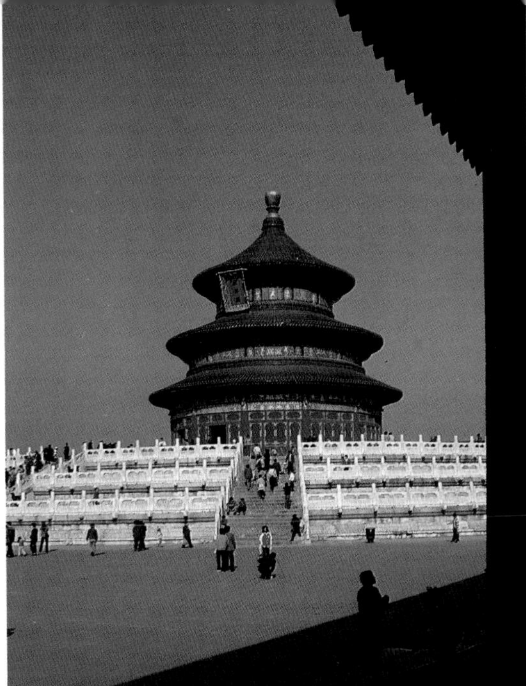

Echo chamber
The Temple of Heaven is renowned for its acoustic qualities. Most famous is the Echo Wall, where your whispered words are amplified to a listener opposite. In the same compound is the Imperial Vault of Heaven, before which are several flagstones – depending upon where you stand on them, the sound made by clapping your hands will echo once, twice or thrice. If you stand talking at the centre of the Imperial Altar your voice will return louder.

The Hall of Prayer for Good Harvests, Temple of Heaven

Imperial City (which still stands) there were two more gates on today's Chang'an Avenue and another, to the south, where the Qianmen now stands. It was surrounded by a vermilion wall beside which ran a covered corridor for use by officials. To the east and west were the imperial ministries. After 1949 most of this was torn down and replaced with what you see today.

The **Tiananmen Gate** has survived since 1651. The brick base is set on a foundation of white marble. The central bridge over the Outer Golden Water Stream forms part of the Imperial Way used on ceremonial occasions and over which only the emperor could pass. Two ornamental columns are surmounted by dishes containing a lion-like creature in stone. The dishes were supposed to catch the 'jade dew' imbibed by the emperor to ensure longevity, while the lions were to watch over him if he were away from the palace.

Along the spine of the square, north to south, are the **Monument to the People's Heroes** (1958), **Chairman Mao's Memorial Hall** (where Mao lies in state), the **Arrow Tower** and **Qianmen**. The west side is dominated by the **Great Hall of the People** – opposite is the revamped **Museum of the Chinese Revolution** and the **Museum of Chinese History**, one of the most important in China but with few concessions made to those who do not speak Chinese.

*A watchful 'lion' atop one of the ceremonial columns (*huabiao*) in front of the Tiananmen Gate*

The East is Red
Before the break with the USSR in 1960, Mao was confident of a shared, bright future. In Moscow in 1957 he said: 'I believe it is characteristic of the situation today that the East Wind is prevailing over the West Wind. That is to say, the forces of socialism have become overwhelmingly superior to the forces of imperialism.'

Polyglot inscriptions in Mongolian, Manchurian, Tibetan and Chinese welcome visitors to the Lam Temple

An equinoctial sphere, one of the beautiful scientific instruments to be seen at the Ancient Observatory

Other sights
Lama Temple (Yonghegong)▶▶ Open 9–4:30, closed Monday. Built in 1694 by the Kangxi Emperor as a residence for his son, Yinzhen, Yonghegong was partly turned over to the Lamaists for scripture recitation when Yinzhen became emperor. It is an extravagant building of some beauty, with remarkable examples of joinery and craftsmanship, and consists of a series of courtyards and pavilions, many with statues of the various incarnations of the Buddha. In the centre of the **Hall of Infinite Happiness (Wanfuge)**, at the rear, stands the grandest at 26m, a statue of the Tathagagata (Maitreya) Buddha made from a single sandalwood trunk.

The Western Hills (Xi Shan)▶▶ is an area of recreation and worship, excellent both for sightseeing and strolling. Here you may visit the **Temple of the Reclining Buddha (Wofosi)** where a bronze Buddha instructs his disciples from his deathbed. Weighing 250,000kg, it dates from the Yuan dynasty. The **Temple of Azure Clouds (Biyunsi)** dates back 600 years. In the **Hall of Arhats** are 500 statues of Buddha's disciples and at the rear is the **Sun Yatsen Memorial Hall**, where Sun Yatsen, the revolutionary and former Provisional President, lay in state after his death in 1925 (see page 229).

Part of the area is known as the **Fragrant Hills Park (Xiangshan Gongyuan)**, formerly the emperor's pleasure parks. Now it is a recreation area with a cable car and only a few remnants of its imperial past.

Churches▶ The Jesuits, who became active in China during the Ming dynasty, bequeathed several churches. The grandest (Nantang) is found at 181 Qianmen Xidajie; it was first erected in the 16th century, but the current version is from 1904. Another is at 74 Wangfujing. The North Cathedral is on Xishiku.

The Ancient Observatory (Guanxiangtai)▶ Open 9–11 and 1–4, closed Monday. Not far from the Friendship Store, mounted on a section of old wall just off Jianguomenwai Avenue, are the remnants of an observatory whose history goes back to the Yuan dynasty. It was built between 1437 and 1446 to provide astrological predictions. Within is a display of navigational equipment and reproductions of ancient Chinese maps and other items relating to the stars. Outside, on the parapet, are instruments designed by the Jesuits who in 1601 gained permission to work with Chinese scientists eager to learn about European firearms. The emperor, impressed by the Jesuits' scientific knowledge, later appointed them court astronomers in place of his Muslim advisers. The instruments are not all original but are of considerable beauty.

Beijing Zoo▶ Open 7:30–6. Although the zoo itself is hardly an example of enlightened animal management, the animals look healthy enough, and there are several examples of China's rarities, notably pandas (giant and red) and Golden Monkeys.

Underground City▶ A network of tunnels honeycombs Beijing's subterranean depths, a result of the fear in the 1960s of a Soviet attack. Part of the system is now shops and even a hotel but the main interest lies in the entrances, several of which are concealed beneath sliding floors in busy neighbourhood shops.

Other temples▶ The ruins of the former imperial temples can still be seen in Beijing – in the north is **Ditan (Temple of Earth)**; to the south is **Taoranting (Happy Pavilion Park)**; to the east is **Ritan (Temple of the Sun)**; and to the west is **Yuetan (Temple of the Moon)**. Although these resemble parks more than temples, hints of their past abound and they are interesting places to observe Chinese life, especially in the early morning. The **Confucian Temple (Kongmiao)** is on Guozijian Jie, an interesting street

Examination hell
Opposite the Ming observatory, to the north, were the former imperial examination halls – 8,500 brick cells where, every three years, candidates were locked in for three days and two nights to take the first stage of the civil service examinations which led to high office. In operation for over 2,000 years, these examinations ceased in 1900 and the halls were demolished in 1913.

Beitang, the North Cathedral, with its defiantly European façade, stands stiff behind curving Chinese roof profiles

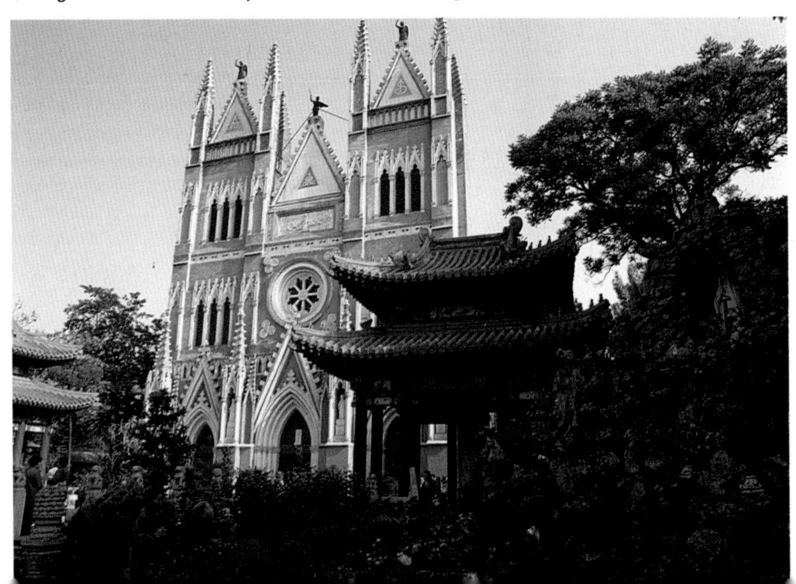

Echo Wall, within the Temple of Heaven Park

Handfuls of dust
One of the quirks of Beijing weather in the spring is the dust that arrives in clouds from the Gobi Desert – it is at this time that women wrap scarves across their faces much as bank robbers are supposed to do.

The open space of Longtan Park provides a peaceful setting for early morning meditation

spanned by commemorative arches, just off Yonghegong Dajie. The **Baiyun Temple (White Cloud Temple)** on Binhe Lu near the southwest corner of the old city was once the centre of Taoism, whilst the **Niujie Mosque** is in the Muslim area in the southwest of Beijing. The **Five Pagoda Temple (Wutasi)**, in the Hindu style, is northwest of the zoo, whilst the **Great Bell Temple (Dazhongsi)** on Beisanhuan Xi Road has a 47.25 tonne bell, cast in 1406.

About 48km west of Beijing is the ancient **Tanzhi Buddhist Temple▶▶**, the largest in the area. It dates back to the 3rd century AD and contains decorative features not found elsewhere in Beijing.

Marco Polo Bridge (Lugouqiao)▶ This bridge 16km southwest of Beijing, mentioned by the Italian traveller, dates back to the late 12th century, although most of the present edifice is from the 17th century.

Qing Tombs▶ The tombs of the Qing imperial family are divided into two groups – Western Qing (Xiling) and Eastern Qing (Dongling). The former are 112km southwest of Beijing and include the excavated tomb of Emperor Guangxu at Chongling, the last tomb to be built (between 1905 and 1915). The latter are 128km east of Beijing and are more impressive, having a spirit way with bridges and guardians. Two tombs are open – those of Emperor Qianlong and the Empress Dowager Cixi.

Other parks▶ Beijing boasts a number of parks. The **Longtan Park (Longtanyuan)** is east of the Temple of Heaven; the **Purple Bamboo Park (Zizhuyuan)** is west of the zoo; and the **Yuyuantan Park** is in the west of the city. The area around the moat of the Forbidden City is also popular.

Other Museums and Galleries▶ The **Song Qingling** Museum (**Song Qingling Guju**) is the former residence of the wife of Sun Yatsen, the founder of the Republic of China. The **China Art Gallery (Zhongguo Meishuguan)** is of interest particularly when there are temporary exhibitions. The **Lu Xun Museum (Lu Xun Bowuguan)** is dedicated to the career of the revolutionary writer.

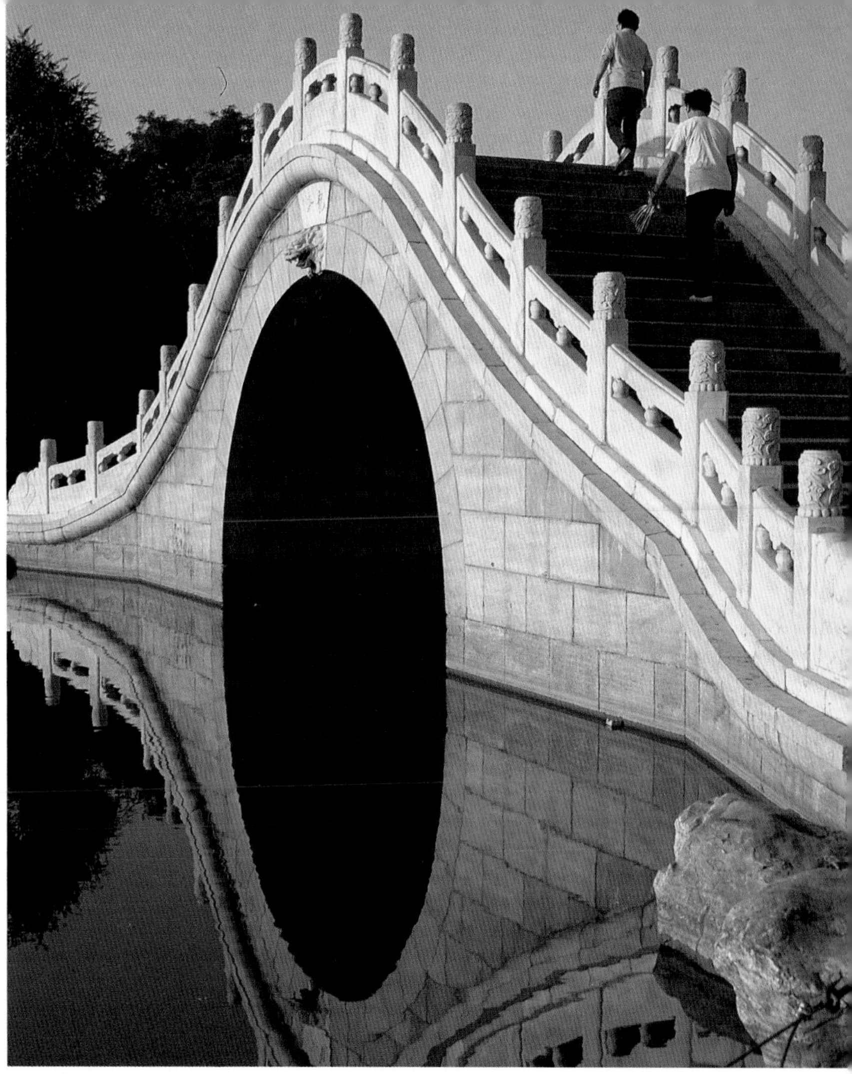

Perfection of form and proportion in Longtan Park

Cycle ride From Tiananmen Square

See highlighted route, page 49.
Bicycles can be hired from most hotels very cheaply. Start near Tiananmen Square and go up Beiheyan Street, just east of the Forbidden City. At a main junction (Wusi St) turn left and then right, by Jingshan Park. Follow the road as it goes left and then turn right along Di'anmennei, cross a junction and continue to the old Drum Tower. Bear right, then left and then take the second lane on the left to bring you to Jiugulou, near the Bamboo Garden Hotel (Zhuyuan Binyuan), former home of a Qing official. Turn south down Jiugulou and then right and left along narrow streets to cross Qianhai Lake. Go left, to Di'anmen Xi Street; turn right and then left and follow streets south beside Beihai Lake and Nanhai Lake to return to the start.

Accommodation

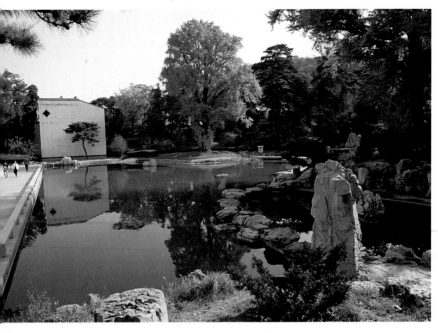

The garden of the beautiful Fragrant Hills Hotel outside Beijing, designed by Sino-American architect I M Pei

The five-star Guoji (International), typical of Beijing's new hotels

The standard of accommodation is now high in Beijing – almost too high since there is a lack of middle-range or budget hotels. However, the improvements have been remarkable – there are now some 130 hotels receiving foreigners, of which 12 are five-star standard. The main criticism, apart from that of expense, is their general lack of character.

A central location in some respects is less important than in other major cities – many of the principal sights are outside the city altogether and the worsening traffic can make a journey across Beijing frustratingly long. However, nobody would quibble with a hotel within easy walking of Tiananmen Square. There are two. The Beijing Hotel has three sections – the original Wagons Lit hotel, built in 1901, another section added in the 1950s, and the third in the 1970s. Although not truly luxurious, it exudes a sort of grandness and is comfortable, well equipped and has some excellent if expensive restaurants. Some of the rooms boast views across the roofs of the Forbidden City. Adjoining the Beijing Hotel is the Grand Hotel Beijing, of a higher grade, but with less character.

There are several other luxury hotels, some grouped in the northeast corner. The Great Wall Sheraton, with its striking exterior, is efficient, expensive, comfortable and rather soulless. Nearby are the Kunlun (the Sheraton's Chinese cousin), the Kempinski and the Hilton. In the same area is the less glamorous Zhaolong, representing fair value for money.

The Jianguo has a reasonably central location near the Friendship Store and although it was the first foreign-designed hotel to appear in Beijing (in 1982), it remains one of the best. Next door to it is the Jinglun (Beijing-Toronto), of equal standard but somehow less inviting, despite its excellent Tao Li restaurant. The Guoji

Modern luxury – Jinglun (Beijing-Toronto) Hotel ...

(International) has a central location on Jianguomennei Dajie but is huge and impersonal. Nearby are the 5-star Otani and the 4-star Gloria Plaza. The Shangri-La, in the northwest corner of the city, has a good reputation. Apart from the Beijing Hotel, the hotels with the best central locations are the Holiday Inn on Wangfujing and, nearby, the luxury Palace. Other central quality hotels are the Taiwan, the Peace, the Novotel, and the China World.

The Lido Holiday Inn is not in the luxury bracket but is comfortable enough and is well located for the airport, even if not so convenient for the city centre. There is a Mövenpick at the airport itself.

There are a number of cheaper hotels built in the 1950s, before the open-door policy, by the Chinese themselves or with the help of the Russians. The Friendship Hotel is a sprawling building on the road to the Summer Palace originally constructed for Russian experts in the 1950s. Set in attractive gardens, it now houses many of the new wave of 'foreign experts' as well as visitors and is reasonably comfortable. The Qianmen (Front Gate) is another modernised hotel from the Russian period and has a good location on Yong'an Lu in a colourful part of the city centre.

Outside the city there is the luxurious Fragrant Hills Hotel (Xiangshan Hotel) in the park of the same name – a charming position it is also convenient for the Summer Palace and the Great Wall, though somewhat less so for Beijing city.

At the cheaper end of the market there are a few reasonable propositions – the Ritan, the Guanghua, the Beiwei, the Hademen, the Desheng, the Shangyuan, and the Leyou, 13 Dongsanhuan Nanlu, Chaoyang. There are also some hotels with dormitories: the Feixia Building, 5 Xili Xibiangmen, Xuanwuqu; and the Qiaoyuan, Dongbinhe Lu, Yongdingmen. Such hotels are very cheap, but the dormitories, although clean, provide no privacy.

There is a hotel desk at Beijing Airport beyond customs for those arriving without reservations.

Housing shortage
When Beijing first opened to foreigners, there was a severe shortage of hotels. As tourism expanded in the early 1980s, things got out of hand. Groups of tourists landed at Beijing airport only to be placed on the next flight out because there was nowhere to accommodate them. Or they arrived to be told that they were staying in Tianjin (several hours away) and would be driven to Beijing each day for sightseeing.

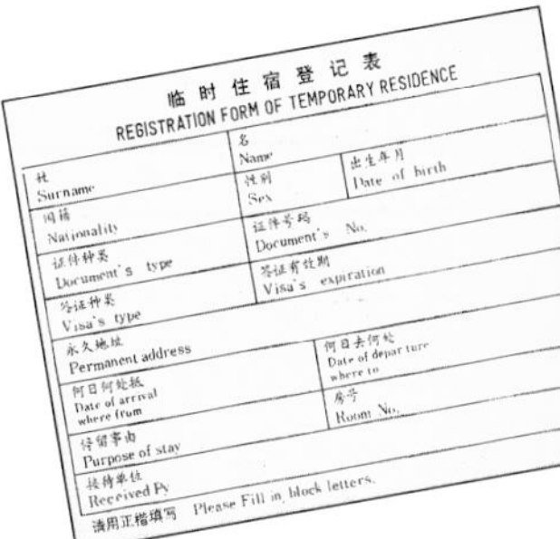

临时住宿登记表
REGISTRATION FORM OF TEMPORARY RESIDENCE

姓 Surname | 名 Name
性别 Sex | 出生年月 Date of birth
国籍 Nationality | 证件号码 Document's No.
证件种类 Document's type | 签证有效期 Visa's expiration
签证种类 Visa's type
永久地址 Permanent address | 何日去何处 Date of departure where to
何日何处抵 Date of arrival where from | 房号 Room No.
停留事由 Purpose of stay
接待单位 Received By
请用正楷填写 Please Fill in block letters.

... traditional style – the Bamboo Garden

Food and drink

East meets West: Coca-Cola – made in China

In Beijing it is now possible to sample most styles of Chinese and foreign cooking but it remains difficult to categorise the average restaurant for quality – most reliable restaurants are still to be found in the main hotels, although Beijing Tourism Administration is placing plaques on the doors of those restaurants it recommends. On the whole it is fairly difficult to eat badly, even in some of the shabbier establishments. Many ordinary restaurants have two floors – a utilitarian ground floor and an upper floor where the food usually will be more sophisticated, better presented, and more expensive. If you want a full meal then upstairs is a better proposition; if a snack, then don't allow yourself to be propelled any farther than the ground floor. The streets, meanwhile, are still filled with stalls where plates of excellent noodles or pancakes can be bought for next to nothing.

Whilst Beijing cuisine is in the robust and rustic northern tradition, it has been subject to many influences throughout its long history, and also has its own specialities, the most famous of which is 'Peking Duck'. Air is blown between the skin and the flesh, and then boiling water. The skin is covered in a malty solution after which the duck is hung and then roasted in a fruitwood oven. It is eaten with scallions (a type of shallot) and a bean sauce wrapped in a small pancake, and is delicious. There are a number of restaurants specialising in this dish, notably the Qianmen and Hepingmen branches of the Quanjude Kaoyadian (duck restaurant).

Another speciality of Beijing (in winter) is the Mongolian Hotpot. Thinly sliced mutton from Mongolia is cooked with vegetables and other ingredients by the diner himself at the table in a pot filled with a vertical funnel containing burning charcoal which keeps the cooking liquid constantly on the boil. The most famous restaurant for this is the Hongbinlou.

Of the other famous Chinese restaurants one of the most interesting is the Fangshan established in 1925 by a

'Do-it-yourself' dining: one of the Mongols' few tangible legacies, the Hotpot

'Peking Duck', complete with pancakes, scallions and bean sauce

former imperial cook on the site of an imperial dining-room on the island in the lake at Beihai Park. It specialises in imperial-style banquets or Manchu-Han feasts which include 'all known or available delicacies from land and sea'. For example, the Eight Marine Delicacies include shark's fin and sea-cucumber, the Eight Mountain Delicacies camel's hump and deer tendons. You must book well in advance.

Other recommended local restaurants are the Fengzeyuan at 38 Zhushikou Xidajie, famous for seafood and soups and good for Beijing-style cooking; the Ren Ren at 18 Qianmen Dongdajie specialises in *dim sum*. The Sichuan at 51 Rongxian Hutong, popular among high-level government officials, is housed in the palatial former mansion of a Qing prince and serves the excellent spicy food of Sichuan province. Other recommended restaurants are the Cuihualou (Shandong), the Xiangshu (chicken specialities), the Laozhengxing (Beijing and Shanghai style), the Ritan Park (Beijing style) and the Guangdong (Cantonese). The Kaorouji, which is just north of Beihai Park on the east bank of Qian Lake, specialises in Mongolian barbecued food.

The standard of the best Chinese restaurants (mostly Cantonese style) in the hotels is very high, with good service and presentation and prices to match. European and American food is of varying standard and usually disappointing but all types are represented from Portuguese to Vietnamese, mostly in the hotels. Otherwise most hotels have coffee shops, some of which stay open until 11pm or later. There is a branch of McDonald's on Wangfujing, a Kentucky Fried Chicken on Tiananmen Square and a Pizza Hut on Dongzhimenwai Dajie.

Proverb
An enigmatic saying in China goes 'If you rattle your chopsticks against the bowl, you and your descendants will always be poor.'

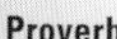

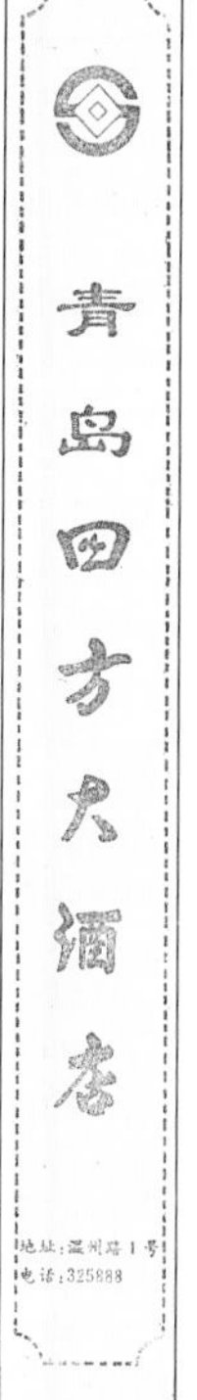

Chopstick envelope from a restaurant

Feast food
Imperial hospitality, like many things in old China, was rigorously graded. Dukes were to be treated to three morning meals and three evening banquets; counts to two in the morning and two in the evening; barons to one in the morning and one in the evening. Morning banquets were usually simply a matter of protocol; but in the evening guests were expected to 'remove their shoes and drink until wine-rapt'.

Watch out
It is worth looking out for interesting fob watches in antique shops. Many were left by foreign residents living in China before 1949 and although a good one will not be cheap, the price may compare favourably with the cost at home.

Not long ago the only place where you could buy high-quality goods was the Friendship Store on Jianguomenwai Dajie. It remains one of the best shops in China with three floors of merchandise including silk, antiques, books, carpets, arts and crafts and so on. Within are two good food areas, one a supermarket for daily needs, the other selling foreign and domestic-made packaged foods and drinks. There is no bargaining here.

There has been a shopping revolution of late. The once-gloomy traditional shopping streets have been transformed into emporiums filled with consumer goods and often staffed by people eager to sell them. Don't therefore feel compelled to buy in hotel arcades – try the local shops along Wangfujing Street selling daily necessities well-designed clothes in cotton and silk at reasonable prices, jewellery, toys, antiques and arts and crafts. The

Guanyuan bird market in northwest Beijing

Foreign Languages Bookstore is at No 235, and No 275 is the excellent Beijing Department Store Toy Shop. Other shops sell more pedestrian items but you may be able to get your camera fixed here, or buy film more cheaply than in the Friendship Store.

Liulichang Street is lined with 18th-century antique and craft shops, restored in 1981. It has plenty of atmosphere and although you will be hard pressed to find a bargain, the quality is generally high.

The Qianmen area, south of Tiananmen Square, is the nearest that you will get to the bustling and colourful lanes of old Beijing. Many shops retain their original façades, carved or decorated with wrought iron, especially along the narrow lane of Dazhalan. Here are shops selling stationery, silks, Mongolian 'hot pots', everyday clothes, pharmacies with selections of often bizarre remedies using fungus, deer antlers and items stranger still – the best known is the Tongrentang on Dazhalan.

Specialist shops are dotted all over the city. The most famous shop for silk is the Yuanlong Silk Store at 55 Tiantan Lu; another is the Beijing Silk Store at 5 Qianmen. For teas you might try the Beijing Tea and Honey Shop at 78 Xuanwumennei Dajie. For carpets visit the Huaxia curio shop at 12 Chongwenmennei or the Qianmen Carpet Factory at 44 Xingfu Dajie. If you want something out of the ordinary then try the shop at 130 Qianmen Dajie – it specialises in costumes for opera performers but also has items like embroidered shoes, or black cotton boots .

Whilst Beijing's street markets are not the most colourful, they are not without interest and it is worth having a look round them for a couple of hours or so. At the northeast corner of the Temple of Heaven is the Hongqiao antique market and the Chaowai antique furniture market is to the north of Ritan Park; whilst along the northeast wall of the same park is a livestock market. The bird and fish market (*niao shi*) is near the zoo on Xizhengmeng, a little way west of the Pinganli intersection; whilst the Shichahai Market on the south of Houhai deals in flowers and birds. There is a very popular clothes market at Xiushui, just east of the Friendship Store.

'I climbed the Great Wall' is the ubiquitous T-shirt slogan

Second-hand shops
An interesting diversion for the jaded shopper is a visit to Commission Shops, which deal in second-hand goods and can provide the occasional bargain. Try the one at 113 Dongdan Beilu or at 119 Qianmen Lu.

Antique shops on atmospheric Liulichang Street

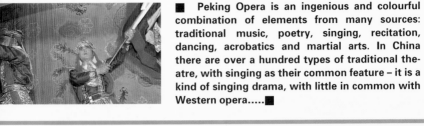

Peking Opera

Peking Opera is an ingenious and colourful combination of elements from many sources: traditional music, poetry, singing, recitation, dancing, acrobatics and martial arts. In China there are over a hundred types of traditional theatre, with singing as their common feature – it is a kind of singing drama, with little in common with Western opera.....

Peking Opera: fascinating as a spectacle, it can be extremely trying for Western ears

Lacklustre star
One of the greatest practitioners of Peking Opera was Mei Lanfang who died in 1961. As a student he felt that his eyes were insufficiently lustrous for stardom. To remedy this he exercised his eyes relentlessly by gazing at the flickers of an incense flame in a darkened room, by staring at soaring kites against a blue sky, and by keeping pigeons so that he could follow their flight. This, he reckoned, gave him a pair of bright, keen, expressive eyes.

History Each type of Chinese opera uses the dialect of a particular area; Peking Opera is one such and grew out of several types of opera being staged in Beijing some 200 years ago. The demands for the performer are great – he must be good-looking or attractive when appearing in make-up, of pleasing physical proportions, with a pair of expressive eyes and a rich variety of facial expressions. A professional must train for up to 12 years.

Gestures and symbols Symbolism is all-important in Peking Opera, for the stage is generally bare. Gestures signify the opening of a door, entering or leaving a room, climbing a mountain or crossing a stream. Riding in a carriage is suggested by attendants holding flags painted with a wheel design on each side of the performer. Walking in a circle indicates a long journey; a spotlight on two men somersaulting represents a fight at night, and so on. A Chinese proverb goes: 'Small as the stage is, a few steps will bring you far beyond heaven.'

The action is accompanied by relentless percussive music from the wings. The main instruments are gongs and drums and clappers of hard wood and bamboo. A distinctively strong rhythmic pattern is produced; and the drummer, who is also the conductor, is able to suggest any emotion in co-ordination with the performer. The stringed instruments are the *jinghu* (Beijing fiddle) and the *erhu* (fiddle); the *yueqin* (moon-shaped mandolin); the *pipa* (a four-stringed lute) and *xianzi* (three-stringed lute). Sometimes a horn and a flute are used.

The words are both spoken (stylised) and sung (high-pitched). The spoken parts use Beijing dialect for clowns, frivolous female roles and children, and the dialect of Hubei and Anhui for grander, more serious roles. The melodies are set to a fixed pattern and are adapted from provincial folk-tunes, arranged to suit the action.

Roles The characters are classified according to age and personality. Female roles are *dan* and subdivided into 'quiet and gentle', 'vivacious or dissolute', and so on. Male roles are *sheng* and subdivided into 'old', 'young', and 'warrior'. The third role is *jing* (the painted face), people who are rustic and simple or crafty or dangerous. These are subdivided into principal, minor, civilian and warrior and are distinguishable by the colours and patterns used in the make-up (rather heavy because originally opera was an open-air event) and costumes (based on those of the Ming dynasty). The clown (*chou*) is depicted by a dab of white on his face. Thus the moral standing of the characters is known immediately. In fact the plot is in a way insignificant – the appeal of the drama lies almost wholly in the spectacle, and in the skill displayed by the performers.

Action Westerners are likely to find Peking Opera unendurable at first. The spectacle is impressive, the reactions of the audience fascinating (there is no formality and much movement and comment) but the singing is seemingly unmelodious, a piercing, relentless howl. It is not without its subtleties, however, and is an integral part of the drama itself. Peking Opera is special in another way, too, for in many of the dramas the action is presented by means of tumbling acrobatics, often more spectacular than a circus performance.

Where to see Peking opera
Performances are frequently held in Beijing in the Liyuan Theatre, in the Qianmen Hotel. Enquire at your hotel reception desk.

Status symbol
In Peking Opera, an umbrella draws attention to an important or prestigious character. Attendants hold umbrellas over the heads of emperors, and officials sit under them when conducting their affairs of state. Even fairies carry umbrellas in their train for aesthetic reasons. Curved handles have more status than straight ones.

Yuxian paper cut: a traditional opera figure as portrayed in folk art

Highlife
Some members of the Beijing community will be relieved at the gradual improvement in recreational facilities. There were reports in the early 1980s that the alcohol problem among foreign residents was one of the worst in the world due to the paucity of cultural life and the repressive atmosphere.

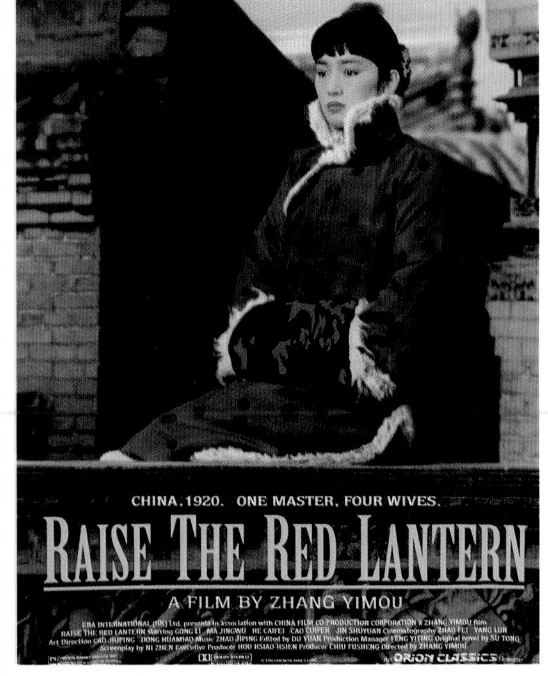

CHINA. 1920. ONE MASTER, FOUR WIVES.
RAISE THE RED LANTERN
A FILM BY ZHANG YIMOU

Poster for a Chinese film being shown with English subtitles, starring Gong Li. Zhang Yimou is China's most famous film director

Entertainment Beijing is not famous for its evening entertainment, although the situation has improved considerably in recent years. For the casual visitor interested in sampling traditional culture, however, there is more than enough to satisfy. To find out what is going on you should look in *The China Daily* (the English-language newspaper) or refer to three new publications – the quarterly *Welcome to China, Beijing*, the monthly *Beijing This Month*, or the weekly *Beijing Weekend*, any of which should be available from your hotel.

There are a large number of theatres in Beijing, although the Guanghe theatre at 24 Qianmen Dajie is the only old one. Performances are cheap, unlikely to set you back more than a few *yuan*, particularly if tickets are bought direct from the establishment concerned. At any one time Beijing's theatres are likely to have on offer Peking Opera (frequently in the theatre of the Qianmen Hotel), a dance drama (a story – usually traditional – told in dance and music), various types of concerts (of classical Western music; or ethnic music and dance from different parts of the country; or Chinese pop music, which is usually impressive for its dreadfulness; or a mixture of all of them); or acrobatics (highly recommended) and puppetry. A new feature is a revival of Chinese music-hall at the Tianqiao Happy Tea Garden. The cinema is popular – some of the films being produced in China have received international acclaim ('Yellow Earth', 'Farewell My Concubine'). Although the language barrier is a problem, a visit to the cinema can still be entertaining. Sometimes the International Club shows Chinese films with English subtitles, and the Friendship Hotel sometimes shows old foreign films.

Beijing traffic jam. The number of vehicles on Chinese roads has increased phenomenally in recent years

Most of the major hotels have discothèques, and karaoke bars abound. The only bars of any note are in the hotels, although small independent versions are springing up along Wangfujing and elsewhere. There are tennis-courts, a swimming-pool, snooker and table-tennis at the International Club. There is a golf club near the Ming Tombs and, oddly, an international shooting range.

Practical matters Beijing is a vast city and the best way of getting about is by taxi. There are different price scales more or less according to size – but the cheapest taxis are the small yellow ones which buzz all over the centre. Hail and make sure that the meter is in use. You are advised not to use the pedicabs, certainly not without agreeing the fare in advance, which may require hard bargaining. To obtain a taxi in advance telephone the Capital Taxi Company on 557461. To hire a car with driver telephone 863661 or the Beijing Car Company on 594441. The local bus service is comprehensive and cheap but the buses are often uncomfortably crowded (numbers 1, 4, 37, 52, and 57 run east–west along Chang'an Avenue). The underground has only two lines but is often less packed than the buses. The most useful is the circle line with stops including Beijing Railway Station, Qianmen (Tiananmen), the zoo, and the Lama Temple.

Hiring a bicycle is feasible but it is advisable to spend a little time observing the traffic first.

Emergency numbers are 110 (Police), 119 (Fire) and 120 (Ambulance). Many hotels have clinics and there is a First Aid Centre on Xuanwumen Dong Dajie, just west of Tiananmen. Among several hospitals the most central is the Beijing Medical College Hospital, 1 Dong Shuaifuyuan Hutong, tel: 553731, ext: 214. The Sino-German Policlinic, tel: 5011983, in the Landmark Tower offers 24-hour medical and dental treatment.

Although most postal matters can usually be taken care of in hotels, some special services may require a post office – the main one is to be found on Yabao Lu, just north of Jianguomen overpass.

The head office of China International Travel Service (CITS) is at 103 Fuxingmennei Dajie, tel: 6011122.

Medical warning
One of the less savoury stories to come out of money-mad Peking in the 1980s was one concerning nurses who, it was alleged, were extorting high payments from patients before offering treatment. This situation has now changed but do check in advance how much you may be expected to pay.

Pedicabs, prolific in most Chinese cities, can be useful in heavy traffic, but be sure to agree the fare in advance

A typical early morning scene on the east coast: a Shandong fishing fleet back at the harbourside

THE NORTH

Chifeng
Fuxin
SHENYANG
Fushun
Weichang
Laoba He
Chaoyang
LIAONING
Benxi
Jinzhou
Liao He
Anshan
Chengde
Jinxi
Yingkou
Yalu Jiang
Liaodong Wan
Dandong
KP
Liaodong Bandao
Great Wall
Qinhuangdao
Shanhaiguan
Beidaihe
Xinjin
TIANJIN
Tangshan
Jinzhou
TIANJIN SHI
Dalian
Tanggu
Bohai Wan
Bo Hai
Cangzhou
Longkou
Yantai
Chengshan Jiao
Dongying
Laizhou Wan
Shandong Bandao
Weihai
Rongcheng
Laiyang
Zibo
Weifang
Jinan
Qingzhou
Laoshan
Taishan
Zhucheng
Qingdao
Tai'an
SHANDONG
Qufu
Shijiu
Jining
Linyi
Huang Hai
Zaozhuang
Weishan Hu
Lianyungang
Xinyi
Binhai
Xuzhou
Da Yunhe (Grand Canal)
Huaibei
Qingjiang
Suzhou
Hongze Hu
JIANGSU
Xinghua
Guo He
Bengbu
Gaoyou Hu
Dongtai
Fengyang
Huai He
Huainan
Yangzhou
Taizhou
ANHUI
Zhenjiang
Nantong
Nanjing
Changzhou
Hefei
Ma'anshan
Wuxi
SHANGHAI
Chaoxian
Suzhou
Yixing
SHANGHAI SHI
Lu'an
Wuhu
Tai Hu
Chao Hu
Dingshu
Tongcheng
Huzhou
Jiaxing
ZHEJIANG
Tongling
Hangzhou Wan
Anqing
Chang Jiang (Yangtze)
Hangzhou
Zhoushan
D
E

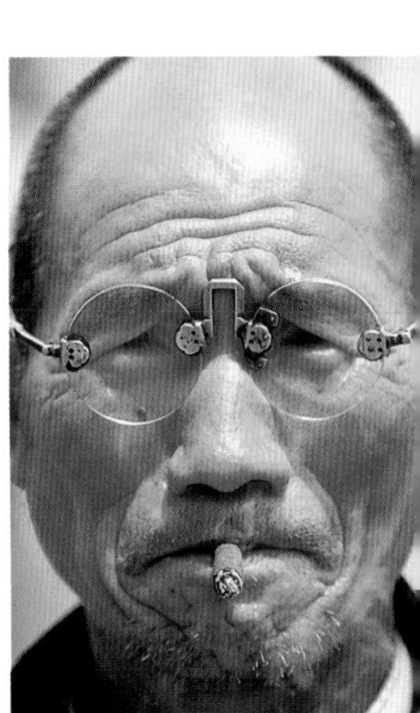

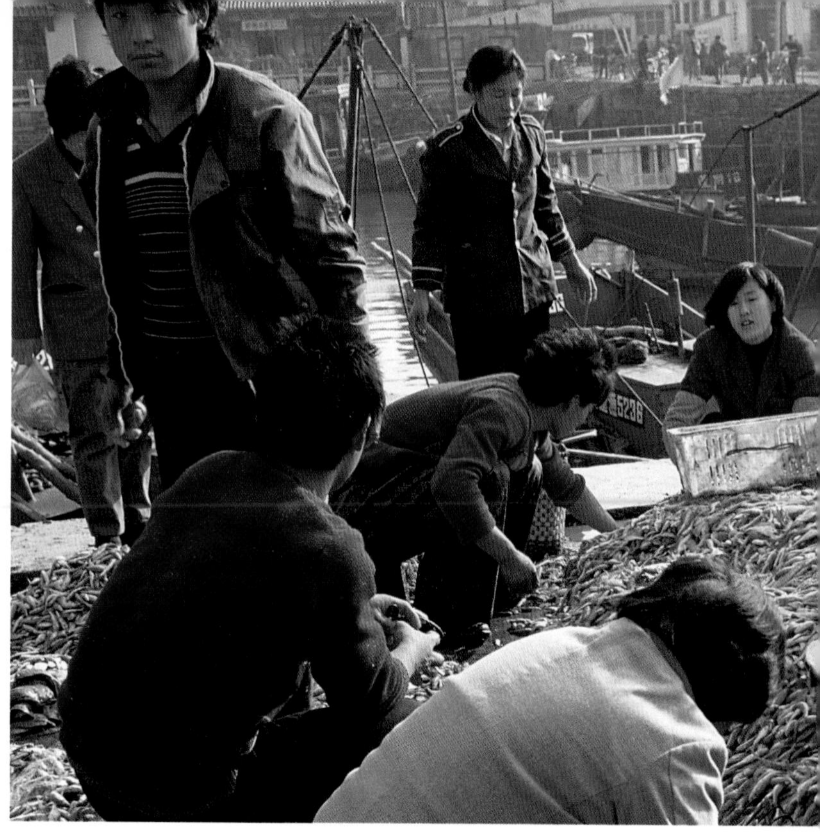

Slow but sure
Stone tortoises bearing stelae were first used in the 6th century AD. Symbols of longevity, their use was restricted to the highest grades of officials. When such stelae were surmounted with dragons, they were still more potent.

China's heartland
I love this wretched country,
This age-old country,
This country that has nourished what I have loved:
The world's most long-suffering
And most venerable people.
– Ai Qing, 'The North', 1938

The North China proper – that is, excluding Tibet, Xinjiang and Inner Mongolia – can be broadly divided into two: the area north of the Yangtze and that south of the Yangtze. Since the geographical and cultural reality is more complicated than that, the north is generally taken to mean the area comprising the floodplain of the Yellow river (Huanghe), where Chinese civilisation is believed to have started. Its boundaries are theYangtze valley in the south, Inner Mongolia to the north, Manchuria to the northeast, and Gansu province, which is the corridor to the desert areas, in the northwest. It is composed of the provinces of Hebei, Shanxi, Henan, Shaanxi, Shandong, and parts of Jiangsu and Anhui.

Crops and the climate Climatically, the region is one of extremes. Summers are very hot, with average temperatures of 25°C during July (over 36°C is not uncommon). Winters, however, are long and cold (state housing is provided with heating in the north, but not in the south), with average January temperatures well below freezing. Snow is a rarity, but in spring northerly winds bring in sand from the Mongolian Gobi. The short autumn from September to October is the most pleasant time to visit.

Despite the heat, rice is not grown in the north because of the absence of water – instead wheat, millet and barley are cultivated, and cotton after the harvest of winter wheat in June. Other crops include sorghum, maize, sweet potatoes and seasonal vegetables, especially cabbages, aubergines, beans, peppers, leeks and onions. Mulberry bushes are grown for the manufacture of silk, tobacco is an important cash crop, orchards are noted for apples, persimmons, pears and pomegranates, whilst rape, sunflower, sesame, and peanuts are grown for oil.

Houses are traditionally of one storey with all the windows facing on to a courtyard. In the cities these have largely been replaced by high-rise flats, but in the countryside many survive and are still built.

The character of the region The northern areas of China are still the most purely Han, or ethnic Chinese, since with the exception of the Muslim Hui people, there are no minorities in the region. Certainly the Confucian sense of China is most apparent in the north. Not only does it remain China's political heartland, it is the most conservative part of the country and the most resistant to change, unlike most other countries whose capital cities are often the first to produce or adopt new ideas. It is hard to believe that Canton, which has known contact with foreigners for centuries, is in the same country as Beijing.

And yet the north shares many characteristics with the rest of China, for the culture of the Han Chinese has been remarkably successful in maintaining continuity over the entire area of China for many centuries. But that character was formed in the north of China and it was under the leadership of a northern state, the Qin, that China was unified. It was further shaped by the constant threat of the barbarians from beyond the northern frontiers and the fickle nature of the Yellow river.

Penglai, Shandong province: early morning shrimp harvest ...

.... and a temple guardian figure

A glut of palaces
The Manchu rulers of the last imperial Chinese dynasty were spoilt for choice as far as summer palaces were concerned. There were the two on the outskirts of Beijing as well as Chengde, also called the Summer Palace. The first two were favoured towards the end of the dynasty but during the 17th and 18th centuries the court spent most of the summer at Chengde.

▶ Anyang *80C2*

Anyang lies between Zhengzhou and Beijing in the north of Henan province. It lies close to the site of the last capital of the Shang dynasty, and has a well-preserved old quarter with alleyways, quiet courtyards and low-eaved houses. In 1899 ancient oracle bones used to predict the future were found here, and later excavations confirmed the existence of a 3,000-year-old city. There are few upstanding remains at the site of **Yin** – just the merest outline of a city – but the original excavations produced much from the tombs. A possible excursion from Anyang is to the **Red Flag Canal** (see page 92 under Linxian County).

▶ Beidaihe *81D4*

China's foremost beach resort is a 5-hour train ride from Beijing. It first became famous at the end of the 19th century when it was patronised by foreigners living in Tianjin's concession areas or the legations of Beijing. Much of the architecture, with its European villas, reflects the period. Indeed Kiessling's restaurant still exists, serving cakes and reputedly the best bread in China. The seawater is clear and the **three beaches▶** (formerly divided into one for foreigners, one for Communist Party hierarchy, the third for anybody at all) are clean. There are a number of scenic spots in the area offering unusual rock formations and views. The train from Beijing leaves you 14km from the resort but there is a bus link.

Fine ceramic figure on the Putuozongsheng, one of the collection of temples at Chengde, the Qing emperors' summer palace

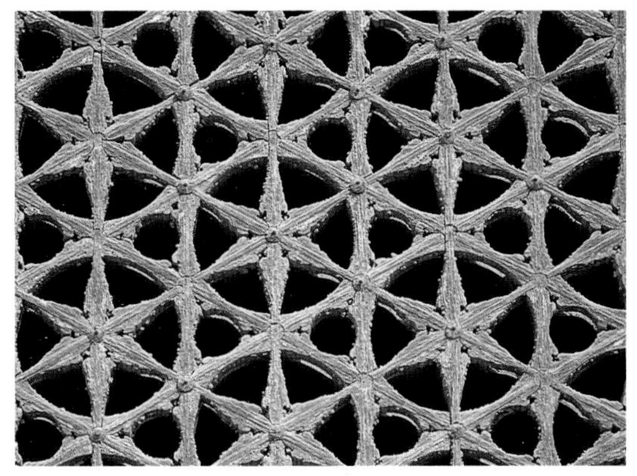

The last Imperial General
Yuan Shikai, who tried to restore the Qing dynasty with himself as emperor in 1915, is buried just outside Anyang. A traitor through and through, he betrayed the 1898 One Hundred Days of Reform movement to the Dowager Empress Cixi and then, realigning himself to progressive factions, was appointed President in 1911, before declaring himself Hongxian Emperor. He died in 1916.

►► Chengde *81D4*

Sometimes known as Jehol, Chengde was the 18th-century summer palace of the Qing emperors, close to the mountains and forests of their northern homeland. It has the largest imperial gardens in China and is only six hours by train from Beijing.

At first a country seat, it soon became an important centre of government. Many of the pavilions were built in the style of the religious architecture of the minority peoples in China – especially the Mongolians and Tibetans – partly to impress their envoys and partly to use Lamaism to control these potentially troublesome peoples.

In the mid-19th century Jehol witnessed many dramatic events as hostilities between China and the foreign powers increased. It had been abandoned as a summer retreat in 1820, following the death of the Jiaqing Emperor but in 1860, as the British and French forces approached Beijing, the Xianfeng Emperor fled here, accompanied by his favourite concubine, the ambitious Cixi. Concerned that the emperor might die without naming their son as heir, she forced her way into his bedroom to extract the promise that was to make her the most powerful person in China. The emperor died shortly afterwards.

The palace►►► consists of a villa within a park and a number of outer temples. The entrance through the Lizhengmen (main gate) takes you to the Front Palace, now a museum of imperial memorabilia. Beyond is the Misty Rain Tower (Yanyulou), an imperial study. The Wenjin Chamber (Wenjinge) housed the Sikuquanshu (Complete Library of the Four Treasures of Knowledge), an anthology of literature and philosophy. Outside the main park are the **Eight Outer Temples**, built between 1750 and 1780. The largest and most impressive is the Putuozongsheng, a miniature facsimile of the Potala in Tibet, although the most interesting is the Pule, built for Mongolian envoys in a style that is partly Buddhist and partly Islamic.

Window screen detail, Puning Temple, Chengde

Tibetan-style roof ornament at Chengde

Yungang Caves: the broken-hearted son of Emperor Daiwu, represented as a Buddha in Cave 20

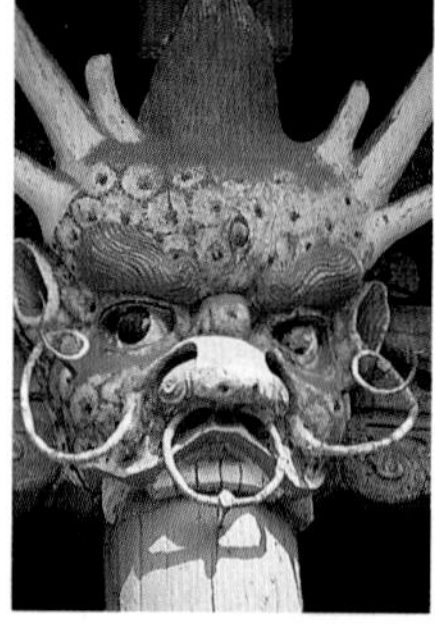

Detail from one of the Yungang cave façades

Ancient pagoda
Not surprisingly there are few original wooden pagodas still standing in China today. The earliest is the Yingxian pagoda some 70km south of Datong. It was built in 1056 and is 67m high.

►► Datong *80C4*

Datong is a grimy coal town in Shanxi province. It lies west of Beijing, not far from the Mongolian border, on the route of the Great Wall (of which there are several decaying remains in the vicinity) and of the railway to Mongolia and Siberia. The interest of this poor industrial city derives from its Buddhist shrines, created in the 5th century AD, when Datong was briefly capital of the Northern Wei. During this period, the town prospered and the Buddhist religion, actively fostered by the Wei rulers, flourished, producing some of China's finest Buddhist art. Over 51,000 stone carvings are still extant, the greatest sight in Datong.

The **Yungang Caves►►►** are 16km west of the city. Originally the entrance to each was concealed by pagoda-like buildings. The idea of sculpting the rock into Buddhist shrines came from India and there is plenty of evidence of Indian, Persian and even Mediterranean influence in the decorative features of the caves. The peculiarly Chinese styles are seen in the bodhisattvas, dragons and apsareses (angel- or wraith-like creatures). The original caves were carved with images of the first Northern Wei emperors but the site was abandoned after the imperial capital was moved to Luoyang. Caves 5 and 6 are the most impressive, the first with a 17m Buddha, the second with the life-story of Buddha carved on the east, south and west walls. The statue in cave 19 is of the Emperor Daiwu, a one-time champion of Buddhism but who later rejected it in favour of Taoism, persecuting Buddhists in the process. Cave 20 offers the best view of a Buddha statue, supposed to represent the son of the emperor Daiwu, who died of a broken heart as a result of the misdeeds of his father.

Datong has an interesting **old centre►**, one of the better preserved ones in China, worth a stroll even if you are not attracted to the two monasteries or the dragon screen. **The Huayan Monastery►►** is the more interesting of the monasteries, with an atmosphere of antiquity lacking in some others. Its main attraction is the Bojiajiaocang Hall with architecture and 31 clay figures from the Liao period (AD907–1125). The **Shanhua Monastery** also has Ming sculpture in its main hall. The Nine Dragon Screen, built in 1392 on Dadong Jie and one of only three in China, was supposed to have offered protection to the mansion of the 13th son of the first Ming emperor, Hongwu, who was viceroy of Shanxi.

The **Datong Locomotive Factory**▶▶▶ was, until 1989, the only one left in the world making steam locomotives; now it produces diesel and electric engines. A tour of the factory is still possible through CITS and the museum houses seven steam locomotives. The **Mass Graves Exhibition Hall** commemorates atrocities carried out by the Japanese in the 1940s.

A worthwhile day trip from Datong is to the **Hanging Temple (Xuankongsi)**▶▶, constructed on the side of a cliff, about three hours' drive from the city. The temple's precarious location is spectacular enough but the loess landscape and villages *en route* are also worthwhile.

▶ Gongxian *80C2*

Gongxian County is famous for two things – the Buddhist caves at the foot of Dalishan dating back to AD517 and, above all, the **Song Tombs** of seven of the nine Northern Song emperors. Here 700 stone statues of animals and military and court officials line the sacred avenues which lead to the ruined tomb buildings, scattered over an area of 30 sq km. Stylistically, there are several clear distinctions varying from Tang influence at first, to the more naturalistic features of the later Song.

Imperial capital
Although Datong's heyday was during the Wei period, it was also the capital under the Liao rulers, a Mongol people who had given up their nomadic lifestyle and controlled the extreme north of China in the 10th to 12th centuries. Although they attempted to overthrow the Song dynasty, they were eventually conquered by the Jin rulers, ancestors of the Manchus.

The gravity-defying Hanging Temple (Xuankongsi), well worth the 3-hour journey from Datong

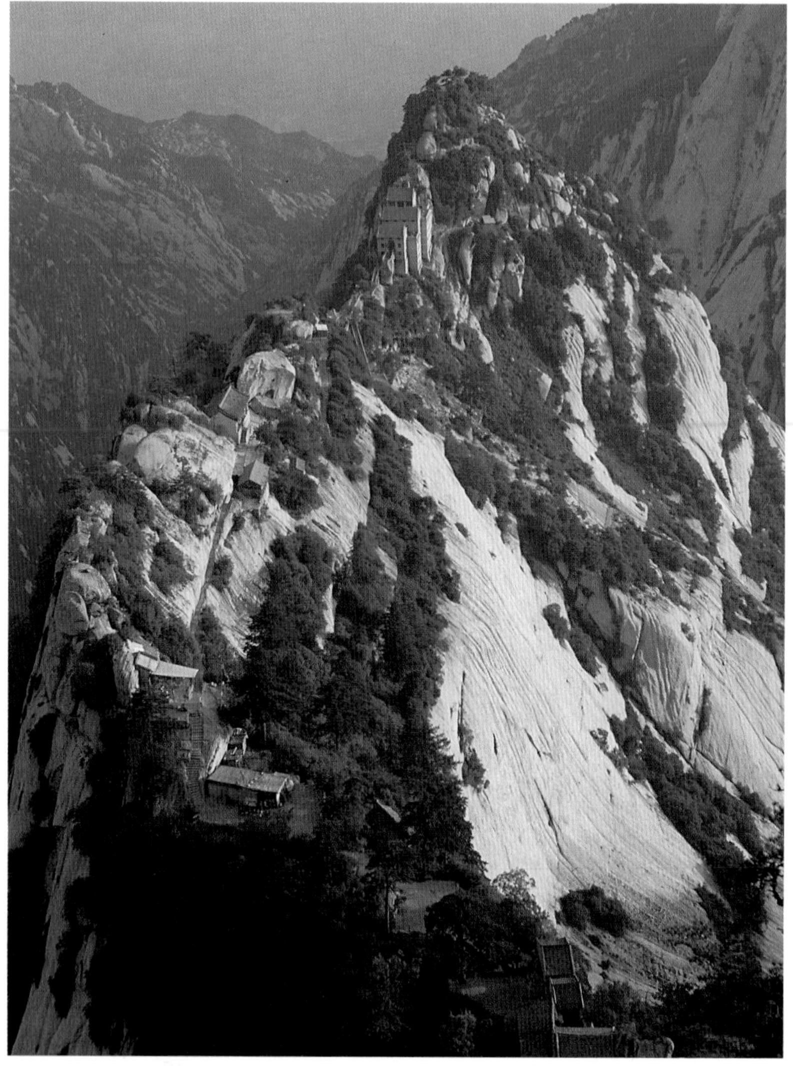

Taoist temples cling to holy Huashan

▶ Huashan *80B2*

Huashan (Flowery Mountain), 2,200m in height, 112km east of Xi'an, is one of the five mountains in China sacred to Taoism which were to some extent also adopted by the imported religion of Buddhism. The single crowded route to the top can be followed in a day and there is accommodation at the summit for those wishing to stay overnight. The mountain is composed of five peaks, of which the Middle Peak is supposed to offer the best view of the 'Sea of Clouds' at sunrise.

▶ Jinan *81D3*

As capital of Shandong province, Jinan is an important city politically and industrially but not of much interest to the visitor, although it was a major commercial centre under the Tang and Song. It is well known for its springs –

Gushing-from-the-Ground Spring, Black Tiger Spring, Pearl Spring, and Five Dragon Pool – surrounded by gardens. The **Shandong Provincial Museum**▶▶ has a fine collection of sculptures, and artefacts from Longshan.

The **Four Gate Pagoda (Simenta)**▶, the oldest stone pagoda in China, dating back to the 7th century, is 35km out of Jinan. Beyond Simenta is the Song dynasty **Longhu ta (Dragon Tiger Pagoda)**, which is surrounded by a small forest of stupas (burial-chambers) built as a memorial to the monks who lived at the nearby Shentong Monastery. The **Thousand Buddha Mountain (Qianfo shan)** has good views and statues from the Sui dynasty.

Lively detail from the glazed tiles that face the Iron Pagoda in Kaifeng

▶ Kaifeng *80C2*

An imperial capital during the Northern Song dynasty, Kaifeng is particularly interesting for the presence of a Jewish community, one of several in China before the establishment of the foreign concessions in the major ports during the middle of the 19th century. Although their presence in Kaifeng is well documented, the origin of their arrival is a mystery. The heart of the Jewish quarter was **Beitun Jie**, where some of the street names commemorate the former occupants.

One of Kaifeng's principal attractions is the **Xiangguo Monastery (Xiangguosi)**▶▶. Founded in AD555, the current buildings date back only to 1766, the originals destroyed in the deliberate flooding of the Yellow river in 1642 in an attempt to stop the Manchu invasion. There is a magnificent bronze bell and a gingko wood Guanyin of a Thousand Arms and Eyes.

The **Iron Pagoda (Tieta)**▶▶, of 1049, 54m high, is made of bricks covered in glazed tiles that give the edifice a metallic look. It is said to house relics of the Buddha.

The **Dragon Pavilion** is a fine Qing hall on the site of the old imperial palace, and is the only building not destroyed by the flood of 1642.

The **Yuwangtai (King Yu's Terrace)**, with a collection of Tang memorabilia, just southeast of the old wall, was the haunt of Tang musicians and poets. The nearby **Fan Bo Pagoda**, built in 977, is the oldest building in Kaifeng. Just northeast of Kaifeng is **Long Temple**, containing an Iron Rhinoceros of 1466, supposed to prevent flooding.

Near the **Liuyuankou Ferry** is a lookout across the Yellow river.

Some of the Iron Pagoda's 13 storeys

The Yellow river

■ The Yellow river (Huang He) is 5,460 km long and the second longest river in China. The birthplace of Chinese civilisation, this temperamental waterway – named after the colour of its silty waters – has earned itself the epithet 'China's Sorrow'......■

Old trick
Almost 300 years after the Ming officials at Kaifeng deliberately breached the Yellow river to halt the Manchus, the nationalist leader, Chiang Kaishek, did the same at Zhengzhou when he tried, but failed, to prevent the Japanese invaders utilising the railway in 1937. Hundreds of thousands of Chinese died.

Riverside ox at Shengzhou, meant to placate the river

Route The Yellow river emerges from the Bayan Har Mountains in Qinghai. By the time it reaches Lanzhou it is already of considerable size; then it winds across north China, kinks up into Inner Mongolia, returns to China, and today debouches into the Gulf of Bo Hai in the Yellow Sea.

Heavy water The Yellow river is infamously temperamental. The quantity of water that it carries varies drastically from season to season and from year to year, a reflection of the strongly seasonal rainfall of north China, three-quarters of which occurs between June and August, to be supplemented by snow melting in Qinghai as late as June. The river's characteristic hue is produced by thick deposits of filtered soil (loess) picked up in Gansu, Shaanxi and Shanxi, blown there from the deserts of Central Asia. When the river reaches the sea the water is coloured for miles by the same ochre paste and indeed the coastline is constantly expanding further northeast as the silt finally settles.

No ships Despite its size, the Yellow river has never been important as a waterway. The density of the silt, erratic water flow, and the difficulty of mapping the shifting shoals have made this impractical. Even in areas quite close to the mouth the river is shallow, and in the severe northern winters it often freezes. So it tends to be used for local fishing, ferries from bank to bank, and some commerce over short, sure distances. This lack of commercial potential has been compensated for by the smaller **Huai** river to the south, which is navigable, the man-made **Grand Canal**, and the **Wei**, the Yellow river's principal tributary (also of considerable historical significance), navigable almost as far as Xi'an.

Temperament The Yellow river has been most important as a source of irrigation, but at a price. When it floods, it does so with a vengeance. Time after time whole towns have been washed away and even now it is not remarkable to see the bodies of animals, and even occasionally of humans, bobbing through the middle of Lanzhou, for example. On the whole, however, the construction of dykes has kept the river in check.

In 1855 severe flooding altered the course of the river near its mouth, shifting it some 350km to the north. For 500 years previously it had joined the Huai in Jiangsu province, from where they had flowed together to the sea. This change, which had the effect of almost

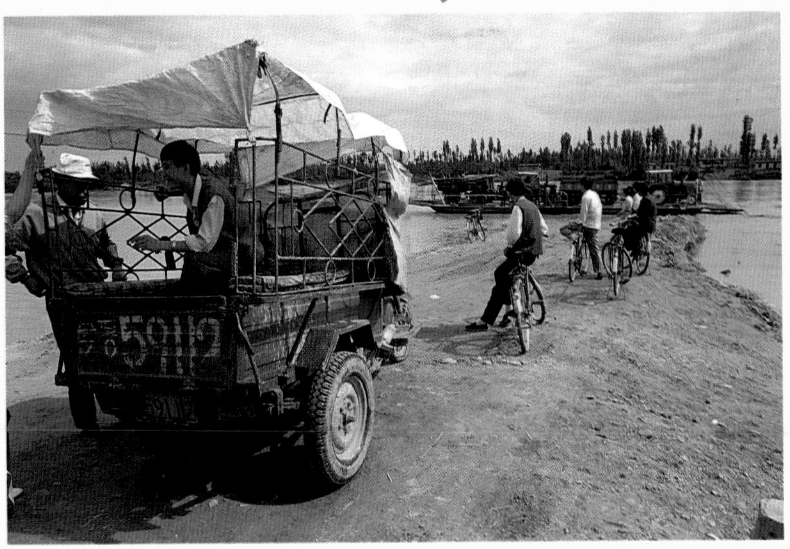

emptying stretches of the Grand Canal, was by no means the first, for from the 7th century BC until AD11 the river in its lower reaches became a series of divided channels, all of which flowed into the sea to the north of the mouth today. Construction of dykes at that time to create a single major channel reduced the frequency of floods but accelerated the deposit of silt. This made the floods, when they came, far worse, for the water between the dykes was higher than the surrounding plain. It has been recorded that the river has burst its banks on some 1,500 occasions during the last 3,000 years.

It was the silt (37kg carried in every cubic metre of water) which made the area attractive to the first Chinese cultures. It is very fertile and easily managed with primitive tools. Traces of neolithic settlements are legion along the river's banks and the first recorded dynasty, the Shang, had an early capital near Zhengzhou.

Ferry crossing point at Zhongwei in the Autonomous Hui Region of Ningxia

The Yellow river at Huaxuankou near Zhengzhou. Mao's words: 'Control the Yellow river' are inscribed on the wall

Laoshan water

Dropping out
During the 12th century, Luoyang was famous for the 'Seven sages of the Bamboo Grove', a group of scholars who abandoned politics in favour of a bohemian lifestyle discussing Taoism, writing poetry, playing music and drinking wine. According to legend one of them was constantly shadowed by a servant bearing wine flagons, and a spade for his burial should he drop dead.

Former governor's residence, Qingdao

► Laoshan *81D3*

To the east of Qingdao, in Shandong province, Laoshan is a mountain area of scenic spots and fine views, famous for its mineral water, which is used in the production of China's best-known beer, Qingdao (Tsingtao). The mountain is also noted for its **Taiqing Palace**, a Taoist monastery from the Song Dynasty.

► Linxian County *80C2*

Close to Anyang in the northwest of Henan, Linxian is a rural area held up as a model for the tenets of Maoism, for here is the **Red Flag Canal** (**Hongqiqu**), built collectively by hand to receive a river rerouted through a mountain by means of a tunnel. Over 1,500km of canal throughout the country were to be built in the effort to demonstrate the feasibility of a self-reliant China.

►► Luoyang *80B2*

Although a major city historically and industrially, Luoyang is comparatively little visited. There is, however, plenty to see in the vicinity. The site, strategically placed with hills on three sides and bisected by four rivers, was inhabited from neolithic times. In 771BC it became the main Zhou capital and legend has it that Confucius studied here and Laozi was the keeper of archives. Capital again under the Later Han, it was the starting-point of the Silk Road. Buddhism was introduced into China from India via Luoyang, and it hosted a number of Chinese inventions, including paper.

After the fall of Han the city remained capital for several dynasties and was the scene of a cultural flowering. The Northern Wei dynasty moved its capital from Datong to Luoyang and carved its monuments to Buddhism at nearby Longmen. But the Wei rulers suddenly abandoned the city in 534; it lay in ruins for about 70 years before becoming the capital again, under the Sui. It was a secondary capital under the Tang, too, after which the focus of Chinese life moved elsewhere and Luoyang, though capital of Henan province, became a backwater until its industrial revival after 1949.

Luoyang has a certain quiet appeal. It is not beautiful, yet a walk in the old town, around **Zhongzhou Donglu**, with its well-preserved timbered houses and market atmosphere, pleasantly evokes the past. Luoyang is

Heavenly guard and demon warrior on Fengxian Temple, Longmen Buddhist Caves near Luoyang

famous for its peonies which bloom in early April, particularly in Wangcheng Park or Zhiwuyuan. It is said that in AD800 Empress Wu Zetian, angry that peonies refused to bow to her command to bloom in the snow, banished them from Xi'an.

Most of what has been uncovered of Luoyang's past is in the **museum▶▶** near Wangcheng Park, where there are some fine examples of work from most periods, especially the famous Tang polychromatic figures, and models of the Sui dynasty grain silos discovered north of the old town. In the park a pair of Han tombs and one from the Jin with interesting murals are open to the public.

Luoyang's main claim to fame lies outside the city. The **Longmen Buddhist Caves▶▶▶** are among the finest in China. On a splendid site by the Yi river, the earliest caves were carved soon after AD493, although the majority date from the Tang. There is a spectacular array of niches, statues, carved pagodas and inscriptions, among which the most striking is the 17m-high Buddha flanked by statues of leering guardians.

The Han dynasty **Baimasi (White Horse Temple)▶**, 10km from Luoyang, is China's earliest Buddhist temple.

▶ Qingdao *81D2*

See following page for town map and walk.

China's fourth port, no more than a fishing village in 1897 when the Germans annexed it in order to compete with other Western powers, is an interesting place. It was returned to China only in 1922. It is a popular resort and is home to China's most famous **brewery▶**, which can be visited through CITS. There is a modern Qingdao but the well-preserved old **German Concession▶▶**, with its cathedral, is worthwhile for its central European atmosphere. The **Qingdao Museum▶** has a good collection of paintings and large stone Buddhas. A day excursion to **Laoshan** from Qingdao is possible from here by boat or by bus.

China's premier export beer, is brewed in Qingdao (Tsingtao) using Laoshan mineral water

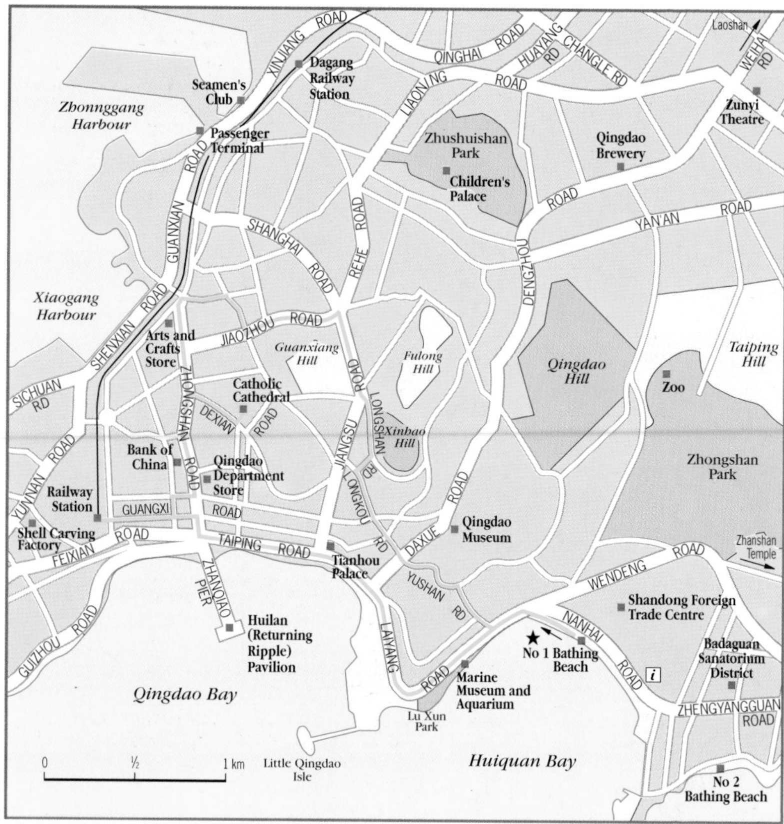

Walk The heart of Qingdao

Start at the No 1 Bathing Beach and walk towards the town centre along the waterfront. Pass the **Marine Museum and Aquarium**▶ and Lu Xun Park and continue to the pier. The Huilan Pavilion is perched at the end.

Opposite the pier is Zhongshan Road, the main street. Walk along it for a short distance and turn left along Guangxi Road to see the busy railway station and famous reconstructed clock tower.

Retrace your steps to Zhongshan Road, continue past the many shops, visit the Roman **Catholic Cathedral** on the right, and then continue past the skyscraper department store opposite the Jianglinglu alley to Jingchen market on the right. Walk through the market and bear right up a rising street; then bear left and then right. At the main street turn left and at a junction by an old church turn right into the heart of the old but well preserved **German Concession area**.

Continue down, keep to the left of a small park and then at a clearing bear rightish towards another church and then left before it, down Longkou Road.

Cross another junction with a Chinese wall on the left, climb up and then bear right by some trees. Follow the road as it curls left around a building with a tower and then right with the tower to the left. This road will eventually deposit you back on the waterfront.

▶ Qufu

81D2

Qufu, with its quiet charm, is famed as the birthplace of Confucius and as the home of his clan, the Kong. The **Kong Mansion▶▶**, built during the Ming dynasty, was home to the clan until 1948 and is one of the finest extant examples of an aristocratic mansion in China, providing a fascinating insight into the life of an eminent mandarin family.

The **Kongmiao (Temple of Confucius)▶▶** dominates the town. Across the moat is the Guiwenge, which used to contain the Confucian library. In the Great Courtyard is a tree, allegedly planted by Confucius, the Xingtan Pavilion, and the Dachengdian, built during the Qing dynasty and one of the largest wooden structures in the world.

The **Konglin▶▶▶** is the family graveyard, set amid trees just outside the town. In this, the most charming part of Qufu, amid the many pavilions and statues, Confucius's grave is simple and dignified.

Pope's view
The master's fame reached far and wide. 'Superior and alone, Confucius stood, Who taught that useful science, to be good'.
– Alexander Pope, 'The Temple of Fame' 1715

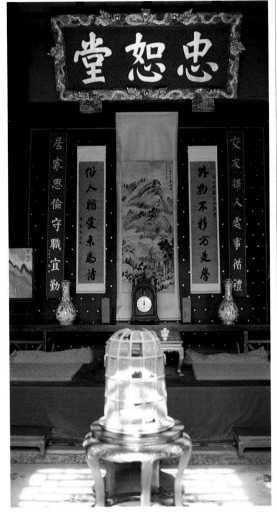

Confucian wine improves the mind

Politically incorrect
The opinions of Confucius, who was himself fairly high born, on women and the lower classes would have been given short shrift these days. 'Women and people of low birth are very hard to deal with,' he said. 'If you are friendly with them, they get out of hand, and if you keep your distance, they resent it.'

One of the residential rooms in the Kong Mansion, Qufu, family seat of Confucius's clan, the Kong

■ China's railway system is of particular interest for a number of reasons, not least because China's withdrawal from the world stage for so many years aroused curiosity among train buffs, who tend to have an insatiable desire for detail.....■

Travelling 'hard seat class' in Inner Mongolia

Revolution and the railways
It is possible that the railways in China played a contributory role in the downfall of the last dynasty. Railway construction in the decade up to 1911 had been financed largely by foreign organisations in co-operation with provincial governments but had been less profitable than before. The Chinese government, already badly short of funds, was compelled to service railway debts and consequently took control of the system. Resentment of this action in the provinces led to rallies among all enemies of the state, sparking off the 1911 revolution.

A difficult start The reasons for the fascination of the Chinese railway system are several: the expansion of the railway network; the fact that until recently steam locomotives were still being manufactured in China (and are still widely used); and because China's train service is a good way to meet the Chinese.

The history of China's early railway system is characterised by Chinese intransigence and imperial manoeuvrings. The first attempt to introduce railways to China was made by a consortium of Chinese and foreign companies in 1863, but since this was in the thick of the Taiping Rebellion it is scarcely surprising that the application was refused. In 1864 a further application was made to the governor of Jiangsu, Li Hongzhang, a man aware of the advantages that dealing with foreigners could bring to China. But he felt that the time was not yet right, despite agreeing with the Europeans that the railways were a key to prosperity. This did not stop the illegal laying of a track from Shanghai to Wusong in 1876 (after negotiations with landowners and families whose ancestral graves were likely to be affected), which was subsequently torn up.

Official approval However, the Chinese were slowly coming around to the idea and the next line to be built, with official approval, was for a coal mine near Tianjin. The train was initially pulled by mules, but the Beijing government soon turned to steam traction, recognising its military possibilities. Indeed, it was fear of Russian and

Japanese aggression that led to plans for new lines in Manchuria and between Beijing and Canton. Henceforth railway construction became increasingly entangled with the fates of the Western powers whose presence in China was increasingly unwelcome.

Foreign pressure Some Western powers felt that China was fated to be carved up among them; others disagreed. The result was several spheres of influence, each economically dominatd by one power. China constantly found herself caught in the middle of their competitive struggles. In some ways this was to her advantage. Railways were built, but usually under some sort of pressure, for the Chinese government had no money. The first contract was signed in 1896, with France, for a railway near the Vietnamese frontier and this was followed by more with other countries. The eagerness to build railways was founded less on the desire to make money (they were hardly profitable) than on the need of each power to obtain concessions before any of the others did.

Shortfall After the Boxer Rebellion the Chinese enthusiasm for railways increased and various agreements were ratified. In 1911, trunk lines were removed from provincial to central imperial government control. When Sun Yatsen came to power efforts were made to standardise the various railway systems which had tended to reflect the countries involved in their construction. Apart from the logistical challenge, standardisation was difficult because of China's great climatic and geographical extremes.

Wars For the next 40 years, despite civil war and invasion by the Japanese, the railways continued to function. With the help of private Chinese capital and the Boxer Indemnity Fund, but mostly using revenues generated by the railways themselves, the system was improved. The resumption of civil war after the Japanese withdrawal brought everything to a halt, however.

With the communist victory in 1949 railways became a priority. Collaboration with the USSR produced many more lines as well as the construction of the railway bridge across the Yangtze at Wuhan. After the split in 1960, concern for defence led to the construction of still more lines and the Yangtze bridge at Nanjing. Nowadays electrification and new lines to remoter areas (for example between Kunming and Dali) are a priority.

Until 1989 steam locomotives were produced just for the home market. Opposite, top: a steam train in the desert at Dongsheng. Above: Manchurian steam in Heilongjiang

Beijing Railway Station in grandiose fifties style

The 17th-century town gate of Shanhaiguan, inscribed: 'First Pass Under Heaven'

Sacred peaks
The five holy mountains represent the five directions sacred to the Chinese (north, south, east, west and centre), hence the link with the emperor who was viewed as the son of heaven and who lived at the centre of his kingdom.

▶ Shanhaiguan (The Pass between the Mountains and the Sea) *81D4*

Shanhaiguan is where the Great Wall meets the East China Sea. The town is a charming place and, although the wall is less picturesquely preserved than at Beijing, it is a good deal less crowded. The 1639 town gate is inscribed 'First Pass Under Heaven'. A temple 7km out of town is dedicated to Meng Qiangnu. The wife of a man conscripted under the Qin to build the Great Wall, she followed him only to find that he had died. Her tears brought the wall down to reveal his skeleton within.

▶ Shaolin *80C2*

The **Shaolin monastery▶** (west of Zhengzhou) was founded in AD495. It was said to have been visited by the founder of Zen Buddhism, Bodhidharma, in AD527, after he had failed to persuade the emperor of the nothingness of everything. Having crossed the Yellow river on a reed, he sat facing a wall for nine years. He rejected doctrine in favour of meditation and indeed Shaolin is best known for its *gong-fu* monks, a martial art developed to enhance meditation which has found fame in spectacular films. Shaolin is also noted for its Ming frescos, as well as its forests of stupas (burial-chambers) and its collection of stelae, one of which dates back to 683.

The 'Forest of Stupas', Shaolin

▶ Shijiazhuang *80C3*

The capital of Hebei province is an important railway junction and noted as the burial-place of the Canadian doctor Norman Bethune, one of the foreigners honoured by the Chinese communists. He arrived in China in 1938 but died of septicaemia the same year.

About 12km north of here is Zhengding, site of the **Longxing Temple**, famous for its 22m bronze of Guanyin.

Massacre of missionaries
Taiyuan was a major centre for anti-foreign Boxer activity in 1900. Xenophobia reached a climax when the local governor rounded up all the foreign missionaries in the area and publicly executed them.

▶▶ Taishan *81D2*

Taishan (south of Jinan) is perhaps the holiest of the five Chinese holy mountains devoted to Taoism and the cult of the emperor. Of the two possible routes to the summit, the middle one is the most popular. Make your way through the **Daizongfang**, and begin the 1,515m climb up the 5,500 steps. The journey up should take four to five hours if you are reasonably fit. You can also take a bus to Zhongtianmen, about half-way up, where there is a cable

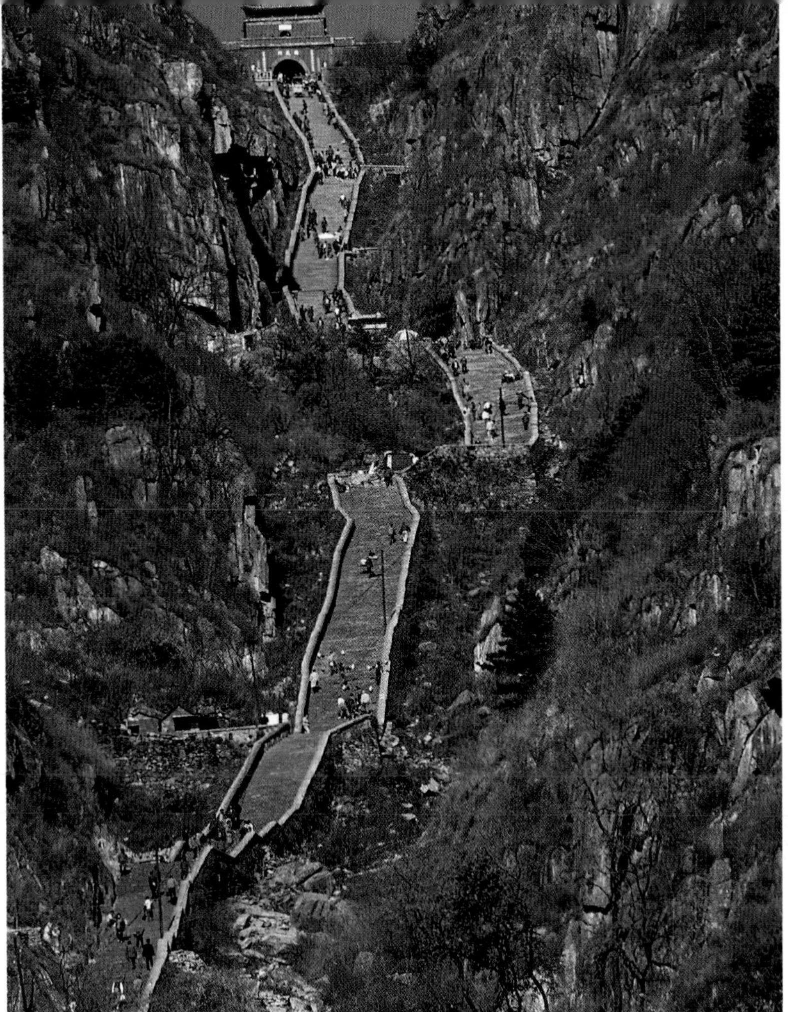

Stairway up the holy mountain of Taishan

car to the top. There is a hotel at the summit.

The mountain is covered in temples and scenic spots and if the weather is clear enough you can watch the sun rise from Dawn Watching Peak. It is possible to return by the more circuitous western route, which also offers excellent views over the mountainside.

The number of temples and historical places along the route defies description here but the **Taishan Temple** at the foot of the mountain is one of China's great, ancient, palace-style buildings.

Yellow earth
The provinces of Shanxi and Shaanxi not only have similar names but are both covered in thick deposits of yellow loess, sometimes to a depth of over 100m, which characterises the landscape. In some places, troglodyte cave-houses have been cut into the perpendicular valley sides which, though primitive, are cool in the summer and warm in winter.

► Taiyuan *80B3*

The capital of Shanxi province is an industrial city boasting several interesting features. The **Shuangta Temple►►** is one of China's finest examples of Ming architecture, whilst the **Chongshan Temple►** was once part of the largest Buddhist monastery in China. Other temples include the magnificent **Jinci►►**, about 25km southwest of Taiyuan, with some fine examples of Song dynasty architecture. About 90km south is the Song dynasty **Shuanglin Monastery►►**, a worthwhile day trip.

Gong-fu

■ '*Qi*' in Chinese denotes a vital breath within us which also animates the cosmos. Although it is a loose term, according to Chinese philosophy – notably Taoism – the secret of inner strength lies in harnessing this mysterious force.....■

Gong-fu *is about self-discipline, both as a form of exercise (above* taijiquan*) and as a martial art*

Natural alliance The secret of outer strength lies in using *qi* to unleash latent power that depends not on physical strength but on knowledge. *Gong-fu* is the cultivation of *qi* and its use as a fighting technique.

Taoism claims to be able to demonstrate its superiority through movement, based on the notion that the human body is the universe in miniature. But the movements themselves are to be based on acquiescence, not confrontation, made in tune with nature.

In martial arts there are two categories, external and internal. Both aim to tap into the flow of *qi*. Of the former, karate, concerned with skills of self-defence, is a well-known example . Internal forms are more concerned with the body as a vehicle of spiritual development; among these *taijiquan*, or shadow-boxing, is the best known.

Meditation To do this it is essential to be able to concentrate the mind so that the movements made are in tune with it. This meditation in action is considered essential by Taoists because it involves the whole human being, body and soul. At the same time the practitioner must be aware of his actions, so that the weapon, whether it be hand or sword, is directed to strike but does so almost intuitively, having sensed in advance the movement of an opponent. The mind is flowing, and this is *qi* .

At the same time the relationship between the two types of breathing, physical and spiritual, is vital. Perhaps this could be described as 'tranquil', but the word is

inadequate because it fails to imply the level of alertness essential for success. *Taijiquan* is supposed to be able to teach both the calmness necessary in everyday life and the added awareness needed for fighting.

Rhythms In *taijiquan* the spine should be erect, the abdomen relaxed and the centre of gravity lowered. The breath must be allowed to find its source in an area a few centimetres below the navel and identify with the inner breath of *qi*; to concentrate on control of physical breathing alone is to inhibit one's natural, instinctive strength. There must be no strain, for to strain is to go against nature. Energy should be stored and only unleashed at the right moment, as the arrow from the bow. Observing the Chinese people will show that these lessons have been absorbed and used in ordinary life, for the Chinese person is rhythmical in everything he does until speed is demanded of him, in which case the reaction is intense and accurate.

It is all too easy to become pretentious when describing a naturalistic process that is in a way no more than refined common sense. In fact for Taoists it is merely a question of *qi*, which is the essence of essences. In the martial artist the concentration of *qi* should produce the innocent mental state of a child – no preconceptions, focused only on the immediate circumstances but within the larger framework of the universe. This state is illustrated by the following account of a *gong-fu* contest taken from Peter Ralston's *Consciousness and the Martial Arts*: 'For example I would start to move and my opponent would throw a kick and I would realise that I was moving out of the way of a kick. But I was doing it before I knew why! I just moved, and they would throw a kick and miss! '

Gong-fu *as an aid to meditation: sculptures in the temple at Shaolin Monastery and (top, opposite) a wall painting portraying 13 monks practising the art before the Tang Emperor Li Shimin in the 7th century* AD

A world of shadow-boxers
David Rice, in his book *The Dragon's Brood: Conversations with Young Chinese*, describes Chinese shadow-boxing: 'From five o'clock in the morning, in every street-corner park, in front of every apartment block, and in the woods around the Temple of Heaven, there were thousands of people, some in groups, some alone, all performing what seemed to be slow-motion ballet, making strange, slow, graceful movements with limbs and torso. It was eerie, yet strangely beautiful.'

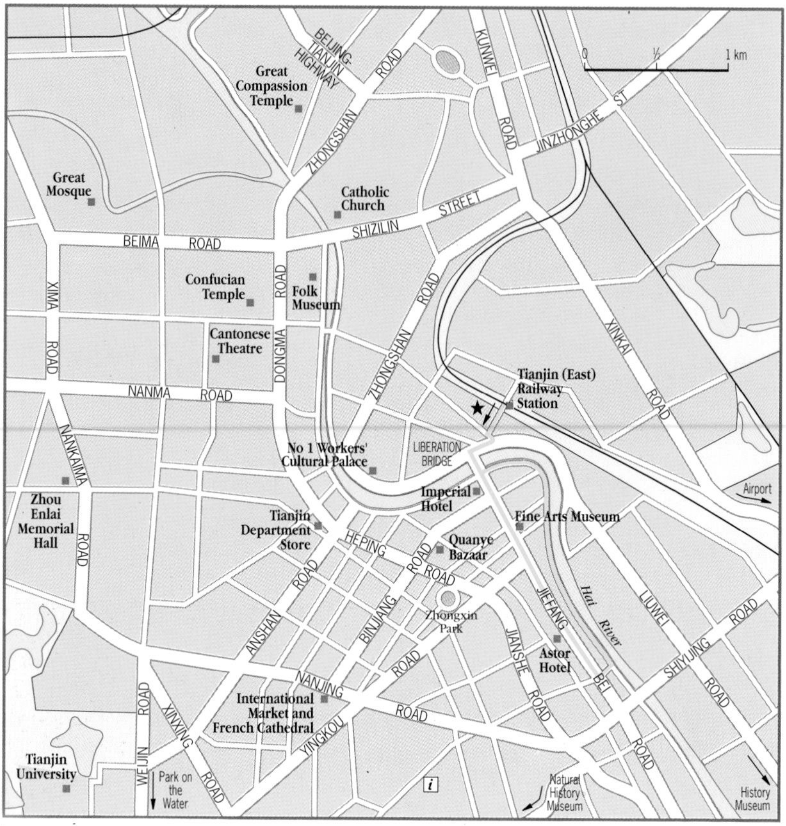

Walk Tianjin's foreign concessions

A stroll through the foreign concessions reveals a surprising degree of Westernisation. Walk from the east railway station towards the river. Cross Liberation Bridge and continue along Jiefang Road, passing the old Imperial Hotel on the right. Continue through the former **French Concession** to the Fine Arts Museum. Yingkou Road marked the beginning of the **British Concession** but continue along Jiefang Bei Road to the Astor Hotel and the former Victoria Park. Turn left to the river and return along the waterfront, passing the old French and British consulates and the Customs House.

▶▶ Tianjin (Tientsin) *81D3*

One of China's major ports, with a population of 7 million, Tianjin was one of the treaty ports controlled by the Western 'great powers' from the 19th century. In 1976 it was badly hit by an earthquake but has since recovered to become China's third city, with the status of autonomous municipality (along with Beijing and Shanghai), similar to that of a province.

Never as glamorous as Shanghai, Tianjin none the less has retained much of its European atmosphere, although the various concessions granted to the foreign powers in

1860 never merged, as they did in Shanghai, to form an International Settlement. Each preserves a distinctive flavour, particularly the British, French and German. Broadly speaking the old Chinese town is to the north of the city, the concessions to the south.

Other than the **concessions▶▶** there are several places of interest. The **Dabeiyuan (Great Compassion Temple)** is a Buddhist temple which used to contain the cranium of Xuanzang, the 7th-century monk who made a celebrated journey to India. **Wenhua Jie (Ancient Culture Street)▶** is a pleasant area of restored traditional Chinese shops, just west of the river in the northern part of the city. It is close to the **Tianhougong (Hall of the Heavenly Empress)**, originally a temple, now a **Folk Museum▶**, with many examples of the mud craft peculiar to Tianjin, and of the woodblocks made in the nearby village of Yangliuqing. The **Fine Arts Museum▶** at 77 Jiefang Bei Road has both old and new paintings. The 18th-century **Great Mosque (Qingzhen Da Si)▶** is in the old Chinese city. The old **French cathedral▶**, outside the former French Concession, is worth a look. Also interesting is the southern style **Guangdong Guildhall (Guangdong Huiguan)▶**, built in the 1920s as a centre for traders from that province.

Chinese whispers
China has always had secret societies which, dedicated to the overthrow of the government of the day, were often no more than criminal gangs. Tianjin in the 19th century was the headquarters for many, including the White Lotus, which was influenced by Buddhism and Manichaeism. These societies were active in the early 20th century, setting fire to Esso storage tanks in 1929. It is said that they still exist today.

French Concession architecture along the former rue de France, Tianjin's old banking district

▶ Wutaishan *80C3*

Wutaishan in the north of Shanxi province is one of the four holy peaks of Chinese Buddhism. It is a cluster of five peaks, the highest reaching just over 3,000m. There is an abundance of temples, many concentrated at the town of **Taihuai**. The Yuan dynasty **Nanchan Temple** is decorated with frescos of the classic 'Journey to the West' made by the monk Xuanzang, who travelled to India. The **Luohou Temple** contains an imposing wooden lotus flower on a mechanism which, when rotated, opens the petals to reveal carved Buddhist figures.

Strength through wisdom
Wutaishan is supposed to have been the home of the Bodhisattva Manjusri, the god of wisdom. Riding on the back of a lion, he carries a sword with which to fight ignorance.

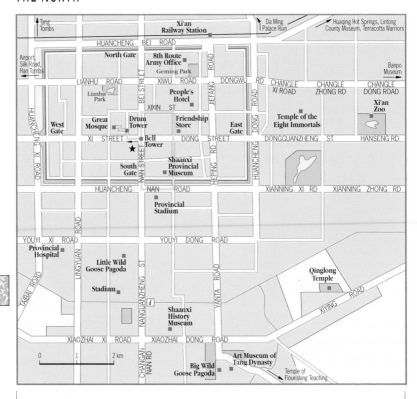

Tang Tombs
Xi'an Railway Station
Da Ming Palace Ruin
Huaqing Hot Springs, Lintong County Museum, Terracotta Warriors
HUANCHENG BEI ROAD
Airport, Silk Road, Han Tombs
North Gate
8th Route Army Office
Geming Park
JIEFANG ROAD
Banpo Museum
LIANHU ROAD
XIWU ROAD
DONGWU RD
CHANGLE XI ROAD
CHANGLE ZHONG RD
CHANGLE DONG ROAD
Lianhu Park
BEI STREET
People's Hotel
XIXIN ST
Xi'an Zoo
HUANCHENG XI ROAD
West Gate
Great Mosque
Drum Tower
Friendship Store
East Gate
DONG ROAD
Temple of the Eight Immortals
XI STREET
Bell Tower
DONG STREET
DONGGUANZHENG ST
HANSENG RD
South Gate
NAN STREET
Shaanxi Provincial Museum
HEPING RD
HUANCHENG
HUANCHENG NAN ROAD
XIANNING XI RD
XIANNING ZHONG RD
Provincial Stadium
YOUYI XI ROAD
YOUYI DONG ROAD
Provincial Hospital
LINGYUAN ROAD
Little Wild Goose Pagoda
NANGUANZHENG ST
YANTA ROAD
Qinglong Temple
TAIBAI ROAD
Stadium
i
XIYING ROAD
Shaanxi History Museum
XIAOZHAI XI ROAD
XIAOZHAI DONG ROAD
0 1 2 km
CHANGAN NAN RD
Art Museum of Tang Dynasty
Big Wild Goose Pagoda
Temple of Flourishing Teaching

Walk Xi'an, taking in the Muslim quarter

The Bell Tower near the city centre is a good place to start. From here head west along Xi Street until you come to the **Drum Tower** at the beginning of the Muslim quarter. Turn right beneath the tower and then turn left along a narrow, stall-lined street, following it as it bears right and then left to the **Great Mosque**. After that return to the main road and walk left along it, passing a number of attractive traditional houses. At the top bear right along Xixin Street until you come to the old main square. A little further on is the People's Hotel. Return to the square and turn south, pass the Friendship Store and continue on to the Shaanxi **Provincial Museum**. Turn right to the South Gate and then right back to the Bell Tower.

Worshipper at the Great Mosque in Xi'an's Muslim Quarter

The Bell Tower stands in a pivotal position at the centre of Xi'an's Ming period street-plan

▶▶▶ Xi'an *80A2*

One of the greatest cities in the history of civilisation, Xi'an (Sian) had declined to a provincial backwater before the discovery of the Terracotta Warriors in 1974. Since then it has become one of the most important tourist destinations in the world and its prosperity has increased correspondingly. Its history is long and illustrious. A capital during the early Zhou dynasty, it became the first capital of a united China under the First Emperor, Qin Shihuang. It was, however, during the Tang dynasty that Xi'an became the centre of the greatest flowering of Chinese culture. It is thought that the population may have reached 2 million, at a time when commerce with the outside world had reached unprecedented levels. The modern city, however, is based on the Ming street-plan.

Although the **Terracotta Warriors▶▶▶** (see pages 108–9) must be the highlight of the visit, there is much else to see in and around the city. The **city wall▶▶▶**, over 11km in perimeter, dates from the early Ming. Made of rammed loess on a base of earth, lime and glutinous rice, faced with grey brick, it was completely restored during the 1980s and is an awesome sight, particularly in the misty early morning or at sunset. It is possible to mount the wall, 12–14m wide at the top, at different points.

The old **Shaanxi Provincial Museum** was housed in the former Confucian Temple at the foot of the wall in the south of the city. Part of it still is; the rest is now in a new museum on Xiaozhai Donglu. The **old museum▶▶** (8:30–6, closed Mondays) houses the famed Forest of Stelae, a collection founded in 1090 of inscribed stone tablets, some dating back to the Han. Some have pictures of scenery or illustrations; others carry the text of the 13 Classics. One testifies to the arrival in Xi'an of a Nestorian Christian priest and the foundation in 781 of a chapel.

The **new museum▶▶▶** has a magnificent display of locally discovered Zhou bronzes, marvellous Tang ornaments, and a variety of stone sculptures including four of the carved horse reliefs from the tomb of Li Shimin, the founder of the Tang dynasty. Two of these are now in the Metropolitan Museum in New York.

Peasant art

The brightly coloured quilted jackets embroidered with stylised designs that are now for sale all over China originate from the countryside around Xi'an. A more recent development is the art in naïve style from Huxian, a nearby town. Vivid paintings of agricultural themes, they became popular in the late 1950s and are now widely sold in the area.

Warriors by night

The sudden surge in the numbers of tourists after 1980 caught Xi'an unawares, and it became a notorious blackspot for a while. The old airport (happily now superseded) had an especially bad reputation since it seized up at the merest hint of bad weather. At least those stuck in Xi'an visited the highlight of their tour to China, the Terracotta Warriors, by day – others whose arrival was badly delayed often ended up seeing them by torchlight.

Part of the Forest of Stelae in Shaanxi Provincial Museum

The Journey West
The 'Journey to the West' (*Xiyouji*) is the name of a fable written in the Ming dynasty, based on the pilgrimage made to India by the Tang monk Xuanzang, in honour of whom the Xi'an Big Wild Goose Pagoda was built. In the story of his adventures, he is accompanied by a pig, symbol of greed, and a magician monkey. There are many stories based on the characters, some of which appear in a delightful television series.

The city's symbol is the 60m **Big Wild Goose Pagoda (Dayanta)▶▶▶**, first built in AD652 to house the sutras collected by the wandering monk, Xuanzang, from India. The top offers fine views across the city. The **Little Wild Goose Pagoda (Xiaoyanta)▶** is a similar, smaller, more delicate structure from 707.

Xi'an has a Muslim population of about 30,000, a hangover from the Silk Road. On Huajue Xi'ang in the Muslim quarter is the **Great Mosque (Qingzhensi)▶▶**. It was founded in 742, though the present buildings, heavily restored in recent years, are in Ming style. It is a charming place particularly the garden and prayer hall.

Near the Mosque is the **Drum Tower▶**, in an interesting area of shops and houses. Its twin, the **Bell Tower▶**, is a little way to the southeast. Moved here in 1582, it was built in 1384, originally standing at the centre of the Tang city, two blocks west.

The route to the Terracotta Warriors takes the visitor past several places of interest. The area around Xi'an has been important to man from the earliest times. **Banpo▶▶▶**,

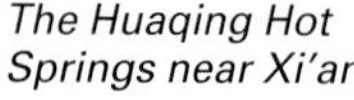

The Huaqing Hot Springs near Xi'an

discovered in 1953, is a covered excavation which clearly shows the layout of a neolithic village of the Yangshao culture. The foundations of several dwellings (thatched roofs supported by timber columns), kilns and graves, some of which were filled with urns containing the bones of children, can all be viewed. The pottery discovered there shows an interesting progression of pattern from representations of man and fish to more abstract geometric design.

The **Huaqing Hot Springs▶**, a scenic spot in the shadow of Li Mountain, have been patronised for their mineral content by emperors since the Zhou dynasty, but are particularly associated with the Tang emperor Xuanzong and his concubine Yang Guifei, whose fate is a perennial subject of Chinese art. The baths are being reconstructed in the Tang style. The springs are also associated with the 'Xi'an incident' of 1936. Chiang Kaishek had come to Xi'an to continue his offensive against the communists, choosing to ignore pleas for a united front against the invading Japanese. A warlord, Zhang Xueliang, though allied to Chiang's nationalists, saw the urgency of the situation and captured him here, chasing him from his office (still standing just above the spring) up the hillside. Chiang was forced into an alliance though he later obtained his revenge on Zhang by imprisoning him.

Not far from Huaqing is **Lintong County Museum▶**, frequently overlooked by tourists but with an interesting display of Buddhist relics discovered on Li Mountain and other sites found in the area.

There are several sites not normally included in a visit to Xi'an but worthwhile if at all possible. The **Han dynasty Tombs▶** (none of which has been excavated) lie 35km west of Xi'an. The most interesting is that of Huo Qubing which has a series of fine, lively, stone animals, which would once have graced the spirit way and are now under cover. There is a museum devoted to items discovered in the area. Not far away is the tomb of the Tang concubine Yang Guifei. The main **Tang Tombs▶▶**, however, are some 80km northwest of Xi'an. The grandest is **Qianling** (unexcavated), the tomb of the third Tang emperor and his wife Wu Zetian, one of the three notorious women rulers of Chinese history (the others being Empress Dowager Cixi and Gang of Four member Jiang Qing), who assumed power on the death of her husband and became a ruthless, though effective, ruler.

The location of the tomb, on a natural hill, is impressive. It is approached along a spirit way running between two mounds, flanked by a succession of winged horses, birds, human figures and stelae. Beyond is a congregation of headless statues, the foreign envoys who attended the emperor's funeral. Nearby are several lesser tombs, some excavated, notably those of Princess Yongtai and Prince Zhanghuai, covered with beautiful court paintings. East of Qianling is the **Zhaoling** group of tombs – it was from the tomb of Taizong, the second Tang emperor, that the famous horse panels now displayed in the provincial museum were taken.

The **Temple of Flourishing Teaching (Xingjiaosi)▶** is 25km southeast of Xi'an. It is a flourishing temple, spectacularly located on the side of a hill overlooking a village and a wide, tree-sprinkled plain. The temple is famed as the burial-place of the travelling monk, Xuanzang.

A cosmopolitan capital
Despite the magnificent city walls, which date from the Ming dynasty, Xi'an's greatest days were already long past by then. During the Tang the city was much larger – an array of markets was closely controlled by a sophisticated government bureaucracy whilst the inhabitants lived in walled districts which were closed at night. Life in Xi'an was international – the city was filled with traders from as far away as the Middle East, perhaps even Rome, who came to deal in horses, jewels, exotic fruit, silks and porcelain, and who had their own mosques, and Manichaean and Zoroastrian temples.

Detail: Little Wild Goose Pagoda, Xi'an

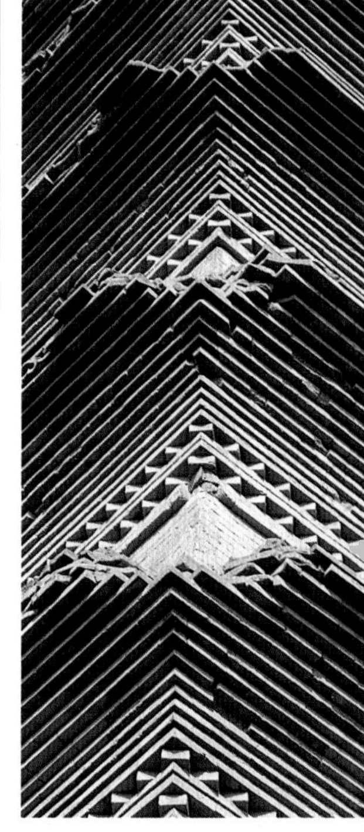

The Terracotta Warriors

The discovery of the Terracotta Warriors in 1974 by local farmers who were digging a well has turned out to be one of the most significant archaeological finds of the 20th century.....

From emperor to queen
Such is the beauty of the bronze chariots on exhibition at the site of the Terracotta Warriors that Queen Elizabeth II was given an exact copy of one of them when she visited in 1987. She is also one of the few foreigners ever to have been allowed to stand in the pit among the warriors.

Construction The First Emperor, Qin Shihuang, whose as yet unexcavated mausoleum lies beneath a hill 1.5km from the site, was a figure of almost legendary stature. The scale and nature of this find reveals a level of material civilisation remarkable for its self-confidence.

Work was begun on the mausoleum in 246BC, as soon as the First Emperor became ruler of Qin, and involved the labour of nearly 750,000 conscripts. According to historical records, the mausoleum itself is filled with models of palaces and a China in miniature where the waters of the Yellow and Yangtze rivers are of mercury and can even be made to flow by means of a special mechanism. The whole is protected by automatic crossbows. Outside the mausoleum there was a perimeter fence and villas occupied by guardians of the site.

The army So far interest has focused on the army of life-size terracotta soldiers arrayed in pits to the east, the largest, Pit 1, now protected under a vast hangar. It consists of 11 parallel underground corridors from which earthen ramps lead to the surface. Each was paved with bricks and protected by a wooden roof covered in straw matting and clay. The mausoleum was sacked by rebel soldiers following the First Emperor's death, probably as a result of the tell-tale mounds of excavated earth.

The soldiers stand in military formation in infantry battle order facing east. They have some armour but no helmets (which were reserved for officers). The vanguard at the east end consists of bowmen, unarmoured for mobility,

The celebrated Terracotta Army, in battle formation in the vast Pit 1

who are separated from the foot soldiers by chariots and mobile infantry unarmoured for rapid deployment. Armour was unnecessary since ferocity and bravery were considered sufficient protection for infantrymen such as these. Thus in the narrow north and south corridors soldiers guarding the flanks face outwards, shieldless. The terracotta warriors did, however, carry real arms, made of bronze, many of which were removed by the rampaging rebel army.

Sculpture The statues themselves were made of local clay. No two faces are alike – each is a personal portrait. Each body was made separately. The legs are solid but each torso is hollow and hands and head were added later. Individual details such as beards and ears were sculpted afterwards, then the whole was brightly painted. It is uncertain quite why so much trouble was taken but one theory is that the different faces, many of which belong to what have become minority races, are a celebration of the first unification of China. Another argues that they demonstrate the power of the ordinary citizen, a view which smacks more of 20th-century Marxism than serious empirical analysis. But certainly these men were clearly highly esteemed by the First Emperor even if their presence here represents no more than the egotism of a powerful man.

Exhibitions Pit 2 contains a unit of cavalry and war chariots, Pit 3 contains a war chariot, 68 warriors and numerous bronze weapons, whilst Pit 4 was empty. Only Pits 1 and 3 are currently open to the public.

In separate exhibition halls there are examples of the soldiers under glass, and in yet another hall you can see a pair of scaled-down bronze chariots of quite remarkable precision and beauty, discovered in 1980 just west of the tomb itself.

It is forbidden to photograph or video the exhibits in Pits 1 and 3, a rule that is vigorously enforced. Photography is permitted elsewhere, however. There is an interesting free market outside the site gates.

Each of the life-sized warriors is said to be an individual portrait

Royal rage

The First Emperor was a driven man. In about 218BC he found crossing the Yangtze difficult due to a gale. He blamed the river-goddess whose temple was on a nearby mountain and so, to punish her for inconveniencing him, he ordered 3,000 slaves to fell all the trees on its slopes.

A deserted back street near the waterfront in the old part of the port city of Yantai, Shandong province

▶ Yan'an (Yenan) 80B2

Yan'an (Shaanxi province), the Communists' headquarters during the Anti-Japanese war, holds an honoured place in recent Chinese history, not least because it was also the finishing-point of the Lóng March. The area of arid hills is not without interest for its local cave architecture, quite apart from its revolutionary associations.

▶ Yantai 81E3

Known as Chefoo to 19th-century foreigners, Yantai in Shandong province is a fishing-port, notable for its **Fujian Guild Hall and museum▶**, built by traders from Fujian in 1884 as both lodging- and meeting-place.

▶ Zhengzhou 80C2

The capital of Henan province is thought to have been a Shang dynasty capital. Although it remained a city of middling importance for the next 3,000 years, it is only recently that it has regained its stature, but as a manufacturing centre of considerable ugliness. It was here in 1938 that Chiang Kaishek breached the Yellow river dykes to hold back the Japanese, allowing hundreds of thousands of Chinese to die in the process. There is a commemorative tablet at Huaxuankou on the road to the Yellow river.

The **Provincial Museum▶▶** on Jinshui Lu has a remarkable display of local finds from the neolithic to Ming periods. Nearby is the **Yellow River Exhibition Hall** which tells the story of the river and the efforts to control it. The **Temple of the City God (Chenghuangmiao)▶**, of the Ming dynasty, on Jiefang Donglu, is dedicated to the city protector, a tradition supposed to date back to the reign of the legendary Yao Emperor, 4,000 years ago. At the east end of the same street are the remains of the **Shang city wall** which, it is estimated, was 9m high and 20m wide.

Railway strike
In Communist folklore, Zhengzhou is inextricably linked to the revolution because of the strike which started on the railway in 1923. This arose because of the local warlord's opposition to the establishment of a united trade union, not least because the railway line was vital, he felt, to the movement of his troops. Thirty-five workers were shot, and the strike that followed is considered to be one of the first major steps taken by the Workers' Movement.

The Long March

■ In 1930 Mao Zedong, with the assistance of Zhu De, founder of the Chinese Red Army, and others destined to play a considerable role in the New China, founded a Chinese soviet republic in the mountains of Jiangxi, in southeast China.....■

Breakout Chiang Kaishek, aware of the growing threat to his nationalists posed by the communists in southern China, mounted five campaigns against them in the years 1931–4. Only on the fifth occasion were Mao's forces compelled to break out. The communists decided to retreat from Jiangxi to Yan'an, a remote town far off in the northwest, in Shaanxi province. From October 1934 for two years almost 100,000 marchers lived off the countryside making their way over mountains and difficult terrain to Yan'an, a distance of almost 8,000 miles. Peasants were converted to the cause *en route*, but the ordeal and battles with local warlords took their toll and only a fraction of the original number completed the journey.

The march, however, was an important milestone in Mao's career – it enabled him finally to achieve the leadership he sought and in 1935 he was elected chairman of the Party's Central Committee. Simultaneously, the march had temporarily benefited the nationalists, for much of the burden of fighting had been passed on to the warlords. At the same time there was a good deal of factional fighting among the communists themselves and it was only Mao's emergence as leader that settled those differences once and for all. Once the communists had arrived in Yan'an, it became their capital until 1945.

Revolutionary base areas

- 1934
- 1935
- 1936
- Guerilla zones

Long March routes

- First Front Army
- Second Front Army
- Fourth Front Army
- Sixth Army Group
- 25th Army Corps

1. Central Soviet Area
2. Hunan-Jiangxi
3. Hunan-hubei-Sichuan-Guizhou
4. Sichuan-Shaanxi
5. Fujian-Zhejiang-Jiangxi
6. Hunan-Hubei-Jiangxi
7. Hubei-Henan-Anhui
8. Hubei-Henan-Shaanxi
9. Shaanxi-Gansu-Ningxia

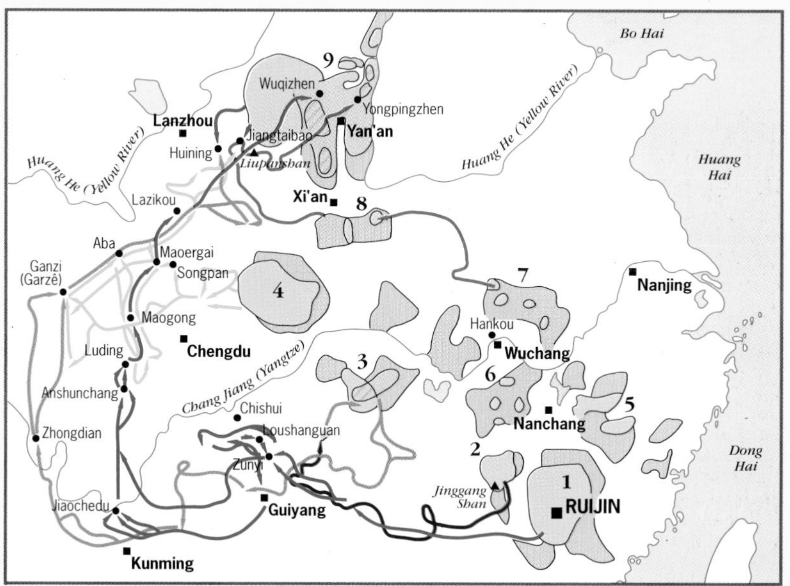

SU
MN
KP
NEI MONGOL ZIZHIQU
(INNER MONGOLIA)
HEILONGJIANG
JILIN
LIAONING
HEBEI
Mohe (Xilinji)
Tahe
Huma
Ergun Zuoqi
Ergun He
Jagdaqi
Heihe
Manzhouli
Hailar He
Hailar
Hulun Nur
Nenjiang
Nen Jiang
Xiao Hinggan Ling
Wudalianchi
Heilong Jiang
Bei'an
Laha
Zalantun
Da Hinggan Ling
Yichun
Tongjiang
Hegang
Fujin
Qiqihar
Zhalong
Jiamusi
Shuangyashan
Daqing
Suihua
Anda
Wusuli Jiang
Sban
Ulanhot
Zhaodong
Jiang
Yilan
Qitaihe
Hulin
Wanda
Baicheng
Da'an
Songhua
Harbin
Mishan
Taonan
Fuyu
Shangzhi
Linkou
Jixi
Xingkai Hu
Mudan Jiang
Mudanjiang
Changchun
Jilin
Jingpo Hu
Tongliao
Shuangliao
Songhua Hu
Dunhua
Siping
Liaoyuan
Tumen
Yanji
Chifeng
Meihekou
Liao He
Tieling
Fuxin
Hunjiang
2750m
Changbaishan
Tumen Jiang
Chaoyang
SHENYANG
Fushun
Benxi
Tonghua
Jinzhou
Anshan
Liaoyang
Jinxi
Yingkou
Yalu Jiang
Fengcheng
Dandong
Qinhuangdao
Liaodong Wan
Bingyu
Xinjin
Liaodong Bandao
Dalian
Bo Hai
0 100 200 300 km
A B C
1 2 3 4

Right: women workers shovel snow off the streets of Harbin

Centre right: the Throne Room of the Manchurian Imperial Palace, Shenyang

Far right: children enjoy an ice sculpture on a riverbank in Harbin

THE NORTHEAST

A detail from the Imperial Palace, Shenyang

Mighty Manchus
Such was the Manchus' prestige when they took control of China in 1644, that the fifth incarnation of the Dalai Lama journeyed to Beijing from Lhasa in person to acknowledge the suzerainty of the new Qing dynasty. He ordered the building of the White Dagoba there in 1651 (it still stands today in Beihai Park) perhaps because he had a premonition about the future – a hundred years later Qing China had expanded to the Nepalese border and Tibet had become a Chinese protectorate.

The Northeast Although the northeast region of China has much in common with north China, it nevertheless has its own character, a mixture of China, Manchuria, Siberia and Korea.

This is partly because the frontier here has fluctuated considerably over the centuries. Indeed it is only during the last 20 years that agreement has finally been reached between the Chinese and the Russians to prevent the sniping across the banks of the Heilong Jiang (Amur) river which had previously been a feature of the region. Residents of this region may now go about their daily business without fear of invasion, and foreigners also benefit since they may travel more freely here.

The region, consisting of the provinces of Liaoning, Jilin and Heilongjiang, is the northernmost part of China proper. It borders Siberia in the north, Korea in the southeast and Chinese Inner Mongolia in the west, and is washed by the Yellow Sea to the south. On the whole it is a marked contrast to the rest of China, for it is an area of freezing winters, of fir-clad hills and mountains, of rivers and lakes, and of the minority peoples. These days its major cities are vital components in China's industrial life.

Off the beaten track From the visitor's point of view, the northeast is usually considered a fringe attraction. This does not mean, however, that it is devoid of interest, only that it demands more research and more effort. For the lover of nature, particularly, the northeast has much to offer; but the determined traveller can discover much else. After all, China was ruled by people from this region for the last 300 years of her imperial history.

Its history, as might be expected in frontier country, is a chequered one, and rather obscure. Of the many peoples to have made their home in the northeast perhaps the best known are the Manchus or Manchurians, who gave a political shape to the region. They, it seems, were originally a Jürchen tribe of Tungusic stock. The Tungus inhabited the northeast, living by a mixture of hunting and agriculture. The Manchu dynasty arose out of the Aisin Gioro clan which held the hereditary chieftainship of one of the Jürchen tribes. By the usual tactics of marriage into and alliance with other tribes, Nurhaci, the leader of the Manchus (whose son subsequently inaugurated the Qing dynasty), developed a power base in the Liaodong peninsula and created a united front against the Chinese, with whom relations had for long been uneasy.

By the time Nurhaci was sufficiently powerful to invade China he had inculcated a sense of statehood into his people. The economy was solidly based on ginseng and horses whilst the state bureaucracy, no doubt influenced by that of China, was conducted using a new script based on the Mongol alphabet. Shenyang became the capital of the new Manchurian state, which was then absorbed into China.

The Manchurian state was later reincarnated briefly and ingloriously in the 1930s as Manchukuo, a spurious attempt by the invading Japanese to give legal substance to their own ambitions.

The ginseng and the horses remain, and so do some 10 million Manchurians, one of China's 55 minority peoples. The northeast is not China's heartland but is none the less an integral part of the modern Chinese state.

China in a modern world
A fascinating aspect of China is its contradictions: a Third World country that makes its own nuclear weapons; a socialist country that encourages farmers to earn more; a country that pioneered great inventions (gunpowder, the magnetic compass, printing) yet lags behind modern technology; and that has strict measures for population control yet relies on manual labour for agricultural production.

A winter vendor of baked yams, in Harbin

Feature film
Changchun is advertised as the cradle of New China's film-making industry but most of the films that have come to international attention in recent years have been made elsewhere. *Yellow Earth* and *Red Sorghum* made in the Xi'an studios, received widespread acclaim in Europe and America, whilst *Farewell My Concubine*, made with Chinese talent and Hong Kong money, was nominated for an Oscar in 1994.

▶ Anshan *112A1*

Anshan produces over 20 per cent of China's steel and, although important industrially, has little aesthetic appeal. To the southeast of the city, some 10km distant, are the **Tanggangzi Hot Springs**, where Puyi, the Last Emperor, used to bathe with his empresses. About 20km to the southeast is **Mount Qian (Thousand Lotuses Hill)▶**, a well-known beauty spot of green peaks and, among the conifers, Taoist and Buddhist monasteries dating back to the Ming dynasty.

▶▶ Changbaishan *112B1*

The remote Eternally White Mountains form China's largest nature reserve, a vast area of dense forest and tundra, noted for its varieties of plant and animal life, from wild ginseng to Manchurian tigers. It is within the Yanbian Korean Autonomous Prefecture, home to the Korean minority. Its most famous beauty spot is the volcanic crater lake of **Tianchi (Heavenly Lake)▶▶**, at a height of over 2,000m. Almost 13km in circumference and with an average depth of 204m, it is the deepest lake in China. Formed in an eruption of 1702, it glistens in the shadow of wild peaks and is a 1- or 2-hour climb from a 60m waterfall, the point where most visitors arrive. There is some hiking from late June to September, which is the only time when it is possible to enter the area unless you hire a snowmobile.

▶ Changchun *112B2*

Between 1933 and 1945 Changchun, the capital of Jilin province, was the capital of Manchukuo, the artificial state created by the Japanese to be ruled over by the puppet Last Emperor, Puyi (see page 119). His former **imperial residence▶▶** has become a museum and exhibition

The harbour at Dalian. The maritime climate here means that the waters never freeze, making Dalian one of China's most important ports, as well as a popular summer resort

hall. Otherwise, Changchun is famous for its car factory (which produced the Red Flag limousine) and for its film studio. Tours of both can be arranged by CITS.

► Dalian *112A1*

Formerly known as Dairen and Luda, Dalian is the only real port in the northeast and is comparatively attractive as modern Chinese cities go. It is clean and uncrowded and, as an Open Coastal City, has an air of prosperity not commonly found in most of the rest of China. Strategically important because of its deep-water, ice-free harbour, under the Japanese it was a rival to Hong Kong; before that it was of interest to the Russians, who wanted to build a thriving alternative to Vladivostok, which becomes ice-bound. Under the terms of the Yalta agreement in 1945, the Japanese gave up Dalian to the Soviet Union, whose occupation ceased only in the 1950s. The occasional Russian street sign is a reminder of that time.

It is not an exciting place to visit, however. A tour of the port is possible and there are some excellent beaches. The shopping streets are lively and the **Natural History Museum**► is of interest, but Dalian's main attraction is its fish restaurants. Specialities are sea-cucumber stew, yellow croaker in sweet-and-sour sauce, pike in soybean sauce, soft-fried sea conches and phoenix shark's fin.

About 200km to the northeast of Dalian stretches a chain of mountains. Here the valley of **Bingyu (Ice Valley)**►► winds through a 5,000-hectare primeval forest, and a river meanders through a landscape of sheer rock formations. Places of interest in the valley include the Skylark Peak, Xiaoyu (Small Valley), the Yingna river, and the Longhua (dragon splendour) and Huaguo (orchard) Mountains.

Ore down under
Iron was first discovered in China in about 600BC, followed quickly by the development of cast iron, so that there was a flourishing iron and steel industry by the Han dynasty. China still has huge reserves of untapped iron ore, mostly of low quality with an iron content of about 30 per cent. A great deal of high-grade ore is therefore imported from abroad. To secure supplies the China Metallurgical Import and Export Corporation bought a 40 per cent stake in a mine at Channar in Western Australia.

Steel works at Anshan, Liaoning province. The smoking furnaces highlight China's serious pollution problem

Puyi, the Last Emperor

■ The tragi-comic life of the Last Emperor has been colourfully brought to world attention by the Italian director Bernardo Bertolucci in his film *The Last Emperor*. Puyi's story was a travesty but in many ways he personified the decline and fall of a once great civilisation.....■

Reformation
For the Western reader the first part of Puyi's autobiography (on which the film was largely based) is fascinating for its insight into the way of life inside the Forbidden City. The second part, dealing with the Last Emperor's re-education, is less colourful. None the less, it too is of interest for it shows how Puyi was used as an example to the people: the book closes with the words, 'Only today, with the Communist Party and the policy of remoulding criminals, have I learnt the significance of this magnificent word ['man'] and become a real man.'

Puyi's story as told by himself

Early start Puyi was born in Beijing on 7 February 1906, in the mansion of his father Prince Chun, who had inherited the title from Puyi's grandfather the seventh son of the Emperor Daoguang (reigned 1821–50). He was not yet 3 when in November 1908 he was made emperor at the behest of the dying Dowager Empress Cixi, in whose shaky hands the destiny of China had lain for several lack-lustre decades. He ascended the throne as the tenth and last emperor of the Qing dynasty on 2 December. On 12 February 1912 he was forced to abdicate by the newly installed revolutionary government, but his retirement was not to be a quiet one.

Premature retirement On the contrary, the years after his abdication are of greater interest than those of his juvenile reign. His life under the Republic was at first governed by the Articles providing for the Favourable Treatment of the Great Qing Emperor after his Abdication. His title of dignity was to be retained; he was to receive an annual allowance of 4 million taels; he was to continue to live, temporarily, in the Forbidden City; the sacrifices at his ancestral temples and imperial tombs would be maintained for ever; the uncompleted tomb of the Emperor Guangxu would be finished according to the original plan; although no further eunuchs were to be engaged, all persons of imperial grade would continue to be employed at the palace; the former emperor's private property would enjoy the protection of the state; and the existing palace guard would become part of the Republican Army.

Palatial existence Puyi remained in the Forbidden City, complete with imperial retinue, until 1924 when the nationalists, concerned at the threat of restoration, forced him to leave. It was as if he lived in a continuous theatrical production – outside, the China that had sustained dynastic rule for 2,000 years was attempting to come to terms with notions of incipient democracy, something altogether at odds with Chinese tradition; whilst, simultaneously, Puyi lived a barely diluted imperial existence in the palace. Everywhere he went – whether to study, carry out imperial duties or to stroll in the garden – he was pursued by his retinue of eunuchs and attendants. He called this 'the daily pomp'.

Above: Scene from the film The Last Emperor, *directed by Bernardo Bertolucci*

Restoration There was surprisingly widespread support for the monarchy in early Republican China, and Puyi was restored to the throne for just 12 days in 1917. The idea of restoration was never entirely relinquished, particularly by the Japanese who thought that popular support for an emperor might play a useful role in their own ambitions for a Pan-Asian empire.

After his expulsion from the Forbidden City in 1924, Puyi took refuge in the Japanese Legation. He was later made puppet emperor of Manchukuo, an artificial empire created in northeast China by the invading Japanese. After the war he was captured by Soviet troops and lived in Russia until Mao's victory in 1949. After his return he underwent political indoctrination before becoming a gardener in the Botanical Gardens in Beijing. Public humiliation followed during the Cultural Revolution and he died in 1967.

A formal portrait of Puyi, last representative of 2,000 years of imperial rule

Sun dried
The name 'Harbin'comes from the Manchu language and means 'a place for drying fishing nets in the sun', which is an indication of the city's lowly status before being discovered by the Russians, when it was no more than a remote village.

▶ Dandong 112B1

A border town with North Korea, Dandong is one of the most important ports in the region. It is also an important centre of light industry – watches, foodstuffs and so on. It is another pleasant, clean town with little to offer other than its proximity to North Korea for which a visa is necessary, possibly available in Beijing. However, it is possible to see North Korea without a visa by taking a boat ride along the Yalu river, or by going up the hill in Jinjiangshan Park. About 50km from Dandong is **Fengcheng** where the 840m Fenghuang Mountain is covered in temples from various dynasties.

Autumn mists on Taoist Fenghuang Mountain, near Dandong

Bear necessity
One of China's rarest and most famous exotic dishes is perhaps found only in Harbin. This is Bear's Paw, often associated with the 4th-century BC philosopher Mencius who said: 'Fish I love; bear's paw I love; If I cannot have both I'll forgo fish for bear's paw'.

▶ Daqing 112B3

One of the country's success stories since 1949, Daqing in Heilongjiang is China's most famous oilfield and one of the largest in the world. Before then it was no more than a chill swamp but with the help of the Soviet Union drilling commenced. After the Sino-Soviet split the Chinese continued until oil was finally discovered in late 1959. The town, originally a series of self-contained villages, is interesting only as an example of one of the occasional successes the communists had in mobilising the masses.

▶▶ Harbin 112B2

Architecturally speaking, Harbin, in Heilongjiang province, is unique in China. This is because of Russian influence – not from the alliance with the Soviet Union in the 1950s, but from the days when Harbin was an important junction on the Russian Manchurian Railway. As a result Harbin's skyline is shaped by the onion domes and traditional roofs of a pre-Revolutionary Russian town.

Walk Harbin

Start by taking a ferry across the river to **Sun Island** and then return, walking through the Stalin Park eastwards, noting the **Flood Control Monument**, until Shangzhi Street on the right. Walk down here with Zhaolin Park on the left. At the main junction turn right and then right up Zhongyang Street with the Modern Hotel on the right. At the top turn left then first left to the junction with Jingwei Street. Take the second left for the **cathedral,** then head south towards Fendou Road and Dong Da Zhi with its markets and shops.

Harbin: winter in China's far north

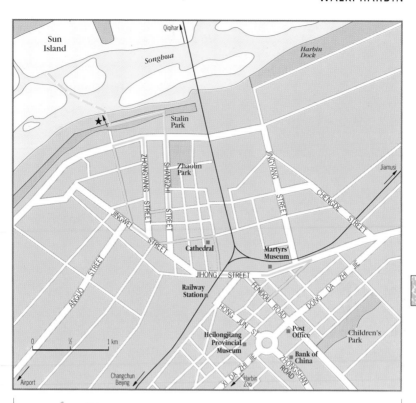

One of the glowing ice sculptures, London's St Paul's Cathedral, created for Harbin's extraordinary ice festival held in Zhaolin Park every year

Before the 1890s Harbin was a moderately sized fishing village on the Sungari (Songhua) river. With the construction of the railway a large number of Russian engineers and merchants moved in, followed by Chinese in search of work. After 1917 the population swelled to about 200,000 as refugees from the revolution in Russia escaped over the border.

There are still a few Russians left in Harbin but their numbers are fast dwindling. Their influence can be seen most clearly in the **Daoliqu**►► area, near Zhongyang Dajie, which is also of interest for its shops and markets on the banks of the river.

Harbin is well known for two other reasons. The first, dismal reason is that during World War II Harbin was home to a Japanese Germ Warfare Experimental Base, now a museum, which is some 30km away at the town of Pingfang. It shows the sadism of experiments carried out on Chinese, Soviet, British, and Korean prisoners of war who were injected with bubonic plague, frozen alive, and roasted alive amongst other unspeakable horrors.

The other more cheerful reason to visit Harbin is for the **ice-festival**►► in January–March. The Chinese have learnt to create ice and snow sculptures which are wrapped around lanterns so that dragons, bridges and traditional pavilions glow in the dark. The sculptures are concentrated mostly in Zhaolin Park. There is also a ballroom dancing competition, a food sampling fair, as well as the chance to ride on sledges and on snow motorcycles.

Sun Island is a sandbank on the Songhua river popular with sunbathers in the summer. A snow sculpture competition is held there in January.

Cold comfort
Although the people of Harbin are well known for their friendliness, the city has a typical Siberian climate. In the winter temperatures fall to -38°C but in the summer can climb to over 30°C.

► Heilong Jiang (Heilong or Black Dragon river) *112B3*

The river, which has given its name to the province, is more familiar by its Russian name – Amur. It forms the border between China and Russia and has been the scene of border disputes and skirmishes. Now that the border has been settled once and for all, the area is open to foreign visitors. Boat tours run between **Heihe**, **Huma**, and **Tongjiang**. This is a region of minority peoples: the Hezhen, numbering about 1,500 at the last count, live by fishing and, like their Eskimo cousins, use dog sleighs. They used to wear animal hides, although the Chinese proudly boast that they have converted them to woven clothing. Another minority people, with a population of just over 4,000, are the shamanistic Oroqens, who also live across the border in Inner Mongolia. Although many lead settled lives now, they are by tradition nomadic forest hunters, raising reindeer and making their utensils from birch bark.

Mohe is China's most northerly town from where the aurora borealis can be viewed.

A northeastern treasury
The three treasures of the northeast are antlers, furs and ginseng. There is also frog oil, extracted from the female frog's ovary which, when served in soup or with chicken, is supposed to have curative properties.

► Jiamusi *112C3*

A large manufacturing town, Jiamusi is of interest for the farms where ginseng is grown and where red deer are bred for their antlers, used in Chinese medicine.

Manchurian ginseng and tree fungus, used in traditional Chinese medicine

► Jilin *112B2*

A major chemical centre with a population of over 1 million, Jilin (formerly Kirin), although not of particular interest, has nearby ski slopes, a **ginseng farm**►, and a **museum** containing a large meteorite that fell in 1976. There is also an ice-festival in January.

Songhua Lake is 14km southeast of Jilin, in a scenic area of 550 sq km.

►► Jingpo Lake *112B2*

Some 110km from the town of Mudanjiang is this S-shaped lake surrounded by high mountains. A good place for fishing (equipment may be hired), it is 90km square and the result of a volcanic lava flow which dammed up a gully. The area is a **national park**►►, with volcanic craters, karst caves and waterfalls, including the 40m-wide Diaoshuilou.

►► Shenyang 112A1

Now a city of 6 million, and the capital of Liaoning province, Shenyang was by the beginning of the 17th century the capital of the Manchurian empire. In that same century the Manchus overran China, making Beijing their capital and relegating Shenyang (formerly known as Mukden) to a secondary position. At the beginning of the 20th century it was a Russian railway town; then it alternated between China and Japan during the first Sino-Japanese War (1904–5). During the next 45 years it was in the hands of various warlords, the Japanese, the Russians, the Guomindang and finally the communists. Nowadays Shenyang has an industrial output to rival that of Shanghai – aircraft and textiles are among its many industries.

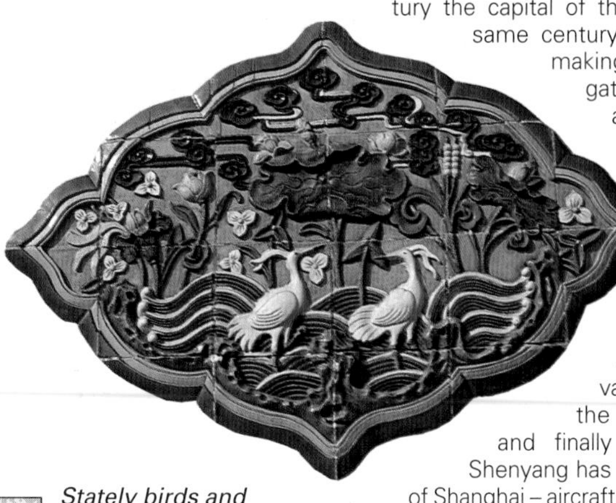

Stately birds and elegant lotus blossoms adorn an ornamental feature in the Imperial Palace in Shenyang, Liaoning province

The city's main sites are the **Imperial Palace►►**, the **Qing tombs►►** and the **Shisheng Temple►**. The **Imperial City** is a Manchu version in miniature of the Forbidden City in Beijing. It was originally named the Palace of the Prosperous Capital (Shenjing Gong), but was renamed the Travelling Palace of Upholding Heaven after Beijing became the capital in 1644. Although additions were made during the 18th century, the palace was initially completed between 1625 and 1636. There are some 300 rooms and 10 courtyards within its walls, all

Map of Shenyang

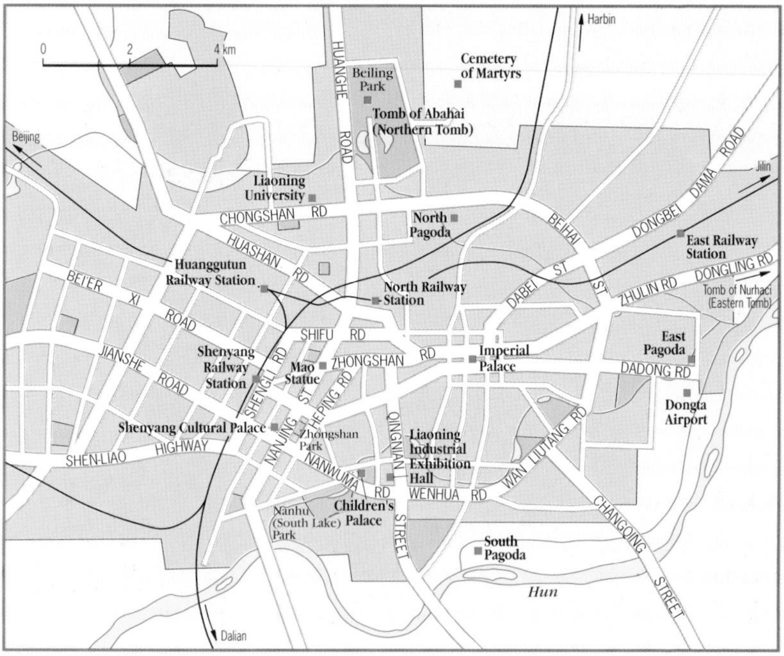

Roofscape, Imperial Palace, Shenyang

arranged on three axes – middle, eastern and western. The arrangement of the buildings of the eastern axis is most typically Manchu. On the western axis is the Wensuge (Hall of the Source of Culture), built in 1782 to house a manuscript edition of the 3,450 classical works which made up the Complete Library of the Four Treasures of Knowledge.

The **Tomb of Nurhaci** (**Dongling** or **Fuling**), founder of the Manchu tribal group, is 12km northeast of Shenyang. An avenue of stone animals leads to a wall enclosing a tower and the circular mound beneath, in which are buried the emperor, his empresses and concubines.

Beiling or **Zhaoling**, in a wooded park in the northern part of the city, is the tomb of Abahai, the second Qing emperor. It is better preserved than Dongling – there are stone horses and lions, bridges, and a fine *pailou* (canopied gateway) in black stone, as well as a stele bearing Abahai's calligraphy.

The **Shisheng Temple**, on Heping Lu, was built in 1638 and was the main lamaist temple in the city.

▶ Wudalianchi *112B3*

This nature reserve comprises five linked lakes, formed in 1720 when volcanic activity forced lava into the Bei river. The mineral springs are said to cure almost any ailment.

▶▶ Zhalong *112B3*

Another nature reserve, established in 1979, Zhalong is at the edge of an immense area of marshland that lies on an important bird migration route from the Arctic to southeast Asia. Some 180 species of bird pass through between April and October, among them the almost extinct red-crowned crane, the traditional Chinese symbol of longevity.

Stocks and shares
In 1986 Shenyang was the first city in China since 1949 to boast a stock exchange; and in the same year a Shenyang company was declared bankrupt, unheard of in a socialist economy.

Charismatic cranes
For the Chinese, animals are either to be eaten or worshipped. Such was the reverence accorded the red-crowned crane by the Duke Yi of Wei that he paid them a salary and allowed them to travel in carriages. This irritated the Wei generals who asked, 'Since the cranes are so highly honoured, why not let them do the fighting?'

■ For Westerners, traditional Chinese medicine is invariably associated with acupuncture, but acupuncture is only one of several applications, all of which are based on the precepts of Taoism.....■

A Yunnan herbalist passes on his knowledge to his son

Slow but sure
Chinese medicine usually comes in the form of a variety of pills and potions with a plethora of bewildering instructions. Tempting though it is to ignore them, patience and careful observance of the directions often leads to good results, but Chinese medicine does not act as quickly as its Western counterpart.

In the pharmacy of the Hospital of Traditional Chinese Medicine, Tianjin

Vital essence Chinese medicine is considered rather unscientific and imprecise by Western practitioners; however, a Chinese doctor might well argue that its imprecision – or flexibility – is in fact its strength. The Chinese refer to organs, but when they do so it is not the organs themselves that are important but their function in the distribution of vital essence (or *qi*) throughout the body. The 11 organs by which health is judged are the bladder, circulation, gall bladder, heart, kidney, large intestine, liver, pancreas, small intestine, stomach, and something called the triple burner, which has no material existence at all but is a driving force. Over the centuries hundreds of points were located on the body which were linked to these organs. By joining them together, meridian paths were drawn which traced the flow of *qi*.

Harmony There are 12 of these meridians, each corresponding to one of the five Chinese elements (metal, earth, fire, water, wood) and each best treated at a certain time of day. A further eight meridians are important in Taoism but of less importance to clinical medical treatment. What concerns Chinese medicine is not the state of the heart itself but the invisible motor that drives the heart to beat. Illness results from a disharmony between mind and body, which can arise when emotional strain, for example, distorts nature's balance.

Diagnosis The Chinese doctor examines the state of the flow of *qi* through the body's meridians by checking the pulse. He uses three fingers to read the six different pulses in each wrist which correspond to the 12 meridians and, by applying different levels of pressure with the fingers, will notice irregularities. Having read the pulse, the doctor will ask questions of the patient in order to decide upon the appropriate treatment.

Treatment His aim is to stimulate the flow of *qi* in the blocked meridian using acupuncture (*zhenjiu*), acupressure (similar to acupuncture), heat treatment with needles in conjunction with the burning leaves of mugwort (moxibustion), or massage (*anmou*). The most precise and efficacious of these is acupuncture which is particularly good for the relief of pain.

Diet is considered vital to health and is part of the Chinese obsession with food. Taoist teaching recommends abstinence from a variety of foods and stimulants from aubergines to vinegar, although a less rigorous version of the diet suffices for most. Only food that relates to the organs and the elements associated with them is eaten, so that hot foods are recommended for the lungs, for example.

Much of this, although not scientifically expressed according to Western lights, does correspond to Western ideas and there is no doubt that Chinese medicine, even if based on amorphous theories, is extremely effective for some diseases. Some aspects, however, like the use of talismans and incantations, are less likely to win over sceptics; but Chinese medicine in general deserves serious consideration.

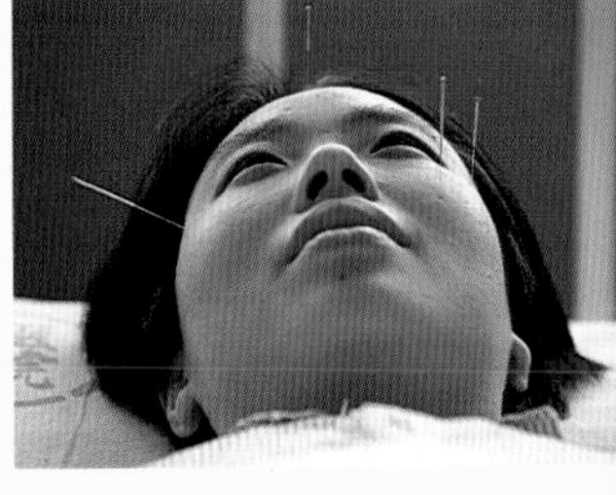

Acupuncture

Skin tonic
Taoists believe that following a strict diet for three years will result in the regeneration of skin tissue throughout the body; after ten years the teeth and bones will be renewed.

Medicine market, Chengdu

SU
KK
MN
KG
TA
AFG
IND
4374m
Youyi Feng
Altay Shan
Altay
Burqin
Fuyun (Koktokay)
Tacheng
Ulungur He
Karamay
Junggar Pendi
Sayram Hu
Ebinur Hu
Huocheng
Kuytun
Ürümqi (Urumchi)
Yining (Gulja)
Shihezi
Tianchi
Bezeklik
7439m
Tian Shan
Aksu
Kuqa
Kizil
Yanqi
Turpan (Turfan)
Hami (Kumul)
Bosten Hu
Kashi (Kashgar)
Korla
Kuruktag Shan
Tarim He
7719m
Kongur Shan
XINJIANG UYGUR ZIZHIQU
GANSU
Ejin
Shache (Yarkant)
Tarim Pendi
Lop Nur
Yecheng (Kargilik)
Mogao Caves
Dunhuang
Yumen
Jiayuguan
Taxkorgan (Tashkurgan)
Taklimakan Shamo
Qarqan He
Ruoqiang (Qarkilik)
Karakorum Shan
Hotan
Altun Shan
Lenghu
Qilian Shan
Zhangye
8611m
Qogir Feng
Hotan He
Qiemo (Qarqan)
Yutian (Keriya)
Da Qaidam
Tianjun
Kunlun Shan
7723m
Qaidam Pendi
Qinghai Hu
Golmud
Gonghe
Hob Xil Shan
5442m
XIZANG ZIZHIQU (TIBET)
QINGHAI
Xiahe (Labrang)
Bayan Har Shan
Tongtian He
Tanggula Shan
0
200
400
600 km
A
B
C
1
2
3

INNER MONGOLIA AND THE SILK ROAD

Heilong Jiang
Mohe
HEILONGJIANG
Ergun Zuoqi
Jagdaqi
Ergun He
Bei'an
Manzhouli
Hailar
Zalantun
Qiqihar
Hulun Nur
Da Hinggan Ling
Daqing
Ulanhot
JILIN
Jarud Qi
Tongliao
Xar Moron He
NEI MONGOL ZIZHIQU (INNER MONGOLIA)
Erenhot
Xilinhot
SHENYANG
Chifeng
LIAONING
Duolun
Taibus Qi
Anshan
Chengde
Jining
Zhangjiakou
Hohhot
Great Wall
Tangshan
Linhe
Baotou
BEIJING (PEKING)
Datong
Dalian
Wuhai
Dongsheng
TIANJIN
Bo Hai
Shizuishan
HEBEI
SHANXI
Yantai
3556m
Helan Shan
Yinchuan
Yellow
Shijiazhuang
Qingtongxia
Taiyuan
Dezhou
Zhongwei
Handan
Jinan
Qingdao
NINGXIA HUIZU ZIZHIQU
Yan'an
Fen He
Da Yunhe
SHANDONG
Huang He
Anyang
Jining
Lianyungang
Lanzhou
Houma
Pingliang
Zhengzhou
Linxia
Xuzhou
Luoyang
JIANGSU
Baoji
Tianshui
Xi'an
ANHUI
Maijishan
Luohe
SHAANXI
Bengbu
Nanjing
HENAN
Hefei
Hanzhong
Suzhou
D
E
HUBEI
Xiangtan
Xinyang
Wuhu

Minorities and nomads
As well as the Uygurs with whom Xinjiang province is usually associated, there are the nomadic Kazaks of the mountains, fine horsemen who live in yurts; and the Kirgiz, also nomadic, who keep herds of camels. The Xibo Manchus, who live near the Russian border, are descended from Qing dynasty garrison troops.

Inner Mongolia (Nei Mongol) and Xinjiang Although these vast areas have quite separate histories, there is a tendency to place them together along with the province of Gansu, gateway to the Silk Road oases, and the autonomous region of Ningxia. Perhaps this is because of their locations either side of the Gansu corridor; or because both, like Tibet, are outside the mainstream of Chinese life (much as Beijing would like to believe otherwise); or perhaps because there is a tendency for tour companies to combine the two as a package.

It will be interesting to see how these areas develop in the coming years. As far as the peripheral regions of the Chinese empire are concerned, the world's emotions have been focused on Tibet. But both the peoples of the Mongolian grasslands and the Muslims of the northwest chafe at Chinese rule from time to time, as well. The Mongolian People's Republic (known in the past as Outer Mongolia) is itself a sovereign state which may yet yearn for reunification with Chinese Inner Mongolia. The Muslims of the northwest have plenty of close relatives across the border in the former Soviet republics – the growing Islamic movement may strengthen ties with the old oasis towns of the Silk Road.

Chinese rule Both areas are comparatively recent acquisitions by China. After the fall of the Mongolian empire at the end of the 14th century the Mongol tribes returned to their nomadic, tribal ways, but under the Qing dynasty the Mongol homelands were absorbed into the Chinese empire, the Chinese at last allaying their fear of the barbarian across the Wall. This huge area was difficult to subjugate and the Russian empire lopped off the northern, 'outer' part of Mongolia as a protectorate. Inner Mongolia remained part of China until 1911 and the fall of the last

Wrestlers in the grasslands outside Hohhot. Mongolian wrestling expresses the joy of manhood

Struggling up the 'singing sands' – dunes near the oasis town of Dunhuang, Gansu province

Hui Muslim from Ningxia

dynasty. The two Mongolias were then reunified for eight years. China subsequently reclaimed Inner Mongolia while Outer Mongolia declared itself the Mongolian People's Republic in 1924. The Japanese occupied much of the area during the 1930s, but after World War II the Chinese declared Inner Mongolia an autonomous region within China, recognising Outer Mongolia as a separate state in 1946. Inner Mongolia has a population of 20 million, of which a mere 2 million are ethnic Mongolians.

Xinjiang ('New Territory'), was brought under Chinese rule at various times during the Han and Tang dynasties but again it was the acquisitive Qing dynasty which finally brought the region to heel in the 18th century. The Muslims never accepted Chinese rule and with the fall of the dynasty in 1911, the region came under the control of a succession of warlords. An attempt in 1945 to form an independent Turkestan Republic failed and the communists absorbed the area into China with little difficulty in 1949. Now more than half its population of 13 million is Han Chinese.

In both regions, although some concessions have been granted to cultural differences, on the whole Chinese rule is paramount. None the less, daily life for many of the natives of these areas is quite different from that of their compatriots behind the Great Wall and thankfully this is still very much in evidence, particularly in the towns of the Silk Road or at the annual Nadam Fair in Mongolia.

Over the border

In the mid-1980s a little-reported phenomenon was taking place in the remote border regions of the Mongolian People's Republic and China, for many years a sensitive area because of their traditional enmity. The infrequent trains between the two were crammed with Chinese who had been living in Mongolia and who, as a result of tension between the two countries, were being unceremoniously bundled across the border back to China. Belongings and food were piled high in the compartments, only to be confiscated at the frontier.

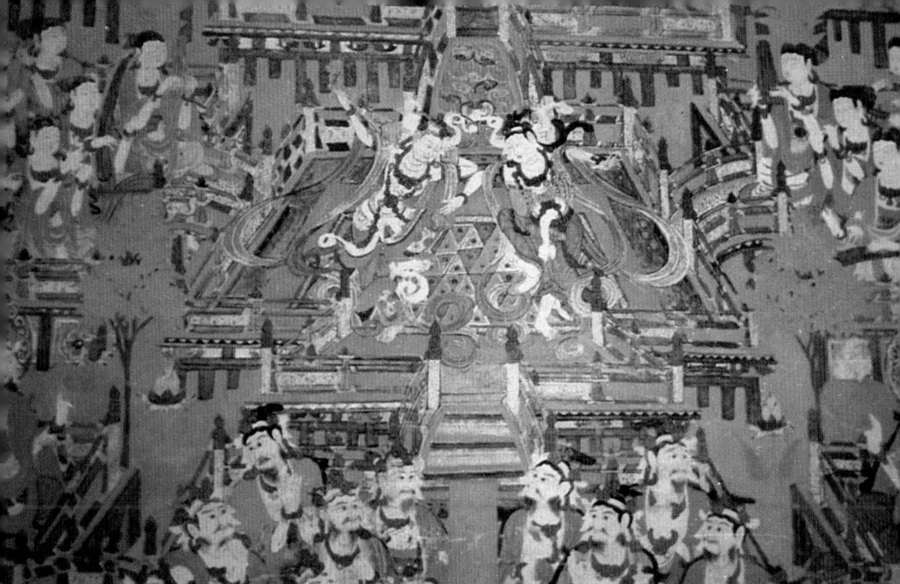

Buddhist dancers depicted in the Mogao caves (Cave 112). Though imaginary, the scene shows factual elements of upper class culture with its assimilation of Western influences

Sutras and documents
Sir Aurel Stein's finds at Dunhuang consist mainly of manuscripts written out as acts of devotion, as well as the Diamond Sutra (now in the British Museum), claimed to be the world's earliest known printed book (AD866); some of the documents were of a secular nature – tax and census returns, and bills of sale, for example – which appear to have been sealed in the caves for safe-keeping, and there is also a manuscript fragment containing musical notation for the lute.

▶▶▶ Dunhuang *128C2*

A small oasis town in Gansu province, Dunhuang (which means 'blazing beacon') is the most important site on the Silk Road itinerary because of the magnificent array of early Chinese Buddhist paintings in the nearby **Mogao caves**▶▶▶ (25km). Dunhuang was made a prefecture in 117BC by Emperor Han Wudi and some of the beacons made of yellow earth which were part of the Han extension of the Great Wall are visible on the road between the town and the railway station at Liuyuan, the nearest point of arrival.

The cave paintings, accumulated over several centuries, were the legacy of the pilgrim monks on their way to India and of merchants and nobles who made their own artistic contributions as a blessing for their caravans and salvation for their souls. The painters themselves were sometimes locals, sometimes masters brought in for the purpose. The cave temples were excavated by monks from AD366; their walls were covered in mud and then layers of dung, plaster, and animal hair, and kaolin was added to provide a suitable surface on which to paint. As the Silk Road declined the caves became less important and in the 10th century were sealed. In 1900 they were rediscovered by a monk who made it his life's work to return them to their former glory. Soon after, the Anglo-Hungarian explorer Sir Aurel Stein persuaded the monk to part with a remarkable collection of manuscripts and silk paintings, now dispersed in the British Museum and the Bibliothèque Nationale, Paris.

The caves (open 8:30–11:30 and 2–4), were made a national monument only in 1961. All told there are about 1,000 of them, of which about 40 are considered worth visiting. Two visits, morning and afternoon, are necessary for a full appreciation.

The earliest caves date back to the 4th century AD (Northern Wei dynasty). A good example is Cave 257, famous for paintings on the west wall depicting the story of the Buddha who, as Deer King, was betrayed by a man whose life he had saved. It also features a very early landscape. The later Western Wei is represented in Cave 249, with some beautiful landscape paintings featuring animals and entertainers.

Cave 428 was decorated during the Northern Zhou with portraits of figures who had sponsored sacred paintings – these are beneath the story from the life of Buddha found on the east wall.

The finest caves of the Sui dynasty are 150, 244, 410, 420 (with a spectacular temple painted on the ceiling) and 427. By now foreign influence (Indian, Central Asian) had been replaced with a more purely Chinese style.

Dunhuang's art reached its zenith during the Tang dynasty when religious traditions were combined with observation of real life. Murals vary from grand scenes from the sutras to portraits of individuals. The finest examples are in Caves 1, 16, 17, 51, 70, 96, 130, 139, 148, 172, 202, 209, 320, 321, 323, 328, 329, 332, 365, 387. The later dynasties were less productive, with the possible exception of the Northern Song represented in Caves 55, 256, and 454.

The other attraction in Dunhuang is the **Crescent Lake**▶▶ (7km south), a spring-fed pool surrounded by giant sand-dunes (called 'the singing sands') which can, with difficulty, be climbed. Camels and drivers are available at the site for transportation, for a fee, to the base of the dunes.

Guardian of the caves
Sir Aurel Stein bought most of his documents from the Taoist Abbot Wang Yuanlu, who devoted much energy to obtaining funds for the restoration of the caves. According to Stein, his efforts were not very successful: they showed 'only too plainly how low sculptural art had sunk in Dunhuang'. However, he admired the efforts of the Abbot 'whose devotion to this shrine and to the task of religious merit which he has set himself in restoring it, was unmistakably genuine'.

A Tang Dynasty 'Apsara', celestial angel, in Cave 44

Perfect statuesque tranquillity at Dunhuang: seated Tang Buddha in Cave 328

Inner Mongolia

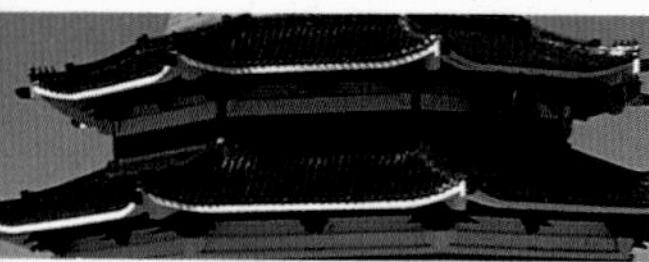

■ Inner Mongolia (Nei Mongol) was absorbed into the Chinese empire in the 18th century. The history of the Mongolian people before that is long and occasionally illustrious.....■

Above: the tomb of Genghis Khan

Beneath the grasslands The attractions of Mongolia for the Chinese are concealed below the earth's surface. It holds first place in the country for rare earth minerals and there are at least 60 verifiable mineral ores in 500 different locations, including coal, iron, chromium, copper, lead, zinc, gold, mica, salt, and mirabilite.

The Lamaist Wudangzhao Monastery, north of Baotou

Nomads For centuries the Mongols were a loose confederation of nomadic tribesmen based on the banks of the Onon river, and a constant threat to the Chinese, who constructed the Great Wall to keep them out. In the early 13th century the various tribes united under Genghis Khan, and under his leadership conquered most of the known world. The Mongols ruled China (the Yuan dynasty) for over 100 years, but with Kublai Khan's death in 1294 the empire began to disintegrate, and although minor khanates continued to exist in isolated parts of the former empire, the Mongols returned to their homeland and nomadic ways.

Grasslands Something of the traditional Mongol way of life is still evident on the grasslands. Round felt tents, or 'ghers', and herdsmen on horseback can sometimes be seen, particularly in the north, but visitors are discouraged from discovering the grasslands for themselves, other than through sanitised tours organised by CITS. However, foreign travel companies organise interesting specialist trips; or you might try to hire a taxi or jeep to take you out to the grasslands.

Highlights Inner Mongolia is not without interest – it has its own atmosphere, and there are a number of places worth visiting, particularly in summer when the weather is pleasantly but not excessively warm. The capital is **Hohhot (Huhehaote)** where the main attractions are the **Inner Mongolia Museum▶▶** which features a 'gher', all the artefacts of traditional Mongolian life, and a locally discovered mammoth; the **Old Town▶▶**, with its low houses and markets, and sprinkling of temples and mosques; and the **Five Pagoda Temple▶**, which is unique in China for its Classical Indian style. Tours can be arranged to the grasslands.

Xilinhot has little to recommend it in itself but is a good centre from which to arrange a visit to the grasslands.

Baotou is the largest city of Inner Mongolia. Its main attraction is **Wudangzhao Monastery▶▶**, 72km to the north. The best surviving example of a Tibetan-style monastery in the region, it was built in the 13th century. Set on the side of a hill, the monastery consists of temples, houses, a hostel and lamas' living quarters. It is a place of considerable atmosphere and well worth the drive from Baotou.

The Five Pagoda Temple, Hohhot

Hailar, on the banks of the Heilong Jiang (Amur river), is another good starting-point from which to visit the grasslands.

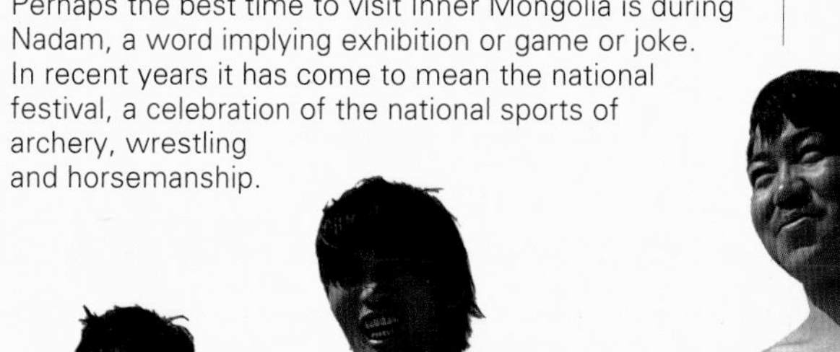

From Dongsheng, south of Baotou, it is possible to reach **Genghis Khan's Mausoleum** via Ejin Qi. The Mausoleum dates only from 1954, when the Khan's ashes were returned from safekeeping in Qinghai. He remains an object of veneration to Mongolians and ceremonies are held here several times a year.

Perhaps the best time to visit Inner Mongolia is during Nadam, a word implying exhibition or game or joke. In recent years it has come to mean the national festival, a celebration of the national sports of archery, wrestling and horsemanship.

A harsh climate makes for tough people: Mongolian wrestlers

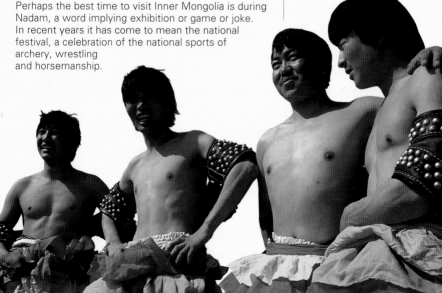

News from Kashi
Perhaps the most entertaining account of Kashi before 1949 is to be found in Peter Fleming's *News from Tartary*, for many the ultimate travel book. He stayed in the former British Consulate: 'a pleasant house with a lovely garden, standing on a little bluff outside the city. From its terrace you looked across the green and chequered valley of a small river towards the too seldom visible mountains.' The bazaar was filled with 'slant-eyed Kirghiz and bearded Tadjiks from the hills [who] moved with a hint of swagger among the self-effacing Turkis'.

Above: traditional Kashi cloth. Below: Jiayuguan Fort entry ticket

►► Jiayuguan *128C2*

This small town is at the far end and narrowest point of the Gansu Corridor, marking the western extremity of the Great Wall and the traditional boundary of Han China – 'one more cup of wine for our remaining happiness. There will be chilling parting dreams tonight' wrote a 9th-century poet on a parting at Jiayuguan. Just outside the town is an imposing **Ming fort►►►** built in 1372 in a dramatic setting between two ranges of mountain, which crowd in on the pass. It arises in spectacular fashion – crenellated walls 10m high surmounted by towers with elegant roofs – from an area of flat stone desert. The **Heishan rock carvings►**, reputedly made by the Huns about 1,500 years ago, are 20km to the northwest.

►►► The Karakorum Highway *128A2*

The route between Pakistan and China was opened in the mid-1980s using what was once a branch of the Silk Road. It is a magnificent way of leaving or entering China. From Kashi, a day's drive through awesome mountain scenery, passing rippleless lakes and crumbling caravanserai, takes you to Taxkorgan (an uncomfortable overnight stop); from there the road winds up to a height of 4,500m before crossing the border into the mountain valleys of Pakistan.

►►► Kashi (Kashgar) *128A2*

Conjuring up a host of magical images, Kashi, or Kashgar as it is more widely known, manages to come up to expectations in many ways despite emasculation by steady historical decline and Chinese indifference to local culture. Its importance grew from its location as an oasis at the point where the northern and southern arms of the Silk Road converged, forming a natural gateway to the mountain passes leading to India and Russia. Although in Chinese hands periodically since AD78, by the tenth century it was firmly in the Islamic world where it remained until the Chinese reconquered the area in the 18th century. In 1865 a Central Asian named Yakub Beg declared himself Khan of East Turkestan and signed treaties with leading Western powers. His domain did not last but Kashgar became a focal point for the rivalry between Russia and Britain, a tussle for hegemony in Central Asia known as 'the Great Game'. Kashgar became a haven for spies of both empires, both of which opened consulates (the former British one stands at the back of the Chini Bagh Hotel grounds, the former Russian one is the Seman Hotel).

There are several places to see. The **Id Kah Mosque►** is the largest in Xinjiang, with room for at least 6,000 worshippers. Founded in the mid-18th century, its present appearance dates from 1838. The **Abakh Hoja Tomb►►**, in the eastern suburbs, contains 72 tombs of the family members of Abakh Hoja, a saintly man of the 18th century, whose daughter was the legendary 'fragrant concubine' (so-called because she was supposed to have naturally secreted perfume) abducted by the Emperor Qian Long. She defied the emperor, whose mother forced her to commit suicide.

The **market▶▶** in the town centre is a colourful daily event and worth lingering in for a couple of hours; but try to be in Kashi on a Sunday for the **Sunday Bazaar▶▶▶**, a meeting-point for all the farmers in the area who come, much as they have done for centuries, to sell their wares, from melons to horseflesh. Hot and dusty, it provides a fascinating glimpse into local life.

The final frontier
The Inner City of Jiayuguan town, the last Chinese outpost on the Silk Road, with its 10m-high wall, was a citadel which housed the Chinese military commander. Beyond were the 'barbarian' tribes. Outside the west gate there is a stele inscribed with the characters: 'The Greatest Barrier Under Heaven'.

Sunday in Kashi: preparing for the weekly bazaar

Paradise lost
The Kingdom of Kuqa was an extraordinary place, exciting the wonder of seasoned travellers like the 7th-century Tang monk, Xuanzang. It measured 500km by 320km and was blessed with luxuriant oases where even corn and rice grew. The orchards were filled with grapes and pomegranates, the ground with gold and copper. Above all the air was soft and the people, who were gifted above all others in the playing of the lute and pipe, were honest.

The 27m high Tang dynasty Future Buddha in Bingling Buddhist caves, Gansu province

►►► Kuqa 128B2

Formerly known to Westerners as Kucha, Kuqa is the second largest town in the central part of Xinjiang and was once the capital of the kingdom of Qiuqci. Taken by the Chinese in the 7th century, it was an important centre for Buddhism and the home of one of the greatest translators of Sanskrit works into Chinese, Kumarajiva by name, who was ultimately to head a translation bureau employing over 1,000 monks. Kuqa had its own Indo-European language, lost for more than 1,000 years until the script was discovered by the sinologists Paul Pelliot and Albert Von le Coq, respectively French and German, on items in the caves at Kizil at the turn of the century. The manuscripts found here, on palm leaves, paper, bark, and wood, were removed and deciphered in Paris.

Kizil►►► is just over an hour's drive from Kuqa and the caves are in cliffs above the Muzart river. Decorated between AD500 and 700, before Chinese stylistic devices had reached this far, the influence is both Indian (since the stories are mostly taken from the life of Buddha and related subjects) and Iranian, as we can see from the decorative detail. Of the 236 caves, originally named by the European archaeologists according to their subject-matter, but now numbered, about 70 are reasonably preserved. Many of the best frescos were removed by Albert Von le Coq to Berlin, where some were destroyed by bombing during World War II, although others can still be seen there, in the Museum of Indian Art.

►► Lanzhou 129D1

The capital of Gansu province lies on the upper reaches of the Yellow river. A former staging-post on the Silk Road, Lanzhou has become a major industrial city of remarkable ugliness. Within the city itself there are a few items of note. The **Gansu Provincial Museum►►** contains the finest display of Yangshao (early

neolithic) pottery in China, and some marvellous bronzes from the Han dynasty tomb of General Zhang, as well as the famous 'flying horse' in full, ethereal gallop, its hoof poised on a swallow's wing from another Han tomb. It has become a widely used symbol of the area.

The **Five Springs Mountain** (**Wuquanshan**)▶ park, opened in 1955, attempts to reconcile concrete with traditional Chinese architecture, with some success. Within it is the Chongqingsi, a 14th-century temple with 13th-century iron bell, and several other, later temples.

The **White Pagoda Mountain Park**▶, opposite the Iron Bridge which marks the centuries-old crossing-place of the Silk Road, consists of several temples including the **White Pagoda** itself, which was first constructed during the Yuan dynasty.

But the main reason for a stop in Lanzhou is to visit the **Buddhist caves at Bingling**▶▶▶, 100km from the city. Trips to the caves are dependent upon the unpredictable river-water level, and involve a 2-hour bus journey and 2 hours more by boat. *En route* you are likely to visit the **Liujia Gorge Dam**, one of the largest in China, designed with the help of the Russians in the 1950s.

The 34 caves at Bingling, in a superb setting, contain several hundred statues (the largest, a Tang Future Buddha, is about 27m high) and a great many paintings. The earliest caves date back to the Northern Wei period, and continued through the Tang, the period of greatest activity, to the Qing. Some of the best work is in Caves 4, 10, 11, 82 and 114.

It is also possible to visit **Xiahe** and the **Labrang Monastery** (described on pages 146–7) from Lanzhou, although the journey will take some seven hours.

Yellow peril
The Yellow river carries heavy deposits of silt down from the loess region of the northern steppe which for centuries have caused severe flooding and drainage problems. Construction of the dam at Sanmenxia in Gansu province first began after 1949, but later the reservoir became clogged up with the river's sediment and it had to be rebuilt.

View across the Yellow river over the city of Lanzhou from White Pagoda Mountain

Ningxia Huizu Zizhiqu is the Autonomous Hui Region of Ningxia and very similar to Gansu province, of which it was once a part. Its landscape varies from the arid and mountainous south to the northern desert region (the Tengger Desert, part of the Gobi), bisected by the Yellow river.....

Northwestern frontier trouble
The Western Xia (Xixia) were a northern Tibetan (Tangut) tribe who had become the dominant force in their homelands. They invaded the Chinese northwest in 1040, at first with considerable success, but the sheer size of the Chinese army and its sophisticated hardware, which included early hand grenades, in the end was too much for them. The Song dynasty none the less was compelled to pay tribute to the Xia, as well as to the Khitan (another barbarian state threatening Chinese stability) as the price of peace. The Xia were finally vanquished by Genghis Khan in 1227.

Discussing religion at a Ningxia mosque. The Hui, whose antecedents came from the Middle East, are an Islamic people

The Hui Ningxia is one of the poorest and most backward areas of China – it was not so long ago that stories were circulating about impoverished male villagers who were still wearing pigtails, as if the revolution of 1911 had failed yet to penetrate these remote reaches.

Ningxia has a population of 4 million, of whom about one third are Hui people. They are Muslims, with Chinese features, perhaps rather darker skinned, and are descended from Arab and Iranian traders who came to China along the Silk Road during the Tang dynasty and intermarried with the local population. Their numbers swelled further during the Yuan (Mongol) dynasty, when many more arrived from Central Asia. During the Muslim Uprisings of 1862–78 the Hui played a major role, but were mercilessly punished by the imperial troops. Ningxia was originally created as a separate administrative region in 1928; it was then absorbed into Gansu in 1954, re-emerging as an autonomous region in 1958.

Highlights Ningxia is far from being a major centre for tourism, yet it is not without interest. The provincial capital, once the capital of the 11th-century Western Xia dynasty, is **Yinchuan▶▶**. Set amid irrigation canals said to have been used since the Han dynasty, the city does not have a great deal to recommend it, although the old town still has a few items to show off – the 400-year-old Yuhuang Pavilion, the Drum Tower, several mosques, the West Pagoda, the North Pagoda (which dates back to the 5th century but was rebuilt in 1771 following an earthquake), the South Gate and a Catholic church built around the turn of the century.

More enticing is the resort of **Gunzhongkou▶▶**, about 16km west of Yinchuan, among the Helanshan mountains which reach over 3,500m in height. Here are the Twin Pagodas and the Western Xia Mausoleum. The mausoleum was constructed by the founder of the Western Xia dynasty, Li Yuanhao.

Below: sheepskin coracle on the Yellow river
Bottom and top, opposite: details from Gao Temple, Zhongwei

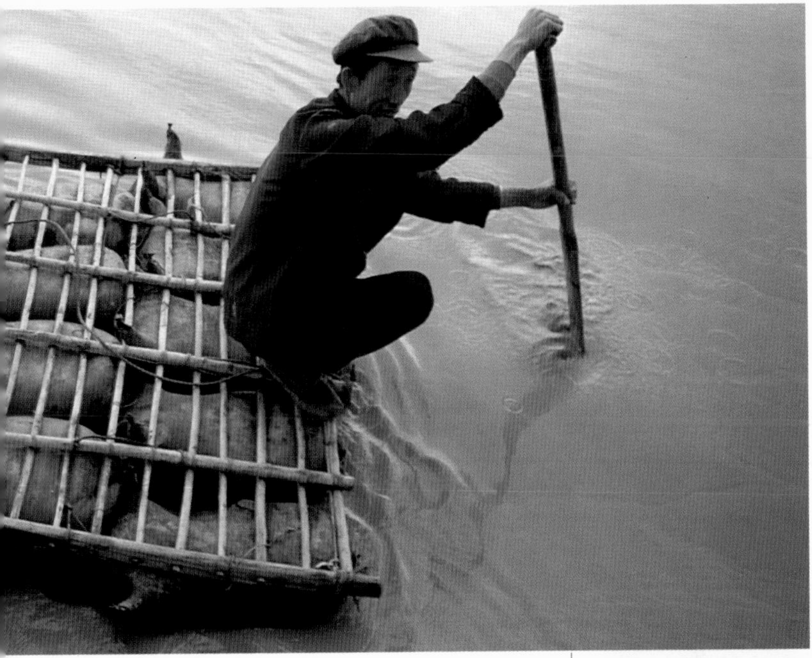

About 100km from Yinchuan is the group of 108 white Dagobas near **Qingtongxia▶▶**, mysteriously built in the shape of a triangle during the Yuan dynasty.

Zhongwei▶ is a small but ancient town. Legend has it that the old walls had no north gate, because there was no more China beyond them. In the town is the Gao Temple, an unusual edifice in wood constructed for use by Buddhists, Confucianists and Taoists. East of the town are remains of the Great Wall and on the edge of the Tengger Desert, at Shapotou, is the Desert Research Centre. Its original brief in 1956 was to find ways of preventing the desert sands from encroaching on the railways and it seems to have met with some success.

Like Yinchuan, Zhongwei is watered by ancient irrigation canals. Rafts made of sheep leather, a traditional method of transportation on the Yellow river similar to the yak-skin rafts of Tibet, can sometimes still be seen at work.

Maijishan: the name means 'Corn Rick Mountain'

Clay sculptures in the spectacular Maijishan Buddhist caves

▶ Linxia *129D1*

Another former Silk Road town in Gansu province of interest because of its minority inhabitants – the Hui, Dongxiang and Uygur peoples.

▶▶ Maijishan *129D1*

The **Buddhist caves** on Maijishan, a mountain about 30km southeast of Tianshui in the south of Gansu province, rank with those at Datong, Dunhuang and Luoyang as the most important in China. Joining a group with a guide is recommended and a torch is useful. The caves, in a dramatic setting high up on the cliff face, are reached by a network of precipitous stairways.

The earliest ones date back to the 4th century AD. In all some 200 remain, many of those on the west side untouched since the Song dynasty – notable among them are caves 100, 133, and 165. On the less well-preserved east side the most interesting caves are 4, 7, 13, 72a, 102, 133 and 191.

▶▶▶ Turpan (Turfan) *128B2*

Turpan is perhaps the most delightful town along the Chinese Silk Road. It boasts a number of interesting sights but perhaps more importantly it still exudes, with its trees and traditional Uygur mud-brick houses, a tranquil, old-world atmosphere rare in China. Although most of the inhabitants are Uygur, much of Turpan's historical importance is pre-Islamic. The Uygurs, originally nomads from Siberia and Central Asia, settled in the area after the 9th century, when they were converted to Islam. They still retain much of their way of life, wearing traditional clothes, building trellised courtyards and small kilns for drying the famous grapes from the area, and following a diet – mutton, flat bread, dried fruit, pilau rice – quite distinct from that of Han China.

Most of the places of interest lie just outside the town but there are a few things of worth within the walls. Turpan's **market▶▶**, with its dried fruit, exotic medicines, and gleaming rolls of cloth, is endlessly fascinating. The **Imin Minaret▶▶**, part of a former mosque, was built in 1778 and is made of beautifully decorated brick in the tapering Iranian style.

Outside the town are some remarkable ruins, graves and caves, many of which were disturbed by turn-of-the century archaeologist adventurers. The **Cave Temples at Bezeklik▶▶** (48km northeast), part of a monastery that existed between the 6th and 14th centuries, were carved out of the cliff face above the Murtuk river in a desert setting. There are some fine paintings remaining (in an Indo-Iranian style with Chinese influence) but many were removed by Albert Von le Coq to museums in Berlin, and some were subsequently destroyed by Allied bombs.

To the west of Turpan is the abandoned town of **Jiaohe▶▶▶**, and to the southeast the ruined city of **Gaochang▶▶▶** and the ancient graveyard of **Astana▶▶**. Jiaohe was originally a Han garrison town, taken by the Uygurs and abandoned in the Yuan dynasty perhaps because of a lack of water or because of Muslim fanaticism towards Buddhist remains. It is both poignant and spectacular in its clifftop setting, as is Gaochang, another Han garrison town, which was the Uygur capital between 840 and 1209. It was abandoned at the beginning of the Ming dynasty.

Astana is a graveyard used between the 3rd and 8th centuries. Well-preserved bodies have been discovered here as well as documents, coins, and pottery, now displayed in Turpan and Ürümqi museums. Three of the graves are open, one showing two of the occupants, the others with charming Tang wall paintings.

Also worth visiting near Turpan are the **Flaming Mountains▶**, which glow at sunset, and **Grape Valley▶**, centre of grape production.

Flaming Mountains

Low life
Turpan lies in the Turpan depression (Turpan is a Uygur word meaning 'lowland'), one of the lowest landfalls on earth, descending to 154m below sea-level at its deepest point. Depressions such as this are a characteristic feature of the northern part of western China. Encircled by mountains, the oases high up are fed by melting snow in summer, while the centres of the basins remain true desert.

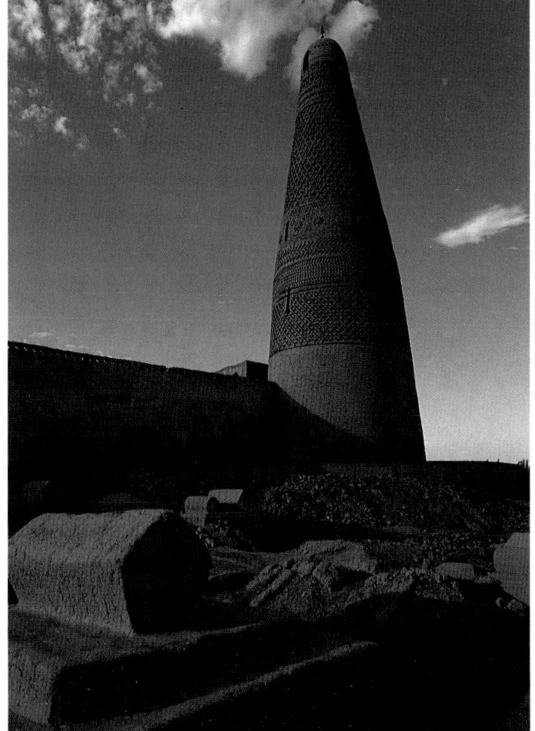

Imin Minaret, Turpan

Well-watered desert.
Turpan is noted for its underground water channels known as *karez*. These carry water formed by the melting snow from the nearby mountains and prevent it from evaporating in the intense heat of the summer. The system is thought to have been imported from Persia 2,000 years ago.

The Silk Road

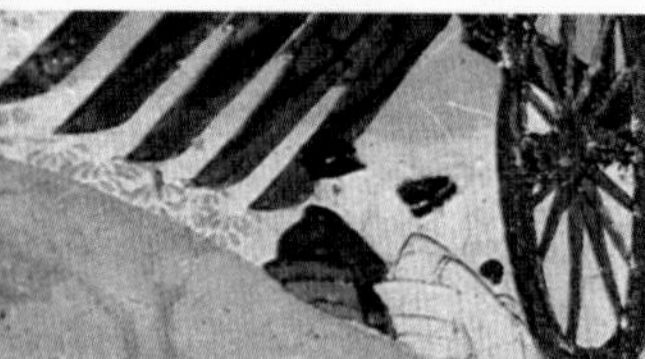

■ The Silk Road is the collective name given to a number of trade routes linking the Chinese and Roman empires. All sorts of commodities passed along it but silk was for centuries one of its mainstays because its production remained a mystery outside China (see pages 182–3).....■

Detail from a mural in Mogao Caves, Dunhuang

Flying horses
General Zhang Qian's mission west took 13 years, during which time he was taken prisoner twice by the Xiongnu barbarian tribe. One of his most significant discoveries was the existence of the so-called 'flying horses' of Ferghana, in Uzbekistan, which were altogether more powerful than the horses familiar to the Chinese and which were taken in large numbers to build up the Chinese cavalry.

Exploration The Silk Road was opened up during the reign of Emperor Han Wudi, who in 138BC had despatched General Zhang Qian on a mission to seek an alliance with peoples west of China against the northern barbarians. The information he brought back about Central Asia led to the westward extension of the Great Wall along the oasis towns of the Gobi and Taklimakan deserts which were to become vital links in Silk Road trade. Beyond China much of what was to be dubbed the Silk Road had been in use for centuries, since communication between the fringes of the great civilisations of Egypt, Mesopotamia and northern India was already possible, if not commonplace. When Alexander the Great marched east many Western ideas found their way east as well and vice versa, with Zhang Qian's mission forming the final link in the chain; and the Romans unified the Mediterranean area, which was linked to Central Asia by means of the imperial highways of the Persian empire. The Silk Road was to remain in constant use until about the mid-14th century.

Merchants The traffic went in both directions – China imported grapes, glass, amber, saffron and, during the cosmopolitan Tang dynasty, a variety of alien faiths including Manichaeism and Nestorianism, as well as Buddhism from India and, later, Islam. The starting-point for Chinese exports was the imperial capital of Xi'an (or Chang'an as it was then). Very few, if any, of the merchants would have accompanied their merchandise all the way to its final destination. Goods were transported by camel through Gansu and Xinjiang from oasis to oasis, through many middlemen, most notably in the Middle East. In Xinjiang the route went north or south of the Taklimakan, meeting at Kashi, from where it went west via either Balkh or Samarkand and Bukhara.

Kashi market: trade still flourishes along the Silk Road

Tea shop on the road between Turpan and Kashi

Foreign influence The centuries passed and governments, rulers, and dynasties changed – the Parthians and the Sassanians succeeded the Persian empire; the Roman empire fragmented and Byzantium emerged in its place, along with the kingdoms of western Europe – but the Silk Road continued as a commercial artery. The greatest upheaval was the gradual expansion from the 7th century onwards of Islam throughout Central Asia to the borders of the Chinese heartlands, a movement which had the effect of binding a vast area together in faith. The Silk Road was probably most open to trade between China and the West under the Mongols during the 13th century, the period when Marco Polo's great journey to China was made.

Decline By the 16th century the Silk Road had lost its significance, as the great empires declined and as maritime trade took the place of caravans. The desert swallowed some towns; radical Islam made travel difficult for infidels; and the Chinese became more inward looking after the Tang. Oasis towns, whose existence had depended on trade, were left to bask in the desert sun until their rediscovery by 19th-century adventurers and the current generation of travellers.

Just deserts
The Taklimakan ('go in, not come out') Desert in Xinjiang province, which separates the northern and southern arms of the Silk Road, was conquered by the archaeologist-explorers Sir Aurel Stein and Sven Hedin in near impossible circumstances in the late 19th century. A hundred years later, Taklimakan has again been subjugated, this time by an Anglo-Chinese expedition, led by Charles Blackmore in 1993–4, which has discovered many lost towns previously hidden under the sands.

Modern-day tourist caravan at Dunhuang

Infamous warlord
After 1911, Xinjiang was for several decades ruled by a succession of warlords. The most infamous of these was Yang Zhengxin. His ferocity was legendary, manifested particularly in a tendency to behead his enemies at banquets to which he had cordially invited them in a spirit of reconciliation. In the end he had his just desserts, for he was himself shot at another banquet in 1928.

▶ Ürümqi (Wulumuqi) *128B2*

The capital of Xinjiang, with a population of about 1 million inhabitants, is rather uninspiring in appearance, although there are good reasons for going there – in fact its position as capital and transportation hub make a visit almost inevitable. Despite an unprepossessing exterior and a lack of any precise centre, the city is of interest for its 'minority' quarters, where many of the Hui and Uygur peoples live with their own markets and restaurants. The excellent **Minority Peoples' Museum▶▶** on Xibei Lu imaginatively explains the ways of life of the various nationalities in the area and is well worth a visit. Otherwise there is **Hongshan Hill** with its Qing pagoda and view; and factories which produce carpets, jade and musical instruments.

Ürümqi's main attraction lies outside the city – **Tianchi (Heaven's Lake)▶▶▶** is cradled 100km away at an altitude of 2,000m among the Tian Shan (Heavenly Mountains), which rise to over 6,000m. It is a beautiful (if popular) sight, worth the journey just to gaze upon; if you have the time and the inclination you can go on horseback with a Kazakh guide to the snowfields above and spend the night in a yurt.

From Ürümqi it is also possible to visit the beautiful **Nanshan grasslands** (Baiyanggou) 70km south.

▶▶ Xiahe and the Labrang Monastery *128C1*

Xiahe is almost 3,000m above sea-level in eastern Gansu, some 150km from Lanzhou and within striking distance of the old Tibetan northeastern province of Amdo. It is a place of exceptional interest, home to one of the six major Tibetan monasteries, the **Labrang Tashi Khyll**

Kazakhs in the summer meadows of the Heavenly Mountains, Baiyanggou

(Labulengsi)►►►, an important place of pilgrimage for Tibetans who flood here in their distinctive finery.

The monastery was built in 1709 by Jamyang Zhepa (a renowned abbot of Drepung Monastery in Lhasa). At one time there were 4,000 monks (reduced to 1,700 now) filling the six institutes of Esoteric Buddhism, Medicine, Law, Astrology, Higher and Lower Institutes of Theology, and the various halls and residences. The monastery has had to withstand fire (in 1985) and the Cultural Revolution but its reputation and pull as a religious centre have apparently survived intact, and this is never clearer than on religious holidays when followers of Tibetan Buddhism pour in to mix with the monks in religious celebrations. The Great Prayer Festival (Monlam) takes place just after the Tibetan New Year (based on the lunar calendar and therefore variable) either in February or March, and there are some fascinating celebrations on the 13th, 14th, 15th and 16th days of the month in question.

► Yining *128A2*

Yining, centre of the Ili Kazakh Autonomous Prefecture, is a town near the Russian border that has only recently opened to foreign tourists. Nearby, in the Ili Valley, **Almalik** is thought to have been the capital of the empire (today's Xinjiang) inherited by Chaghatai, the second son of Genghis Khan, in 1227. The northern arm of the Silk Road ran through here on its way to the great oasis towns of Central Asia.

There is little to see in Yining unless you are lucky enough to witness a **traditional celebration by Kazakh horsemen►►►** in the nearby pastures, a performance of high-spirited horsemanship that is great fun and likely to include gymkhana-style races and a peculiar chase on horseback with a dead goat.

The surrounding countryside is beautiful, however, particularly in the region of the **Sayram Lake►►►**, on the road to Urumai, whose waters are the colour of sapphire.

Monks at Labrang Monastery, Xiahe

Border party
The border of Kazakhstan (in the former USSR) is very close to Yining. Since the 1950s, Westerners have been forbidden to cross it but in 1985 an international group of tourists was allowed across in celebration of 2,000 years of the Silk Road. A bar was set up on the Russian side of the frontier (after customs) and Beatles music was broadcast across the wilderness. The travellers were met by a prancing dragon on the Chinese side.

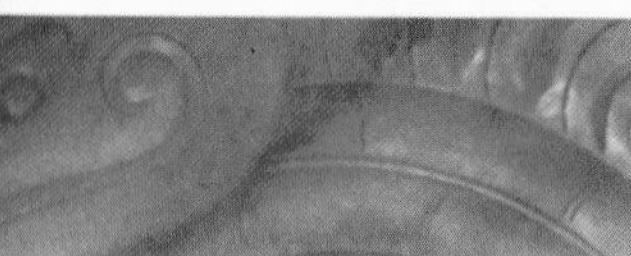

Jade ('*yu*') is the stone most often associated with China. Usually thought of as a deep green colour, in fact it has an unexpectedly wide variety of hues, ranging from creamy white to almost black.....

Toad grease
The oily substance which blends the abrasive mixture used in jade cutting was called 'toad grease', and according to Chinese texts was produced from toads killed in a special way. In fact the grease has always been tallow from mutton or lard from pork.

A jade craftsman in Yangzhou, Jiangsu

History The point just outside Dunhuang where the northern and southern arms of the Silk Road divided was known as Yumenguan or 'the Jade Gate', and jade has long been associated with both imperial and magic powers and known for curative properties, particularly for kidney diseases. It was one of the principal items of tribute payable by barbarian princelings to the Chinese emperor.

Nature Just what is jade? And how do you tell good from bad, or even good from less good? The oldest jade is a calcium-magnesium-aluminium silicate with a hardness of 6.5 according to the Mohs' Scale – this is classical nephrite, found most particularly in Hotan, the old Silk

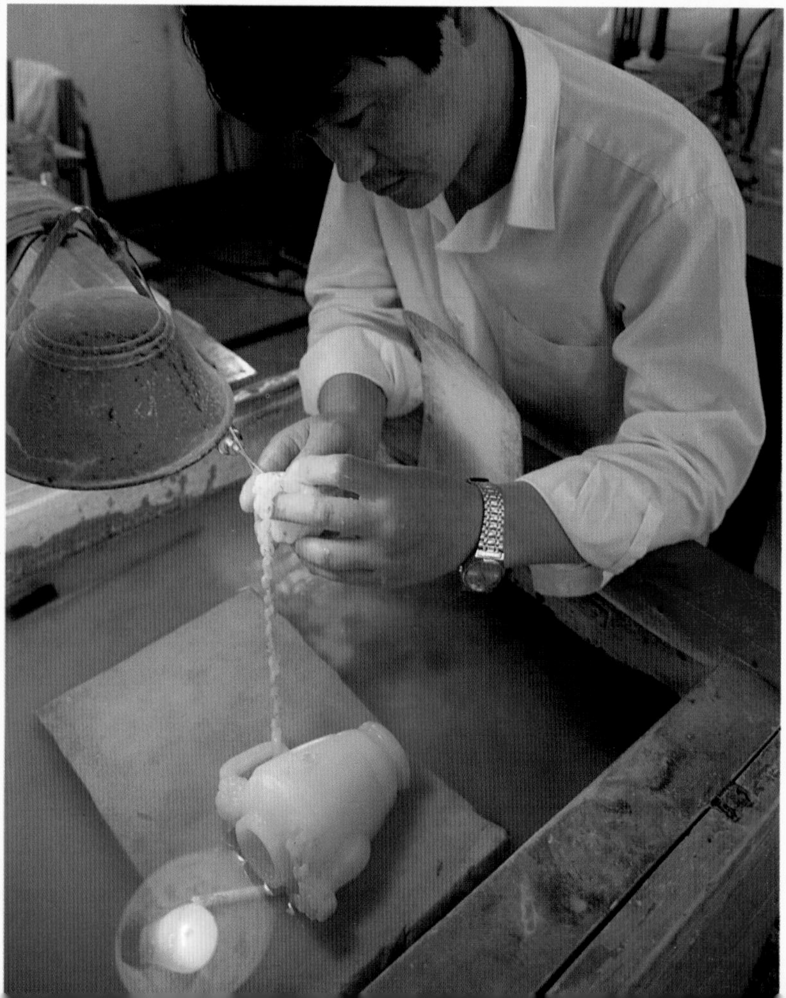

Road town of Khotan. In the 18th century the brilliant green jadeite from Burma became popular. Other stones, particularly serpentine, are sometimes also called jade. What passes for jade in shops in Hong Kong is often no more than fluorite, a soft stone which, compared with jade, is of little value; for it is jade's hardness that is one of its distinguishing features and what makes it valuable to the Chinese.

Colours Nephritic jade was originally found in the form of pebbles from alluvial deposits in Chinese Turkestan (Xinjiang) and was first mined from rock in the 12th century. Curiously, for a mineral so treasured by the Chinese, it is not found in China proper at all. 'Its fascination derives from its subdued smooth brilliance which can be redolent of the deep waters of a mountain lake or of the mistiness of a distant summit.' White jade, which is slightly opalescent and translucent, is known in China as 'mutton-fat' jade. Nephritic jade occurs in a wide variety of colours due to the presence of metallic oxides or silicates, most usually iron, which endows it with shades from grey to, rarely, black. Ferrous silicates produce shades of green ranging from pale to almost black and, very occasionally, blue, while ferric silicates bring browns and oranges and, most prized of all, yellow. Streaks in the jade are caused by trace elements – manganese, for example, produces pale jade with threads of pink or purple. The most common colour – and widely considered the loveliest – is the pale smoky green, called Cabbage Jade by the Chinese. Jade can also change with age, giving added depth to the colour.

Hard dark green jade, the colour of an emerald of the deepest hue, is more likely to be jadeite. Although very similar in appearance to nephritic jade, jadeite has a different chemical composition, and was for long considered by the Chinese as being of inferior value. Jadeite can also be a brilliant red, due to the presence of chromium, which is never found in nephritic jade; the presence of manganese produces a lilac colour.

Heaven Jade is still commonly used in the manufacture of jewellery and ornaments but its use for tribal objects goes back to neolithic times – the jade *pi* will be seen in many Chinese museums. This flat disc, with a large central hole, is often said to represent Heaven and is thought to derive from ancient sun cults. The oldest known example dates back to 2000BC. What is most remarkable is its perfectly formed central hole, suggesting that the Chinese already knew how to use a primitive lathe.

Appeasement
The Chinese believed that various earthly spirits remained in the body after death, once the Celestial Spirit had departed. It was feared that such spirits might become angry, leave in a huff and torment the relatives. To prevent this the body orifices were plugged with jade and offerings were made to encourage them to leave peacefully.

A jade 'pi' with decorated surface. A 'pi' was a ritual disk symbolic of heaven

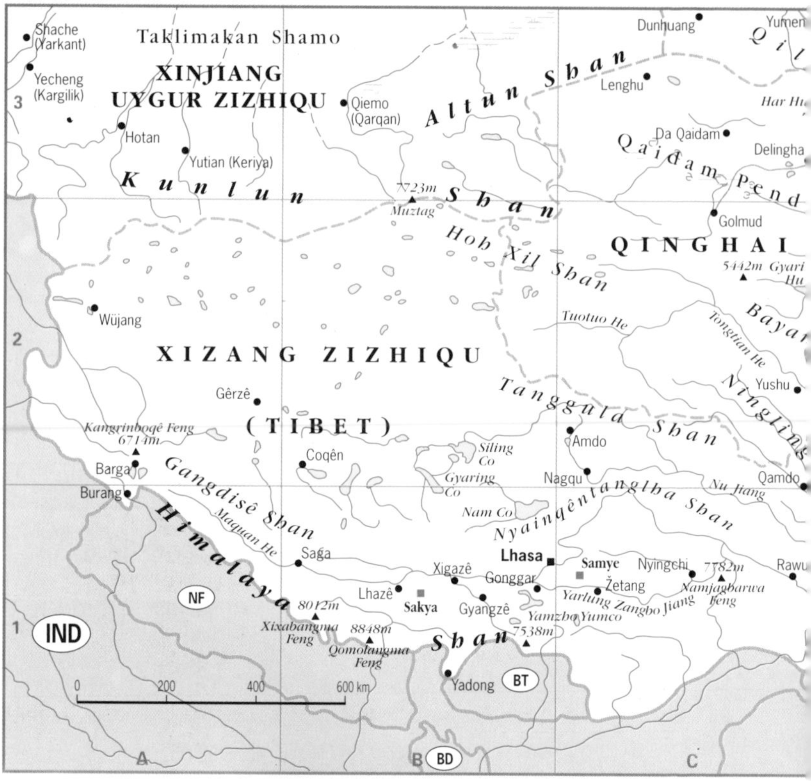

The terraced rice fields of western Sichuan, gateway to Tibet

SICHUAN AND THE TIBETAN PLATEAU

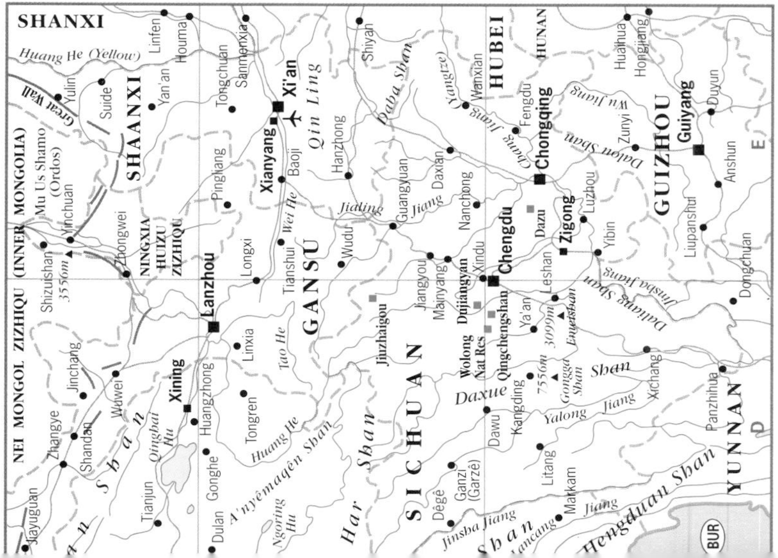

NEI MONGOL ZIZHIQU (INNER MONGOLIA)
SHANXI
Jiayuguan
Zhangye
Shandan
Jinchang
Shizuishan
3556m
Yinchuan
Mu Us Shamo (Ordos)
Great Wall
Yulin
Huang He (Yellow)
Suide
Wuwei
Zhongwei
SHAANXI
Tianjun
Qinghai Hu
Xining
NINGXIA HUIZU ZIZHIQU
Yan'an
Linfen
Houma
Dulan
Gonghe
Huangzhong
Lanzhou
Pingliang
Tongchuan
Sanmenxia
A'nyêmaqên Shan
Tongren
Linxia
Longxi
Xianyang
Huang He
Ngoring Hu
Tao He
Tianshui
Wei He
Baoji
Xi'an
GANSU
Qin Ling
Hanzhong
Har Shan
Wudu
Jialing
Shiyan
Jiuzhaigou
Daba Shan
SICHUAN
Guangyuan
Jiangyou
Mainyang
Daxian
Dêgê
Ganzi (Garzê)
Daxue Shan
Wolong Nat Res
Dujiangyan
Xindu
Nanchong
(Yangtze)
Wanxian
Jinsha Jiang
Dawu
Qingchengshan
Chengdu
Chang Jiang
HUBEI
Kangding
Ya'an
Fengdu
7556m Gongga Shan
3099m Emeishan
Leshan
Dazu
Chongqing
HUNAN
Litang
Yalong Jiang
Zigong
Markam
Luzhou
Lancang Jiang
Daliang Shan
Jinsha Jiang
Yibin
Dalou Shan
Wu Jiang
Zunyi
Huaihua
Hongjiang
Hengduan Shan
Xichang
GUIZHOU
Liupanshui
Guiyang
BUR
Panzhihua
Anshun
Duyun
YUNNAN
Dongchuan
D
E

An endless cycle – the wheel of life

Sichuan and the Tibetan Plateau It may seem odd to place a province (Sichuan) which is part of China proper in the same chapter with Tibet which, although part of the modern state of China (as the 'autonomous' region of Xizang), remains quite separate as far as way of life, culture and attitudes are concerned. There are two reasons, one practical, the other geographical and historical. First, the majority of visitors to Tibet enter on direct flights from Chengdu in Sichuan. Secondly, Sichuan is located at the foot of the Tibetan Plateau, and indeed much of the western mountainous area of the province forms part of it. Furthermore, in the distant past some of what is now Sichuan was ruled by Tibetan tribes and consequently traces of Tibetan culture remain in the area. Chongqing and Dazu, however, are discussed in the Yangtze valley chapter (pages 170–3) since they are usually visited only by those making the journey through the Yangtze Gorges.

Sichuan, the largest and most populous (over 100 million people) of China's provinces, is quite distinctive. The vast Chengdu plain is one of the country's most important rice-producing regions. Sichuanese food – some of the best in China – is hot and spicy. Most famously, Sichuan is associated with the giant panda – a few are found in neighbouring provinces, but Sichuan is their preferred home. The cultivated valleys give the province a particular beauty and there is an astonishing array of flora. Its mountainous nature has allowed it to enjoy a degree of independence during the centuries of Chinese rule. Although linked to China since the 4th century BC, it previously enjoyed an advanced civilisation of its own, affiliated to the cultures of

Writing on the wall: 'Fu', the character for 'happiness' or 'luck', Baoguang Temple, Chengdu

That old gang of mine
The architect of China's recent prosperity and democratic reforms, such as they are, is Deng Xiaoping, who is a Sichuanese. Indeed so many of the people associated with his period of rule are from Sichuan that they are sometimes referred to as the Sichuan Gang.

A Tibetan woman in Songpan, northern Sichuan, heavy with amber, coral and turquoise jewellery

southeast Asia. Sichuan, now one of China's fastest growing areas, continues to retain an independent spirit.

Tibet Dogged by the tag of Shangri-la, shielded by its isolated location within the highest mountains in the world and its determination to exclude outside influence, Tibet, until recently, remained an enigma. Its history before the early 7th century AD is obscure, but in AD625 Songtsen Gampo became the first king of a unified Tibet, his empire spreading into China and India. The fact that he married Buddhist princesses (as well as Chinese) seemed to strike a chord in the Tibetan mind – for within a century, following a debate between an Indian sage and Bon priests, the native Bon religion had been ousted in favour of Buddhism. After years of internecine struggle the notion of the reincarnation of religious leaders was introduced, but Tibetan Buddhism remained divided into three rival schools. Finally, in the 14th century unity was established by the Gelukpa (yellow hat) sect, which built the great teaching monasteries.

In 1720 the Chinese took Tibet and, despite British interference, more or less held it until 1911. Tibet then became independent until 1951, when the Chinese re-established control. Repression followed and the current Dalai Lama fled to India in 1959. The Cultural Revolution saw the destruction of hundreds of monasteries, and although the material existence of Tibetans has now improved, there is still repression. Yet Tibetan traditions continue, the monasteries function and Tibet remains one of the most naturally beautiful places on earth.

Monkey business
There is a colourful explanation of the origins of the Tibetans. It is said that the Sakyamuni Buddha, observing that there were no humans in Tibet, elected to confine his work to India. The responsibility for dealing with Tibet was passed to Avalokitesvara, who assumed the form of a monkey and descended on to a mountain in Tsetang. After he mated with a demoness, six offspring were born, half human and half monkey, the first Tibetans.

'Pure Land'
The most popular form of Chinese Buddhism is called *jingtu* (PureLand), which is unknown in India or Central Asia. It teaches that the Pure Land is a kind of heaven or nirvana that can be achieved merely by repeating the name 'Amitabha Buddha' (the Buddha of the future), hence its mass appeal. Most of the Buddhist temples stlll operating in China today are of this type.

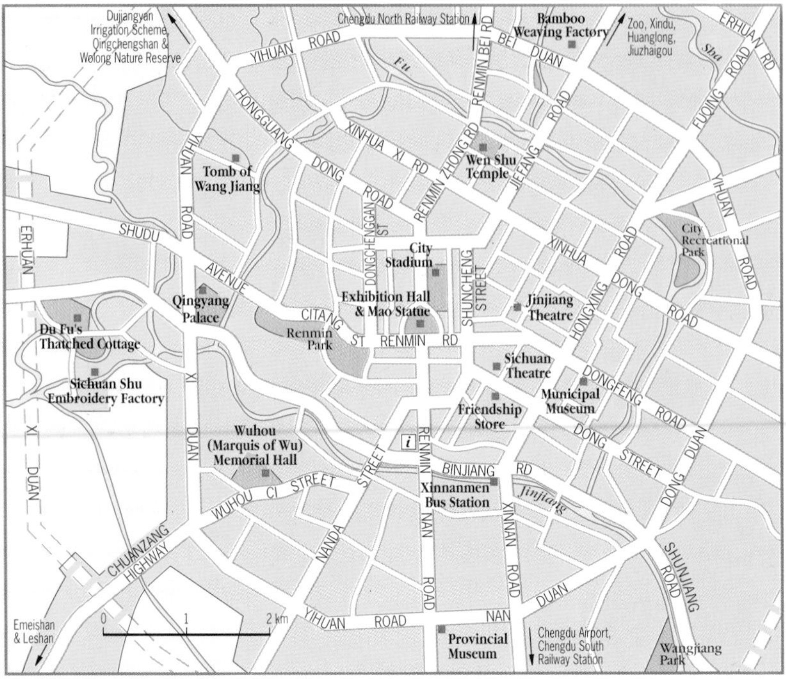

Pagoda at Xindu's Monastery of Divine Light, near Chengdu

▶▶ Chengdu *151E1*

The provincial capital of Sichuan combines modern tree-lined avenues with narrow streets of traditional half-timbered houses, and is one of the fastest growing cities in China. Though renowned for its prosperity from silk, goldwork, silverwork and lacquer, it has always lain outside the mainstream of Chinese life, perceived as a place of refuge by poets and rulers alike. Marco Polo was impressed by the level of commercial activity and industry here; and indeed it remains a busy city, important industrially and academically.

Although there are a few items of interest to visitors, Chengdu's main attractions are a sense of well-being unusual in modern Chinese cities, and the streets themselves. There are also several notable places to visit outside the city.

Du Fu's Thatched Cottage▶▶ is a memorial to one of the greatest of Chinese poets, Du Fu, a minor official under the Tang Dynasty who was forced to flee from Chang'an (Xi'an) after a rebellion and spent four years in Chengdu, where he wrote many of his best poems. He is particularly highly regarded because his poetry was compassionate in an age when compassion was rare. The memorial, constructed 200 years after his death, is set in a pretty bamboo garden where there is a museum containing early versions of his poetry.

Of the several temples in Chengdu, the most interesting (much patronised by locals) is the **Wenshu▶▶**, with four halls and a tea-house in the garden. The **Provincial Museum▶**, frequently overlooked, is important for its displays of Sichuanese culture. **Chengdu Zoo▶▶** has a large number of breeding giant pandas.

There are several fascinating excursions from Chengdu. About 16km away is **Xindu▶▶**, a town associated with colourful basketware and the Monastery of Divine Light (Baoguangsi), dating from the Tang dynasty though reconstructed in the 17th century. It boasts some pretty gardens and courtyards, a 13-storey leaning pagoda and a fine tablet from AD540 bearing a frieze of 1,000 Buddhas.

Of unique interest is the ancient **Dujiangyan Irrigation Scheme▶▶** at Guanxian, about two hours' picturesque drive west of Chengdu. Begun in 256BC by the governor of the state of Shu to tame the Min river, it is a remarkable precursor to modern dams – a stone and bamboo dyke divided the river into an 'inner' and 'outer' channel while a second dyke was built to divert water in case of flood. Expanded over the centuries, the system now irrigates more than 7.5 million acres. The best view is from the nearby Subdued Dragon (Fulong) Temple, or the Two Kings Temple (Erwangmiao); below the latter is the Anlang chain bridge.

Also worth a visit is the **Qingchengshan Taoist Mountain▶▶** (a less crowded alternative to Emeishan), which can be climbed in one day. Its highest temple (Shangqinggong) stands at over 1,500m. The going is not too hard and the Taoist belief in harmony with nature gives a rustic feel to the buildings *en route*. Trips to **Emeishan** and **Leshan** (pages 156, 160) are also possible from here, but involve long drives and an overnight stay.

Finally there is the **Wolong Nature Reserve▶▶▶**, some nine hours' drive from Chengdu, established in the 1970s for panda conservation and now China's largest reserve. For a visit here to be worthwhile you need both time and a willingness to trek.

Spice of life
Sichuanese food is famed for its spicy qualities. One of the best dishes is Ma-Po Donfu (beancurd), a red-hot stew made famous by a pock-marked female (ma-po) chef-pedlar. Another is Bang-Bang Chicken, cold chicken topped with spiced sesame sauce.

A meeting
How long does youth last?
Now we are all grey-haired,
Half of our friends are dead,
And both of us were
surprised when we met.
– Du Fu (712–70)

Bamboo culture: tea house at the People's Park, Chengdu

Prayer flags on the summit of Emeishan

Flora and fauna
Emeishan is attractive not only for pilgrims searching for 'the way' but also for its wide variety of animal and plant life. Apart from the monkeys there are the famous bearded frogs, 200 species of butterfly, silver pheasants, lesser or red pandas, medicinal herbs, tea bushes, rhododendrons and an array of colourful flowers.

Kumbum stupa at Palkhor Monastery, Gyangzê

► Dêgê 151D2

This town on the road from Chengdu to Lhasa is famous for its 250-year-old Bakong Scripture Printing Lamasery, which houses the last surviving copy of a woodblock history of Buddhism in 555 plates.

►►► Emeishan ('Lofty Eyebrow Mountain') 151D1

One of the holy mountains of Buddhism, the abode of Samantabhadra the Bodhisattva of pervading goodness, Emeishan, in the southwest of Sichuan province, rises to well over 3,000m. It makes a magnificent sight, a pair of peaks with a green fir coat, and frequently a topcoat of dense mist at various levels. From the base to the summit is a distance of some 50km but, although it may require two days to complete the pilgrimage (ascent or descent), no special climbing skills are necessary, even if the height and distance involved render it quite arduous. A minibus goes up to Jieyindian, at 2,400m, and from there you can continue either on foot or by cable car to the summit. If you have the time and inclination you can descend the whole way on foot, spending the night in one of several temples *en route* which offer accommodation (for example, the Hongchun or the Qingyin). The weather often obscures the spectacular view from the summit itself, but some pilgrims like to stay the night here for sunrise, others to enjoy the rainbows and fantastic shadows, called 'Buddha's Glory', which sometimes appear on the clouds below during the late afternoon. Lower down is the famous Xixiangchi (Elephant Bathing Pool), where the elephant belonging to Samantabhadra was believed to have bathed; here the moon is supposed to cast an eerie light. Note that footwear with a good grip (the steps can be slippery) is essential and a light waterproof and perhaps a staff would be useful. The mountain is famous for its monkeys (especially on Xianfeng, or Fairy Peak), which can be fierce and should not be approached.

It is also possible to combine a visit to Emeishan with one to **Leshan** (see page 160), which is only a short distance away.

▶▶ Ganden Monastery *150C1*

About 40km to the east of Lhasa lie the remains of what was once one of the most important monasteries in Tibet. Ganden, which means 'the Pure Land of Tushita', where Maitreya the Future Buddha currently resides, was founded by the great 14th-century reformer Tsongkhapa (or Je Rinpoche), who is generally depicted wearing monk's robes and a yellow hat. The main hall of the monastery was not consecrated until 1417 and its founder died here in 1419. The head of the monastery, the Ganden Tripa, is also the head of the Gelukpa order. By 1959 there were 5,000 monks but the Cultural Revolution reduced the monastery to ruins.

The monastery, spectacularly and romantically located on the slopes of Mt Drokri, is being painstakingly reconstructed. Among the most interesting buildings are Tsongkhapa's Golden Tomb and the Amdo Khantsen. A path leads behind the hill, offering breathtaking views.

In a stupa
Stupas (known as 'chorten' in Tibet) are as fundamental to Buddhists as the cross to Christian. They probably evolved in India as prehistoric burial-chambers for local rulers, but under Buddhism they acquired a sacred status as the symbol of Buddha himself. Subsequently, they became burial-places for the ashes of saints or repositories of holy scriptures or relics. In Tibet stupas have square bases (earth), surmounted by a globe (water), a triangle (fire) and a crescent moon (air) and sun (infinite space).

▶ Ganzi (Garzê) *151D2*

The capital of the Ganzi Tibetan Autonomous Region (as distinct from the Tibetan Autonomous Region), in remote Sichuan, is home to the Ganzi Lama Monastery.

▶▶ Gyangzê (Gyantse) *150B1*

A small Tibetan town (formerly the centre of the wool trade) at a height of 3,777m and about 80km east of Xigazê on a rough road in magnificent scenery, old Gyangzê forms a street of traditional Tibetan houses dominated by the **Palkhor Monastery▶▶▶**, built in 1429. Originally it was much larger, but only the main temple and a nine-storey stupa, Tibet's largest, decorated with the stern eyes of Buddha outside and beautiful murals within, now remain. It is overlooked by the old fort set astride a pinnacle. In 1904 Gyangzê was the scene of one of Britain's less glorious military exploits, when Francis Younghusband, sent on a mission to enforce a trade agreement, allowed the massacre of 700 Tibetans. The fortress was captured and a trade mission was then established.

The Five-Colour Pool, Jiuzhaigou

▶▶ Jiuzhaigou *151D2*

Comparatively little known, this scenic area in the Aba Autonomous Prefecture of Sichuan, some 300km north of Chengdu, rivals Guilin for its beauty, with the added attraction of Tibetan and Qiang minority settlements. It is an area of lakes, mountains and waterfalls, as yet unspoilt by tourism. A tour of the area by road will take a week.

■ Although it is the giant panda that has received the most publicity over the years, China is also home to a number of other endangered species.....■

Hairy monster
Not strictly speaking an endangered species, the yak is found in any number only in the Tibetan region. It is so well adapted to high altitudes and the bitter cold that it could not survive in mild, lowland areas. Bulky yet nimble, it needs a daily supply of fresh water, snow being an inadequate substitute.

Giant panda Whilst it is impossible to know just how many pandas remain in the wild, it is thought that the number is no higher than 1,000, insufficient to guarantee its survival. The giant panda is found mostly in Sichuan but there are a few in the neighbouring provinces of Shaanxi and Gansu; in these provinces 13 reserves have recently been established dedicated to its preservation (no easy task where even the death penalty fails to deter the rapacious Chinese from trapping and skinning pandas). Live pandas were only discovered in 1896, although remains dating back over 600,000 years have been found. They prefer altitudes of between 2,000 and 3,000m,

Above: giant panda, hypersensitive to its environment
Top: Père David's deer, now found only in captivity

consume some 20kg of a specific variety of bamboo per day, and are very sensitive to their environment. When supplies of bamboo failed in the 1970s, up to 200 were estimated to have died of starvation. Their mating habits are mysterious – captive breeding has met with only limited success, and the birth rate in the wild is not much better. The future for the giant panda remains bleak.

A Manchurian (or Siberian) tiger. The tiger is a Chinese symbol, yet is almost extinct

Père David's deer The outlook is more optimistic for some of China's other rare animals since efforts are now being made to ensure their survival. One of the most intriguing is the Père David's deer, first discovered in the imperial hunting-parks by the French priest and zoologist Père Armand David in 1865, although already extinct in the wild. They are thought to have come originally from Manchuria and Kokonor. By 1900 there were none left in China, even in the parks, but the species has survived at Woburn Abbey in England where a breeding herd has been established by the Dukes of Bedford. In 1985 20 were presented to the Chinese Government to live at Chengdu, but it is unlikely that they will ever be re-established in the wild.

Tiger China has three subspecies of tiger – the South China tiger, the Manchurian (or Siberian) tiger, and the Bengal tiger. The South China tiger, unique to China, may no longer exist in the wild, for at the last count there were only about 50 left, an insufficient number to ensure its survival. It has been the victim of political campaigns to rid the countryside of vermin. The Manchurian tiger's chances of survival are even lower according to a recent survey, which recorded no more than 30 individuals, although there are a few more in Siberia. The Bengal tiger, which is still found in Yunnan, is not much better off, although exact statistics are hard to come by.

Unfortunately for tigers, some parts of their anatomy are thought to have properties crucial to Chinese virility; trade in these organs is so lucrative that the law banning it is almost impossible to enforce.

Others There are other animals and birds in the same precarious position: the alien-looking golden monkey, the Yangtze alligator (smaller than its cousin in the USA), the red-crowned crane and the Yangtze river dolphin. Efforts are being made by the Chinese, in co-operation with the Worldwide Fund for Nature and others, to ensure their survival but sadly the Chinese accord them low priority and the future for many of these creatures remains grim.

Mosquito boast
Despite its climate, China is remarkably free of mosquitoes. This is one of the success stories of the Communist Party, who have initiated a determined programme to eradicate malaria. Similar efforts were made to cull the sparrow population, which had risen to alarming proportions. It is said that Chairman Mao exhorted citizens to step out regularly with dustbin lids and make such a clatter that the birds would never return. Although sparrows were the target, millions of other birds were, literally, scared to death too.

Acclimatising to Tibet
Since Tibet lies at an average altitude of about 4,000m you can expect to suffer from a shortage of breath because of the thin oxygen supply. This affects everyone to a greater or lesser degree, regardless of age or levels of fitness. To minimise the discomfort, you are advised to rest for a few hours after your arrival, no matter how healthy you feel. This gives the body time to acclimatise at a gradual rate. Increase your fluid intake by drinking plenty of water or tea, but avoid alcohol.

Rippling waters
Lhasa's original name was Rasa, from 'ralasa', the sound made by the wind and the waves ruffling the waters of the lake around which the city was built. The lake is no more, filled in and covered by the Jokhang in the 7th century.

The Buddha's head, Leshan, of cathedral-like proportions

▶▶ Kangding *151D1*

Sometimes known as Dardo, Kangding in Sichuan province stands at an altitude of 3,000m, yet is dwarfed by mountains of up to 7,500m. Tibetan in flavour, the town has several monasteries and some excellent walking in the area. You can also trek along the nearby **Hailuogou Glacier**, said to be the lowest in Asia.

▶▶▶ Leshan *151D1*

One of the most impressive places in Sichuan, if not in the whole of China (5 hours by road from Chengdu and 90 minutes from Emeishan), this small town, with its old cobbled streets, has considerable charm in itself, but its principal attraction is the colossal **Grand Buddha (Dafo)▶▶▶**, carved out of the cliffs at the confluence of the Min and Dadu rivers. In a sitting posture, the position favoured by Maitreya the Future Buddha, it is the largest Buddha in China (perhaps the world), towering to over 70m – one of the toes alone is 8.5m long. The Buddha was started in AD713 as a placatory offering to the dangerously swift-flowing river. It took 90 years to complete and contains a drainage system to prevent excessive weathering. A magnificent sight (though recently repainted in somewhat gaudy colours), it sits primly at the side of the river. Narrow twisting stairs to the right of the figure take you up on to the Buddha's head, and above the right shoulder are the **Grand Buddha Temple▶** and Song dynasty **Lingbao Pagoda▶**.

The **Wuyou Monastery▶▶**, dating back to the Tang dynasty, is charmingly located on Wuyou Hill, a short ferry-ride away from Leshan dock. Opposite the temple, on the same bank as the Grand Buddha, are several tombs, and a crudely fashioned Buddha which dates from AD159, about the time that Buddhism was introduced to China.

The Potala Palace seen from Chokpuri through prayer flags

The endless knot, Buddhist symbol of eternity, adorns the roof of Jokhang Temple, Lhasa

▶▶▶ Lhasa 150B1

The Tibetan capital since the unification of the country in the 7th century, dominated by the magnificent Potala, Lhasa may have been shabbily treated by the Chinese but it still manages to convey much of its unique character if only because of its remote, ethereal location – its name means 'Ground of the Gods'. For the 600 years between the end of the first Yarlung dynasty in the 9th century and the era of Dalai Lamas in the 15th, Lhasa was capital in name only, as Tibet was torn by civil war and religious schism. Since the arrival of the Chinese in 1951 there have been many further changes, very few, if any, aesthetically for the better.

Lhasa has a wealth of fascinating things to see, most of them concerned with Tibetan religious life. The first place to visit is the **Barkhor (Intermediate Circuit)▶▶▶** the oldest part of the city forming a quadrangle of streets surrounding the Jokhang Temple, the most revered and ancient of Tibetan temples. The Barkhor teems with religious and commercial activity – pilgrims doing clockwise circuits, frequently on their hands and knees, and street vendors selling their wares from stalls. This is the heart of old Tibet and, although about one third of it has recently been gutted in order to build shopping malls and other horrors, it nevertheless still manages to retain something of its old flavour.

The **Jokhang (Shrine of Jowo)▶▶▶**, facing the newly built and unsuitable 'plaza', is open from 9 to 12 noon. Only some woodwork on chapel doorways and the statue of Jowo Sakyamuni, given to King Songtsen Gampo by his Chinese wife and believed by Tibetans to have been made by the celestial artist, Vishvakarman, date back to the foundation in the 7th century. The atmosphere here is similar to, but more intense than any other temple in Tibet – the smell from the thousands of flickering candles fills the gloomy air, and pilgrims prostrate themselves before altars. The main chapel, and the most elaborate, is the Chapel of Jowo Sakyamuni

The last Panchen Lama
The last Panchen Lama who died in 1989, was the tenth in his line. In 1959, when the Dalai Lama fled to India, the Panchen Lama found himself in China, unable to escape, and remained in the hands of the Chinese government from that time on. Although many saw him as little more than a quisling, his pro-Tibetan statements led to his imprisonment and probable torture during the Cultural Revolution.

The Time Wheel dagoba at Taer Monastery, Huangzhong, Qinghai

China's gulag
Qinghai is a bleak and in many ways forbidding place, a reputation not helped by the fact that the Chinese government has built labour camps here for criminals from all over China. Nobody knows for certain how many criminals are imprisoned in them, but it is alleged that the Chinese undercut most of the world's export prices with the aid of cheap labour both in these camps, and many others all over China.

whose statue is laden with brocade and jewellery. There are dramatic views across the city from the roof.

The **Potala Palace ►►►** (open 9–12 noon except Sunday, although independent visitors may be confined to Wednesdays and Saturdays, 10–4), named after a holy mountain in India, was first built on this site in the 7th century but the current structure dates from 1645. It has been the home of successive Dalai Lamas and their winter home since the construction of the Summer Palace in the 18th century. It is of an ineffable beauty – the best view is from the Kyichu river. Several chapels, part of the living-quarters, and the tombs are open to the public.

The **Norbulingka (Summer Palace)►►** (open 9–11:30 and 3:30–5; closed Sunday) is in the west of Lhasa and has been used as a summer palace since the 8th Dalai Lama. More of a park than an estate, it has a tranquil, bucolic air. Architecturally less imposing than the monasteries and the Potala, its domestic atmosphere allows an insight into the more homely aspects of theocratic rule. It is from here that the Dalai Lama escaped in 1959.

The other principal monasteries here, both of which deserve extended visits, are the **Sera►►** (5km north of Lhasa) and the **Drepung►►** (8km west).

►► Qinghai Province *150C2*

Formerly the Tibetan province of Amdo, Qinghai forms part of the Tibetan Plateau but has provincial status separate from the Tibetan Autonomous Region. An area of high grassland, mountain ranges, and salt marshes in the northwest, it includes the sources of three important rivers: the Yellow river, the Yangtze and the Mekong. The largest town is Xining, interesting only for a 14th-century **mosque►**, the largest in the region, and the excellent **West Gate market►►**. Some 25km southwest is one of the most venerable of Tibetan monasteries, the **Taer at**

Huangzhong▶▶▶, noted for its yak-butter sculptures. The second town, Golmud, a centre for potash, has nothing to recommend it.

Qinghai's main attractions are the scenery, the peoples and – perhaps most spectacularly – **Kokonor (Qinghai Lake)▶▶▶**, China's largest salt-water lake and a bird-lover's paradise. Huge flocks of migrating birds land here, particularly during March to June, the mating season and best time to see them.

▶▶ Sakya *150B1*

About 140km southwest of Xigazê the focal-point for the Sakyapa sect, founded in the 11th century, was established here. There are two monasteries: the northern one was almost entirely destroyed during the Cultural Revolution whilst the southern monastery, an imposing fortress-like building, still stands complete with magnificent assembly hall and fine chapels.

▶▶▶ Samye *150C1*

The first monastery built in Tibet (AD770) is in a marvellous location on the north bank of the Brahmaputra river (Yarlung Tsangpo), 40km northwest of Zêtang. An irregular ferryboat takes 1½ hours to make the river crossing and a lorry takes you to the monastery. It is worth the effort.

▶▶▶ Xigazê (Xigatse) *150B1*

Tibet's second town, and the site of one of its greatest monasteries, the **Tashilhunpo▶▶▶**, is spiritual home of the Panchen Lama (the incarnation of Buddha Amitabha), second to the Dalai Lama. The monastery dates from 1447 and is outstanding architecturally, even if the same cannot be said about its spiritual life, particularly under the last Panchen Lama, who died in 1989, and was widely regarded as a Chinese puppet.

Sakya rooftops, excellent for drying crops and yak dung, and for hoisting prayer flags

Taking the ferry to Samye across the Yarlung Tsangpo (the Brahmaputra)

Suppression of a culture
Traditional Tibetan culture may never recover from the damage inflicted by the Chinese after the revolt of 1959. The Cultural Revolution of the 1960s and 1970s saw the brutal suppression of religious life, and the destruction of many of Tibet's cultural treasures, and during the 1980s there were demonstrations and violent clashes against Chinese rule. Material aspects of life have improved, however, although the Tibetans' appetite for Western pop music and films further undermines their traditional unique way of life, which can now never be re-established.

Tibetan Buddhism

Buddhism took root in India and spread throughout Asia. In Tibet it competed with the native shamanistic religion (Bon) which it eventually absorbed whilst retaining some of its symbolism.....

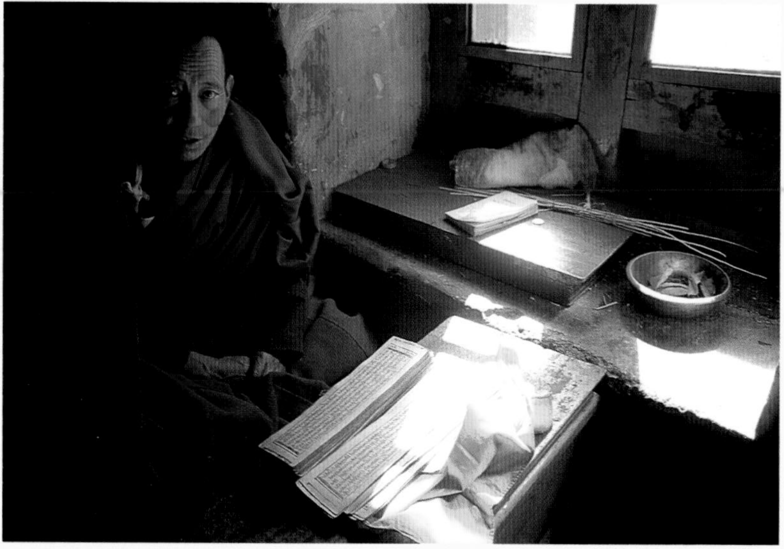

Monasteries (above, Ganden) hum with the recitation of sutras

Jewels Buddhism is the following of the path to self-awareness and enlightenment, a way of dissolving the emotional confusion within ourselves that is seen as the source of human strife. The Buddhist must commit himself to the 'Three Jewels' – to the Buddha (Sakyamuni, the manifestation of the ideal of enlightenment); to the Dharma (the way revealed by Buddha); and to Sangha (devotion to the religious community). And in Tibet there is a fourth 'jewel', devotion to a spiritual teacher, or lama.

Monk business
Monks who choose to follow the full course of philosophical training are required to study a range of subjects over a period of up to 20 years. The basic course lasts two or three years, followed by further study of the five main subjects of Buddhist philosophy eventually leading to the degree of Geshe, or Doctor of Divinity. The remaining years are devoted to tantrist studies.

Vehicles There are three types of Buddhism. The first is known as Hinayana ('the lesser vehicle'), which presents the basic teachings of the Buddha himself; its practice required a high degree of moral discipline combined with meditation. As the number of devotees grew, so the monasteries expanded, requiring more complex adminis-

Devotees prostrating themselves in front of Jokhang Temple, Lhasa

tration on the part of the monks which in turn was to have political implications. Gradually Tibetan government became theocratic, a process reinforced by the custom whereby families made a contribution to the Buddhist order by offering a son as a monk.

Mahayana ('the greater vehicle') is based on Hinayana but asserts that the search for enlightenment (nirvana) should not require complete detachment from the world but also find expression in compassion and love. Compassion is one of the central themes of Tibetan Buddhism, embodied in the 'bodhisattva', the disciple who refrains from entering nirvana in order to save others. In Tibet the most important bodhisattva is Chenrezi, manifested in human form as the Dalai Lama. You can see Chenrezi in many temples, sometimes with four arms, sometimes a thousand, and as many faces. The vocal expression of compassion is 'Om mani padme hum', which you hear murmured everywhere you go. Sometimes the chanting is accompanied by the beating of a drum to ward off the supplicant's ego, for his quest is to know emptiness, to be free of all prejudice in his interpretation of himself and of the world around him.

The third type is Vajrayana ('the diamond'), also based on the twin objectives of compassion and enlightenment but through the teaching of Buddhist tantras. Sutras are the words spoken by Buddha for all, but tantras are vouchsafed only to a select few. Tantrist Buddhism sees the human condition as more than making moral choices. Internal energy if misdirected adds to the store of human misery but by channelling it in the correct way, you achieve nirvana. Studying the tantras helps speed up the way to enlightenment.

A devotee rotates a prayer wheel at the foot of the Potala, Lhasa

Tashilhungo Monastery: typically, its size and site reflect the significance of monasteries in Buddhist culture

Temples Tibetan temples are filled with images. Mandalas are a series of coloured squares within a circle and are used as an instrument of meditation. You must shed all preconceptions about reality, and imagine you are a deity and that the mandala is your world. The wheel of life, often seen at temple entrances, represents the eternal universe, seen by Buddhists as an infinity of systems inhabited by humans, animals, giants, ghosts, devils and celestials. Existence without enlightenment is a meaningless cycle of reincarnation from one to the other. Liberation is achieved by breaking out of this cycle.

Tantras and tangkas
Buddhist terminology can be confusing for the uninitiated. It is easy, for example, to confuse tantras with tangkas, although they are quite dissimilar. Whilst tantras are prayers and teachings, tangkas are simply painted scrolls, usually depicting lamas and deities and various events from their lives, serving as an aid to meditation.

Lamas and monks
Lamas and monks are not necessarily one and the same. A lama does not need to be a monk, for a lama is someone spiritually qualified to lead others on the path to enlightenment.

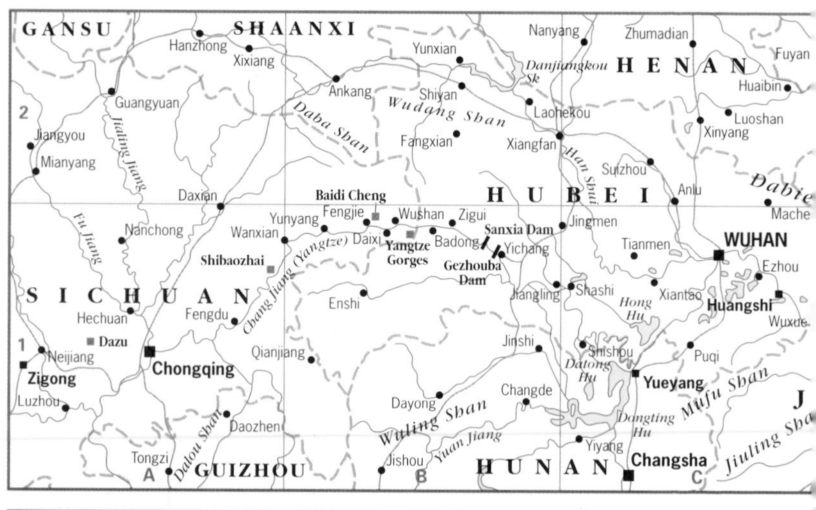
GANSU
SHAANXI
HENAN
HUBEI
SICHUAN
GUIZHOU
HUNAN
Hanzhong
Xixiang
Yunxian
Nanyang
Zhumadian
Fuyan
Danjiangkou Sk
Huaibin
Guangyuan
Ankang
Shiyan
Wudang Shan
Laohekou
Luoshan
Xinyang
Jiangyou
Jialing Jiang
Daba Shan
Fangxian
Xiangfan
Han Shui
Mianyang
Suizhou
Dabie
Daxian
Baidi Cheng
Fengjie
Wushan
Zigui
Anlu
Mache
Fu Jiang
Nanchong
Yunyang
Wanxian
Daixi
Yangtze Gorges
Badong
Sanxia Dam
Yichang
Jingmen
Tianmen
WUHAN
Shibaozhai
Chang Jiang (Yangtze)
Gezhouba Dam
Ezhou
Enshi
Jiangling
Shashi
Hong Hu
Xiantao
Huangshi
Wuxue
Hechuan
Fengdu
Dazu
Neijiang
Chongqing
Zigong
Qianjiang
Jinshi
Shishou
Datong Hu
Puqi
Yueyang
Mufu Shan
Luzhou
Dayong
Changde
Dongting Hu
Daozhen
Wuling Shan
Dalou Shan
Yuan Jiang
Yiyang
Tongzi
Jishou
Changsha
Jiuling Sha
A
B
C
1
2
J

166

THE YANGTZE REGION

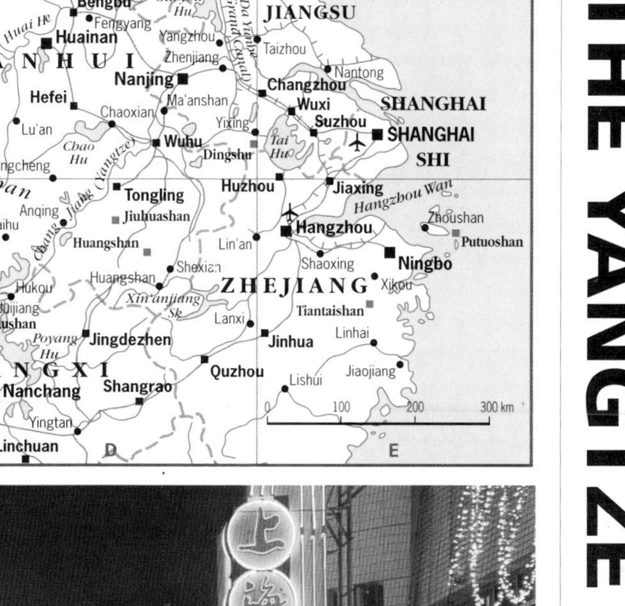

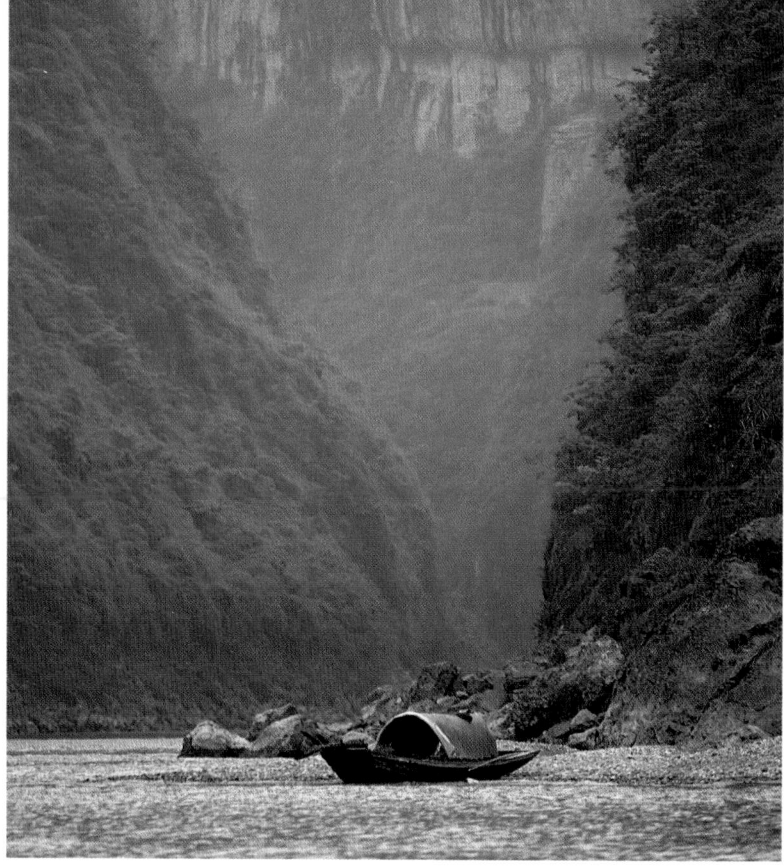

The Yangtze river, the heart of China: one of the three lesser gorges along the Daning river

The Han river
The Yangtze's longest tributary is the Han (1,530km) which rises in the Qingling mountains in Shaanxi province. Like the Yellow river, it is temperamental and given to flooding. In 1488 it changed its course, separating Hanyang from Hankou (two of the cities which make up modern Wuhan).

The Yangtze region In a sense this region does not exist. The course of the Yangtze river neatly divides China into north and south, passing through eight quite separate provinces, but the reason for creating this artificial region and for classing so many heterogeneous places together is simple: they are all destinations that are likely to be visited on the same trip, their common link being the Yangtze river.

The Yangtze (Yangtze is a corruption of a local, Yangzhou area, pronunciation of Chang Jiang, which means 'the long river'), 6,300km in length, is the third longest river in the world, after the Nile and the Amazon. It rises in Qinghai province, part of the Tibetan Plateau, and disgorges into the Yellow Sea. It is joined by some 700 tributaries along its course and is divided into three sections. The Upper Reaches, possibly the most spectacular part, run from its source across the Sichuan Basin, through the Three Gorges (discussed on pages 194–5), to Yichang in Hubei province. The Middle Reaches are between Yichang and Hukou at the mouth of Boyang Lake in Jiangxi province, where the river, wide and sluggish, flows through flat, low land, fed by waters from the Dongting as well as Boyang Lake. The Lower Reaches run from Hukou to the estuary, a landscape characterised not only by its flatness but also by the network of canals which crisscross it. Known as the 'Land of Fish and Rice', it is home to a third of China's population producing some

40 per cent of national grain output (including 70 per cent of paddy rice), 33 per cent of cotton, 50 per cent of freshwater fish and 40 per cent of industrial output.

Navigation Although it was once a vital navigation artery of the Chinese empire, the arrival of the railways almost emptied the Yangtze of the traditional sanpans ('three planks'), wupans ('five planks') and junks which used to throng its length as far as Chongqing. Nowadays ocean-going vessels penetrate upriver as far as Wuhan and local traffic is much in evidence. Not so long ago boats had to be pulled by trackers through the treacherous rapids, gruelling toil that was little better than slavery. Instructions were relayed to the harnessed trackers, heaving on ropes, by means of a beating drum. Some craft could require as many as 400 trackers to pull them. Isabella Bird, the indefatigable Victorian traveller who, aged 64, made a journey along the Yangtze in 1896, observed 300 trackers dragging a junk without making perceptible progress in two hours. 'Suddenly the junk shivered, both tow ropes snapped, the lines of trackers went down on their faces, and in a moment the craft was spinning down the rapid; and she flew up into the air as if she had exploded.' The towpaths carved into the rocks are still visible here and there. The main obstacles to safe navigation were blown up after 1949.

After 1861 the annual tea races were held on the Yangtze, when competing clippers from foreign companies raced to bring the freshest tea from China to Britain, the USA and Russia. After the China tea trade collapsed, the Yangtze impinged on Western consciousness only in 1949, the year of the Yangtze incident. The *Amethyst*, a British frigate, was fired on by the communists, who were about to launch a final offensive on the nationalists, remaining under siege for a tense three months. Her daring nocturnal escape is now part of naval folklore.

The Yangtze, the greatest river in China, remains a powerful symbol of Chinese civilisation, and much that is most fascinating about the country is still to be seen in this region.

Dongting Lake
Dongting Lake was once China's largest freshwater lake. Now, because of the accumulation of silt from the four rivers which feed it, it is only the second largest. Flood-prevention schemes (over 6,000 irrigation or drainage channels and 15,000 sluices) mean that the surrounding area is productive all year round, the lake acting as a reservoir for flood-water in the summer. At its centre is an island where Junshan Silver Needle Tea is grown, once presented as tribute to the emperors.

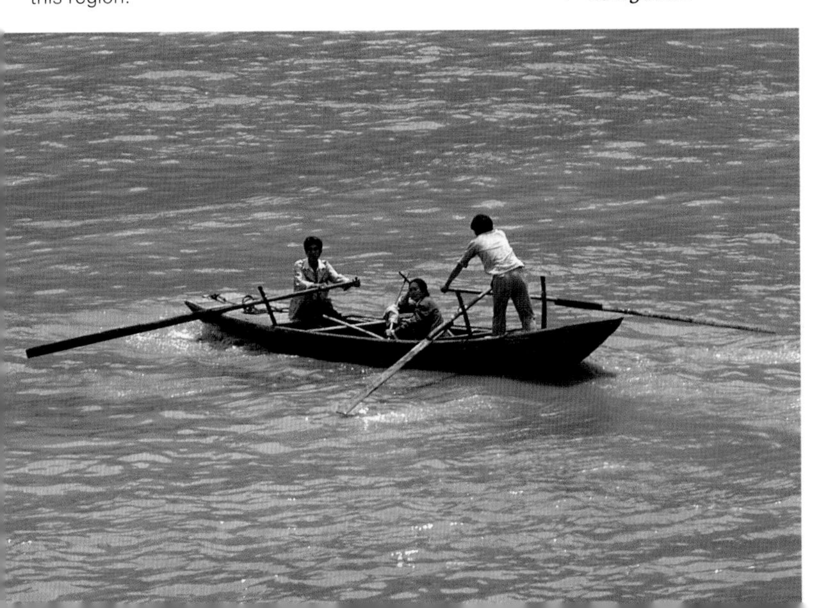

The Yangtze's treacherous nature demands careful navigation

Chongqing cable car

▶▶ Changzhou 167E2

Although it does not have the willow-pattern charm of Suzhou, and there has been much redevelopment here, the old centre of Changzhou with its relatively few tourists, still has much to commend it. Situated on the Grand Canal, with a network of smaller canals spanned by little stone bridges, and a maze of narrow streets and alleyways, it has a quaint atmosphere of its own. The restored **Tianningsi (Temple of Heavenly Tranquillity)▶▶**, founded 1,300 years ago, is a beautiful example of temple art, with its elegantly curving eaves and shining plum-coloured lacquer. Behind it is the **Red Plum Park (Hongmei Gongyuan)▶**, with two pagodas and a tea-house. The **Ma Garden (Mayuan)▶** off Dongheng Jie is worth a visit; and the **Mooring Pavilion (Yizhouting)** has literary associations with the Song dynasty poet Su Dongpo. Dong Dajie and Nan Dajie, the main streets, reward exploration. Tours around Changzhou's ornamental comb factory are on offer to visitors, and it is occasionally possible to visit the hospital of traditional medicine.

Red Plum Pavilion, Changzhou

▶▶ Chongqing

166A1

If you make the journey through the Yangtze Gorges, the chances are that you will start or finish at Chongqing. It is a city of 14–15 million, perched high on the cliffs overlooking the confluence of the Yangtze and the Jialing rivers, which divide the city in three. Although the city is far from beautiful, its position lends it an air of grandeur and as a port it bursts with bustling riverside life. In short, it has character. Now an important industrial and mineral centre, it has always been Sichuan's trade outlet with the rest of China. One of the farthest flung of treaty ports (opened to foreign trade in 1890), Chongqing came to prominence as the Nationalist capital in 1938, after the Japanese took the former capital of Nanjing. Filled with spies it was a crowded, reeking place, the object of continuous bombing missions by the Japanese during World War II.

Chongqing has few specific attractions, but plenty to enjoy. The best park, and the city's highest point, is on **Pipashan (Loquat Hill)▶▶** (entrance on Zhongshan Erlu), offering panoramic views across the city. **Chongqing Museum▶** is in the park, with some fine, if limited items on display – a collection of Han carved tomb-bricks, dinosaur remains and some excellent paintings. Further down, at the end of Xinhua Lu, Shaanxi Lu and Minzu Lu, by the docks, is **Chaotianmen▶▶**, the meeting-point of the two rivers where there is a hubbub of riverside activity. Overhead, to the left, is the cable car, giving spectacular views over Chongqing's rocky promontory (Cangbai Lu and Jinsha Jie are the two stations). Another cable car, at Wanglongmen, spans the Yangtze to the south.

South of Minzu Lu, near the junction with Cangbai Lu, is **Luohan Temple▶**, founded in the Song dynasty. The main shopping streets (for good entertainment value) are at the junctions of Zourong Lu, Minquan Lu and Minzu Lu, around the Liberation Monument Clocktower.

Just to the north of the Renmin Hotel, on the south bank of the Jialing river, is **50 Zengjiayan** where Zhou Enlai lived and worked when he was the secretary of the South China Bureau of the Central Committee of the Chinese Communist Party (CCP) between 1939 and 1946.

Air raids and flowers
The writer Emily Hahn was in Chongqing during World War II. 'Chungking. What does the name evoke in my mind? Air raids. Oranges. Szechuan food, good, full of strong pepper, probably to warm up the blood on the cold, wet, muddy days ...Yet Chungking is a place of flowers. You can have roses in your garden all the year round. I am not kind in my description ... but I liked it.'

Taking home the new washing machine, Chongqing docks

Vision of Hell, Baodingshan, Dazu

 **Dazu** *166A1*

If you stay any length of time in Chongqing, do visit Dazu. Although it is just possible to get there and back in a day, it is far better to stay overnight in the basic but acceptable hotel. Trips to Dazu from Chengdu are also possible.

Dazu is famous for its Buddhist **stone carvings►►►**. Set in lush, picturesque countryside, and less formal than the other major groups at Datong and Luoyang, thousands of the sculptures and reliefs exhibit a colourful liveliness peculiar to Sichuan, in which the story-telling element is as important as orthodox religious iconography. The carvings are in two principal areas – Beishan (North Hill); and the more interesting Baodingshan (Precious Summit), where the carvings were completed according to a plan and follow the area's contours. Mostly Buddhist, the carvings also carry elements of Taoism and Confucianism.

The carvings at Beishan, within walking distance (2km) north of Dazu, were begun in the 9th century; work continued for about 250 years, and some 10,000 statues were made. The earliest caves are numbers 2, 3, 5, 9 and 10. Cave 245 contains over 600 figures and many scenes of everyday Tang life. In Cave 113 a divine Avalokitésvara (he became Guanyin in Chinese Buddhism) gazes in rapture at the moon's reflection. In 136, the largest cave, Samantabhadra (Bodhisattva of pervading goodness) rides an elephant, with Manjusri (Bodhisattva of wisdom) on a lion, while Sakyamuni is surrounded by representations of Guanyin, goddess of mercy and bringer of sons. Other caves of interest are 101, 113, 125, and 279.

Baodingshan lies 14km northeast of Dazu. There are two groups of carvings here – Xiaofowan and Dafowan, of which the latter is the more colourful, with lively scenes from Buddhist scriptures. The carvings were

Classic Purple Sand teaware from Yixing. The teapots, it is claimed, retain both the colour and the flavour of the tea

completed between 1179 and 1249, and are in a horseshoe-shaped gully reached down a flight of steps by some reconstructed temple buildings. 'A fierce tiger coming down the mountain' greets you at the bottom right. Niche 3 reveals the Wheel of Life with the founder of the site, Zhao Zhifeng, at its centre; above him is the Pavilion of the Western Paradise, flanked by the animals that represent stages of rebirth. Niche 8, the Dabei Pavilion, contains the figure of the 1,000-arm Avalokitésvara, the largest ever carved in China. In niche 11 is the famous reclining Buddha, 31m long, whose posture symbolises entry into nirvana. Try to make time to see niches 14 (Buddha Teaching), 15 (Requital of Parental Kindness), 21 (Eighteen Layers of Hell) and 30 (Cowherds with Oxen, a symbolic story of taming the passions).

▶▶ Dingshu *167D2*

About 75km to the west of Wuxi is Yixing county, dotted with tea-plantations, bamboo-groves and miniature lakes. The area is famous for its pottery and underground caverns. Although the hotel is in Yixing town, the place of greatest interest is **Dingshu (or Dingshan)▶▶▶**, which has specialised in the production of glazed ceramics since the Han dynasty. Its Purple Sand pottery is seen all over China, particularly as teapots. The shops are filled with modern pottery at very low prices, and a stroll around the streets is well worth while. Factory tours are usually possible, whilst the **Exhibition Centre** displays older and more sophisticated examples of Dingshu ware.

Excursions are also offered to the three groups of **caves▶▶**; wear shoes with a good grip, and take waterproofs and torches. All the caves are filled with neon-lit rock formations. The **Shanjuan** group is 25km southwest of Yixing. You leave the caves by boat along a subterranean stream. The **Linggu**, 25km south of Yixing, is the largest group. **Zhanggong Cave** is 18km south of Yixing.

Lost art
Despite claims to the contrary, it seems that the Chinese have almost lost the art of making beautiful porcelain. Cheap, practical, occasionally interesting porcelain is manufactured by the ton, but little has any true beauty. It is possible to find exact replicas of famous museum pieces in stores aimed at the foreign tourist and museum shops, and these are bargain purchases.

The Sixth Patriarch
Zhao Zhifeng, who founded the Buddhist site at Baoding (Dazu), was from the nearby village of Miliang. Between 1179 and 1249 he supervised the carving of thousands of images in the mountain face representing the teachings of Buddhism, making Baoding one of the most important centres of Tantrist Buddhism in China.

Wheel of Life, Dazu, with Zhao Zhifeng at the centre

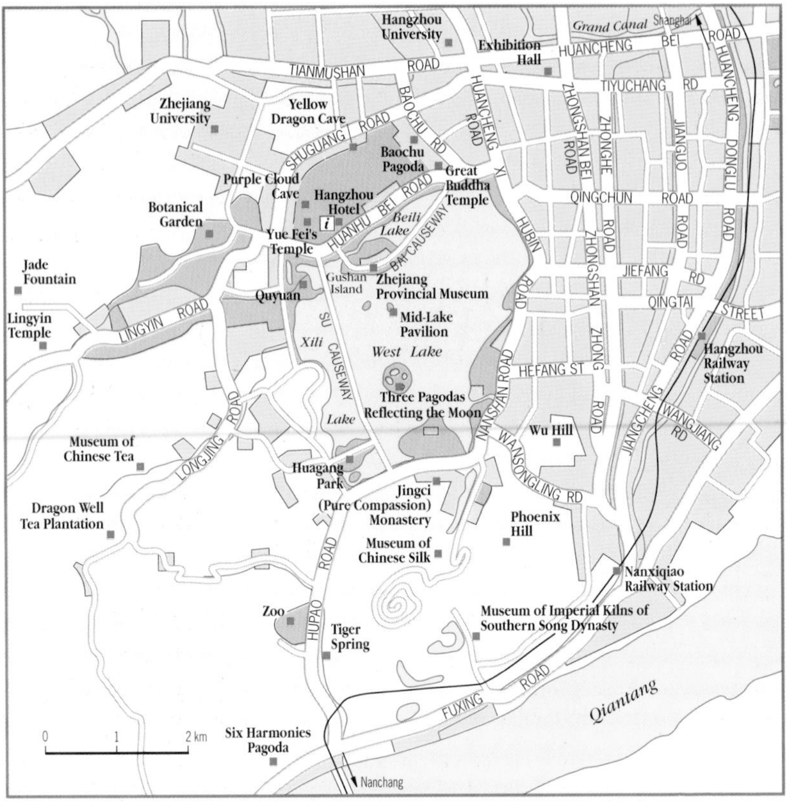

►► Hangzhou

167E1

The capital of Zhejiang province, Hangzhou lies on the banks of Qiantang river, about 95km from the sea. Famous above all for the West Lake, it is also the southern terminus of the Grand Canal (see page 176), which reached Hangzhou during the Sui dynasty and is a testament to the former importance of this now comparatively provincial town. Renowned for its scenic beauty, Hangzhou is a favourite honeymoon destination, but its reputation as a place for leisure and sensual pleasures goes back to the Song dynasty, when it succeeded Kaifeng as capital of the Southern Song. Marco Polo wrote about its captivating women and the loveliness of its temples and gardens. Under the Qing, Hangzhou remained one of the richest towns in China, but in the mid-19th century, during the Taiping Rebellion, much of it was razed to the ground. Foreign concessions were established in the late 19th century and new industries sprang up to complement the traditional ones of silk and brocade manufacture. Although many historic buildings have been destroyed, parts of the town have not changed for centuries and the lake and surrounding hills retain their reputation as one of China's best-known beauty spots.

West Lake (Xihu)►►► was originally a shallow inlet off Hangzhou Bay. In the 4th century AD silt deposits from the Qiantang river built up, creating a barrier and forming the present lake. Two sections of the lake are enclosed by

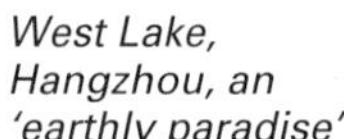

West Lake, Hangzhou, an 'earthly paradise'

two causeways, the result of water-control work during the Tang and Song dynasties.

The Bai Causeway encloses the Beili Lake and runs from near the Hangzhou Hotel on the north bank to Gushan Island and then back to the north bank further east. This makes a good walk with fine views from both the Duanqiao (Broken Bridge, so-called because snow melts first at the bridge's hump giving the impression of a gap) and from the top of Gushan. A Qing pavilion houses the **Zhejiang Provincial Museum▶▶** which includes one of the hollow bricks, complete with ancient printed sutra found within, from the collapsed Leifeng Pagoda, the oldest finds associated with rice and silk culture in China, and ancient maps of the city. At the eastern end, the Pavilion of the Autumn Moon on a Calm Lake is, unsurprisingly, perfect for watching the moon, though it doubles as a tea-house.

Detail from the Lingyin Temple

The Su Causeway links the north shore with the south (at the Huagang Park, filled with fish-pools) and encloses the Xili. Near the north end is the **Tomb and Temple of Yue Fei▶**, a much-venerated Song general.

No visit to Hangzhou is complete without a boat excursion around the lake. Steamers depart from Gushan, the east shore (Hubin Lu), and Huagang Park for tours of the islands, including the renowned **Three Pagodas Reflecting the Moon** (**Santanyinyue**) island, which contains four miniature lotus-covered lakes.

The **Lingyin Temple▶▶** is a celebrated Chan (Zen) Buddhist temple, founded in AD326. The current structures date from the late Qing dynasty. Its highlights are the flourishing Great Hall, with its 20m camphor-wood statue of the Buddha, and the Feilaifeng (Peak Flying From Afar), a hill opposite the temple covered with inscriptions and reliefs carved into the rock dating from the 10th to the 14th centuries, the most important such site in south China.

Other places worthy of attention are the **Six Harmonies Pagoda▶**, the **Dragon Well Tea Plantation▶** and the **Silk Spinning Factories▶**.

Heavenly walk
Hangzhou is a delightful town in which to stroll. Apart from the obvious walk around the lake, you can explore the hills by following a path behind the Yuefei Temple, or wander along the canals at the eastern end of the town.

One of the two Laughing Buddhas, here with entourage, on the 'Peak Flying From Afar'

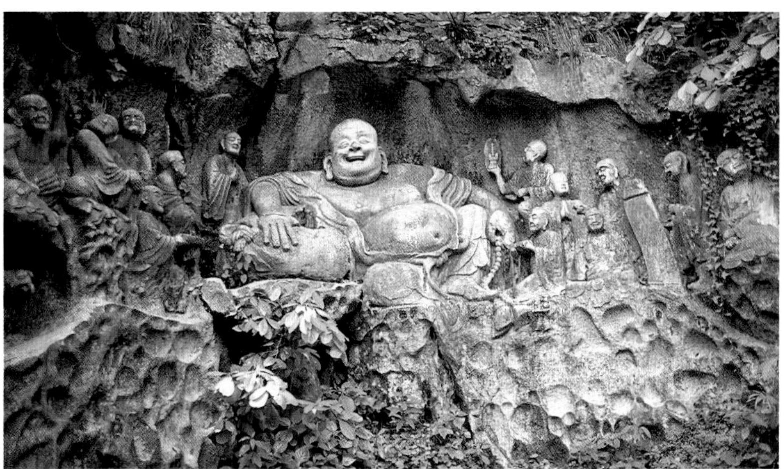

The Grand Canal, a commercial success: above, traffic at Suzhou and, opposite, a train of barges at Wuxi

▶▶▶ The Grand Canal (Da Yunhe) *167E2*

A cruise along the Grand Canal is one of the easiest and best ways of seeing what makes China tick. In half a day you can travel between Wuxi and Suzhou, for example (or vice versa), through a jostling floating hubbub that has barely changed in over a thousand years.

The Grand Canal, which in parts dates back to 400BC, is still the world's largest man-made waterway. The early sections were built in the north for the movement of troops but it was the Sui Emperor Yangdi who undertook the construction of the main canal in the 7th century AD, with the labour of 5.5 million conscripted men – in some places this meant all the commoners between the ages of 15 and 55. They worked under the supervision of 50,000 police, and those unable to finish their work quotas were flogged or forced to bear neck weights. The Sui emperor celebrated the completion of the canal by arriving amidst a flotilla of beautifully decorated dragonboats pulled by teams of the loveliest girls in the empire.

The emperor's original aim in building the canal was to link his two capitals, Xi'an and Luoyang; he then decided to extend it as far as Hangzhou, so as to connect the four major trading rivers – the Yangtze (which it crosses by means of locks), the Yellow, the Qiantang and the Huai – thus linking the rich area of the Yangtze valley, the rice-bowl of China, with the more heavily populated north. Normal trade was not its only function – it was also used to convey tribute to the imperial court: 'nine thousand

Water borne
One of the features of the Grand Canal is the string of barges following each other nose to tail. In the past, entire families lived aboard but apparently nowadays factories own most of the boats and allocate flats to the boatmen they employ. However, judging by the family atmosphere on some of the barges – children, pets, cooking all in evidence – it is more than likely that the new liberal approach to the economy is encouraging the re-emergence of old habits.

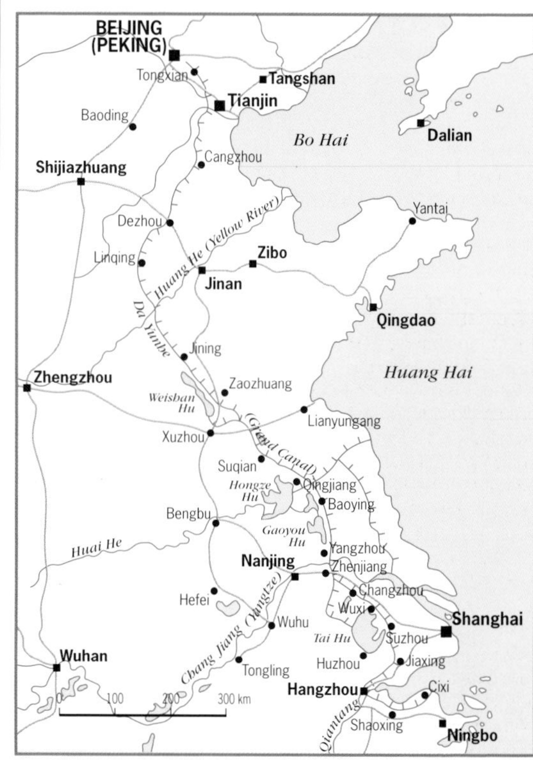

The Grand Canal

barques conveying tribute to the emperor', as a contemporary wrote to convey the frenetic activity on the canal.

From the 12th century China's economic focus moved to this region and the towns bordering the canal grew in status. During the Mongol dynasty, the canal's importance was such that it was extended to the new capital, Beijing; although the decadent Qing dynasty liked to suppress shipments of grain in favour of imperial pleasure-barges, the canal did not lose its supremacy until the beginning of the 20th century, when the course of the Yellow river altered, the railways proved more efficient and coastal shipping began to be used more widely. In 1793–4 the first British embassy to China, under Lord Macartney, returned to Macao from Beijing by way of the Grand Canal (and several rivers), a journey of 3,200km of which a mere 80 had to be travelled over land. In 1896 the traveller Isabella Bird described the canal as 'wonderful even in its dilapidation'; on arriving at Tianjin (Tientsin) from Tungchow 'my boat took two days and a half to make its way through the closely jammed mass of cargo and passage boats at the terminus'.

Since the 1950s the Grand Canal has undergone a renaissance. The southern stretch between Zhenjiang and Hangzhou is navigable all year round and a cruise in comfortable boats, some equipped in imperial livery, is a pleasant diversion for foreign visitors.

China's culture
One of the commodities commonly carried along the Grand Canal is bamboo. China's culture is sometimes said to have been founded on bamboo, a sentiment illustrated by the following remark by the poet Su Dongpo (1036–1101): 'I would rather eat a meal without meat than live in a place with no bamboos. Without meat one may become thin: without bamboos one becomes vulgar.'

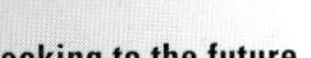

Looking to the future
There are plans afoot to improve the northern stretches of the Grand Canal, which have been silted up for centuries, by diverting water from the Yangtze to the more arid regions of the north and dredging some sections to enable navigation by vessels of up to 2,000 tonnes. .

Moon tight
A famous drunk, the poet Li Bai met a most romantic end, or at least one in keeping with his philosophy ('With three cups I penetrate the Great Tao. Take a whole jugful – I and the world are one'). He drowned while drunkenly leaning overboard trying to embrace a reflection of the moon.

► Hefei 167D2

Hefei is the capital of Anhui, a comparatively poor province created in 1662. The town can boast only an excellent **museum►►**, its highlight being a Han dynasty jade burial suit. It is the nearest point of departure for a visit to the tomb of China's most eminent poet, Li Bai (701–62), who is buried near the place where he drowned. Some 100km northeast of Hefei, near Fengyang, are the **remains of the capital built by the first Ming emperor►** close to his birthplace before he realised that Nanjing was a better site. Only the foundations are visible and, a short distance off, the impressive spirit way to the tomb of the emperor's parents.

►► Huangshan (Yellow Mountain) 167D1

One of a range of 72 peaks in south Anhui, the highest reaching 1,800m, Huangshan is considered the most beautiful mountain in China. Its slopes are covered with pine trees, and swathed in cloud. It is a strenuous but not difficult climb to the summit. There are several routes but the best is to take the eastern, shorter route up, and the longer, more spectacular western route down (just about possible in 10 hours). A bus takes visitors to the main path which starts from the lower cable car terminal. If you

Huangshan, featured in innumerable paintings and even on stamps

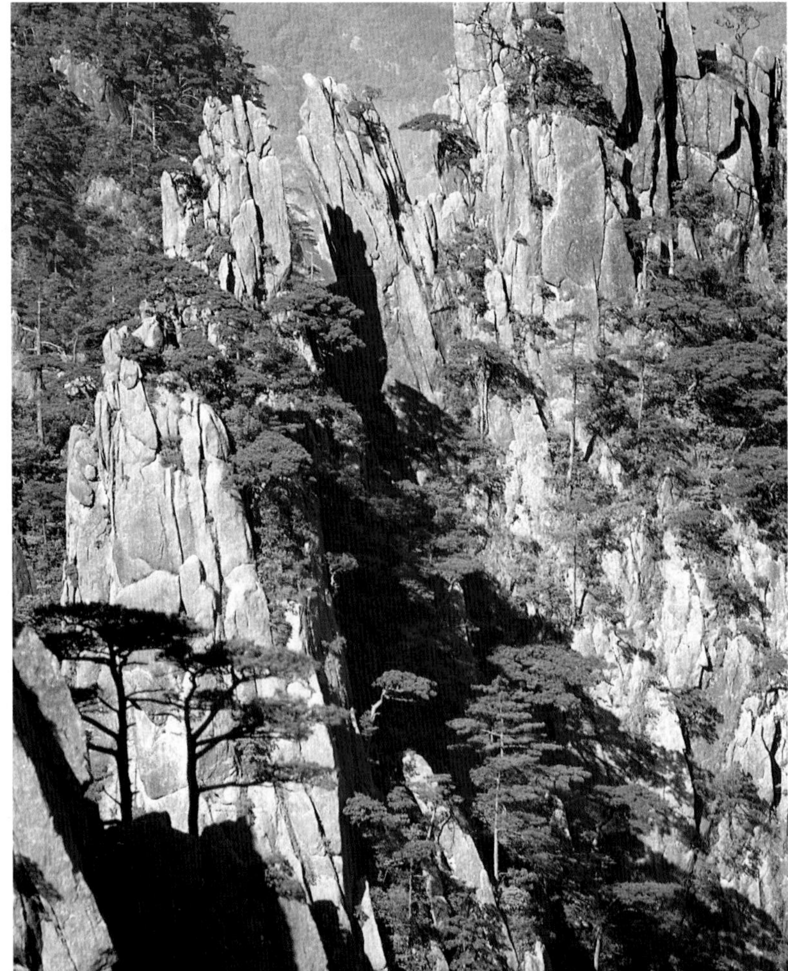

want to watch the famous sunrise, there are hotels at the top where you can stay overnight. South of Huangshan, 70km away, is Shexian, which is well known for its Ming dynasty houses.

▶ Jiuhuashan *167D1*

Jiuhuashan, the southern holy Buddhist mountain in Anhui province, is revered as a place of pilgrimage for the bereaved. Not as spectacular as Huangshan, it is none the less a splendid sight and the 1,400m climb can easily be accomplished in a day. You can get there from Nanjing by train (7 hours) and then bus (another 8 hours); or by boat from Nanjing to Wuhu (a day), and then by bus (another day).

Nº 0092160
黄山风景区交通费
票价 25 元
(报销凭证)

▶▶▶ Nanjing (Nanking) *167D2*

The capital of Jiangsu province lies on the south bank of the Yangtze and is one of the most delightful Chinese cities, despite the usual sprawl of unimaginative modern buildings. The city centre retains its Ming street plan, the old city wall is largely intact, the surrounding countryside is pretty and an air of dignified calm, often absent elsewhere in China, pervades its tree-lined streets.

It has been a capital at various times during the last 2,000 years – of the kingdom of Wu after the collapse of the Han, of local dynasties when China later fragmented, of imperial China under the early Ming, and of Republican China under the nationalists between 1911 and 1949.

Nanjing is a pretty even mix of imperial and revolutionary China. The city centre is the area around Zhongshan Lu and Hanzhong Lu. But let us start with the **Ming city wall▶▶▶** which ignores the usually rigid rectangle, by necessity following instead the contour line for 33km, the longest city wall in the world. Much of it is still complete. There are good views of it from the park surrounding the **Xuanwu Lake▶**, whilst it can be examined in detail on the road to the **Purple and Gold Mountains Observatory▶**, the largest in China. The **Zhonghua City Gate▶▶**, made of stone and clay bricks (each stamped with the name of its maker), has three inner gates designed to trap would-be attackers who had breached the first gate in a compound. Steps lead up to the ramparts which command fine views over the city. There is usually a cluster of people selling the local polished stones (which are a Nanjing speciality) around the foot of the gate.

Astronomical instrument at the Purple and Gold Mountains Observatory, Nanjing

Just back into the city from Zhonghua Gate, along Zhonghua Lu, are the **Taiping Museum▶** and the **Confucian Temple**. The museum is housed in the residence and garden of one of the leaders of the Taiping Heavenly Kingdom Rebellion (1851–64) (see page 42),

The Yangtze River Bridge, Nanjing, a 5km-long feat of engineering that took eight years to complete

Tomb of the King of Borneo
In 1408 the King of Borneo arrived in Nanjing, along with his extensive family, in order to pay tribute to the Ming court. His mission was evidently not entirely successful for he died there the same year and is buried just to the south of the city walls.

and features exhibits of maps, coins, weapons, documents and other artefacts relating to the Taiping movement. Taiping wall-paintings have recently been found at 74 Tangzi Jie.

The **Provincial Museum▶▶** at 321 Zhongshan Donglu, in an attractive modern building constructed in traditional style, is noted for its Han jade burial suit – jade squares linked by silver thread. Other items on display include ceramics and bronzes from prehistoric times to the Qing.

The ruins of the **Ming Palace▶**, on which Beijing's Forbidden City is modelled, rest anonymously under the trees near the Provincial Museum, a little further west along Zhongshan Donglu. Two sets of five marble bridges remain, and part of the old Meridian gate and some pillar bases. On the other side of the road an attempt has been made to re-create a scale version of the palace.

With the exceptions of the **Ming Bell and Drum Towers▶** (in the centre on Beijing Xilu), Nanjing's other attractions lie on the edge of, or outside, the city. The magnificent **Yangtze River Bridge▶▶▶**, always cited as an example of what the Chinese could do when the Russians said it was impossible, is to the northwest of the city and links south with north China. Before its opening in 1968, trains crossed the river on a special ferry, which took two hours to make the journey. The bridge is a double-decker (rail and road) and, between its extreme points, 2km long. A lift takes you to a viewing tower on the south side.

To the east of the city a road weaves through bamboo groves to the **Tomb of Zhu Yuanzhang▶▶**, the first Ming emperor. The tomb is not open but you can walk down the spirit way lined with statues, less grand than its counterpart in Beijing, but also less despoiled by commercialism. At the end furthest from the tomb itself the road curves away to the right, but walk straight on and, hidden among the trees, is a large brick arch, part of the wall that used to surround the tomb.

Further on, east of the Ming tomb, embedded in the slopes of the Purple and Gold Mountains (Zijin Shan), is **Sun Yatsen's Mausoleum▶▶▶**. Founder of Republican China, he died in 1925 in Beijing, where he was laid out in the Biyun Temple. The competition for the design of his mausoleum was won by Y C Lu, who was influenced by the shape of the Liberty Bell in Philadelphia, USA. The tomb itself is in the uppermost pavilion, reached by several flights of steps. Sun Yatsen's remains are covered with a marble effigy, rather than visible in the crystal sarcophagus originally envisaged.

East of Sun Yatsen's Mausoleum is the curious concrete **Linggu Pagoda▶**, built by an American in 1929. Nearby is the impressive Ming dynasty **Beamless Hall▶▶**, constructed entirely of brick without any wooden beams. It was part of a temple that originally stood on the site of the tomb of the first Ming emperor.

The rape of Nanjing
Between 1937 and 1945, during the Japanese occupation, it is estimated that at least 400,000 civilian residents of Nanjing were murdered or raped with appalling brutality. In the 1980s a school history textbook was published in Japan which gave only a passing mention to this massacre. The Chinese government protested until changes were made.

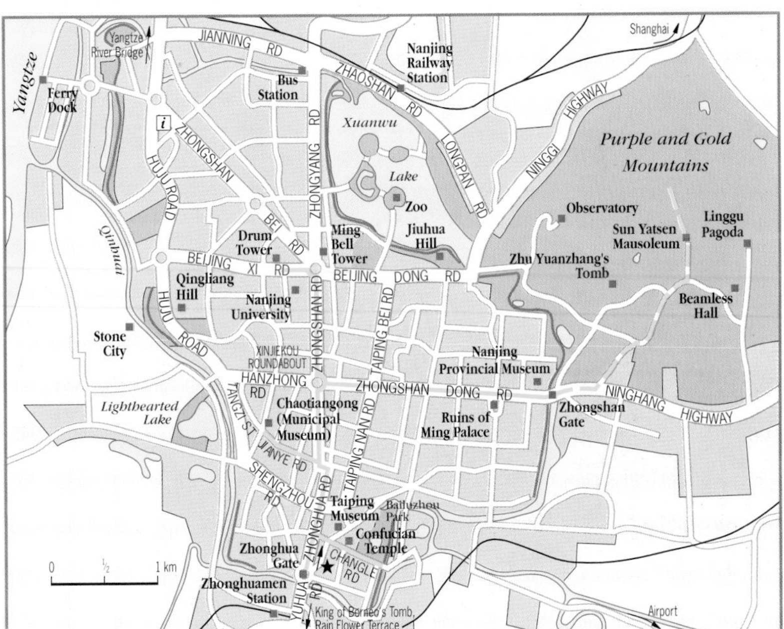

Walk or cycle ride Nanjing

Start from the pretty old wooden-fronted houses outside Zhonghua City Gate and head north along Zhonghua Road. Turning right along Changle Road to Bailuzhou Park leads you to an interesting area of alleyways and old houses. Return to Zhonghua Road, go past the Taiping Museum and ornamental gardens and then turn left along Jianye Road to Chaotiangong, one of the oldest parts of the city and home to the Municipal Museum. Return to Zhonghua Road, go to the Xinjiekou roundabout and up Zhongshan Road to the Drum Tower. East from the Xinjiekou roundabout leads to the Ming Palace site and the Nanjing Provincial Museum. You can continue on to the Purple and Gold Mountains (Zijin Shan) by bicycle.

■ Nobody knows the precise date of the discovery of silk but Chinese tradition ascribes it to the Empress Xi Ling who in the year 2640BC harnessed the natural skills of the silkworm for the advantage of mankind.....■

Sericulture The Chinese kept the secret of silk for 3,000 years until, so it is said, perfidious princesses and cunning missionaries exported it to the West and throughout the Orient. The word 'sericulture' derives from the Greek word for silk, *serikos*, and refers to the raising of silkworms and the production of raw silk. Farmers breed the silkworms and then deliver the cocoons to spinning factories, where raw silk is drawn on to bobbins, ready for commercial use. The silkworm is the caterpillar of the moth *Bombyx mori*, a native of China. One moth may lay 500 eggs, which are hatched in incubators or open trays at about 22°C. The caterpillars are black or grey, later turning creamy white, and are interested only in eating. Mulberry leaves are their preferred diet, supplied to them every three to four hours. After five weeks they have grown to a length of 7cm and are extremely sensitive to smells or noise; when full-grown they reject food and become restless, a sign that they are ready to make their cocoons. Small straw frames are then placed on the trays for this purpose.

The silk is produced by a pair of tubular spinning glands each of which secretes a single fibre. This is joined together with the other by muscular contraction, producing a thread up to 900m long. A gummy secretion holds it all together in its cocoon shape. This process takes about ten days, after which 90 per cent of the cocoons are sent to the factory, while the farmer keeps 10 per cent for breeding purposes.

The factory Once at the factory the cocoons are sorted to reject any that are flawed, and the remainder are then steamed to kill the live chrysalis. The threads from six or seven cocoons are needed to produce a fibre strong enough for weaving; the cocoons are immersed in hot water to loosen the threads, which are then extracted from the water and reeled together as one by machine. The cocoon case left behind is used as an ingredient in traditional medicine.

Top: silkworms and cocoons
Above: a silk embroidered double-sided peony, on display in Suzhou Silk Museum

Old fabric, new style

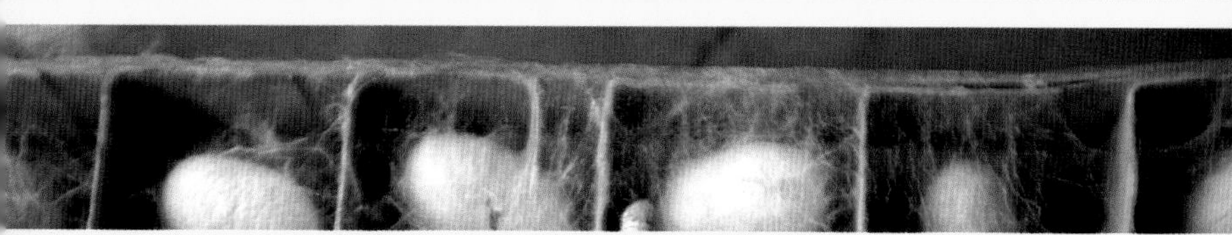

The newly created thread is then transformed into a yarn suitable for weaving by a process of doubling and twisting, known as 'throwing', which gives it durability and strength. The amount of throwing varies according to the use to which the yarn will be put. After a certain point, silk loses its sleekness and is left with a granular surface, known as crêpe.

The twisting is done mechanically – rows of machines transfer the yarn from one bobbin to another, with each bobbin moving at a different speed in order to achieve the amount of twist required.

From here the silk goes to dyeing factories and then to weaving factories to be made into cloth or carpets, or perhaps to institutes which specialise in the production of silk embroidery. The most famous of these is in Suzhou, and there are others in Guangdong and Sichuan.

Silk markets
Much of China's silk production of 45,000 tonnes is exported. China has 90 per cent of the world market for raw silk and is attempting to increase its 40 per cent share of the finished silk market.

A silk-reeling mill in Suzhou

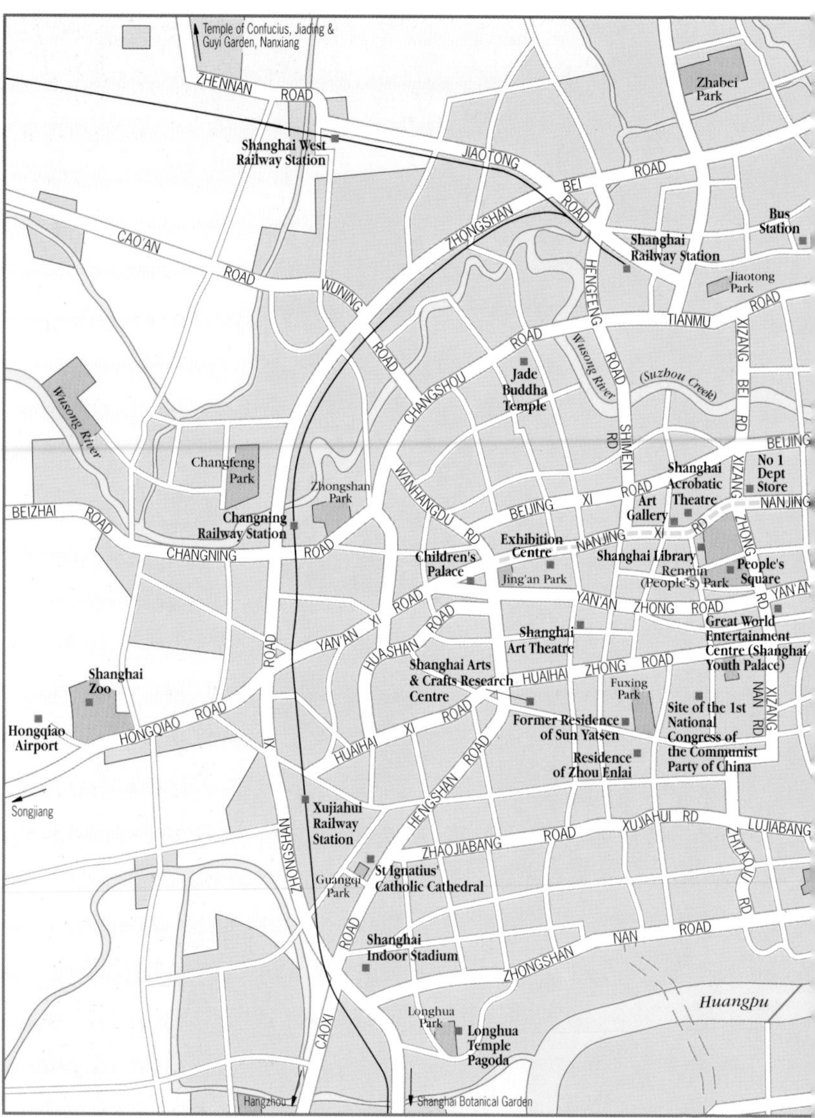

City slickers

In the financial districts of Shanghai the exchange brokers dashed between offices, as the rates fluctuated, in low-slung, four-wheel carriages, drawn by little Mongolian ponies. Each sported a coachman dressed in all his finery.

▶▶▶ Shanghai

167E2

Shanghai, with a population of 13 million, is one of China's largest cities, and as one of China's three municipalities (along with Tianjin and Beijing), is under direct central government control. It was a town of middling importance from the 13th century, when it became a county seat, located in the area now known as the old town, which until the early part of the 20th century had its own wall. In the 19th century the foreign powers recognised Shanghai's considerable potential as a harbour, situated as it is on the banks of the Huangpu, only 28km from the mouth of the Yangtze; the Treaty of Nanjing in 1842 (which concluded the Opium Wars) ceded areas of Shanghai first to the British and then the French and

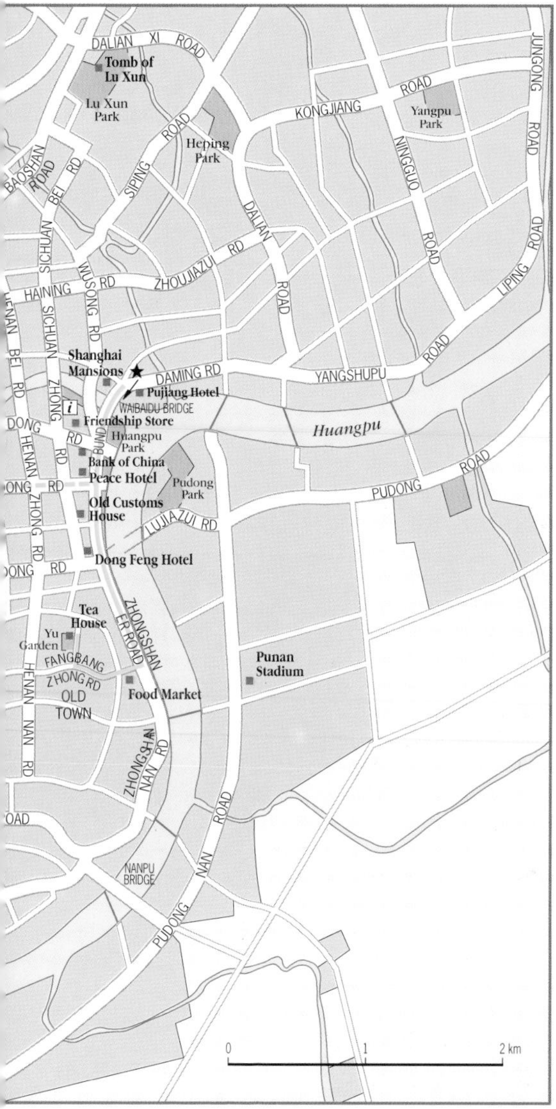

Early morning dance lessons on the Bund, Shanghai

The Great World
At the junction of Yan'an Lu and Xizang Lu is an extraordinary building resembling a wedding-cake, formerly called the Great World. Inaugurated in 1917 it was a cross between bazaar and freak show. Open from noon until late, each floor was devoted to different attractions from the burlesque to the vile sing-song girls and peep-shows, a stuffed whale and imported lavatories with a resident expert on their use. A Great World newspaper kept patrons informed of coming events.

The Great Maloo
The Nanjing Road was originally cobbled and is named after the Nanjing treaty of 1842 which ceded areas of Shanghai to foreign control. For the Chinese it was always the Great Maloo, or Great Horse Road, since it was built for horsemen. It and its western extension, the former Bubbling Well Road, were noted by the writer John Steinbeck as one of the most interesting streets in the world.

Americans, forming what became known as the 'Foreign Concessions'. The British and Americans eventually combined to form the International Settlement, whilst the French Concession remained separate. The rules governing these foreign enclaves were complicated, but essentially foreign nationals were not bound by Chinese law, but were subject instead to the jurisdiction of their own consuls. Foreigners dominated commerce and industry, amassing huge fortunes in banking, trading and shipping. This state of affairs lasted until 1949, although the writing on the wall was visible well before then.

The colonial legacy is a bizarre one. Although Shanghai is a vital part of Chinese industry, and despite visible signs of change, it still looks, with its suburban English or

Far-seeing Jesuits
Shanghai was dominated by foreigners by the second half of the 19th century, but 300 years j184 earlier the Jesuits had already begun to exert an influence there. Occupying the area called Xujiahuie, they set about converting the locals to Catholicism, building a cathedral and observatory on land bought from one of their converts.

French villas and Liverpool-style waterfront, like a European city in a Chinese setting. A walk around the Bund and its neighbouring streets is a good way to soak up its cosmopolitan atmosphere and gain an impression of its former colonial splendour.

The **Jade Buddha Temple (Yufosi)▶▶**, in the north-west of the city on Anyuan Road, is less than 100 years old but has an extremely attractive restored main hall and (in a separate building), the remarkable Jade Buddha itself, brought back from Burma by a local abbot. The temple is particularly lively on the first and fifth days of the lunar month. Shanghai's two other active temples are the **Jing'an▶** on Nanjing Xi Road and the **Longhua▶** at 2853 Longhua Road. There are numerous parks but the most interesting are the Renmin, the Lu Xun, and the Jing'an.

Walk The Shanghai Bund and its neighbourhood

See highlighted map, pages 184–5.
The **Bund▶▶▶** (derived from the Anglo-Indian word meaning quay), about 1km long, is the city's fulcrum. Ideally, a half day should be devoted to a walk through the area – the Bund and the nearby streets, and the Friendship Store (China's largest) – or a day, if you combine the walk with a harbour cruise to the Yangtze mouth (boats leave near the Peace Hotel). At the far end of the Bund, just the other side of Suzhou Creek, is **Shanghai Mansions Hotel**, a 22-storey brick ziggurat, in what would have been the American Concession.

Opposite, on the other side of Zhongshan Dong Road, is **Pujiang Hotel**, formerly the Astor House, and opposite that the **Russian Consulate**.

Cross the Waibaidu Bridge back to the Bund. The former **British Consulate** (1870) at No 33, set in manicured lawns, is now offices. The Bund proper, known as Revolution Boulevard during the Cultural Revolution, consists almost entirely of pre-1949 buildings in grandiose style. No 29 was originally the Banque de l'Indochine and No 31 the former offices of Jardine, Matheson & Co, upon whose opium deals the prosperity of Shanghai was founded.

The outstanding buildings this side of the Nanjing Road are

Huxinting tea house

first the **Bank of China**, with its New York façade and Chinese roof, jostling for supremacy with the **Peace Hotel**. The Peace Hotel was originally the Cathay, built by Sir Victor Sassoon as the finest in Asia. Redolent of the 1930s, it sounds like the 1940s, because an old jazz band still thumps out period tunes in the bar at night.

Nanjing Road▶▶ is a shopper's paradise. One of the busiest streets in China, it has a huge variety of merchandise on sale, often in period buildings. It leads through the heart of the city to the old **Race Course** (now **Renmin Park**), the department stores, the Jing'an Temple and the opulent villas of the former foreign residents.

Continuing along the Bund you pass the old **Customs House** at No 14, with some fine mosaics in the lobby ceiling, surmounted by **Big Ching**, a clock that used to play the Westminster chimes. No 12 is the former premises of the **Hong Kong and Shanghai Banking Corporation**, built in 1921 and then considered to be one of Asia's finest buildings. No 3, the Dong Feng Hotel, was originally the famously snobbish **Shanghai Club** (the British Club), watering-hole of the taipans (bosses of the foreign trading companies), and home to the longest bar in the world.

Yan'an Road was formerly Avenue Edward VII, the boundary between the International Settlement and the French Concession. The waterfront strip (Zhongshan Er Road) was the Quai de France. Walking along here will bring you to the former Chinese Bund, which runs in front of the **Old Town▶▶▶**. Turn right along Dongmen past Waixiang Guajie on the left, site of the main **food market**, worth a diversion. Continue on to Fanbang Zhong Road until, right, you meet the Ming gateway to the **Temple of the City God** (**Chenghuangmiao**), now more or less a bazaar, and beyond it the Tea House and the Yu Garden.

Pass through the gateway and into the heart of the old town, a maze of quaint shops and restaurants reminiscent of old China. In the middle is a small lake, filled with golden fish. The zigzag bridge leads to the 18th-century **Huxinting tea house▶▶**, or mid-lake pavilion, an excellent place for a refreshing pot of green tea.

The nearby Ming dynasty **Yu Garden▶▶** is a fine example of miniature landscaping, built in 1559. The first pavilion is the ceremonial Three Ears of Corn Hall, followed by the Hall for Viewing the Grand Rockery. Turn right as you come out of here, follow the pond shore, then keep right past a series of pavilions, halls and gardens to re-emerge in the old town behind the tea house.

The skyline of the Shanghai Bund

Shanghai is a legend. A generation after the last 'Shanghailanders' relinquished their privileges, the name continues to evoke nostalgia for a way of life that can never be the same again.....

A pre-war survivor, the Peace Hotel jazz band

Fox-hunting memories
Part of the charm of pre-1949 Shanghai was its absurdity, an oasis of unreality in a world that was all too real beyond the boundaries of the Foreign Concessions. For the British, memories of home were reinforced by such events as the paper hunt. A pack of foxhounds would set off in pursuit of a chemical trail with the odoriferous qualities of a fox. Horses and huntsmen galloped across the countryside not far behind, with the last man in the field being responsible for mollifying any outraged peasant farmers.

The old Cathay Hotel, now the Peace, a Shanghai classic

A unique city Shanghai was 'life itself'. It was an extraordinary mix of the very seedy and the very decadent, immense wealth, and terrible poverty. It has even given its name to a verb – to be shanghaied is to 'be drugged and shipped as a sailor, when unconscious'.

This was due to the peculiar circumstances of the city's existence. Written into the Treaty of Nanjing was the notion of extra-territoriality, which meant that foreign nationals in Shanghai were outside Chinese law. Of course each of the concessions had its own laws but in practice almost anything went. Shanghai became a magnet for the dispossessed, seekers of wealth, and adventurers, a city of magnificent extremes.

Shanghailanders Most of what is left of concession Shanghai dates from between 1920 and 1949. The character of the two concessions (the French and the International Settlement) was quite different – not only did you change buses at Avenue Edward VII but also electricity systems. The differences were more subtle than that, however, for in many ways each concession reflected different national personas and attracted different types of character. And Shanghai was full of characters: wealthy Baghdad Sephardic Jews like Sir Victor Sassoon, owner of the Cathay Hotel (today's Peace Hotel), with his stable of greyhounds – for greyhound racing was a passion among expatriates – whose names coincided with his initials ('Very Slippy', 'Veiled Secret', 'Very Soon'); and Silas Hardoon, the wealthiest man in Shanghai, who owned an estate (now covered by the old Russian-style Exhibition Centre) in the heart of the city where he kept his Eurasian wife and colony of adopted children; then

there were the underworld criminals, such as the notorious Pockmarked Huang and Big-Eared Du, who ran the city from the safety of the French Concession. The mixture of propriety and duplicity that was Shanghai is exemplified by the careers of these two – Huang was the Chief Detective of the French Sûreté, while Du would remind those who spurned his offers of protection of their mortality by delivering a coffin to their front door.

Nightlife Above all Shanghai was a nocturnal city. Night started with the tea-cocktail hour, 'tea for propriety and cocktails for pep', and perhaps finished at dawn at Blood Alley (Xikou Lu). Taxi-dancing was an institution – vast dance-halls where hostesses were for hire for whom drinks had to be bought, invariably cold tea but billed as champagne or whatever the lady requested. Then there were the sing-song girls, who provided entertainment at restaurant dinner-parties. Although not above high-class whoring, their main accomplishment was seductive singing, each accompanied by a man playing the *erhu*, a two-string Chinese violin. The sing-song girl was easy to identify in her highly polished lacquer rickshaw; a bell announced her presence whilst a lamp at her feet was angled to highlight her face and the lotus in her hair.

After years of darkness, the nightlife that Shanghai used to be so famous for has returned

After dark
The Russians were an important and volatile element in the make-up of pre-1949 Shanghai, arriving in the wake of the 1917 Revolution. They are credited with the development of the cabaret. Russian girls teamed up with Filipino dance-bands to perform in Chinese-owned cabarets, and were frequently cited in scandalous divorce cases. As a contemporary guidebook pointed out, 'there are three classes of cabaret – high class, low class, and no class'.

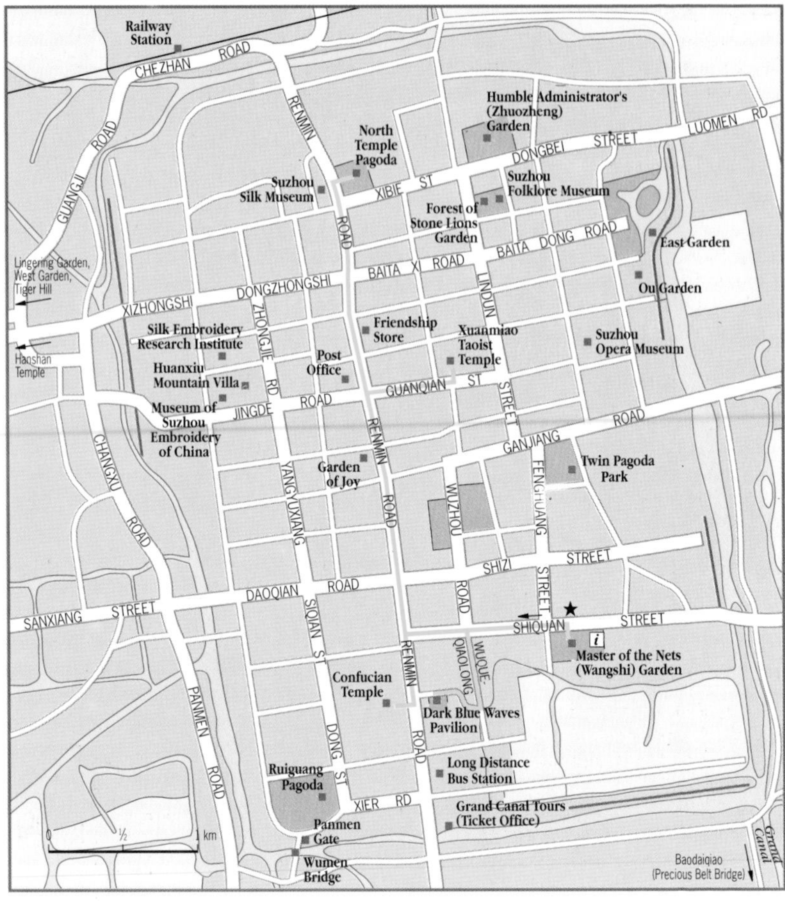

Walk Suzhou's gardens and temples

A short walk introduces you to some of Suzhou's principal sights. In Wangshi Xiang, an alley off Shijin Jie, close to the Suzhou Hotel, is the **Master of the Nets Garden (Wangshiyuan)►►►**, a miniature garden built around a pool and first laid out in 1140. It has several small halls carved in lattice and fretwork on the principle of 'framing a view'.

From Wangshiyuan turn left to Shiquan Street and then first left into Wuqueqiaolong until you come to the entrance of the **Dark Blue Waves Pavilion (Canglangting)►►**, one of Suzhou's oldest gardens, dating back to the 10th century.

Back on Shiquan Street turn left until the junction with Renmin Road, turn left again and continue to the **Confucian Temple►** where you will find an ancient street-plan of Suzhou, the earliest such map extant in China.

Return to Renmin Road, retrace your steps northwards and turn right into Guanqian Street, to reach the Song dynasty **Xuanmiao Taoist Temple►**. Continuing north along Renmin Road will take you past the Friendship Store (no. 504) to the impressive **North Temple Pagoda►►** set in a pretty garden.

▶▶▶ Suzhou *167E2*

A comparatively small town in Jiangsu province, on the Grand Canal, about an hour's train journey from Shanghai, Suzhou is one of China's most charming cities, recognised for centuries for its loveliness. Its fame rests on its silk and its gardens, both of which still flourish, and what were once standard features of Chinese towns in this area – pretty houses overlooking narrow canals spanned by traditional bridges – have now become attractions in their own right.

Suzhou's history dates back to the 6th century BC when it was founded on a network of canals built to control the Yangtze floodwaters. Its subsequent prosperity was brought about by the construction of the Grand Canal and the growth of the silk industry, which flourished under the Tang and became even more important under the Song, with the establishment of the capital at Hangzhou. Later it was known as a great cultural centre but on the whole it has remained relatively unaffected by the convulsions of Chinese politics.

The wealth of Suzhou's officials, scholars and traders was invested in their gardens. The greatest, the 10th-century **Humble Administrator's Garden (Zhuozhengyuan)▶▶▶**, is also the largest, occupying a 10-acre site; the poetically named 19th-century **Lingering Garden (Liuyuan)▶▶▶** is small with delightful rockeries. The **Forest of Stone Lions Garden (Shizilin)▶▶▶**, about an acre in size, has four lakes, rocks, bridges and hills. It is considered one of Suzhou's finest gardens, although to Western eyes it lacks picturesqueness.

At the **Silk Embroidery Research Institute▶▶▶** you can watch craftsmen creating their painstaking masterpieces, sometimes embroidering with a strand that is a mere one-fortieth of a silk thread, as well as buy samples of their work. **Suzhou Silk Museum▶▶**, near North Pagoda on Renmin Lu, offers a fascinating insight into the story of silk with live silkworms and a collection of silk looms, old silk garments, etc.

Outside the city, **Tiger Hill▶▶▶**, a scenic spot, has a Song dynasty leaning pagoda with some Tang features, built in brick to imitate wood architecture. In 1957 workers discovered sutras there and a record of its date of construction (959–61). The low, long **Precious Belt Bridge▶▶** affords excellent views of life on the canals.

Bridges over canals
Handsome bridges spanning the canals are a feature of Suzhou. One of the most impressive is the Maple Bridge, near the Hanshan Temple, the subject of a poem by the Tang poet, Zhang Ji, entitled 'Anchored by night at the Maple Bridge'. Another, offering a classically picturesque view, arches across the old moat near the Panmen Gate.

Wangshiyuan, the Garden of the Master of Fishing Nets

Luohan Hall in the 'Temple of the Return to the Fundamental Principle', Guiyuan Temple, Wuhan

Rebel headquarters
Between 1926 and 1927 Wuhan was the headquarters of a faction of the Guomindang which opposed Chiang Kaishek. The faction commander was Wang Jingwei, who at the time allied himself to the communists, but in 1927, in an abrupt volte-face, he turned on them, murdering 100,000 of their supporters in the Wuhan district. He was eventually to lead a Japanese puppet government in Nanjing in 1940 and to die in Tokyo in 1944.

►► Wuhan *166C1*

Wuhan, capital of Hubei province, is an iron and steel city on the Yangtze made up of the three former cities of Wuchang, on the south bank, and Hanyang and the former treaty port of Hankou on the north. Wuchang was briefly capital of the state of Wu in the 3rd century AD, whilst Hanyang was founded during the Sui dynasty. Hankou was little more than a fishing village until the Western powers established concessions there from 1861. Wuhan was the centre for the revolutionary activity which culminated in the 1911 uprising and overthrow of the Manchu dynasty.

Wuhan tends to be seen merely as an embarkation or disembarkation point for the Yangtze river cruises but the old city centre, improved recently, has some attractions.

The most striking of these is the **Yellow Crane Pavilion (Huanghelou)►**, on Sheshan (Snake Hill) in Wuchang, by the river bridge. Recently restored, it was originally built in the 3rd century AD. Commemorated in many poems, it gets its name from the story of a Taoist priest, Wang Zian, who alighted here on a yellow crane on his journey to become one of the Immortals. If you have time to explore Sheshan a little further, you will find the **Shengxiang Baota** lama stupa, embossed with interesting carvings, and the **tomb of Chen Youjing**, who declared an independent state at the end of the Yuan dynasty, both worth a visit.

Further east is the **East Lake (Donghu)►**, a spacious pleasant place for a boat trip or stroll. Nearby is the remarkable **Provincial Museum►►►**, mostly devoted to the finds excavated from the tomb of Marquis Yi of the state of Zeng, who died in 433BC, and important because it demonstrates the extraordinary richness of Chinese cultural life well before China became a single, unified state. The highlight is a set of 64 bronze bells on racks, supported by bronze soldiers, still sometimes used in concerts of ancient music. The crawling dragon motif is repeated on many of the ritual lacquerware vessels that were also discovered in the tomb. There is a fine collection of ritual bronzes, as well as other ancient musical instruments.

In Hanyang the **Guiyuan Buddhist Temple▶▶** on Cuihui Jie, built in the Qing dynasty on the site of a Ming garden, is celebrated for the 500 figures sculpted by two artists between 1822 and 1831. **Guishan (Tortoise Hill)▶** was once covered in temples and pavilions, some of which have been reconstructed, including the Song dynasty **Guqin Terrace** (**Guqintai**). It was built to commemorate two Han dynasty musicians, Yu Baiya and Zhong Ziqi, who used to play together here. One year Yu arrived to find that his friend had died; having played a farewell tune on his lute, he broke the strings, vowing never to play again.

Hankou▶▶, like Shanghai, is interesting for its European atmosphere, a legacy dating from 1861 to 1949 when the foreign powers were established here. The British Concession went from Jianghan Dadao to the train station; then, in sequence, were the smaller Russian, French, German and Japanese concessions. The old waterfront along Yanjiang Lu evokes a sense of nostalgia with its former European trading houses – Butterfield and Swire, Litvinoff, British-American – as well as the major consulates and the Customs House. **Zhongshan Dadao** is the main shopping area of Hankou (and Wuhan), and there are markets in the Jiefang Dadao area. Jiefang Park and Zhongshan Park were the former racecourses.

Wuhan is a major carpet producer and the factory can be visited by appointment.

The Yangtze River Bridge was completed in 1957. Over 1km long, it carries both rail and road traffic.

Chairman Mao takes a dip
During the Cultural Revolution, Wuhan was the scene of Chairman Mao's famous swim in the Yangtze river. Popular mythology recounts that he swam from bank to bank, an unlikely feat when you look at the width of the river at this point; what he did was to go in and allow himself to be carried by the current downstream a little way.

The Yellow Crane Pavilion, overlooking the Yangtze, Wuhan

■ Although the river itself and the life along its banks are fascinating in themselves, the focal point of the cruise along the Yangtze is the dramatic journey through the Three Gorges.....■

Yangtze gorges
The Three Gorges were formed about 70 million years ago when earth movements caused a vast inland sea draining east to cut into limestone faults in zigzag fashion, creating the celebrated perpendicular cliffs and sharp curves of the gorges.

Transportation For most people the journey along the Yangtze begins or ends either at Wuhan or Chongqing (downstream takes 3 days and 2 nights, upstream 5 days). Between the two cities are the gorges themselves and a host of small towns and villages. As well as the ships run by CITS and those chartered by foreign tour-companies, there are local steamers which have basic passenger accommodation ranging from fairly unpleasant dormitories to two-berth cabins of an acceptable standard with a small lounge. They have restaurants which serve, on the whole, execrable food. But these ships are a slice of ordinary Chinese life and, if you can secure one of the better cabins, tolerate the food, and become accustomed to the booming hooter, are a worthwhile experience.

Sights The Yangtze is lined with evocatively named rocks and hills. About 270km east of Chongqing is the **Stone Treasure Stronghold (Shibaozhai)**, a 30m high rock said to resemble a jade seal, with a brilliant red pagoda against the side. At its summit is an early 18th-century temple. About 48km beyond, **Wanxian** is a typical riverine settlement, high on the banks and reached by a long flight of steps. Long a trading centre, it is crammed with market stalls piled high with fruit, nuts and traditional basketware. There is also a silk-weaving factory. At **Yunyang** the Zhang Fei Temple is dedicated to a Three Kingdoms general renowned for his honesty. Next is **Fengjie** with its Ming walls, then **Baidi Cheng** followed by the Gorges.

The Gorges The Gorges are a spectacular sight. The first is the 8km **Qutangxia (Bellows Gorge)**. As you enter it,

Shooting the rapids in one of the Yangtze's three 'Lesser Gorges' along the Daning river

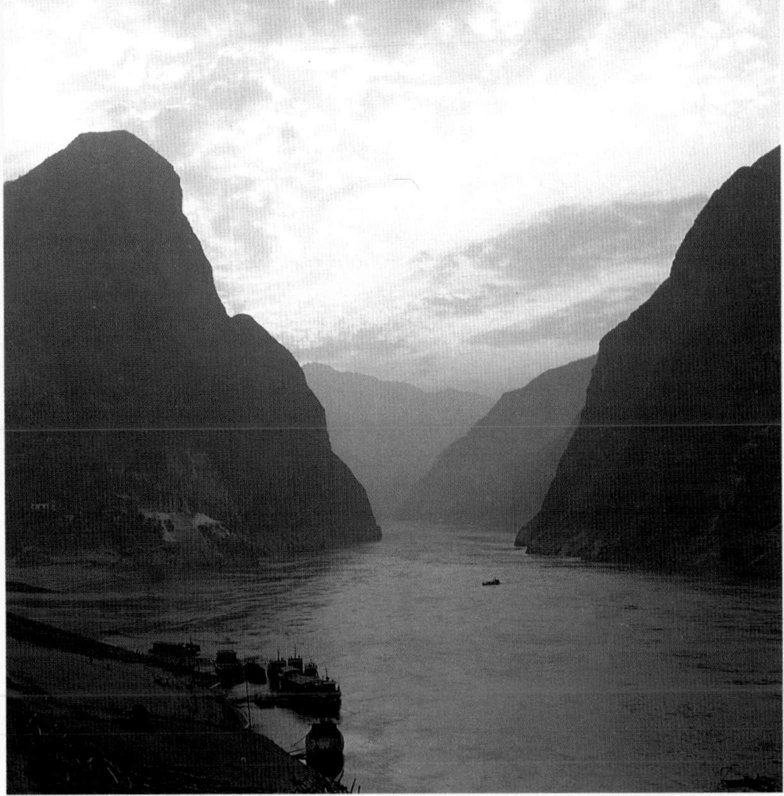

Red Shoulder Mountain appears on the north side, pockmarked with square holes, ancient burial places said to have been used as bellows by the god of carpenters, Lu Ban. On **White Salt Mountain**, on the south bank, are the remains of a 6th-century city. Clinging precariously to the rock face high up on the north side of the gorge is the old towpath. The gorge ends at the town of **Daixi**.

Boats often moor at **Wushan** in order to visit the three small gorges along the Daning river, renowned for their breathtaking scenery.

Next comes the 44km **Wuxia (Witches Gorge)** lined by 12 peaks, six on either side, each with a poetic name based on the legend of Yao Ji, daughter of the Queen of the West, and her 11 sisters. **Zigui** was the home of the 3rd-century BC statesman Qu Yuan of the state of Chu, whose suicide when his advice to resist the rise of the state of Qin was ignored is commemorated in the annual Dragon-boat races. Finally comes the 75km **Xiling Gorge**, which comprises seven smaller gorges. The main ones are the **Gorge of the Sword and the Manual on the Art of War** (named after Zhuge Liang, a 3rd-century minister said to have hidden here his treatise on military strategy); and then the **Ox Liver and Horse's Blood Gorge**, the **Kongling Gorge**, and the **Shadowplay Gorge**, all named after colours and shapes of rocks.

A former treaty port, Yichang is now famous for its **Gezhouba Dam**, completed in 1986 (see panel).

Though the waters are rising, the gorges remain a most spectacular sight

Dam all

The Chinese authorities are building another dam on the Yangtze which will effectively submerge the Gorges for ever. Although there has been an outcry about this project, work has now begun.

Meanwhile, visits can be arranged to the Gezhouba Dam (it produces 14 billion kilowatt-hours annually), as well as to the White Horse Cave and Three Visitors Cave, both of which have impressive rock formations.

Traditional Huishan clay figurine 'fatties', still made in Wuxi

Figures of clay
Wuxi is not only known for its rocks and silk, it also produces the famous Huishan figurines made of local clay. Depicting characters from traditional fairy-tales, operas and plays they may not be to everyone's taste, but even if they do not appeal to you, a visit to the factory to watch them being made is worthwhile.

Attraction of opposites
In *Behind the Wall*, Colin Thubron describes the rocks of Lake Tai as 'a frozen turmoil' which 'concentrated the wild energy of nature'. In traditional gardens rocks represented the hard, masculine 'yang' principle, in contrast to the water, next to which they were usually placed, which was soft, feminine 'yin'. 'Water was stone's antithesis. It was the blood of the earth, drunk by the kings of old legend in search of immortality.'

▶▶ Wuxi and Lake Tai *167E2*

Although there are several places within striking distance of **Lake Tai (Taihu)▶▶**, Wuxi town provides a convenient access point. With an area of 2,200 sq km, Lake Tai is one of the largest freshwater lakes in China, stippled with some 90 islets and, occasionally, fleets of traditional fishing boats. It is famous for its ornamental limestone rocks pierced with holes by the action of the waters, which were highly prized and often adorn traditional Chinese gardens. Brought to the surface, these were cleaned and scoured before being transported as far afield as Beijing as well as to gardens in Shanghai, Suzhou and Wuxi itself.

Wuxi, one of the principal ports on the Grand Canal, has one of the fastest growing economies in the country. Although an old town (its name means 'no tin', given during the Han dynasty when the tin mine on Xishan dried up), its economic expansion dates only to the turn of the 20th century when wealthy Shanghai entrepreneurs established new factories and developed the silk industry, for which it remains famous. A visit to the **Number 1 Spinning Mill▶▶** makes an interesting experience.

There are hotels at the lakeside (some distance out of town) and in the city centre which, although not beautiful, has a lively port atmosphere. The city is dominated by Xihui Hill and Park, where one of the most noted gardens in China, the **Jichangyuan (Attachment to Freedom Garden)▶▶**, stands on the site of an ancient monastery. Such was its fame that the Emperor Qianlong replicated it as the Garden of Harmonious Interest in the Summer Palace in Beijing. Xihui Park was created in 1958 by linking the Hui Mountain, with its nine dragon peaks and spring water, its temple and its Song dynasty bridge, with Xi Mountain and its 16th-century Longguang Pagoda and Temple. There is another garden, the **Liyuan** (Wormy Garden), near the lakeside Hubin and Shuixu hotels – built in the 1920s, its name adequately describes its occupants. **The Meiyuan (Plum Garden)▶**, on the road to the Taihu Hotel, is particularly pretty in the early spring, when its thousands of plum trees are in blossom.

Opposite the Taihu Hotel is **Tortoise Head Promontory (Yuantouzhu)▶**, a beauty spot supposed to resemble a turtle's head where there are tea houses and pavilions in a lovely lakeside setting. It is a good place for idle strolls. From here boat trips to Sanshan Island, pretty enough in the right conditions, are sometimes possible.

During high summer, the lotus flowers in full bloom by the shores of the lake make a splendid sight.

There are frequent boat services across the lake and by canal to, for example, Yixing (Dingshu), Hangzhou, Changzhou, Suzhou and Xidongtingshan, where the ornamental rocks are prepared. Back in Wuxi town itself, there are hints of the past – the central area is bounded by arms of the Grand Canal, and in the bustling main streets of Renmin Zhonglu, Jiefang Xilu and Zhongshan Lu the occasional older house or restaurant (serving the delicious local specialities, whitebait or Wuxi spare ribs) survives.

►►► Yangzhou *167D2*

In Jiangsu province, on the Grand Canal just north of the Yangtze, Yangzhou is a charming town with a cultured past that has bequeathed many poets and painters, gardens, a local opera style and the still-live tradition of recitation of novels in the street. A prosperous town in the past, its wealth derived from salt, rice and silk.

Eternal China: view through a moon gate, 'Five Pavilion Bridge', Yangzhou

The **Xu Garden (Xuyuan)►►**, on the west side of the Narrow West Lake, is noted for the beautiful carved woodwork inside the pavilions. Three other **traditional gardens (Xiyuan, Yechunyuan, Hongyuan)►►** cluster round the moat to the west of the Xiyuan Hotel, near the old imperial jetty. The **Geyuan►►**, on Dongguan Jie, was the 19th-century home of a salt merchant, one of several merchant houses in this area. Another attractive garden is the **Heyuan►►** on Xuningmen jie, small but ingeniously contrived. The **Museum►** is located on Yanfu Xilu in a Qing temple. To the northwest are traces of the Tang city walls, and the **Fajingisi Temple**. The **Slender West Lake** (Shouxi Hu)►► has the famous Five Pavilion Bridge (Wutingqiao); an unusual point of interest is the **Tomb of Puhaddin**, a Yuan dynasty Muslim preacher and descendant of Mohammed, which overlooks the Grand Canal.

Yangzhou eccentrics
Although Europeans associate Yangzhou with Marco Polo, who is supposed to have been governor here, for the Chinese it brings to mind the 'eccentrics of Yangzhou', a group of painters who incurred imperial disapproval. Also known as the Eight Eccentrics, they specialised in simple, dramatic works and one, Gao Qipei (1672–1734), is especially remembered for his works with finger and fingernail.

▶ Zhenjiang *167D2*

Zhenjiang's prosperity was founded on silk and the Grand Canal. Industrial now, in the 19th century it was a treaty port and the **museum▶** is now housed in the former British Consulate in an area of alleyways leading down to the river. Jinshan is dominated by the **Jinshan Temple▶▶**, with its stunning, renovated Main Hall of Golden Buddhas and the **Cishou Pagoda▶**, whilst **Jiaoshan▶** is a bamboo-forested area some 5km downstream with the **Dinghui Temple** and remains of the gun batteries used against various foreign invaders. On **Beigushan▶** are the 11th-century **Iron Pagoda (Tieta)**, the **Sweet Dew Temple (Ganlusi)** and the **Soaring Clouds Pavilion (Lingyunting)**.

Hall of the Golden Buddhas at the Jinshan Temple, Zhenjiang, one of the oldest temples in this region

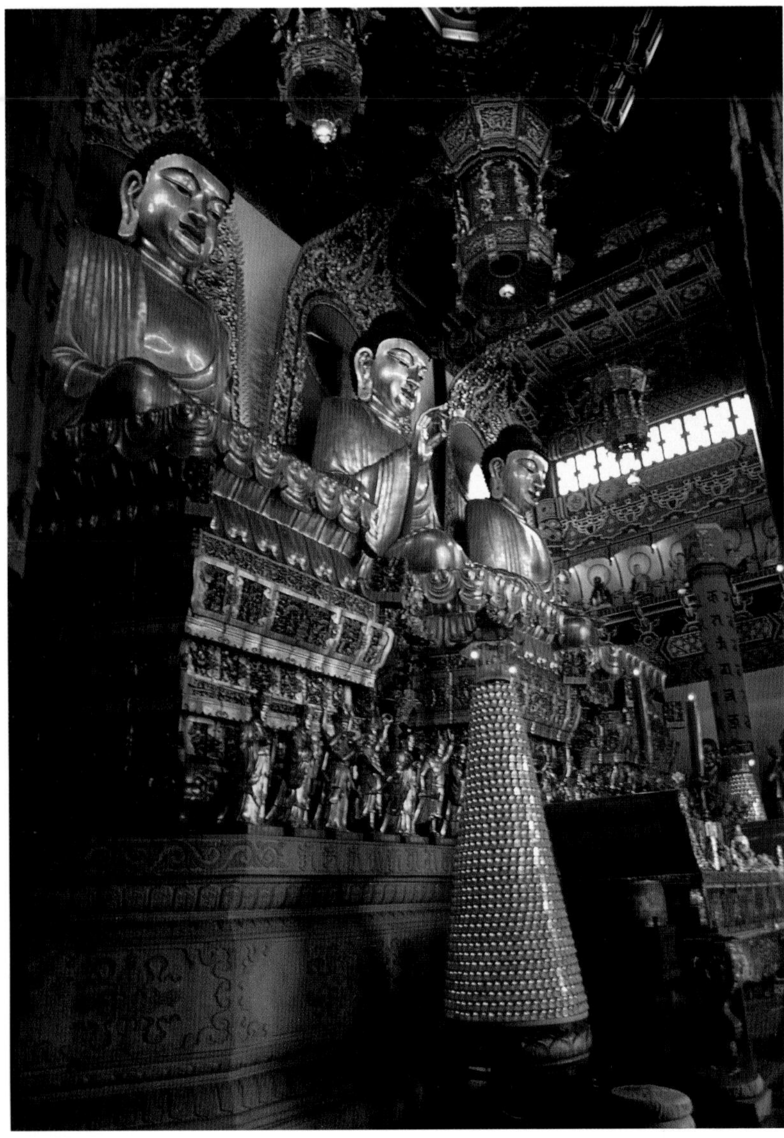

Chinese gardens

■ Chinese gardens are works of art which mirror the Taoist principle of harmony with nature. Imperial parks apart, wealth could not buy the large country estates that it did in Europe, so the Chinese garden was a city retreat for the cultivated scholar-official whose yearnings for rural tranquillity were sublimated in the gentle art of garden-scaping.....■

Balance The most famous Chinese gardens are the miniature gardens of southern China, where ponds become lakes, rockeries mountains and where bridges and pavilions provide the human element. But not all gardens need be small – to the Chinese the Summer Palace in Beijing is a garden where the pond really is a lake, the pavilions are palaces and the rockeries are dwarfed by hills, the natural world in microcosm, an expression both of the wealth and majesty of the emperor and the variety of the world at large.

Top: Taihu rock in the Forbidden City Below: the zigzag pathway in the Master of the Fishing Nets Garden, Suzhou, illustrates the concept of never revealing the whole garden at once

Harmony In a Chinese garden all the emotions experienced in the natural landscape should be aroused. Lofty mountain peaks are evoked by rocks and stones piled up together; ponds reflect clouds and shadows, mirroring the sky; sunlight gives way to shade, paths lead from high to low, all physical expressions of the Taoist precepts of balance and harmony, the co-existence of the natural and the man-made. There are halls for entertaining friends, rooms to sit and muse in, libraries for reading and writing. Bamboo, pine and plum-blossom, pots of flowers, scented shrubs, and intricately cut gateways giving tantalising glimpses of what is to come complete the tranquil scene. The cultivation of his garden was an accomplishment for the cultured scholar-official equal to painting and poetry-writing. It was a place for recreation, contemplation and philosophising, to be enjoyed in all weathers.

Nature and man
Although the Chinese garden intends to imitate, if miniaturise, nature, the hand of man is considered an integral part of a garden landscape. Calligraphy is frequently inscribed on rocks or over doorways; and the fanciful names which are given to pavilions are usually taken from literary sources and supposed to enhance enjoyment of the garden.

SOUTH CHINA

SICHUAN
HUBEI
Han Shui
Suizhou
Anlu
Dabie Shan
Macheng
Tongche
Lu'a
Daxian
Yunyang
Fengjie
Wushan
Wanxian
Badong
Jingmen
Tianmen
WUHAN
Taihu
Chang Jiang (Yangtze)
Yichang
Jiangling
Ezhou
Huangshi
Enshi
Shashi
Hong Hu
Xiantao
Wuxue
Huko
Jiujiang
Guling
Poyang Hu
Lushan
Qianjiang
Jinshi
Shishou
Datong Hu
Puqi
Yueyang
Mufu Shan
Dayong
Changde
Boyan
Daozhen
Wuling Shan
Dongting Hu
Jiuling Shan
Nanchan
Yuan Jiang
Yiyang
Jishou
Changsha
Gan Jiang
2942m
Shaoshan
Xiangtan
Yichun
Linchuan
Wu Jiang
Tongren
HUNAN
Zhuzhou
Huaihua
Lengshuijiang
Loudi
Liling
Pingxiang
Nancheng
Shaoyang
Ji'an
Zhenyuan
Xiang Jiang
Hongjiang
Hengyang
Guangchang
GUIZHOU
Kaili
Jingxian
Xiang
Leiyang
JIANGXI
Duyun
Dong'an
Yongzhou
Suichuan
Wu
Miao Ling
Ruijin
Rongjiang
2142m
Quanzhou
Ganzhou
Dushan
Chenzhou
Daoxian
Dayu
2081m
Guilin
Nan Ling
Lechang
Rongshui
Shaoguan
Longnan
Jianghua
Lianxian
Hechi
Yangshuo
Pingle
Lianping
Meizhou
Liuzhou
Li Jiang
GUANGXI ZHUANGZU ZIZHIQU
GUANGDONG
Bei Jiang
Huaji
Heshan
Qingyuan
Conghua
Heyuan
Pingnan
Wuzhou
Lianhua
Binyang
GUANGZHOU (CANTON)
Zhaoqing
Lufeng
Guigang
Nanning
Xi Jiang
Foshan
Huizhou
Rongxian
Yulin
Luoding
Jiangmen
Shenzhen
Zhongshan
Yunkai Dashan
Yunwu Shan
Kaiping
Qinzhou
Macao (Port)
HONG KONG (UK)
Yangjiang
VN
Maoming
Beihai
Zhanjiang
Leizhou
Haikang
Beibu Wan
Bandao
Xuwen
Qiongzhou Haixia
Nan Hai
Haikou
Wenchang
HAINAN
Hainan Dao
Changjiang
Qiongzhong
Dongfang
1867m Wuzhi Shan
Xinglong
Tongshi
Sanya
Xincun
Luhuitou

5
4
3
2
1

A
B
C

Wuxi
Suzhou
SHANGHAI
Chao Hu
Wuhu
(Yangtze)
Tai Hu
SHANGHAI SHI
ANHUI
Huzhou
Jiaxing
Hangzhou Wan
Tongling
Jiang
Jiuhuashan
Zhoushan
Anqing
Hangzhou
Putuoshan
Huangshan
Lin'an
Shaoxing
Ningbo
Shexian
ZHEJIANG
Xikou (Qikou)
Huangshan
Xin'anjiang Sk
Tiantaishan
Lanxi
Jingdezhen
Jinhua
Linhai
Quzhou
Jiaojiang
Lishui
Shangrao
Shan
Wenzhou
Yingtan
2158m
Pucheng
Yandang
Pingyang
Wuyishan
Fuding
Shan
Shaowu
Zhenghe
Jian'ou
Dong Hai
Jiangle
Nanping
Ningde
Min Jiang
Fuzhou
Sanming
Yongquan Temple
Yong'an
FUJIAN
Putian
Zhangping
Haixia
Quanzhou
Longyan
Zhangzhou
Xiamen
Shan
Zhangpu
RC
Taiwan
Chaozhou
Raoping
Shantou
Dongsha Qundao
RP
0 100 200 300 400 km
D
E

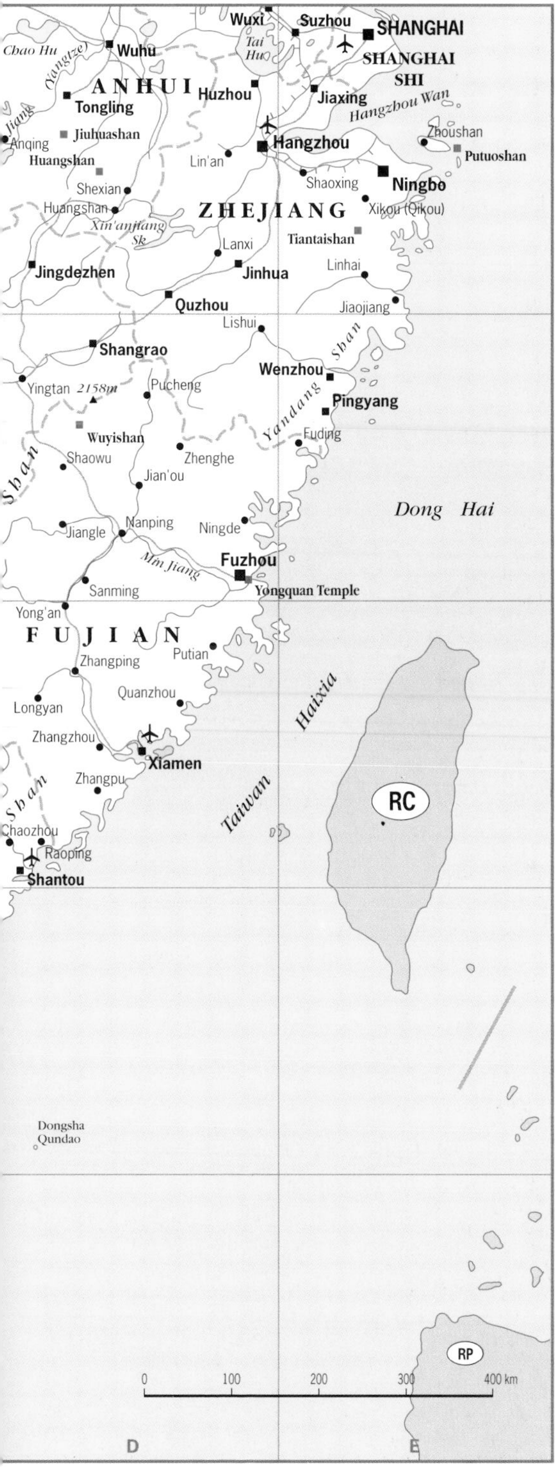

SOUTH CHINA

Big wind
Typhoons (from the Chinese 'da feng', or 'big wind') strike China more frequently than any other country, at a rate of about seven a year. By Chinese standards a gale of force 8–11 is regarded as a typhoon. Generally speaking, they arrive between July and September and can, though rarely, penetrate as far as 400km inland and last several days. On the whole, however, they fizzle out after a few hours.

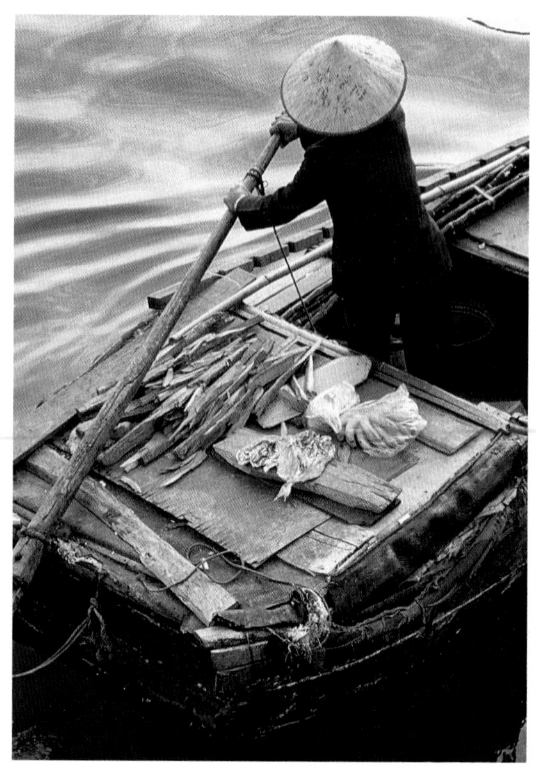

A slow boat in southern China

Chinese 'horoscope'
The 'horoscope' is represented by 12 animals, with one animal governing each year in a 12-year cycle.
Each animal represents one of the Twelve Earthly Branches in Chinese astrology.
Traditionally the Chinese remember each other's ages by the animal sign to which the person belongs ('she was born in the year of the dragon'), calculating their date of birth from there. The 12 animals are: rat, ox, tiger, rabbit, dragon, snake, horse, sheep, monkey, rooster, dog, pig. 1995 is the year of the pig.

South China Broadly speaking, south China is the area south of the Yangtze excluding southwest China as well as a number of towns and cities already included in the Yangtze region, for demographic, historical or geopolitical reasons. What is left is a relatively homogeneous area quite different from the north. The provinces included are Hunan, Guangdong, Hainan Island, Fujian, parts of Jiangxi and Zhejiang, as well as Hong Kong and Macao.

Two thousand years ago the south was populated by indigenous tribes which were only incorporated into a larger China when the first Qin emperor unified the country in 221BC. Even then the area remained marginal – Chinese settlements were sparse and uprisings frequent. It was only in the 12th century, as the threat from northern tribes became more urgent, that the Chinese headed south in greater numbers, massacring the native tribes, or driving them into mountain strongholds or forcing them still further south on to Hainan Island or into Indo-China. The merchant classes, formerly despised, began to prosper in the bountiful south, so that the entrepreneurial spirit, often associated with the Chinese, became very much a southern characteristic. By the early 13th century, with the Southern Song capital at Hangzhou, the focus of Chinese life had shifted south, albeit temporarily since under the Mongols the north was preferred once again, and the following Ming dynasty established its capital at Beijing. The south, therefore, although quite obviously part of China proper, has maintained a separateness which is still evident today.

The major visual differences between south and north are colour and topography. The north is brown and yellow, the colours of earth, sand, dust and silt, the landscape is generally flat and any hills or mountains dry and arid. The south is green, with a wet, steaming climate. Its rolling hills are layered with terraces. Like the north, the south has severely hot summers, with July averages between 25°C and 29°C. Winters are mild with frost a rarity in many areas and in some parts unknown. Rainfall is between 100 and 250cm per year and although summer is the wettest season rain is spread more evenly throughout the year than in the north. Along the coast the summer is also the season of typhoons. The south's most important crop is rice, except in the mountainous province of Fujian where fishing and forestry traditionally take priority. As in the north, the pig is the main meat source and fish are also widely eaten; the water-buffalo, not seen in the north, is used as a draught animal everywhere. Architecture differs too – courtyards are less popular and two-storey houses are more common, often with the upturned eaves and roof decoration which typify traditional Chinese architecture.

Most important are the cultural dissimilarities between north and south. Although the dialects of the more northerly parts of the region are based on Mandarin, and although Chinese characters are universal, the dialects of the south are compounded of many distinctive words, a plethora of tones and implosive consonants. Finally, unlike the insular north, the indented coastlines of Fujian and Guangdong, with their excellent natural harbours, have a tradition of foreign trade which dates back to the arrival of Arab merchants during the Tang dynasty.

Commerce is the lifeblood of the south

Sanya Harbour, Hainan Island: China's 'Water People' have lived on boats for generations

Young Mao
It is difficult to reconcile the Mao of later years with the young man in Shaoshan who threatened to commit suicide when faced with an arranged marriage or the student who failed his art examination by drawing a circle and calling it an egg. However, while a student in Changsha in 1917 he became 'student of the year', simultaneously organising student societies, an experience to stand him in good stead in later life.

►► Canton

See Guangzhou, page 206.

► Changsha *200B4*

The capital of Hunan province, Changsha is a city of little charm, of interest only for its provincial museum and its relative proximity to Mao Zedong's birthplace 100km away at Shaoshan (see page 224). The excellent **museum►►** has a fine collection of neolithic pottery and bronzes from the Shang and Zhou dynasties. But its most famous attraction is the mummified body of the wife of the Marquis of Dai, prime minister to the king of Changsha in 193BC, remarkably well-preserved when unearthed, her skin still supple. For students of the Chinese revolution, there are several links with Mao – for example the **Hunan No.1 Teacher Training College**.

► Foshan *200B2*

Foshan, famous for its Shiwan ceramic ware since the Han dynasty, is 25km from Canton. The **ceramic factory** may be visited by arrangement. In the south of the town is the **Zumiao (Ancestral Temple)►►** founded in the Northern Song dynasty, a Taoist temple devoted to the worship of the demon-slaying Emperor of the North, with complex wooden carving and ceramic roof decoration.

► Fuzhou *201D4*

Fuzhou's importance as a trading port goes back to the Tang dynasty, although its heyday was from the 10th century onwards. Its cosmopolitan nature attracted foreign

Fuzhou: the bustle of Chinese street life

Old habits
Lin Zexu's efforts to deal with the opium trade in the 1830s by confiscating smokers' equipment, forcing addicts to enlist for cures and severely punishing dealers, have parallels in the 1990s. Liberalisation of the economy has resulted in increased drug trafficking, and a government crack-down on those involved. Pushers are shot and suspected addicts sent on compulsory three-month rehabilitation courses.

Lantern maker, Fuzhou

settlers, and it became known as a centre for Nestorian Christianity. Under the Treaty of Nanjing in 1842 it was one of the first cities opened to Western residents. Marco Polo described Fuzhou as 'a veritable marvel' and reminders of its trading past still remain here and there.

Fuzhou sits astride the scenic Min river. Its centre is the streets of Wuyi Lu, Gutian Lu, and Dong Dalu, which is the main shopping street.

The **Fujian Provincial Museum▶▶** is in Xihu Park, site of an artificial lake dug in AD282 for irrigation purposes. The museum includes ceramic figures from a tomb dating to the 10th century, a full-size boat coffin 3,500 years old, a collection of Nestorian crosses and examples of the locally produced Song dynasty black ceramics.

The most noteworthy of Fuzhou's temples is the **White Pagoda▶** on Yushan, first constructed in AD904, although its brick exterior dates from 1548. Nearby is the **Dashi Hall**, once a shrine where city officials prayed for good fortune and now the **city museum▶▶**. The main exhibit is a Song dynasty tomb, with its male and female occupants on view in a tank of formaldehyde.

West of Dashi Hall is the **Black Pagoda**, a little way off Bayiqi Beilu. Built in AD799, it bears some fine carvings.

Other sights include the **Lin Zexu Memorial Hall,** on Xiamen Lu, devoted to the memory of a minister who protested, vainly, to Queen Victoria about the opium trade. The former **Foreign Concession area▶▶** is on the south bank in the Nantai area across the ancient stone bridge. Half way up Gushan, a 1,060m mountain 8km from Fuzhou, **Yongquan Temple▶** has two ceramic pagodas.

The delicate art of Foshan paper cutting

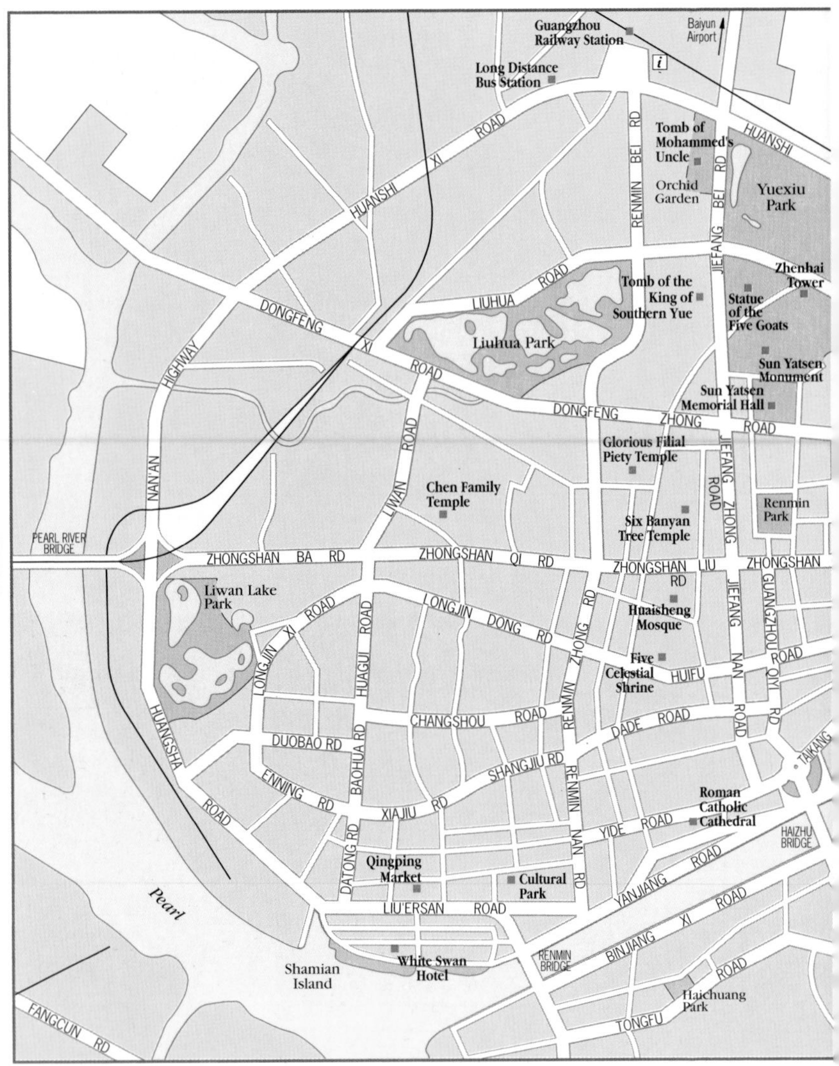

206

Canton or Guangzhou
The origin of the name given to Guangzhou (the Mandarin Chinese name for the city) by foreigners from the 17th century is unclear. It may derive from the English meaning of 'cantonment' as a lodging assigned to troops. A more likely explanation is that it is a corruption of Guangdong, which is the name of the province, not the city.

►► Guangzhou (Canton) 200B2

Guangzhou, or Canton, the capital of Guangdong province, is a major city and port, situated on China's fifth river, the Pearl. It is also the city most used to dealing with Europeans, for they have been trading here for over 400 years. Colonised by the Qin in 221BC, it was only during the Tang dynasty that firm Chinese control was established, and Canton became a major port, attracting foreign traders from as far afield as the Middle East and Central Asia. The Portuguese were the first Europeans to trade here from 1516, followed by the Dutch and the British.

Perversely, Canton is a city that does not receive its fair share of appreciation from contemporary foreign visitors, since for many it is merely a transit stop. As a Special Economic Zone, fuelled by foreign and Chinese investment it is vibrant and lively and has displaced Shanghai as

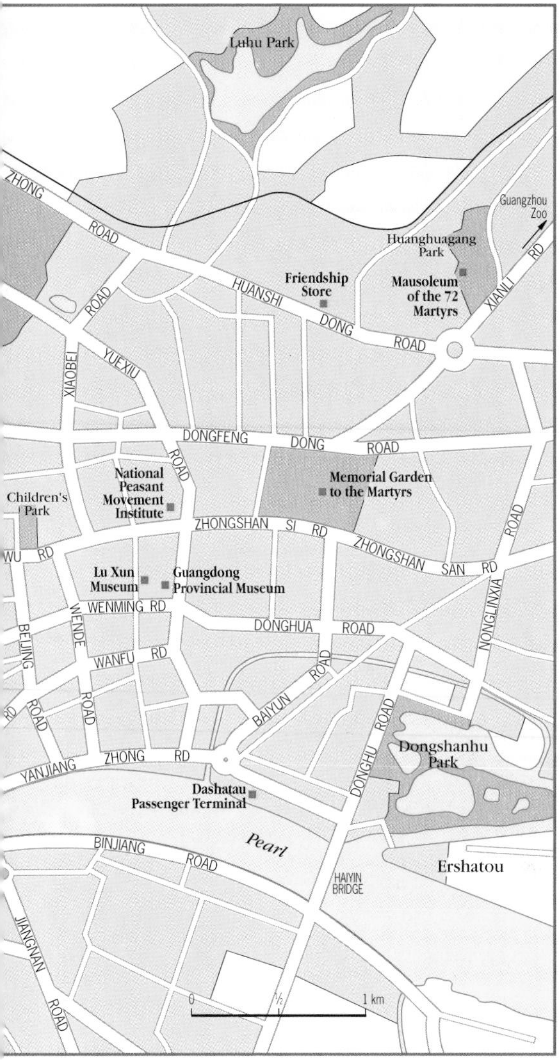

Southern appetite
Although Cantonese cooking is admired throughout China, the northern Chinese are rather contemptuous of the Cantonese people, perhaps a legacy of the Confucianist disdain for trade. The attitude is neatly summed up by a Chinese saying: 'The Cantonese will eat anything that flies except an aeroplane and anything with four legs except a table.'

Snake, it is said, warms you in winter. Try some at Jianglan Lu Snake Restaurant, in Canton

the focus of fashionable living. It is famous for its cooking, and restaurants and shops spill out on to its old colonnaded streets, shaded beneath banyan trees with their distinctive hanging, stringy roots. Furthermore, there are several things to see of interest.

Canton's centre is the area along the riverfront (Yanjiang Road) and the main shopping streets behind – Jiefang, Zhongshan, and Beijing. Also on the waterfront, behind the unmistakable White Swan Hotel, is the former foreign enclave of **Shamian Island▶▶**. Before its acquisition by the British as a concession area following the Second Opium War, foreign traders had been restricted to the city shoreline, their families compelled to live in Macao. Shamian, which was shared between the French and the British, remains a small village, with mouldering European buildings in grandiose colonial style formerly housing the

Colonial architecture on Canton's Shamian Island

Fair Canton
Although present-day China is comparatively open, from the early 1960s, and particularly during the Cultural Revolution when China's borders were effectively sealed, the Canton Trade Fair was the only conduit available to Western traders, journalists and intelligence agencies through which it was possible to glean some idea of what was going on in the country.

French and British consulates, banks, and Protestant and Catholic churches. Walk across the island directly from the White Swan, cross the bridge to Liu'ersan Road, turn right, and you will see on your left the narrow entrance to **Qingping Market▶▶▶**, one of the most fascinating in China. It sells everything imaginable in the way of food-stuffs, spices and live animals. Considering the Cantonese reputation as omnivores, this market may not be for the squeamish but here is the purest Canton, quintessential southern China.

The **Pearl river▶▶** is the city's pulse. To enjoy a simple and brief encounter with it take a ferry to the other shore; or take a cruise on one of the pleasure-boats which sometimes leave from near the Renmin Bridge. During the summer, night cruises sometimes operate.

Sun Yatsen, born in Zhongshan county, was a Cantonese and his **Memorial Hall▶**, on Dongfeng Road, is in the form of an octagonal theatre, built in a garden that was the site of the residence of the Qing governors of Guangdong and Guangxi.

Parks and gardens are one of the charms of Canton. If you are fortunate enough to be here in February, before the humid season, visit the **Orchid Garden (Lanpu)▶▶** (built on the site of the Muslim burial-ground) when the orchids are in flower. A haven of tranquillity with its bamboo-groves, pools and pavilions, it can be enjoyed at any time. Just behind the garden is the tomb of Mohammed's uncle (Muhanmode Mu), who is supposed to have founded the Huaisheng Mosque on Guangta Road.

To see something of the south bank, go to **Haichuang Park▶**, with its remains of the Ocean Banner Monastery. Canton's largest park is the Yuexiu which includes the **Zhenhai Tower▶**, built in 1380, the only part of the city wall to remain and now housing the city museum. Nearby to the south is the **Sun Yatsen Monument**, with his bequest to the nation engraved on its side; and to the west the **Statue of the Five Goats**, the city's symbol. The **Cultural Park (Wenhua Gongyuan)▶** on Liu'ersan Road was constructed in 1956 and built with mass entertainment in mind. Here you can watch rollerskating, carousels, open-air theatre, opera performances and so on. Another attractive park with revolutionary connotations is the **Memorial Garden to the Martyrs (Lieshi Lingyuan)▶** on Zhongshan Road, commemorating a massacre of Communists by the Guomindang in 1927.

Canton also has its fair share of temples. The most interesting exemplifying local architectural styles is the **Chen Family Temple (Chenjiaci)▶▶**, which now houses an exhibition of the best of local craftwork. Built in 1890–4 with monies collected among the Chen clan, it has a long front hall behind which extend several further halls, separated by courtyards. The façade and roof of the entrance-hall are crowded with figures of deities and with colourful and fanciful interpretations of operatic tales. The **Six Banyan Tree Temple (Liurongsi)▶▶** is a working temple on Liurong Road, founded as a home for the Buddha's ashes in AD537. Its name was conferred on it by the Song dynasty poet Su Dongpo, enchanted by the banyan trees (no longer there) in the courtyard. There are panoramic views from the pagoda, parts of which date to the 11th century, whilst in the Hall of the Sixth Patriarch (of the Chan Buddhist sect) is an AD989 bronze figure of the patriarch. **Glorious Filial Piety Temple (Guangxiaosi)▶**, on Guangxiao Road, was founded in the 4th century AD, though most of the buildings date from 1832. It boasts a handsome main hall and a pair of ancient pagodas, one reputed to be built over a hair of the Sixth Patriarch.

The **Roman Catholic Cathedral (Shishi Jiaotang, or 'stone house')▶**, on Yide Road, is a reminder of the 19th-century European presence in Canton. Begun in 1860 by a French architect, it is built of granite on the site of the office of the Chinese governor of Guangdong which was destroyed by the French and British during the Opium War. Its four bronze bells were cast in France.

One of Canton's unacknowledged highlights is the **Tomb of the King of Southern Yue (Nanyuewang Hanwu)▶▶▶**. Before unification under the first Qin Emperor in 221BC, southern China was a loose confederation of the 'Hundred Yue' nationalities known as Lingnan. After the fall of the Qin empire, a breakaway general established the independent kingdom of Yue with its capital in Canton – it lasted until 111BC, spawning five kings before the Han re-established dynastic control over southern China. This is the tomb of the second king, Chao Mei.

You can see the seven-chamber tomb itself but the chief attractions are the tomb's burial goods, including swords, jade ornaments, *pi*-discs, gold seals, musical instruments, cooking utensils, bronze mirrors and silver boxes.

Canton's Qingping market – freshness is everything

Goat City
The symbol of Canton, a herd of five goats, is based on the myth of the city's foundation, a myth which itself aptly reflects the fertility of the surrounding countryside. The legend relates that five celestial beings arrived in the area riding five goats. The goats were bearing bundles of rice, symbols of a promise that the region would never suffer famine.

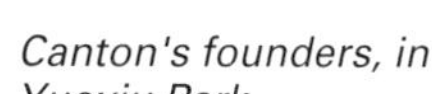

Canton's founders, in Yuexiu Park

▶▶ Hainan Island *200A1*

A large tropical island off the south coast, Hainan has several minority tribes, beautiful scenery, and wonderful beaches, but has traditionally been regarded by the Chinese as a pit of disease, poverty and barbarism. Since 1978 Hainan has been an important military centre but now there are plans to cash in on its potential for tourism.

Hainan was made a province in 1988. The capital, **Haikou▶**, although run-down, has a bustling atmosphere which compensates for its lack of cultural attractions. The liveliest street is Jiefang Lu, criss-crossed by alleys and lanes. Xinhua Nanlu is lined with buildings in Portuguese colonial style. Outside the town you may visit the **Tomb of Hai Rui▶**, a Qing official, or the **Five Officials Memorial Temple**, whilst the best beach is **Shuiying.** Also noted for its beaches (and coconut groves) is **Wenchang**, about 70km from Haikou.

However, the finest beaches are on the south coast, where the main town is the busy port of **Sanya▶▶**. East of Sanya is the resort of Luhuitou and nearby is the lovely **Dadonghai Beach**.

There are good bus services along Hainan's two principal roads – around the coast, and across the mountainous centre via Tongshi, the capital of the Li and Miao autonomous prefecture. The hill villages here are home to the Li and Miao minority peoples who still follow a traditional way of life although this is increasingly under threat from the rapid changes now engulfing Hainan. Further north is **Qiongzhong▶▶** with a lively market and nearby 300m waterfall.

Xincun, on the southeast coast, populated by Danjia people, is the centre for the pearl industry and starting-point for **Monkey Island▶**, a reserve for Guangxi monkeys. **Xinglong** is famous for its fruit and hot springs.

The edge of the world
Just as Jiayuguan was 'The Last Barrier under Heaven' and Shanhaiguan the 'First Pass under Heaven', so Sanya was known as 'Heaven's Limit'. Mountains in the centre of Hainan Island rise to 1,800m, and the subtropical climate allows coconuts, palm oil, rubber and pepper to be produced.

China's tropical island – Hainan

▶▶▶ Hong Kong *200C2*

A few years ago the contrast between Hong Kong and the People's Republic of China was remarkable. The differences are now no longer so marked, not because Hong Kong has become more like China but because parts of China are becoming more like Hong Kong in the run-up to the hand-over of sovereignty in 1997 (see pages 214–15).

There is almost nothing old in Hong Kong. Its pull is its frantic, relentless modernity. Its nature is perfectly illustrated by the fate of the old Repulse Bay Hotel. A rather charming colonial-style building in white, with upstairs veranda open to the sea, it was demolished only to be replaced by an exact replica a couple of years later.

For all that, Hong Kong is a powerful magnet which continues to exert a fascination. Although the island is now linked to the mainland by a modern metro system (MTR), it is worth crossing by the old-fashioned **Star Ferry▶▶▶** to or from Kowloon at least once in order to take in the magnificent skyline of gleaming skyscrapers.

Originally the name Hong Kong ('Fragrant Harbour') referred only to the main island but it now usually covers Kowloon, the New Territories and the Outlying Islands as well. The busiest areas are Hong Kong Island and Kowloon. Standard tours of the island can easily be obtained through the hotels and will include the main sights: **Aberdeen▶▶**, a harbour area crowded with junks and sampans; **Stanley▶▶**, with its market specialising in factory outlet clothes, and the less well-known **Tin Hau Temple**, the oldest on the island, founded by the pirate Chang Po Chai in about 1770; and **Victoria Peak▶▶▶**, the island's highest point, with spectacular views on a clear day, which can be reached either by road or by the old funicular railway.

Hong Kong is home to over five million people

Eccentric view
In 1847 Robert Fortune wrote a book entitled *Three Years Wandering in the Northern Provinces of China*, a journey which also enabled him to form an opinion of Hong Kong. In view of its subsequent history, his verdict is ironic: 'Viewed as a place of trade, I fear Hong Kong will be a failure.'

Suzie Wong
Hong Kong is invariably associated with Suzie Wong, the entrancing prostitute made famous in Richard Mason's book, *The World of Suzie Wong*. Her world no longer really exists for many of the bars of Wanchai have closed and those that remain deal mostly in overpriced drinks.

Money matters – the new Bank of China building

If you are in front of the Excelsior Hotel in Causeway Bay, one of the main shopping areas, at midday, you will still see and hear the firing of the noonday gun which was immortalised in the Noel Coward song 'Mad Dogs and Englishmen'. Going west by tram from here along the north coast of the island will take you through **Wanchai**, the shabby red-light district, to **Central**, the main area of banks, multinational companies and designer shops. Hidden among the skyscrapers are smaller more intimate streets – those off De Voeux Road and Li Yuen, Wing On and Wing Sing streets – filled with market stalls and local shops. On Hollywood Road is the **Man Mo Taoist Temple▶▶**, one of the oldest in Hong Kong.

There are several museums – the **Flagstaff House Museum▶▶▶** on Cotton Tree Drive, in one of the few remaining buildings of distinction, built in 1844, houses a fascinating collection of tea-ware whilst the **Fung Ping Shan▶▶** at the University has a fine collection of Chinese art, ceramics and bronzes. The **City Hall** also has an art museum, and occasional exhibitions.

The **Botanical Gardens▶**, on Garden Road, are a haven of quiet from the hurly-burly. Nearby is another lonely ghost from the past, **Government House**, the residence of the Hong Kong Governor.

The **Tsimshatsui area▶▶** of Kowloon, served by the Star Ferry, is a mecca for those wanting jewellery and electronic goods. Nowadays bargains have to be fought for since Hong Kong is no longer as cheap as it once was.

The story of China tea
Tea is thought to have been first used in the Chinese southwest. It was known during the Han dynasty but became popular only during the Tang dynasty, when the creation of the perfect pot of tea became almost an art form. Rituals developed and tea drinking became a ceremony in itself. While the ceremonial aspect has all but disappeared today, tea-houses remain full. Drivers keep their tin mugs or glass jars on the dashboard all day, half-filled with leaves. Brewed in the cup like this, the second infusion is considered the best, but the leaves can be used again and again.

Ocean Terminal is filled with an extraordinary array of shops but prices are not usually negotiable – for that you need to patronise the shops along and off Nathan Road. One of the most famous landmarks of Kowloon is the Peninsula Hotel, now sadly hidden from the water by newer constructions but still expensively elegant.

North of Tsimshatsui is **Yaumatei** with the rather doubtful jade market on Kansu Street and Temple Street night market. The **Lei Cheung Uk Museum▶** is a Han tomb found in 1954. Going further north still will take you into the rural New Territories bordering China, an area of paddy-fields, hills and little walled villages which originally belonged to single clans. The **Song Dynasty Village**, on the other hand, is a piece of Chinese hokum, but entertaining for all that.

Ferries from piers in Central will take you to the major of the 250 or so Outlying Islands, where life generally is very much quieter than elsewhere. This will eventually change, at least on the largest, **Lantau▶▶**, scheduled as the site of the new airport. Lantau is twice the size of Hong Kong Island and has two small towns (Tai O and Silvermine Bay) and an excellent beach at Cheung Sha. Lantau Peak rises to almost 1,000m, there are scenic walks, and it is possible to find simple accommodation at either the Buddhist or Trappist Monastery.

The other islands of note are **Cheung Chau▶▶** and **Lamma▶▶** which have pleasant beaches, tranquil paths and good, less expensive, seafood restaurants.

Stroll
Although most of old Hong Kong has been destroyed, there are a couple of areas to stroll in which provide relief from the chromium-plated present – along and around Hollywood Road, for example, or Caine Road and Robinson Road, or the streets off Queens Road East. Another interesting place is the Yaumatei Typhoon Shelter in the New Territories, home to many Tanka and Hokla boat people.

Skyscrapers notwithstanding, Hong Kong still exudes a certain exoticism

Two systems, one China

■ **Since the 1970s, when the issue of Hong Kong's sovereignty arose as China re-emerged from the Cultural Revolution, its future, and by extension the future of Macao and Taiwan, has been of prime concern.....** ■

Unrest in Hong Kong
Considering the controversy engendered by the expiry of Britain's lease in 1997, there has been remarkably little civil unrest in Hong Kong. In 1956 there were riots when communist supporters confronted the Guomindang. In 1966, the year the Cultural Revolution began, mobs rioted in protest at a small rise in the first-class fare of the Star Ferry; and in 1967, a series of labour disputes culminated in a siege of the Governor's residence by workers wielding Mao's *Little Red Book.*

Top: Shenzhen, just across the border
Below: Government House, symbolically dwarfed by change

Democracy Hong Kong, Britain's last significant colony and one of the world's foremost centres of capitalism, is an historical anomaly, a residual European colony on Chinese soil. It was ceded to the British 'in perpetuity' under the Treaty of Nanjing in 1842; in 1860 Britain acquired the Kowloon peninsula and then, in 1898, the New Territories on a 99-year lease. In 1984 Britain agreed to transfer full sovereignty of the islands and New Territories to China in 1997 subject to Chinese assurances that Hong Kong's economic freedom and capitalist lifestyle would be preserved for at least 50 years – the 'two systems, one China' agreement. Under this agreement, Hong Kong would become a special administrative region within China, with its own laws, budget and tax system, and would retain its free port status and authority to negotiate international trade agreements. Despite this, the West is concerned that, once the lease has expired, the 5 million citizens of Hong Kong will be unable to withstand undemocratic decisions from Beijing that will be deleterious to Hong Kong's financial standing.

Negotiations between the governments of China and Britain have been long and difficult, and are not yet resolved. Some of the problems are of Britain's own making. Proper representative democracy has never

been accorded to the average Hong Kong citizen, although in 1984 Britain introduced indirect elections to select a proportion of the new legislative council, and direct elections for seats on local councils in 1985. Efforts are being made to improve this situation further but these, predictably, meet with considerable opposition from the Chinese who regard Hong Kong as part of China.

The future All things considered, most people in Hong Kong seem to be convinced that the economic revolution is here to stay and that any attempts to turn back the clock would meet with fierce resistance. At the very least, therefore, Hong Kong's way of life, the quality of which seems to be judged largely according to wealth, will remain intact. As the Chinese prosper, it seems likely that they will eventually demand some form of democracy and Beijing will be forced to grant it. A glimpse into southern China, in particular, where Special Economic Zones such as Shenzhen are almost indistinguishable from Hong Kong, proves that in practice the fundamental contradiction between communism and capitalism can be reconciled. As long as the economy continues to grow there will be little talk of political revisionism since too many people, including high-level government cadres, stand to lose too much. Hong Kong may well continue much as it has done in the past, but with the difference that those residents leading privileged lives will include both the expatriates of America, Western Europe and Australasia, and also the 'professional' classes from Beijing.

Taiwan and Macao China's relationship with Taiwan is gradually thawing. Until recently contact was rare but there is talk of direct flights between the two Chinas and they will inevitably draw closer in many other ways. Under the 'Macao Pact' of 1987, Portugal agreed to hand over sovereignty of Macao to the People's Republic in December 1999 under similar terms to the 'two systems, one China' agreement between Britain and China. It will not be too long before the idea of Two Systems, One China is superseded by One System, One China.

Cultivation in the New Territories, where space is still plentiful

Poisoned bread
In 1857, the baker who provided bread to the British, Cheong Ah Lum, thought he could wipe them out by putting arsenic in the loaves. The attempt failed because his mixture was too strong and the victims vomited the bread up before digesting the poison.

Traffic left to right in 1997

Peak-top villas
Twenty-one of the finest villas on Lushan are currently being restored by the American architect Piero Patri. Controversially, they will then be sold to private investors, mostly Chinese businessmen who left China at the time of the revolution and made their fortunes abroad. However, the leases are good for only 50 years, after which the villas revert to the state.

▶ Jingdezhen *201D5*

This small town in Jiangxi has been famous since the Han dynasty for its porcelain owing to the excellence of the local clay. The imperial kilns were established here from the Ming dynasty, producing ceramics for the court and the blue-and-white ware exported to Asia and Europe from the 16th century onwards. The town's prosperity is still based on porcelain production – there are kilns everywhere which may be visited by arrangement. The **Ceramic Exhibition Hall (Taociguan)▶** on Lianshe Beilu has a good display. Also interesting is the river area at the west end of Juishan Donglu, the town centre around Juishan Donglu, Zhonghua Beilu and Zhongshan Beilu, and the **Ceramic Research Institute▶** in a Ming house west of the river. All around the town are artificial hills created by the waste from ancient kilns.

▶▶ Lushan *200C5*

Lushan is a beautiful 1,500m peak in Jiangxi topped by the hill-town of Guling, and much favoured by foreign residents during the 19th century, and later by Chiang Kaishek, Mao Zedong, and Harry Truman, as a refuge from the heat. Amid fine mountain scenery, peace and quiet there is little in particular to see but plenty to enjoy if you walk around the town and then out to Lulin Lake via the Three Ancient Trees, Dragon Head Cliff and Fairy Cave. At the lake is a museum commemorating the Politburo meeting here in 1970 when Lin Biao, later to die in mysterious circumstances, clashed with Mao.

Lushan, an 'oriental Switzerland' in the middle of China

►► Macao *200C2*

The oldest colony in Asia, Macao was first established as a missionary trading post in 1537, and was leased to Portugal in 1557. It is due to revert to China in 1999. About 65km from Hong Kong, Macao comprises the tip of a peninsula and the offshore islands of Taipa and Coloane (which has fine beaches). Most of the population is Chinese with a sprinkling of Portuguese and Macanese, an intermarried group with their own dialect. As Portuguese influence waned so did Macao's importance, but it still possesses considerable old-world charm. It is worth a day trip by jetfoil from Hong Kong to spend a few hours wandering its cobbled streets lined with a colourful blend of European and Chinese architecture (for example the Largo do Senado and the Rua Central) and sampling the excellent Sino-Portuguese restaurants; or to bet in the casinos (a proscribed activity in Hong Kong) or to relax in the colonial-style Hotel Bela Vista. It is also possible to enter China from here.

Macao's most famous landmark is the baroque façade of **Sao Paolo►►**, built by Japanese Jesuits in 1635 to a design by the Italian, Carlo Spinola. Fire finally destroyed the wooden church in 1835, although many of its fine polychrome wooden figures are now in the Sao Jose Church. Southeast of the façade is the 17th-century **Monte Fortress►**.

The impressive Ming dynasty **A-ma Temple►►**, near the peninsula's southern tip, is dedicated to Guanyin, Goddess of Mercy, who has given her name to Macao. Her colourful feast day takes place on the 23rd day of the third lunar month.

On Estrada Adolfo Loureiro is the 19th-century classical Lou Lim Yeoc garden but perhaps more interesting are the **Camoes Gardens►**, where the great 16th-century Portuguese poet Luis Vaz de Camoes came to relax, and the site of the Casa Villa, a lovely colonial building housing the **museum►►** which has some fine Ming bronzes and Chinese furniture. Nearby is the Protestant cemetery where the painter George Chinnery is buried.

Above: cobbles add to the old-world flavour of a backstreet in Macao

Below: ornate Jingdezhen ware

A Far Eastern painter
George Chinnery was born in London in 1774. After working as a painter in India, he arrived in Macao in 1825 claiming that he was escaping his wife, 'the ugliest woman I ever saw'. His 27 years in Macao were devoted to painting the portraits of eminent persons, although he has also left many pictures of 19th-century life in the Far East.

■ Ceramics have a long history in China. During the neolithic period there were two principal types – a red earthenware, often decorated with black animal and geometric designs, from the Yangshao culture (as seen at Banpo in Xi'an), and black ware from the Longshan culture.....■

A taste for porcelain
As foreign powers started to take an interest in China from the 16th century, so their desire increased for Chinese ceramics. It is recorded that at least 16 million Chinese porcelain dishes were exported by the Dutch East Indies Company between 1602 and 1682.

There is nothing more Chinese than porcelain or 'china'. Top and below: the celebrated Shiwan porcelain from Foshan

Discoveries During the Bronze Age Chinese potters discovered that stoneware clays, when fired to high temperatures, fused to form a waterproof surface much tougher than that of earthenware. In the Han period green lead glazes began to appear on earthenware ceramics used as funerary ornaments.

Decorative porcelain, a finer item than earthenware or stoneware, appeared at about the time of the Sui dynasty (AD581-618). A special feldspar clay was used, found with variations in many areas of China, which was fired to a high temperature (the critical feature which distinguishes it from simple pottery) and simultaneously fused with a glaze. Always resonant, sometimes the porcelain is translucent. By the time of the Tang dynasty, porcelain was widely used and exported in enormous quantities, although its method of manufacture remained a mystery outside China until the 18th century. But it was during the Song dynasty that the production of porcelain achieved an artistic elegance that set a precedent not only for subsequent Chinese dynasties but also for the eventual production of porcelain in Europe.

Specialisation During the Song kilns of different types, both coal-fired and wood-fired, sprang up all over the country, producing both stoneware and porcelain. As production increased, areas began to specialise according to their strengths. In the north, cream-coloured porcelain, often with moulded designs, predominated, although olive-green or greyish-toned glaze ware, known as celadon, was also produced; whilst in the south, where the best clays were found, a 'bluish-white' ware was produced. Production overlapped to some extent, not least because Chinese political life was concentrated in the north until the 12th century, and although each kiln tended to specialise in one type of ware, there is evidence to suggest that they would have produced a certain quantity of the other types as well. Throughout the Song empire, however, all porcelain was distinctive for its simple elegance and monochrome glazes, with the exception of cream Cizhou ware from Hebei which was decorated either with narrative painting or deep carving.

Technology During the Mongol (Yuan) dynasty

the one most important advance was the introduction of blue and white underglaze painting. This used cobalt, imported from the Near East, over a white undercoat of clay, a translucent glaze and high-temperature firing (in excess of 1,280°C).

During the Ming dynasty, considered by many the zenith of Chinese porcelain production, the use of underglaze blue and white painting achieved an unsurpassed elegance. There was also a revival of the three-colour glazes which had been popular during the Tang, and the beginnings of overglaze colouring. The latter allowed greater variation since overglazes were added to the finished product and did not have to endure firing at a high temperature. The new technique permitted a revival in monochromes at the beginning of the Qing, but using rich pastel colours. By the late 19th century, however, design had become heavy and ornate and although porcelain is still produced in vast quantities today, the elegance of the great dynasties has yet to reassert itself.

A Ming dynasty porcelain jar

Early exports
It was during the Tang dynasty that porcelain began to be exported in earnest. Chinese ceramics from this period have been discovered in countries as far afield as Japan, Korea, Borneo and Egypt. Much was taken by camel along the Silk Road. Al b'Isa, 9th-century governor of Khorosan in Persia, offered over 2,000 porcelain vessels as tribute to Abbasid caliph whilst hundreds of shards have been discovered near Cairo. In AD851 an Arab merchant noted: 'The Chinese make pottery clay vessels as translucent as glass. Wine poured into them can be seen from outside.'

Monochromatic porcelain jar of the 18th-century Qing period with animal head handles

Tianyige library, Ningbo

An eminent overseas Chinese
One of Ningbo's most illustrious sons was Sir Y K Pao, the shipping magnate who made his fortune in Hong Kong. Among the many companies he owned was the Star Ferry Company, which provides the service across Hong Kong harbour. Like many overseas Chinese, he invested capital back in China and many of the harbour improvements at Ningbo are due to him. He died in 1991.

► Nanchang *200C4*

The capital of Jiangxi is well known as the temporary home of the 16th-century Jesuit missionary Matteo Ricci and as the site of a communist uprising in 1927. It is rather an uninspiring town overall, but there are two worthwhile excursions. About 10km from Nanchang the **Blue Cloud Text (Qingyun Pu)** is the Taoist retreat of the innovative 17th-century painter Zhu Da, a descendant of the imperial Ming family, whose paintings are displayed in the Shanghai Museum. The Buddhist **Youmin Temple►** has a bronze bell cast in AD967.

► Ningbo *201E5*

From the Song to the Ming dynasties Ningbo was one of China's most important ports, with a foreign trading presence from the 16th century onwards. Under the Treaty of Nanjing in 1842 it became a treaty port, but its position was later eclipsed by Shanghai. Now it is being resurrected as a container port. It is famous for the 16th-century **Tianyige►►**, on Changchun Lu, the oldest surviving private library building in China. Fire has always been a threat (it is made of wood), as well as theft – in the past all the family members had to be present before the door could be opened. Many books have now been lost: in 1808 there were 4,094 items, but by 1930 less than 1,000 remained. Of these, most are now in Hangzhou. The library is tucked away amongst merchant houses dating back to the Ming and Qing dynasties.

The area around the Xinjiang bridge has an exhilarating port atmosphere whilst to its north is the old foreign concession, filled with crumbling Western-style houses. Ningbo's main thoroughfare is Zhongshan Lu; from there Kaiming Jie leads away to the Tang dynasty **Tianfeng Pagoda**, currently under restoration. The **Drum Tower** is just north of Zhongshan Lu leading to Congyuan Lu and its old houses. Outside the town, 15km west, is **Baoguo Temple►**, one of the oldest wooden temples in China dating back to AD1013. **Yuwang Temple**, 24km south-east, is noteworthy for its miniature stupa containing a relic of the Buddha.

A little way off the coast is **Putuoshan►►**, one of the four sacred Buddhist mountains on an island famed for its beauty. A four-hour boat trip from Ningbo, the island is an active centre for pilgrims and has some splendid walks.

► Qikou (Xikou) *201E5*

Qikou, 65km south of Ningbo, was the family home of Chiang Kaishek.

►► Quanzhou *201D3*

A build-up of silt in the harbour has contributed to a decline in the economic importance of Quanzhou, once one of the foremost ports in the world, but it remains one of the most fascinating, if neglected, places to visit in Fujian province, a town of narrow stone-paved lanes and good seafood. Quanzhou's early importance as a trading city led to the presence here of a large Muslim population, who called the city Zaiton, from which is derived the English word 'satin'. The **Qingzhen Mosque►►** on Tumen Jie is one of the oldest in China, dating from

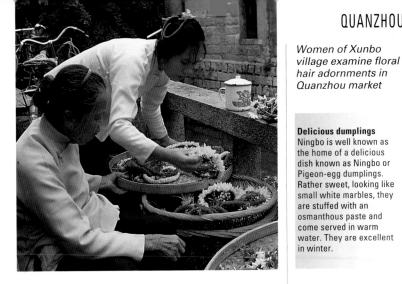

Women of Xunbo village examine floral hair adornments in Quanzhou market

Delicious dumplings
Ningbo is well known as the home of a delicious dish known as Ningbo or Pigeon-egg dumplings. Rather sweet, looking like small white marbles, they are stuffed with an osmanthous paste and come served in warm water. They are excellent in winter.

AD1009, and architecturally intriguing for its absence of Chinese influence.

The **Kaiyuan Buddhist Temple**►►► on Xi Lu dates back to the 7th century AD – its main hall, lined with 100 stone columns bearing delicately carved figures, is a fine example of its kind. A 13th-century 203,200kg sailing vessel discovered in 1974 is housed in the grounds.

The **Quanzhou Museum of Overseas Communication History**►►, East Lake (Donghu), on the outskirts of town, illustrates the religious diversity and cosmopolitan nature of Quanzhou during the Song dynasty. There are tombstones and inscriptions relating to Islam, the Franciscans, Nestorian Christianity and Manichaeism.

Awaiting the faithful, the main Hall of Kaiyuan Temple, Quanzhou

■ The Chinese restaurant, is now a world-wide phenomenon, finding its way into even the smallest village. It is a convenient metaphor for the economic opportunities that have arisen for the Chinese since the expansion of the West into Asia, the Americas and Oceania during the 19th century.....■

Nationals' product
Such is the strength of overseas Chinese ties with the homeland that between 1929 and 1941 remittances home averaged between US$80 and 100 million per year, enough on occasion to offset China's balance of payments deficit.

Early traders From the 15th to the 18th century, Chinese colonies grew up in the trading centres of southeast Asia in the wake of the extraordinary voyages of the eunuch admiral, Zheng He, undertaken between 1405 and 1433. In the last years of the Ming, overseas trade was banned, and individual traders therefore found it expedient to settle overseas. This pattern continued under the Manchus, whose policy of evacuating coastal regions (to undermine Ming loyalists) forced coastal dwellers to seek a livelihood abroad. Eventually foreign trade restrictions were lifted but attempts were made by the Qing rulers to control emigration. Emigrants were classed as criminals – an edict of 1712 declared that the Chinese government 'shall request foreign governments to have those Chinese who have been abroad repatriated so that they may be executed'. This measure was taken partly out of

Chinese in Britain
Most Chinese people in Britain trace their origins back to Hong Kong's New Territories, where Cantonese is the local dialect. For 90 per cent of Chinese in Britain, Cantonese is likely to be the most common dialect in the community although Hakka, Hokkien and *putonghua* may also be spoken. Since 1979 many Hoa (Chinese) people have settled in Britain from Vietnam, speaking Vietnamese as their first language, rather than any Chinese dialect.

China's emigrants have traditionally formed close communities. Right: Chinatown in San Francisco

China or... Chinatown, London

fear of sedition but it also stemmed from the traditional Confucian contempt for merchants.

Provenance The majority of emigrants came from the two southern maritime provinces of Guangdong and Fujian, which by 1500 had less cultivated land per head than anywhere in China. Few came from the ancient Chinese heartlands of northern Mandarin China. Once settled, the emigrant sent for a young son or relation to join him, for the family was to be the mainstay of Chinese exiles' success. This can be seen partly as traditional Confucian filial piety and strong identification with ancestors and the native village; but also as simple practicality. With the help of the family, longer opening hours, and lower wages are possible, although this attitude was later to become a source of friction with emigrants of other nationalities. Chinese communities abroad tended to clan together according to dialect or surname, but whoever they were, the desire eventually to return home a success was paramount, and almost the first thing that they did once abroad was to arrange for the return to China of their body in the event of death.

Nineteenth century Large-scale emigration only started in the late 19th century, when more than 2 million Chinese flooded into ports around the world. There were several reasons for this. One was a huge population explosion; another was the Taiping Rebellion which decimated the country; a third was the arrival of the Western powers who needed reliable manpower to work in their overseas colonies. Whilst some emigrants went as individual seekers of fortune, most were unskilled labourers, the 'coolies'. At first working in the Spanish, Dutch, British and French colonies in the Far East, coolies soon found their way to African mines and South American sugar plantations or guano fields and then to the goldfields and railways of the USA. Theirs was indentured labour of the worst kind – meaningless contracts for years of badly paid, back-breaking work in appalling conditions. Respected companies organised the coolie trade, whilst Chinese agents in treaty ports press-ganged men who did not volunteer. Many coolies died overseas, some returned with pitiful savings, a very few made their fortunes. Thousands died on World War I battlefields. Ultimately large numbers ended up creating sizeable communities in Britain, France and the USA.

Organised crime
Most of the customs that emigrants brought with them from China have enriched the life of their adopted country. One that has not is the Chinese secret society, the Triad, founded originally by Hokkien immigrants to Taiwan. Very hierarchical, the Triad is structured in pyramid fashion, each level given a number or name. For example, the highest authority is Dragon Head or 489, whilst the lowest recruits are called 49 Boys. The origin of the numbers' symbolism is not certain, but they are accredited with mystical qualities.

Overseas Chinese money built the Jinling Hotel, Nanjing

Pennies for heaven
In China, towns become associated with a particular product or trade. Until 1949, Shaoxing produced the 'joss-paper money', imitation lucre which mourners burned to keep the departing soul in comfort in the after-life. Religious belief died after the revolution and the paper-money industry with it; but there are hopes of a revival now that many temples are functioning again.

Old China, alive and well in the old treaty port area around Anping Lu in Shantou

Plenty of fish to fry along South China's coast

► Shantou *201D3*

Known as Swatow to the Westerners who once traded here, this major port on Guangdong province's east coast has a lively, salty atmosphere and its own distinctive cuisine. The British East India Company was present here from the 18th century although formal trading rights were granted only after the 1860 Treaty of Tianjin. The area for walking is the dock area around Anping Lu while the main thoroughfares are Jinsha Lu, Shanzhang Lu, Zhongshan Lu and Waima Lu. Boats leave regularly for **Mayu Island** carrying pilgrims who visit the two temples there.

► Shaoshan *200B4*

Mao Zedong's birthplace is a village in lush countryside about 125km southwest of Changsha. Once a place of pilgrimage for millions, it comes alive now only once a day when the train arrives, and then falls back to slumber. Many workaday items have been given the Mao treatment but the main attraction is Mao's family house; very simply presented with family photographs and domestic chattels, it is surprisingly large given the apparent poverty of his background.

►► Shaoxing *201E5*

Famous for its yellow rice wine, Shaoxing, in Zhejiang province, was the capital of the State of Yue during the Warring States period, and later important during the Song dynasty when the court moved to nearby Hangzhou. A delightfully unspoilt canal town of traditional houses, narrow alleys and hump-backed bridges, its main attraction is the **Lu Xun Museum►**, the childhood home of Lu Xun, the revolutionary writer and philosopher. **Fushan Hill** offers splendid views over the town. From here you can walk east to Jiefang Lu, the main thoroughfare, surrounded by charming streets, and find your way to the 13th-century **Bazi Bridge►**, across a canal lined with picturesque houses. In the small alley of Dacheng, near Jiefang Nanlu, is the **Green Vine Study (Qingteng Shuwu)►►**, the home of the notorious Ming artist Xu Wei, a man whose extraordinary life included the murder of his wife; it has a morbid fascination, but is also one of the loveliest examples of domestic architecture to survive in China. Outside Shaoxing is the **East Lake (Dong Hu)►►**, where boats can be hired to visit the **Temple of Yu**.

▶ Tiantaishan *201E5*

Tiantaishan mountain, reaching 1,060m, is the home of the Taoist-influenced Tiantai Buddhist sect. A number of monasteries are scattered throughout the area, including the **Bajingtai** at the summit. A bus from the Tiantai Gouqing Monastery at the foot of the mountain goes up to Huadingfeng, a short walk from the monastery.

▶ Wenzhou *201E4*

A drab city on the coast of Zhejiang, Wenzhou was a key port servicing Sino-Japanese trade during the Song dynasty, famed for its scenery, hot springs and porcelain. Unable to compete with Shanghai in the 19th century because it lacked a deep-water harbour, Wenzhou drifted into obscurity until 1984, when it was designated one of China's 14 Coastal Open Cities. Since then its development has been rapid. However, its attractions for the tourist are somewhat limited – the **city museum▶**, housed in an ancient monastery on an island in the Ou river, displays some fine examples of local porcelain from the 1st to the 14th centuries. In the nearby **Yandang mountains▶** there are Buddhist shrines and scenic cliffs.

▶▶ Wuyishan *200C4*

This is a comparatively little-visited mountain reserve in a magnificent setting in the north of Fujian. Raft-trips to appreciate its outstanding scenery can be arranged through CITS offices on the spot or in Guzhou or Xiamen.

Cowed by eagles
Wenzhou enjoys the distinction of possessing China's largest dairy. Dairy products are not widely eaten in China since there is little pasture for cows, but in 1926 a Mr Wu Baiheng decided to compete against the only milk available at the time, 'Flying Eagle' condensed milk. Having started the dairy, he called his own brand of condensed milk 'Snatching Eagle'.

Work comes in cycles

Xiamen University

►► Xiamen *201D3*

Called 'Amoy' by the foreign traders who settled here at the turn of the century, Xiamen consists of the island of the same name, and the smaller island of Gulangyu. Xiamen Island is linked to the Fujian mainland by a causeway built in the early 1950s. The town was founded only in the Ming dynasty, and was the stronghold of the Ming loyalist, Zheng Chenggong (Koxinga). With the advent of Westerners in 1842, an international concession was allowed on Gulangyu, whilst a smaller concession grew up on Xiamen itself. Xiamen now prospers as a Special Economic Zone, despite the proximity of the nearby islands which still belong to Taiwan.

In Xiamen itself the **Wanshi Botanical Garden►** on Huyuan Lu has an excellent collection of tropical and subtropical flora. On one side of its lake a large grey stone marks the spot where Koxinga killed his cousin. The **Nanputuo Temple►**, against a mountain backdrop, was originally built during the Tang dynasty, but extensively restored in the 1980s. Gaudily impressive, its roofs are a colourful confusion of flowers, dragons and mythic figures. Tablets in the pavilions either side of the temple's main hall to the rear commemorate suppression by the Qing of secret societies. Steps behind lead up to inscribed rocks; whilst in the summer the lakes in front are covered with lotus flowers, symbols of purity.

Xiamen University, founded in the early 20th century, is on Daxue Lu, close to the temple. There is a small exhibition dedicated to Lu Xun, the eminent writer, who taught here in 1926–7. Nearby are some pleasant beaches. About 2.5km southeast along the coast road is the **Huli Cannon►**, made in Germany by Krupp and placed here in 1891. The **Overseas Chinese Building (Huaqiao Bowuguan)►►** has displays showing the lives of Chinese emigrants, many of whom came from Fujian province (see page 222), as well as bronzes, ceramics and paintings.

Downtown Xiamen centres on the waterfront and Zhongshan Lu. Just opposite where Zhongshan Lu meets the port is the ferry dock to Gulangyu: ferries make the 10-minute crossing regularly, at little cost.

Xiamen and Zhu Xi
The philosopher Zhu Xi is supposed to have preached his Neo-Confucianist ideas in a cave here at the end of the 12th century. His interpretation of the teachings of Confucius became the principles on which the civil service examinations were based until early in the 20th century.

Colonial architecture on Gulangyu Island

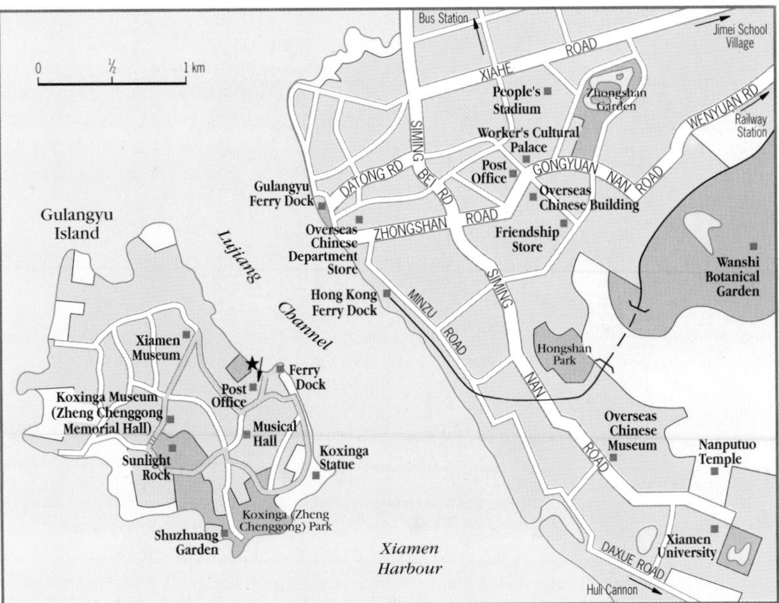

Walk Xiamen: Gulangyu Island

This is a walk to give a flavour of old Xiamen – Sino-European architecture from the earlier part of the 20th century – and one or two key monuments. Having disembarked from the ferry turn left and follow the waterfront with its extensive views across to Xiamen. Eventually you pass a **statue of Koxinga** and the road, bearing right, begins to rise. Stretches of beach are visible before the road begins to descend amid the roofs of the **old colonial houses**. Keep to the same road, passing some **fine door-ways** with interesting motifs. Emerge before a sportsground, with an interesting art-gallery on the corner. Turn left here and continue past some intriguing shops selling antiques and shark's fin; the path will eventually bring you to the sea. Just before the beach turn right and then go up a flight of steps, coming out on to a small square. Here is the entrance to the **Sunlight Rock**, an array of inscribed rocks, terraces with excellent views across the city and, about half-way up, the porticoed **Koxinga Museum**. Return to the entrance and bear left, which will bring you back to the sportsground. Turn left at the corner, left again and then right towards the **Risky Cave**. The next left brings you to a large building surmounted by a cross, the former **Protestant Church**. Then turn back and take the first right and then second left, then right and left up to the domed museum. Then return down to the market-square and, beyond it, the ferry dock.

The pastel shades of former European influence, Gulangyu Island, Xiamen

Timeless landscape in the Lesser Guilin: Seven Star Crags, Zhaoqing

▶ **Zhaoqing** *200B2*

Noted for its scenery, Zhaoqing, 110km west of Canton (Guangzhou), has as its focal point the **Seven Star Crags▶▶**, a group of limestone hills which emerge sheer out of the surrounding countryside. They stand in a park with artificial lakes, concrete walkways and traditional pavilions, and sightseeing can be done either on foot or by boat.

Zhaoqing itself has little enough to see, and can easily be explored on foot. The **Plum Monastery** and the **old quarter** lie to the west of the main street, Tianning Lu, which

leads north to **Seven Star Crag Park** and south to the Xi river and Jiangbin Donglu. By turning left at the river you will come to the **Yuejiang Tower (Yuejianglou)** and beyond it, on Tajiao Lu, amid interesting riverside houses, the **Chongxi (Flowery) Pagoda**.

▶ Zhongshan County and Dr Sun Yatsen

200B2

For those visiting China on a day-trip from Macao, a popular destination is Zhongshan county and the village of Cuiheng, birthplace of the father of Chinese nationalism, Sun Yatsen (1866–1925). His former residence was built in 1892 to his own design; a museum is devoted to the story of his life.

The cult of Mao all but obliterated the part played by Sun, the Father of the Nation, in the establishment of a united China. He studied medicine in Honolulu and Hong Kong, where he developed his Three Principles: the Principle of Nationalism, which implied the expulsion of foreigners from the treaty ports and the dignity of sovereignty; the Principle of People's Democracy, an alien concept in China, meaning that the Chinese government must be responsible to the people, who must be educated and taught how to vote; and the Principle of People's Livelihood, which entailed the nationalisation of basic industries and utilities, and the peasants' right to own the land they worked.

Sun was forced to flee to Hong Kong in 1895 after seeking new recruits in Canton, and later went to Japan where he formed the United League (*Tongmenghui*) dedicated to overthrowing the Qing. He was in America fundraising when the successful anti-dynastic uprising in Wuchang occurred in 1911. He became President but resigned in favour of Yuan Shikai who had no intention of underwriting a republic. Sun died in Beijing in 1925.

Political aides
Sun Yatsen thought that he stood a better chance of achieving his aims if he could enlist the support of the Chinese secret societies. He therefore joined the Hung Men (Vast Gate) society in Honolulu; when he went to the USA in 1904 he went as a society official and was thus able more easily to gain immediate access to Chinese expatriate life.

Place of pilgrimage – Sun Yatsen's birthplace

■ **China's economy is one of the fastest growing in the world, although, as commentators are fond of pointing out, it could hardly be otherwise considering its lowly position before the era of reform.....■**

Corrupting golf
One of the problems accompanying China's economic reforms is the proliferation of corruption. Whilst socialism is still China's nominal guiding ethos, a get-rich-quick mentality is developing at all levels. Nothing could be less relevant to most Chinese than golf-courses; but in 1993 it was discovered that various authorities had given the go-ahead for no less than ten of them, despite the fact not only that every scrap of land is vital for cultivation, but that it is state-owned.

Growth In a comparatively short period miracles have been worked in the Chinese economy and the China we see today is a transformation from the China of only 15 or 20 years ago.

In 1992, while the rest of the world still searched for escape routes out of recession, China's economy grew by a staggering 12 per cent. Industrial production increased by well over 20 per cent. Throughout the 1980s there had been hints of dramatic improvements to come but the legacy of a state-run economy had proved too much of a burden – reforms merely highlighted the deficiencies of a still largely 'socialist' economy. Inflation began to rise as there was nothing to do with earnings except spend them (for example, one woman was reported as having spent all her savings on 2 tonnes of salt). Since then there have been many changes. China recently reported a record US$208 billion in personal bank deposits which can now be sunk into other forms of investment – stocks, bonds and, incredibly, real estate.

Top: challenging the world's economies, Dalian harbour
Above: expanding docks on the Huangpu river, Shanghai

Contradictions The principle of state ownership of land has been sacrosanct in China, with the figure of the landlord cast in the role of wicked villain. Yet in October 1992 the 14th Communist Party Congress gave its blessing to property speculation, an extraordinary about-turn. Local governments have been quick to take advantage of this policy change, and it has been reported that in Wangfujing, Beijing's commercial hub, for example, land is being sold for US$5,200 per sq m. In theory, the land deeds are valid for only 50 years on average, although this has not prevented spiralling prices, possibly because speculators are anxious for the future. Even in Hainan Island (recently touted, with official approval at least at local level, as China's answer to Thailand's sex-industry) the price of a 110 sq m flat has reached US$40,000; and yet the average annual per capita income in cities is a mere US$450.

Optimism Whilst all but the hardest of hardliners in the government now support China's economic reforms to some degree, opinions differ on how they should be implemented. Some who feel that the speed of change is too rapid want to stop reforms now, whilst others – notably, Deng Xiaoping – believe that the only way forward is to allow them to be as wide-ranging as possible. Extravagant property deals do not mean much to the peasant farmers in the poorer provinces whose income, even in the better areas, has increased by a comparatively poor 3 per cent, and the increasing gulf between the very poor and the very rich is a matter of government concern. Yet the fear of a reform 'freeze' is almost tangible in those regions which are prospering, and this, in turn, is giving rise to talk of secession, alarming to the mandarins of Beijing.

The debate has been given new impetus by events across the border in the former Soviet Union, the Chinese government pointing to the chaos there as an example of what can happen when central control is weak. This view may for the time being find favour among many Chinese, who crave stability, but nevertheless it will not be long before state intervention is regarded by most as an unnecessary burden.

The great majority of China's population still work on the land

Stock market in all but name
The currents and cross-currents of the Chinese economy are nowhere better illustrated than in central Chengdu, in Sichuan province, where in close proximity to one of the few remaining statues of Chairman Mao, several thousand people gather each day to trade the shares of Sichuan companies. The stock market is not recognised by central government but the local authorities ignore this and simply charge an entrance fee to each trader.

Cheap, high quality clothing, a mainstay of China's economy

'Floating workers'
About 90 million peasants are believed to have moved from the rural areas to the fast-growing cities and coastal regions, attracted by the Chinese economic boom. In Beijing, already struggling to meet the demands of its 10 million residents, the additional 'floating population' may be as great as 2 million, overloading essential amenities and posing a serious security threat, accounting for 43 per cent of convicted criminals in the capital. Paradoxically, the population's new mobility is essential for the continuing success of China's economic boom.

XIZANG ZIZHIQU (TIBET)
S I C H U A N
Y U N N A N
G U I Z H
Hengduan Shan
Lancang Jiang
Jinsba Jiang
7556m
Gongga Shan
Yalong Jiang
Daxue Shan
3099m
Emeishan
Dadu He
Leshan
Neijiang
Hechuan
Dazu
Zigong
Chongqing
Min Jiang
Luzhou
Yibin
Dêgên
IND
3
Gongshan
Zhongdian
Nu Jiang (Salween)
Lancang Jiang (Mekong)
Muli
Xichang
Dechang
Daliang Shan
Suijiang
Jinsha Jiang
Gaoligong Shan
5596m
Yulong Xuesban
Lijiang
Jianchuan
Zhaotong
Bijie
Qianxi
Dalou
Panzhihua
Liupanshui
Guiyang
Shaping
Erhai
Xizhou
Dali
Yongren
Dayao
Dongchuan
Anshun
Longgong
Huangguoshu Falls
3302m
Tengchong
Baoshan
Xiaguan
Nanhua
Wuding
Wumeng Shan
Panxian
Qujing
Dehong
2
Chuxiong
Kunming
Xingyi
Dianchi
Shilin (Stone Forest)
Luxi
Ruili
Wuliang Shan
Ailao Shan
Yuxi
Nanpan Jiang
Xilin
Tianlin
Lincang
BUR
Shiping
Kaiyuan
Cangyuan
Yanshan
Funing
Bose
Yuan Jiang
Gejiu
Napo
Pu'er
Simao
Lancang
Hekou
Menghai
Jinghong
Xishuangbanna
Daluo
Damenglong
1
Mengla
Pingxiang
VN
0 100 200 300 400 km
LAO
A
B
C

232

Quintessential China: karst scenery along the Li river
Far right: a Hani minority woman, Yunnan province

THE SOUTHWEST

HUBEI
Fengdu
Chang Jiang (Yangtze)
Qianjiang
Jinshi
Hong Hu
Shishou
Datong Hu
Yueyang
Dayong
Changde
Wuling Shan
Daozhen
Dongting Hu
Yiyang
Yuan Jiang
Changsha
Jishou
Zunyi
2942m
Shaoshan
Xiangtan
HUNAN
Tongren
Zhuzhou
Wu Jiang
Huaihua
Lengshuijiang
Loudi
Shaoyang
Zhenyuan
Jiang
Hongjiang
Hengyang
Xiang
Kaili
Leiyang
Jingxian
Dong'an
Duyun
Yongzhou
Miao Ling
Rongjiang
2142m
Quanzhou
Chenzhou
Dushan
2081m
Daoxian
Nan Ling
Guilin
Rongshui
Jianghua
Shaoguan
Hongshui He
Yangshuo
Hechi
Pingle
Liuzhou
Li Jiang
Bei Jiang
GUANGXI ZHUANGZU ZIZHIQU
Huaji
GUANGDONG
Heshan
Pingnan
Wuzhou
GUANGZHOU (CANTON)
You Jiang
Binyang
Zhaoqing
Guigang
Xi Jiang
Foshan
Nanning
Rongxian
Yulin
Luoding
Jiangmen
Yunkai Dashan
Kaiping
Yunwu Shan
Macao (Port)
Qinzhou
Yangjiang
Maoming
Beihai
Leizhou
Zhanjiang
Haikang
Beibu Wan
Bandao
D
E

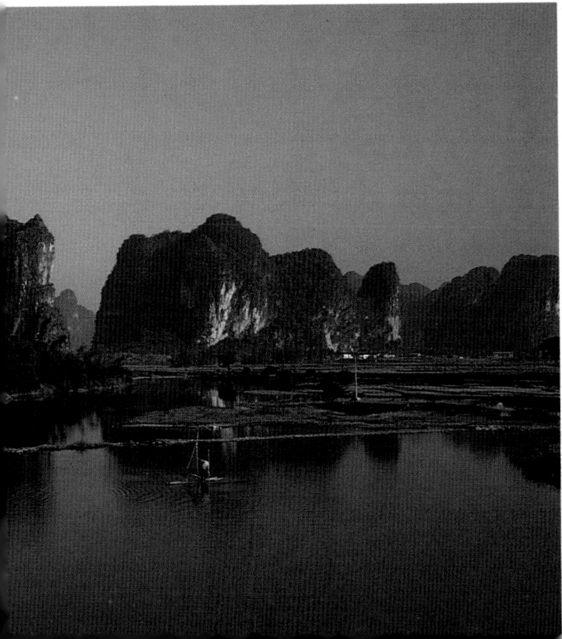

Cormorant fisherman on bamboo raft, Yangshuo

Southern resistance
The continuing resistance in the south to Chinese rule came to a head in the 19th century during the Muslim revolt between 1857 and 1872, which was linked with the Taiping Rebellion. The ensuing slaughter severely reduced the Muslim population. Their leader, Du Wenxiu, declared himself Sultan of Yunnan, and pleaded with Queen Victoria to intervene, a request she declined.

Southwest China In this guide the Southwest is taken to mean Yunnan and Guizhou provinces together with the Guangxi Zhuang Autonomous Region. It is a region of minority peoples who were assimilated into China only centuries after the first Qin emperor had conquered the rest of what was to become China. By the Han dynasty Chinese vanity was satisfied by bestowing imperial titles on the region's local rulers and more or less paying them to protect the southern borders of the Chinese empire. It was not until the 13th century and the arrival of the Mongols that the region was finally and brutally subsumed within China, although it broke away each time that a dynasty collapsed, ensuring that the new rulers would have to go to the trouble of reconquest.

Geographically much of the area is on the Yunnan–Guizhou plateau which rises to an average altitude of 1,000m, reaching 2,000m in the northern part where it meets the border with Burma. The plateau is run through with river valleys (the Red river of Vietnam rises here, as do several major tributaries of the Yangtze) and broken by the occasional towering ridge. The altitude, combined with the region's latitude means that the climate is the most pleasant in China: generally warm and mild, it is known as 'spring at all seasons'. There are areas of upland grazing as well as land devoted to the cultivation of rice, winter wheat, tea, beans, soya, hemp and rape.

At the border with Vietnam and Laos the plateau falls away and the weather is hotter and wetter, ideal for rubber, bananas and sugar; whilst Guangxi has a climate typical of southern China, ideal for the intensive farming of rice and tropical fruits and vegetables.

But southwest China, like everywhere else, is the sum of its parts. In some ways, considering its centuries-old resistance to rule from the centre, it is surprising that the region is not more radically dissimilar to the rest of China. But, although some of the minority peoples may have different facial features or physiques and, sometimes, different dress, there is no doubt that you are in China. Certainly this is the case in the more cosmopolitan parts of the region, and even in the remoter areas, where indigenous customs continue as they always have, life has a very Chinese flavour.

The greatest difference, other than peculiar attractions like the mountains of Guilin or Kunming's Stone Forest, is the pace of life, which is attractively languid, and the countryside, which is lush and colourful – Yunnan, in particular, is the home of many plants familiar to Westerners, like camellias and rhododendrons. Perhaps the other distinctions are more modern – Kunming, for example, has a surprisingly carefree vitality considering its location. An area that was considered a place of exile for centuries, the Southwest has now become quite attractive to northerners who these days are less anxious to return to their staid homeland.

The minority peoples of the area are an important element in the region's charm. Half of China's 55 minorities live in Yunnan alone, whilst Guangxi is home to China's most numerous minority, the Zhuang. As prosperity hastens the disappearance of their traditional ways of life, interest from abroad has taught the Chinese to treat the minorities with more respect. Unfortunately this all too often takes the form of shows for the tourists; but one of the attractive qualities of the minority peoples here is their cheerful acceptance of their fate, which sets them apart from the Chinese.

Sorghum spirit
Guizhou province is the home of Maotai, China's most famous spirit wine. It is usually served at important banquets and although for a time unobtainable, is now merely expensive. Its main constituent is sorghum, which gives it a sharpness that is definitely an acquired taste.

Rooftop view, Lijiang

Sprits and ghosts
In China, spirits or gods (*shen*) were associated with Heaven (which controlled the natural and human world) and the *yang* (male) principle. In folk religion there were *shen* of trees, rivers, rain, thunder, lightning, the household kitchen and - the earth, the latter particularly important in the agricultural society of ancient China. *Gui*, ghosts or devils, were associated with the Earth and the *yin* (female) principle, and were seen as evil beings. To Buddhists they were human beings who had committed evil acts in a previous life and so had been reborn as 'hungry ghosts'.

Opposite, lower right: Jiele Pagoda near Ruili, in the Dehong area

Below: two of the famous Three Pagodas, Dali

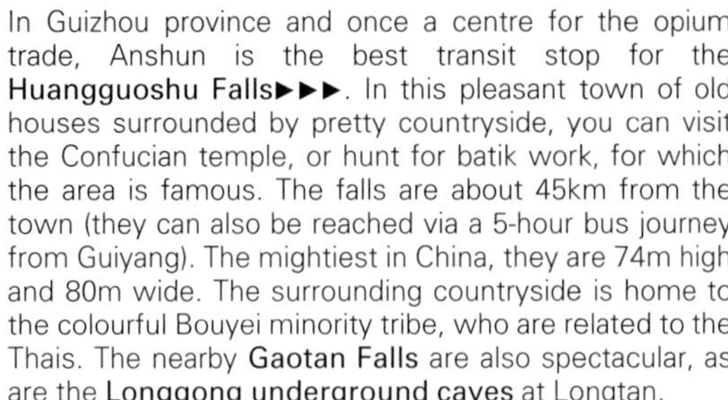

▶▶ Anshun *232C2*

In Guizhou province and once a centre for the opium trade, Anshun is the best transit stop for the **Huangguoshu Falls▶▶▶**. In this pleasant town of old houses surrounded by pretty countryside, you can visit the Confucian temple, or hunt for batik work, for which the area is famous. The falls are about 45km from the town (they can also be reached via a 5-hour bus journey from Guiyang). The mightiest in China, they are 74m high and 80m wide. The surrounding countryside is home to the colourful Bouyei minority tribe, who are related to the Thais. The nearby **Gaotan Falls** are also spectacular, as are the **Longgong underground caves** at Longtan.

▶▶▶ Dali *232B2*

Dali is a pretty town in Yunnan, 11 hours by bus from Kunming, picturesquely situated on Erhai lake beneath Cang mountain, famous for its marble. The main street is Fuxing Lu, at either end of which are the **Qing gates▶**, part of the old city wall. Almost any road to the east off Fuxing Lu will lead you eventually to the **lake▶▶**, where fishermen still sometimes follow the traditional methods of fishing with tame cormorants. The town itself has a simple charm easily enjoyed on foot. Dali's most famous landmarks are the **Three Pagodas▶▶**, just to the north. The largest of them dates back to AD824, is 65m high, and is decorated with buddhas made from the local richly veined marble on each of its 16 storeys. The two smaller and later pagodas are neater and more elegantly classical, with some fine embellishments. Nearby a pool reflects the three in a perfect mirror image. About 10km north is the **Butterfly Spring (Hudiequan)**, a favourite beauty-spot, surrounded by a marble balustrade and overhung by an ancient tree which produces flowers that resemble butterflies. **Zhoucheng**, a nearby village, has an old Qing stage on the main square, once used by itinerant opera troupes, and now the scene of a colourful market. From here it is possible to take a 3-hour boat trip to **Xiaguan** (see page 243), via a small island with a temple. **Shaping**, 32km north of Dali, is famous for its Monday market, but the daily morning market at the charming Bai town of **Xizhou▶▶** is also worth a visit.

▶▶ Dehong *232A2*

The Dehong Dai-Jinpo Autonomous Prefecture, home to the Dai and Jinpo minorities, is a remote area on the Burmese border that has been open to foreigners only since 1990. Its novelty makes a visit worthwhile. Although the Jinpo on the whole are friendly, visits to their villages are not welcome when there has been a death.

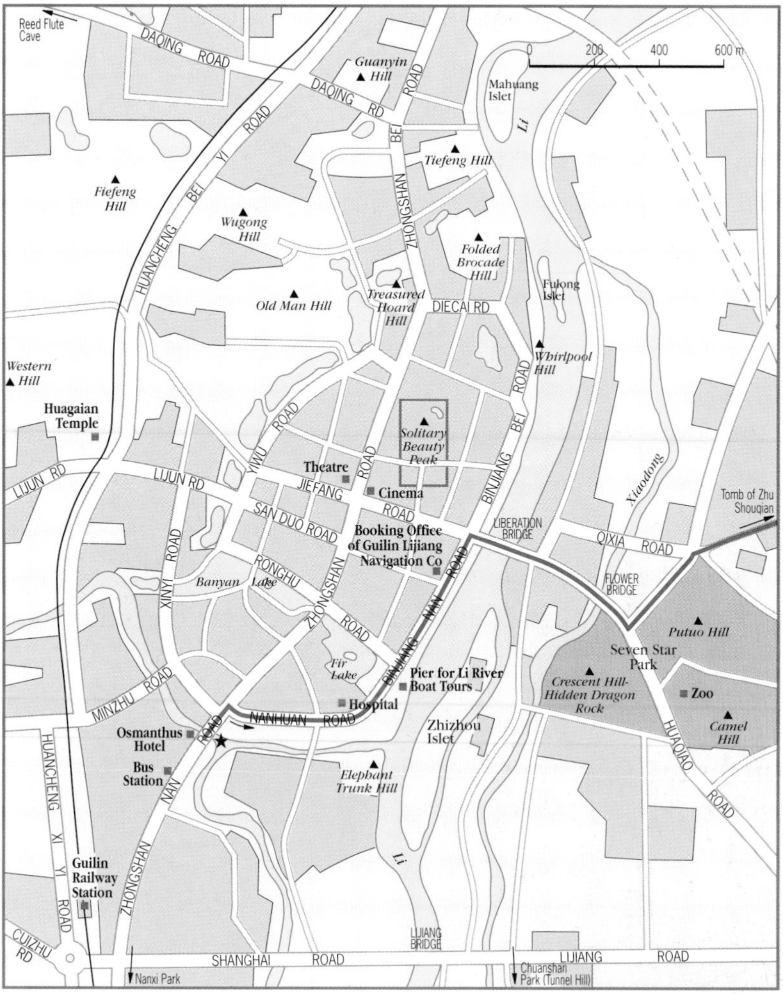

▶▶▶ Guilin *233D2*

Guilin has become one of the stars of Chinese – indeed, world – tourism. Its fame rests on its magical scenery, thousands of square miles of karst limestone outcrops which stand up sheer from a flat plain of paddy-fields and lush bamboo. The area aound Guilin was covered by the sea 300 million years ago and its unique landscape is the result of the movement of the earth's crust, which forced up layers of limestone into the round-topped mountains. Innumerable poems and paintings immortalise the bizarre landscape.

It is alleged that Guilin has been spoilt by 'mass' tourism, but this is a little unfair. True, its attractions have been exploited to pull in large numbers of foreign tourists, hotels have sprung up to accommodate them, and petty crime and corruption are on the increase. Indeed Guilin, which by Chinese standards is little more than a village, feels like a goldrush town, such is the frenzy to make money, but the chief attraction, the scenery, has

River cruise

Down the Li river from Guilin to Yangshuo

This well worth while but rather expensive boat trip begins either in Guilin itself, from the pier on Binjiang Nan Road, or – if the water level is too low, which it frequently is – at a point about 40-minutes' drive downstream, The cruise lasts between four and five hours, and ends at the town of Yangshuo. From Yangshuo, passengers take a two-hour bus journey back to Guilin.

The river passes an endless procession of peaks, each of which has a descriptive soubriquet – Paint Brush Hill, Cock-fighting Hill, Oxen Gorge, Embroidery Hill, and so on. Even in the rain, and this is an all too regular occurrence, the scenery is breathtaking.

Purists will be dismayed at the level of organisation demonstrated on the cruise – flotillas of double-decker boats crammed with tourists (seats are allocated in advance) leave one immediately after the other. However, all this is forgotten as soon as the journey begins and the boats dwindle into insignificance as they are dwarfed by the grandeur of the surroundings.

The shallow river runs clear, past overhanging bamboo fronds and simple villages; fishermen using trained cormorants to catch the fish (see panel, page 239) drift placidly by in bamboo rafts.

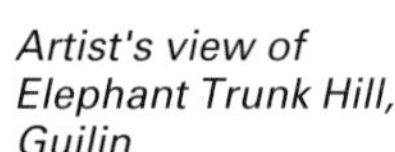

Artist's view of Elephant Trunk Hill, Guilin

remained untainted.

The towering sugar-loaf mountains are apparent as you fly into Guilin. The town itself is attractive, but the highlight of a visit here is a trip on the **Li river▶▶▶** which threads its way through the heart of the mountains (see above).

Guilin started as a garrison town during the Qin dynasty and became a trading centre when the Lingqu Canal linking the Pearl and Yangtze rivers was built. It was the capital of Guangxi from the Ming until 1914, when it was replaced by Nanning. During the Sino-Japanese war in the 1930s, its population was swelled by refugees from the north and the town was heavily bombed, which explains the almost complete absence of ancient buildings. Guilin's name means 'Forest of Cassia Trees' and in the last few

years some million specimens have been planted in and around the town. The trees are in full bloom in autumn, when they give off a lovely perfume, scenting the air all over the city.

Having seen so many peaks in the vicinity, you may also wish to climb some. There are, among others, **Duxiufeng (Solitary Beauty Peak)**, **Fuboshan (Whirlpool Hill)**, which has caves containing ancient statues, and **Diecaishan (Folded Brocade Hill)**, which also has inscriptions and statues. All have superb views from their summits.

A short way outside the town is **Reed Flute Cave▶▶**, an underground cavern of exotic rock formations, its fantastical shapes lit by coloured lights. A path will lead you along a circuit which takes about 45 minutes.

Since the land between the peaks is flat, Guilin is an ideal place for riding bicycles, which can be hired easily and cheaply throughout the town. See below for a suggested cycle ride from Guilin to the tomb of Zhu Shouqian.

Reed Flute Cave, Guilin, gaudy but entertaining

Cormorant fishing
Although a great draw for tourists, who like to be photographed with them, the cormorants of Guilin are not just a pretty sight. The Li river fishermen still use them to catch fish, controlling them by means of a leash tied around the throat which prevents them from swallowing the fish they catch but does not asphyxiate them. When fully trained they are valuable creatures.

Cycle ride **From Guilin to Zhu Shouqian's tomb**

See highlighted map, page 237.
This cycle ride takes about 45 minutes one way, leaving from the Osmanthus Hotel. Cross the bridge (Zhongshan Nanlu) over a tributary and turn immediately right (Nanhuan Road) towards the Li river. Follow the road as it bears left by the river, with Elephant Trunk Hill to your right, until you come to Liberation Bridge. Turn right to cross the bridge, and take the first left on the other side. Follow the road as it curves right, staying with it for some time as it crosses a main road and gradually enters the countryside, passing fields and brick kilns.

Out of the town, not long after passing the first peak, you will come to a track on the left which leads to a graveyard and the statues belonging to the sacred way of the tomb of Zhu Shouqian▶▶, nephew of the first Ming emperor, who established a principality here.

These guides at Stone Forest, near Kunming, belong to the Sani minority

Transportation
Despite, or because of, their comparative remoteness, both Lijiang and Dali are soon to have airports which will make arrival easier but will also undoubtedly affect the area's charm. A railway is also being built from Kunming which will provide a most scenic way of reaching these towns in some comfort.

Celestial temple guardian, Huatingsi, Kunming

► Guiyang *232C2*

The capital of Guizhou province, home to the Miao and Bouyei minorities, Guiyang is an industrial centre with attractive scenery outside town. It is a possible departure point for the **Huangguoshu Falls►►►** (see page 236); otherwise there is the attractive **Huaxi Park** (16km southwest), the **Hongfu Monastery** and **Kanzhu Pavilion**, the graceful **Jiaxiu Pavilion** or scenic **Qianling Park**.

►►► Kunming *232B2*

The capital of Yunnan province has as its main attraction the Stone Forest and is a staging-post for journeys further west but, with its pleasant climate and bustling streets, it is of interest on its own account. It has played an important historical role since 100BC when it became the capital of the Dian, a slave-owning society perhaps related to the peoples of Southeast Asia. It was made provincial capital in 1288. In the early 20th century it became an important railhead when the French built the rail-link from Vietnam to China, and during World War II it was one end of the Burma Road built by the Allies as a supply route.

Most of the main sights lie outside the city but there are some interesting places in the town as well. The **Yunnan Provincial Museum►►**, at the junction of Dongfeng Lu and Wuyi Lu, has an important collection of bronze artefacts from the Dian kingdom excavated in the area; made by the 'lost wax method', and decorated with scenes of Dian life, the bronzes have a distinctive character quite unlike Chinese examples. There is also a display devoted to the province's minority peoples, some of whom still live by hunting in the border jungles. The **Yuantong Buddhist Temple►►** (on Yuantong Jie), founded in the Tang dynasty, is one of the finest temples in China.

A short distance west of Kunming lies Lake Dian, with an area of 300 sq km. On its banks is **Daguan Park►** with the early Qing dynasty Grand View Tower (Daguanlou), famous for its poetic inscriptions by the 18th-century poet Sun Ranweng: 'I am not alone surrounded by

Three of the 500 clay figures (luohans) at the Bamboo Temple, Kunming

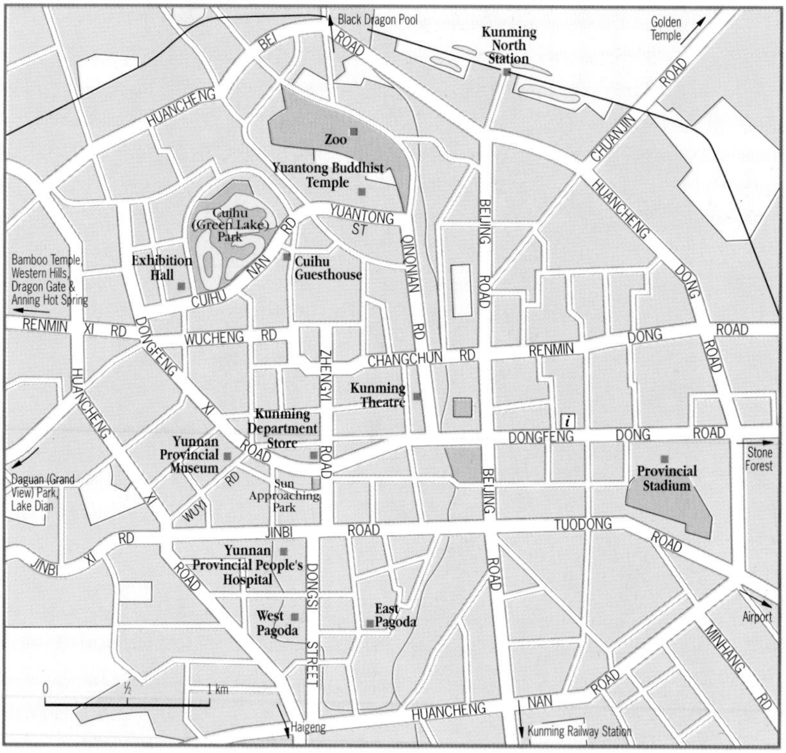

Kunming

green fields of rice, a vast expanse of untainted sand, nine summers of lotuses and three springs of willow.' Boat trips are available here, but there is a splendid view of the lake from the heights of the **Western Hills**▶▶, some 16km from Kunming, and the **Dragon Gate**▶▶, a series of winding steps, tunnels and statue-filled grottoes leading to a lookout point. The latter is approached from the Sanqing Pavilion, a resort built for the Prince of Liang in the Yuan dynasty. The Tang dynasty **Bamboo Temple**▶, 13km northwest of Kunming, thought to be the first Chan Buddhist temple in Yunnan, is known for its hall of 500 clay figures; whilst the **Golden Temple**▶, 6km northeast, has an imitation-timber pavilion in bronze.

The **Stone Forest (Shilin)**▶▶▶, a 270-million-year-old limestone karst formation of tightly bundled grey rocky outcrops, from a distance resembling a petrified forest, is 130km southeast of Kunming. The journey lasts about three hours, through villages built in traditional local style.

A short walk (3km) through this extraordinary landscape is recommended, despite the crowds, for although the colour of the rocks is monotonous, their sharp angles and delineations create strong shadowy contrasts, very good for photography. From the Shilin Hotel turn left and follow the road until you pass **Lion Pond** on the left, and then left to the **Lion Pavilion**. From here continue to a **stone screen**, inscribed with the name of the site. Then take the right-hand path to **Sword Peak Pond**; from here all paths lead back to the starting-point. The local people are Sani – they are cheerful and very persuasive saleswomen.

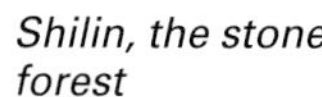
Shilin, the stone forest

The 'Dongba' characters of the Naxi pictorial language, here depicting the Creation Myth and the Rite of Exorcism

Naxi women in traditional dress chatting in a local market

▶▶▶ Lijiang

232B3

The seat of the Naxi minority peoples, Lijiang in the north of Yunnan province lies at 2,500m in a stupendous mountain setting on the border with Tibet, some 11 hours' drive from Kunming. The route passes through a China that is fast disappearing – hills covered in red earth and dotted with traditional-style villages, many still with their local temples. The Naxi peoples traditionally are a matriarchal society related to the Tibetans. Friendship takes the place of marriage, and any children of the union live with the mother, relying on financial support from the father for as long as the relationship lasts. In Lijiang itself this social structure seems already to have broken down, although another day's drive away north the traditional customs are still practised.

Lijiang's **Old Town▶▶▶**, a network of narrow streets lined with small restaurants, intersected by canals, and a lively market square, is utterly charming – take any ascending path for marvellous views across the rooftops. On the edge of the town to the north is the very pretty **Black Dragon Pool Park** with the Ming dynasty **Wufenglou Temple**. In the evenings there are often concerts of Naxi music.

Outside Lijiang you can visit the **Yufengsi Monastery**, perched on a slope overlooking a plain. Indeed, the surrounding countryside, in the shadow of the 5,596m Yulong Xueshan (Jade Dragon Snow Mountain, or Mt

Satseto) is excellent for cycling and walking. Some 88km from Lijiang is **Tiger Leaping Gorge (Hutiaoxia)▶▶▶** on the Jinsha Jiang (Yangtze); 16km long, and between 2,500 and 3,000m deep. It is possible to walk its length along a path high above the river.

▶ Nanning *233D1*

The capital of Guanxi province since 1914, Nanning is a heavily industrialised city made important by the construction of the railway line from Beijing to Vietnam, on which it is the last major town. Although busy, it has little to offer other than the **Guangxi Provincial Museum▶▶** which houses a good collection of tribal and archaeological items. If you have time on your hands, Xinling Lu near the river, or the exotic open market off the main street, Chaoyang Lu, are pleasant places to wander through. The **Nanning Arts Institute▶▶** exhibits arts and crafts of the minority peoples. The **Dragon-boat races** are held on the 5th day of the 5th lunar month (around mid-June). An hour's drive away is the **Yiling Stalactite Cave**.

▶ Xiaguan *232B2*

An industrial town near Dali, Xiaguan has a **museum▶** that is much more interesting than the Dali Museum and well worth a visit. Some say Xiaguan also boasts better shops than those in Dali. There is an ancient Buddhist temple on the slopes behind the town.

Naxi musicians: concerts are regularly given in Lijiang

'Beyond the Clouds'
Lijiang has been the subject of a remarkable documentary called 'Beyond the Clouds', made by an independent British television company and shown on British television. The production team was given permission to live in this remote town and film every aspect of life there for a period of two years. The result was a frank, surprising and often moving insight into the vicissitudes of small-town life in post-Mao China.

■ In China rice is the staff of life. Although you are frequently told that rice is the staple of the south and wheat that of the north, the fact remains that almost everyone in China eats rice and that a Chinese deprived of his daily portion feels uncomfortable and at a loss.....■

Rice research
In the 11th and 12th centuries, Chinese farmers succeeded in producing strains of rice which matured in only 60 days, thus allowing a double, sometimes triple harvest. Eventually, 30-day varieties were developed, reducing the risk of flood damage at a crucial moment in the crop's cycle and thus invaluable in obviating the worst effects of the chronic flooding which used to afflict China.

History A cereal like wheat, rice's distinguishing feature is its immersion in water for part of the year, a feature that conjures up for the foreigner an image that is almost inseparable from the picture of China as a land of straw-hatted peasants toiling under a torrid sky.

During the 1st century AD, the most densely populated part of China was the area around the Yellow river in the north, where rice cultivation was uncommon but where millet was grown, and pigs and sheep reared. Southern China was populated then by Thai-speaking peoples who practised a primitive form of wet-rice farming, and the Chinese of the frontier regions of the Yangtze valley also had a tradition of wet-rice cultivation.Organised irrigation techniques on any scale only began to be introduced in the 3rd and 4th centuries BC. The Chinese of the north were familiar with intensive farming methods, for the use of manure and night-soil was known even if not yet widely practised. In the 4th century AD, when many northerners were driven south as a result of political upheaval, they left behind their sheep but brought their pigs and also their farming techniques, which they then applied to the wet-rice cultivation skills of the southerners, whose use of water buffalo and fondness for poultry were also adopted. By the 14th century, with the shift of Chinese civilisation from the Yellow river to the Yangtze, advanced irrigated cultivation of rice was well established. Fast-growing rice was imported from India, making possible crop rotation. Strains were developed which required less water and could be grown on hillside terraces. Following the shift in population there was also a demand for a greater variety of foods so that sorghum, groundnuts, and later sweet potatoes (from the New World) were introduced.

Top: flooded rice fields in Guangxi province
Below: paddy terraces, Yunnan

To Chinese children, a bowl of rice is what a slice of bread is to a Western child

Cultivation Rice is not a particularly demanding cereal – it tolerates a wide range of soils and gives a high yield in a comparatively small area. Certain conditions must be met, however. Rice needs an average temperature of at least 20°C over a period of three to four months and at least 1,800mm of rain during the growing season. Wet rice, as opposed to upland rice (which can be sustained on rain or spring water), must be submerged beneath water to an average depth of between 100 and 150mm during three quarters of the growing period; the water has to be of equal depth to ensure even growth. For this reason cultivation takes place in small levelled fields (paddies, from the Malay word 'padi', meaning 'rice in the straw') surrounded by low earthen bunds (walls) that keep the water in, and are quickly breached to let it out. Although hillside terracing is often associated with rice cultivation, most of it is grown in deltas or in the lower reaches of rivers where it is inexpensive to level fields and where water is near to hand, and also where the soil tends to be heavy and fine-grained, which prevents excessive drainage.

At the beginning of the season the dykes, bunds and irrigation canals must be repaired and the soil ploughed to reduce it to a muddy consistency. Ten per cent of the fields are set aside as nurseries. After four or five weeks the seedlings are transplanted to the paddies and arranged in rows. As harvest approaches, the fields are drained and reaping begins. Finally the stalks are ploughed back into the field which is then fertilised for the next crop which may be wheat or, in the deep south, another of rice. Paddy-fields do not need to lie fallow, possibly because the water acts as a protection against damage by sun, wind and rain, so the same fields are used year after year.

Staple foods
Although rice is the mainstay of agriculture in China, the Chinese have also imported foreign crops into their agriculture, several from the Americas. Maize and the sweet potato arrived through the Philippines via the Spanish in the 17th century, whilst the potato itself came via the Dutch from Indonesia, as did the mange-tout pea, which is still called 'Dutch bean' by the Chinese.

The Dai
Linguistically and ethnologically the Dai people are closely related to the Thai peoples who are scattered over the very wide area that takes in Thailand, Burma, north Vietnam and Laos, and who once lived in much of southern China. Although the Dai are subdivided into four, all speak Dai which is broadly similar to Thai, although the Dai script differs considerably from Thai writing.

►►► Xishuangbanna *232B1*

Xishuangbanna Dai Autonomous Prefecture, in south Yunnan near the Burmese and Laotian borders, is the home of the Buddhist Dai people, who are related to the Thais. The Dai state was taken by the Mongols in the 13th century and subsequently by the Chinese, and although evidence of colonisation remains, the area retains enough indigenous character from its many minority peoples to warrant a visit, particularly between mid-September and mid-May, when the weather is warm but not stifling.

The capital and main port of entry is **Jinghong**, a pleasant town on the Mekong river, and a useful base. The town centre is modern, but on the southern edge is a **village (Manjing)►** where traditional Dai houses stand in contrast to adjacent, more recent, constructions. A pair of local Buddhist temples adds to the ethnic flavour, whilst every evening performances of the famed Dai Peacock dance take place in several of the restaurants or hotels. There are good small, cheap cafés, one of the best bearing the unlikely name of Natasha's Big Nose Café.

In the centre of town is the **Tropical Plant Research Institute (Redai Zhiwu Yanjiusuo)►**, now open to the public, with a charming display of palms, fruit trees and cascading flowers. But the main items of interest, **the minority villages►►►**, lie outside the town.

Travelling west from Jinghong will soon bring you to the Dai villages of **Manjing Dai** and **Manluan Dian**, where the tradition of weaving bags, rugs and richly coloured cloth still thrives. Beyond is a succession of villages belonging either to the Dai or to the Aini. Whilst most of the inhabitants of the villages near to the road are well used to foreigners, their way of life continues much as it always has. Continuing west will bring you to **Menghai**, a

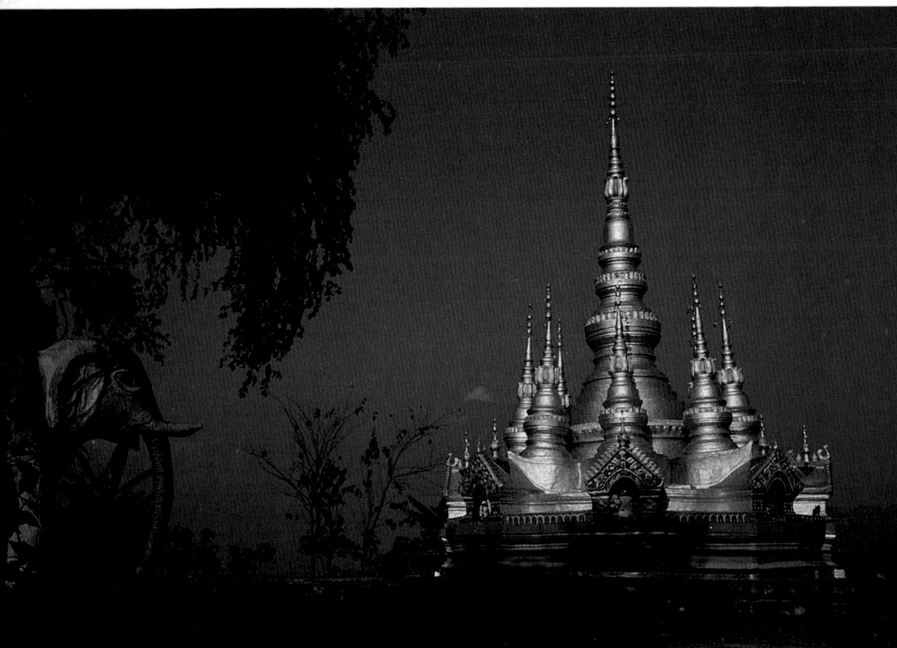

Manfeilong White Pagoda – the Baita, Damenglong, Xishuangbanna

modern town well known for its Sunday market, although the Sunday market at Menghun, 24km southwest, is at least as interesting. After Menghai the road passes the newly restored **Qing dynasty Octagonal Pavilion**, next to a Buddhist school, and continues to **Mengzhe** where the **Wat Gau Temple**, from the Tang dynasty, was rebuilt in 1985. At the western extremity of the region you come to **Daluo,** whose Sunday market is a favourite haunt of Burmese traders.

To the south of the western road is **Nannuoshan**, famous for the King of Tea Trees, apparently the first tea tree to be planted by the Hani 55 generations ago. Further south from Jinghong is the **Manfeilong White Pagoda** at **Damenglong**, built in 1204 in honour of a footprint left behind by Buddha himself.

East of Jinghong, the Botanical Garden in the Dai village of **Menglun** is open to visitors. South of Menglun the road eventually takes you to the Dai and Yao area of **Mengla**; only recently opened to foreigners, its rainforest as well as its villages have a fresh novelty and interest.

Menghan, on the Mekong south of Jinghong, has a market every morning. The nearby Dai village of **Manting** boasts a temple with the tallest Buddha in the area; just southwest of Menghan is the **Wat Ban Suan Men (Manchunman)**, a fine example of Dai architecture.

There are some delightful forest walks among the hills outside Jinghong. The easier walks and a waterfall are at Mandian Jungle, whilst the Tropical Primitive Rainforest Park has more demanding walks for the fit and energetic.

Xishuangbanna is famous for its Water Splashing Festival on 13–15 April, over the Dai New Year, although accommodation is at a premium then.

Name borrowing
'Xishuangbanna' is the Chinese version of the Thai local name 'Sip Sawng Panna', or 'the twelve rice growing districts', the description given to this region when it was ruled by the Dai.

Dai people at Menghan Market, Xishuangbanna

■ **'The very concept of completion is utterly alien to the Chinese way of thinking. The Chinese painter deliberately avoids a complete statement because he knows that we can never know everything.' Michael Sullivan, *A Short History of Chinese Art*, 1967.....■**

Painting *qi*
As in so many other aspects of traditional life in China, the vital force known as *qi* plays an essential role in painting. For the Chinese painter, each living creature, every plant and the oldest, stillest rock is possessed of *qi* which reacts with the *qi* of the painter. One must imagine therefore how it is to look and then put brush to paper at a moment that is both absolute concentration and absolute abandonment.

Top: calligraphy brushes
Below: papier mâché New Year's masks

Painting One of the delights of a visit to China is the opportunity to admire, and buy, Chinese art. A Chinese painting is a distinctive object, based, like so many things in China, on centuries-old traditions. Modern painters in China have found it difficult to escape age-old conventions (and of course political pressures have not encouraged experimentation) but the traditional styles, when executed with real skill, remain enormously attractive.

Traditionally, Chinese painting is done using a brush on paper or silk, often with black ink alone, a monochrome style derived, perhaps, from calligraphy. The ink is made from soot scented with musk or camphor and solidified with animal glue into the form of small inksticks, often decorated with intricate designs. Highly regarded as one of the 'four treasures of the study' (*wenshusibao*, the others being brush, paper and inkstone), the inksticks' colourful, faintly mysterious, presence makes a visit to a traditional Chinese stationer a delight.

Traditional brushes are made of animal hair glued into bamboo. The inkstone, usually black or grey, is a heavy ovoid block made of slate with a shallow bowl often surrounded by carved designs. A little water is placed in the bowl and the inkstick ground into it, with more water added until the correct consistency is reached. Intensely black in its original state, the ink can be diluted to the palest grey.

Painting styles The Song dynasty is considered to have been the greatest period of Chinese painting. Although few earlier examples survive, it is clear that painting in China was already a sophisticated art by the Han dynasty. Painters were either gentlemanly amateurs or professional craftsmen hired for particular occasions. Two styles of painting developed – academic painting, favouring a naturalistic approach to artistic excellence, in which birds and flowers were reproduced in perfect detail; and a more scholarly style which specialised in grandiose representations of nature, concentrating on mountains in particular, where reality is stylised to expose its essence. The art of painting was to grasp reality, not merely the illusion of reality. Such paintings differ from their Western counterparts in that perspective is not from a fixed point, but instead moves between several different viewpoints. Man plays an insignificant role – a tiny figure diminished by mountains might help to direct the onlooker to the correct viewpoint, but it also shows how small is man and how great is timeless nature.

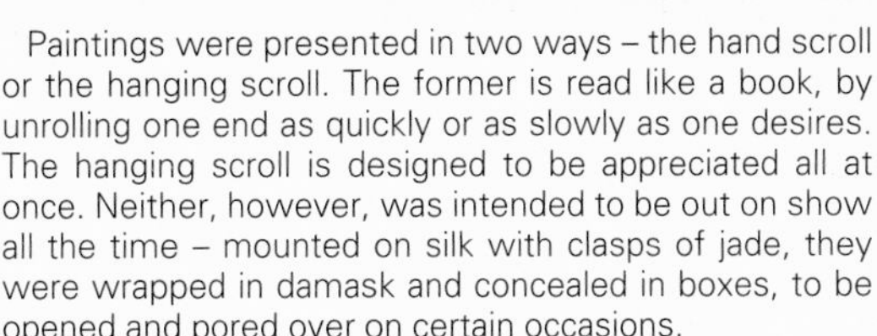

Paintings were presented in two ways – the hand scroll or the hanging scroll. The former is read like a book, by unrolling one end as quickly or as slowly as one desires. The hanging scroll is designed to be appreciated all at once. Neither, however, was intended to be out on show all the time – mounted on silk with clasps of jade, they were wrapped in damask and concealed in boxes, to be opened and pored over on certain occasions.

Lacquerware Distinctively Chinese, lacquer is produced from the sap of the *Rhus verniciflua*, or lac tree, native to China and was originally used as a timber preservative. By the Han dynasty lacquer dishes were used as food containers and it was soon discovered that the addition of minerals produced fine colourings. The typical features of Chinese art – mountains, animals – began to appear on lacquer vessels with a wood or cloth base. Carved lacquer is achieved by cutting through thick coatings of lacquer built up in layers on a wooden or metal base. It is still produced but only rarely with authentic materials.

(*Continued on page 250*)

Painters vilified
During the Cultural Revolution painters, like writers, suffered terrible hardships and ridiculous indignities. The painter Huang Yongyu was sent to work in the countryside; then, after his return, he was accused by Mao Zedong's wife and Gang of Four member, of insulting her by painting an owl with one eye closed. When his accuser was arrested, Huang celebrated by painting a similar owl every day.

Left: a Song dynasty painting, Willows and Distant Mountains, *by Ma Yuan*
Below: the dramatic puppets of Fujian

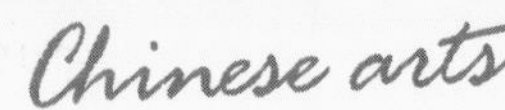

Chinese arts

Chinese carpets
One of the crafts most often associated with China is that of carpet-making. Traditional Chinese carpets are now made in factories in Wuhan, Tianjin and Shanghai whilst other nationalities produce carpets on a smaller scale in Tibet and Xinjiang. Chinese carpets are distinguished by the fact that the pattern is in relief, usually produced by means of a combination of electric scissors and a sure eye.

Right: an example of the peasant painting of Huxian county, Shaanxi

At work in a cloisonné *factory*

Cloisonné A craft that excites contempt as much as admiration is *cloisonné* (from the French, meaning 'cloistered'; *jingtailan* in Chinese).

The technique for this gaudily coloured enamelware, made mainly in Beijing and Xian, was probably first introduced into China during the Yuan dynasty. The process of production is rather painstaking. First, a base is made of bronze or copper – a vase, for example – and then thin copper wires are glued over the surface to produce a network of tiny cells. Into each, by means of a dropper, different coloured mineral paints are added. When dry, the article is fired in an oven, polished with a metal brush, topped up with more enamel, fired again and burnished. The final touch is the gilding of the exposed wires. When the colours are carefully chosen the effect can be very pleasing, although all too often the result is rather vulgar. Antique *cloisonné* is usually more satisfying because the colours are richer but less brash.

Crafts unlimited The number and range of Chinese crafts is almost limitless. Many are clever bits of fun (paper-cuts, or dough-figurine modelling) but all demonstrate intricacy and dexterity. Some cities – Shanghai, for example – boast so-called Arts and Crafts Research Institutes and although not so fashionable for foreign visitors as they once were, a visit is still recommended.

Chinese dynasties and historic events

CHINA	REST OF THE WORLD
600,000BC–400,000BC	
First hominids (Lantian Man and Peking Man)	*Homo sapiens in Africa*
5000BC	
Yangshao culture (red earthenware pots) and Longshan culture (black burnished wares)	*Egyptians invent the calendar of 12 months, each of 30 days*
Xia (2100–1600BC)	
Earliest recorded dynasty *Earliest bronzeware and carved jade objects*	*Pyramids, the Great Sphinx, first great libraries in Egypt* *Minoan culture in Crete*
Shang (1600–1027BC)	
Earliest Chinese characters – 15,000 pictographs carved on oracle bones used in harvest rituals and medical diagnosis *Sophisticated bronze vessels*	*Trojan War (1193BC)* *Moses leads the Israelites to Canaan* *Burial of Tutankhamun*
Western Zhou (1027–771BC)	
Bronze working reaches its technical and artistic peak *Chinese script fully developed* *First mathematical text books*	*King David rules Israel (1000–960BC)* *Carthage founded (814BC)*
Eastern Zhou (770–256BC) Spring and Autumn period (722–476BC)	
Iron replaces bronze for tools and weapons *Confucius (c.551–479BC)* *Laozi, founder of Taoism (c.570–490BC)*	*Rome founded (753BC)* *Homer (700BC)* *Buddha in India (560–483BC)* *Roman Republic founded (530BC)*
Warring States period (475–221BC)	
Metal coinage *The Legalists* *Invention of crossbow, calligraphy brushes, chopsticks*	*Socrates condemned to death (399BC)* *Plato (428–347BC)* *Alexander the Great (356–323BC)* *Mexican sun temple at Teotihuacan (300BC)*

Qin (221–206BC)

Qin Shihuang: first emperor to rule all China
Great Wall completed
Standardisation of weights, measures and coinage
Suppression of Confucianism in favour of Legalist ideas
The Terracotta Army at Xi'an

Hannibal crosses the Alps to invade Italy (218BC)
Cato, the Roman politician (234–149BC)
Death of Archimedes, Greek mathematician (212BC)

Han (206BC–AD220): Western Han (206BC–AD24)

Revival of Confucianism
First civil service examinations
Silk Road opened

First clock (159BC)
Venus de Milo carved (140BC)
Virgil, Roman poet (70–19BC)
Modern calendar introduced (46BC)

Eastern Han (AD24–220)

Buddhism brought to China via the Silk Road
Seismograph invented
Value of pi (π) calculated to the first five decimal places
First treatises on acupuncture and moxibustion

Christ crucified (AD30)
First Christian church in Corinth (AD40)
London founded (AD43)
St Paul's missionary travels begin (AD45)
Gospels written (AD85)
First Mayan monuments (AD164)

Disunity and partition (220–581)

Three clans (Wu, Wei and Shu) fighting for supremacy (221–265)
'Barbarians' (non-Chinese nomadic peoples) conquer parts of China and adopt Chinese customs
Chinese population shifts south to Yangtze valley

Constantinople becomes capital of the Roman Empire (331)
The Roman Empire splits into Eastern and Western empires with two emperors (340)
Alaric the Goth sacks Athens (398) and Rome (410)
Death of British King Arthur (537)
Rats spread plague throughout Europe (542–7)

Sui (581–618)

The Grand Canal built from Beijing to Hangzhou

Petroleum ('burning water') first discovered in Japan (615)

Tang (618–907)

China's Golden Age: flourishing trade with central Asia
China's only empress (Wu Zetian, 690–705)
The poetry of Du Fu (712–70)
First printed books
Arabs defeat the Chinese in the Battle of the river Talas (751)

Mohammed (570–632)
Greek fire (sulphur, petrol, resin and salt) first used in warfare during the siege of Constantinople (678)
Charlemagne crowned first Holy Roman Emperor (800)
Doge's Palace, Venice (814) and St Mark's (828)
Vikings discover Iceland (861)

Five Dynasties and Ten Kingdoms (907–960)

Paper money (910)
Gunpowder (919)

Fatamid dynasty in north Africa
Cordoba in Spain a flourishing centre of Arabic learning and commerce

Song (960–1279): Northern Song (960–1127)

First movable type printing
Landscape painting reaches a peak of excellence
Neo-Confucianism

Arabic numerals first used in Europe (975)
Leif Ericson sails to America (1000)
First Crusade (1096)

Southern Song (1127–1279)

Mongols capture Beijing (1215)
Marco Polo's journeys in China (1271–92)
Celadon porcelain

Earliest European windmills (1180)
First tea imports (1191)
Leprosy imported to Europe by Crusaders (1230)
Paris University founded (1250) followed by Oxford (1263)

Yuan (1279–1368)

Mongol rule in China
Kublai Khan (1214–94)
Drama flourished

Dante (1265–1321)
Black Death in Europe (1347–51)

Ming (1368–1644)

Admiral Zheng He (1371–1433) makes extensive voyages of exploration to Arabia
First Dalai Lama (1447)
First Portuguese explorers reach Guangdong (1514)
First British trade with Hangzhou (1637)

Gutenberg prints the first book in Europe (1450)
Columbus sails to the Americas (1492)
Vasco da Gama sails round the Cape of Good Hope to India (1497)
Luther's 59 Theses spark the Reformation (1517)
Cortes enters Mexico (1519)
Galileo's trial by the Inquisition (1633)

Protecting the Wall for posterity

Qing (1644–1912)

Opium Wars (1839–42) force China to open ports to Western powers
Hong Kong ceded to Britain 'in perpetuity' (1842)
Taiping Rebellion (1850–64)
Boxer Rebellion (1900)
Boy emperor Puyi abdicates (February 1912) ending 2,000 years of imperial rule in China

American Revolution (1776)
French Revolution (1789)
Marx (1818–1883)
Communist Manifesto issued by Marx and Engels (1848)
Industrial Revolution begins in Britain (late 18th century)

The Republic of China (1911–49)

Sun Yatsen first President (1911)
Communist Party founded (1921)
At death of Sun Yatsen (1925), Chiang Kaishek becomes nationalist leader
Massacre of communists in Shanghai (1927). Chiang Kaishek tries to drive communists from China by means of 'Encirclement Campaigns' (1930)
Japan occupies Manchuria (1931)
Mao gathers the surviving communists to begin the long March (1934–5)
War between China and Japan (1937–45)
Civil War (1946–9)
Chiang Kaishek and nationalists flee to Taiwan (1949)

World War I (1914–18)
Russian Revolution (1917)
Hitler becomes Chancellor of Germany (1933)
Wall Street Crash (1937)
Chamberlain's Munich Pact with Hitler (1938)
World War II (1939–45)
Atom bombs dropped on Hiroshima and Nagasaki; Japan surrenders (August 1945)
United Nations created out of the old League of Nations with New York as its permanent headquarters (1945)

People's Republic of China (1949 to present)

First Five-Year Plan (1953–7)
Great Leap Forward (1958)
Tibetan uprising (1959)
Cultural Revolution launched (1966)
President Nixon visits China and establishes diplomatic relations (1972)
Mao dies. Gang of Four arrested (1976)
Democracy movement (1978–9)
Open-door policy launched (1982)
Sino-British agreement on the future of Hong Kong (1984)
Hu Yaobang forced to resign in aftermath of student demonstrations (1987)
Tiananmen Square massacre (1989)

Korean War (1950–3)
Death of Stalin (1953)
Kennedy assassinated (1963)
Vietnam War (1964–75)
Martin Luther King assassinated (1968)
Student riots in Paris and Prague Spring ends in the invasion of Czechoslovakia by Russian tanks (1968)
First Moon landing (1969)
Mikhail Gorbachev becomes Soviet head of state (1988), introduces glasnost (openness) and presides over the collapse of communism in Europe (1989–91)

TRAVEL FACTS

Domestic air travel – modernised but still chaotic

Arriving

By air Most visitors begin their trip to China either in Beijing or Hong Kong. There are direct flights from all over the world both on Air China (formerly CAAC) and other major national carriers to Beijing. All China's major cities are served by direct flights from Hong Kong either on Air China or via the Hong Kong carriers Dragonair. Some cities, for example Shanghai, Canton, Kunming, Xiamen, Dalian and Ürümqi, are served by direct flights from other countries.

By train You can also enter China by train either via Siberia and the Mongolian People's Republic, or through Hong Kong. The former is time-consuming (about six days from Moscow to Beijing) but fascinating (although there have been reports of theft on the Trans-Siberian Express); whilst the journey from Hong Kong to Canton takes under three hours. There is also a newly opened rail link between Alma Ata (Kazakhstan) and Iling, in Xinjiang.

By boat There is a comfortable ship service between Hong Kong and Shanghai (journey time is under three days), leaving at least every five days; and services to most of China's major ports including Hainan, Jiangmen (near Macao), Shantou, Shenzhen, Wuzhou, Xiamen, Zhaoqing, and Zhongshan. Catamaran, ferry and hovercraft services link Hong Kong and Canton. Some cruise ship companies stop at China's coastal cities.

Customs allowances

Two litres of liquor and 600 cigarettes are permitted, plus limitless cash or securities. Pornographic items are forbidden although there is no hard and fast rule about literature or magazines. Travellers are recommended to take no more than one Bible into China.

Departing

A departure tax is payable when you leave. X-ray machines are widespread but are advertised as film-safe.

Entry requirements

Entering the country is straightforward providing visas are obtained

An unusually quiet moment at Beijing railway station

in advance. On arrival in China a simple health form and a landing card (unnecessary for people on group visas) has to be completed. Currency declaration forms are no longer required. In most ports of entry there are red and green channels, but usually only a few luggage trolleys. Taxis are freely available but there are few tourist information facilities except at Beijing airport.

Travel insurance

You are strongly advised to obtain travel insurance sufficiently comprehensive to cover repatriation in the event of serious illness and, ideally, to cover delays.

Visas

If you are travelling in a group you will probably travel on a group visa organised on your behalf by the tour company and held by the group leader.

An individual visa is easily obtained, usually valid for 30 days, travel in China, but easily extended at public security offices in China. To obtain a Chinese visa, contact the consular section of your nearest Chinese embassy; the procedure requires completion of a simple form, a full passport (which must have at least two blank pages and six months' validity) and one recent passport-size photograph. Three working days to process the visa are usually required, although they can be rushed for an extra fee and on the production of airline tickets.

Theoretically, it is possible to obtain a visa on arrival at Beijing airport, but this can be very difficult and visitors should consider it only as a last resort.

In Hong Kong visas can be easily obtained either from **CITS**, (6/F Tower 2, South Seas Centre, 75 Mody Road, Tsim Sha Tsui, Kowloon) or directly from the visa office of the Foreign Ministry of the People's Republic of China, China Resources Building, Wanchai.

Visitors often ask if they can have their passports stamped upon entering or leaving China, but the immigration officers will exhibit a marked reluctance to do so unless the passport contains an individual visa.

Individual tourists wishing to visit Tibet must contact the **Tibet Tourism Office** (10 Renming Beilu, Chengdu; fax: 028 333526) or **China Tibet Qomolangma Travelways Ltd**. (37/F, Times Tower, 393 Jaffe Road, Hong Kong; fax: 834 1535). A special permit is no longer required (just a valid visa for China). However, the government occasionally closes Tibet to individual visitors (because of political disturbances), usually only for a short time. Check with the embassy before setting off.

A typical hallway in a block of flats in Shanghai

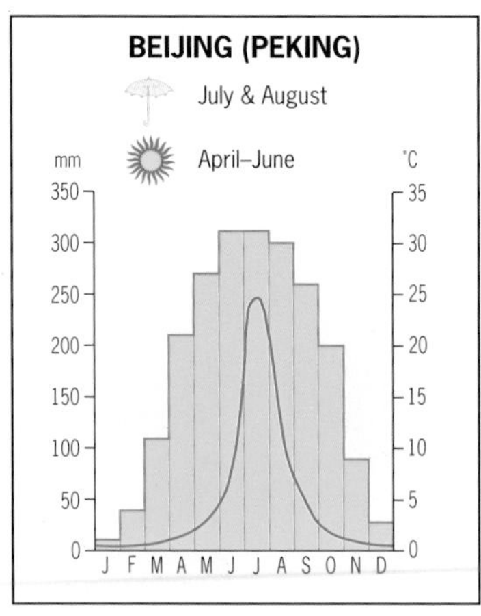

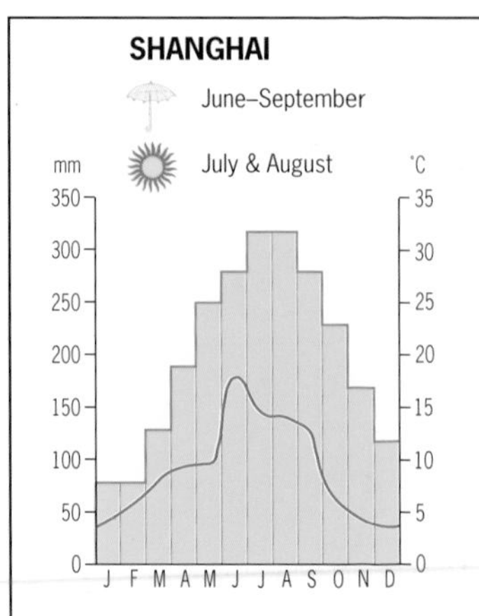

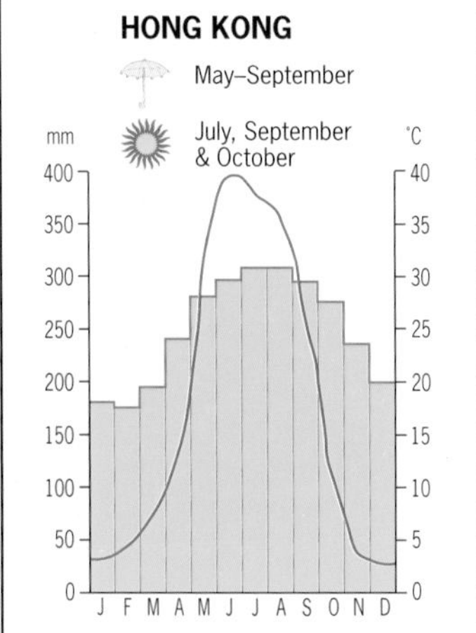

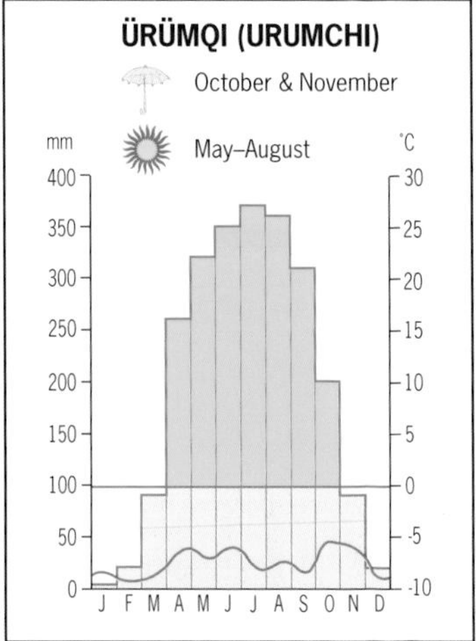

When to go
China is a vast country with very wide-ranging climatic conditions, so a decision about when to go should be based on the regions your trip will cover.

Standard tours usually take in a little of everywhere, so the most comfortable seasons are late spring (May) or early autumn (September to early October). There are other considerations, however: blossom in the north appears in April, orchids in the south in February.

Some national holidays (see opposite), may be attractions or deterrents. Bear in mind that accommodation at these times can be very heavily booked.

Climate
Broadly speaking summers (late May to August) are extremely hot everywhere (except at high altitude, as in Tibet) and very humid in the south. Winters vary from one part of China to another: central China, along the Yangtze, has a short, cold winter (late November to mid-March) whilst the regions to the north are very cold and, in Beijing and northwards, well below freezing. South of the Yangtze temperatures rarely fall below freezing, but vary from cool to warm; in the lowland southwest, winters are very warm. The rainy season runs from May through August. In April sandstorms sometimes occur in Beijing and Inner Mongolia.

Roads like this (in Beijing) remain an essentially urban phenomenon

National holidays
China has nine national holidays: New Year's Day (1 January); Chinese New Year or Spring Festival (the first day of the lunar calendar, usually February) which lasts between three days and a week, when everything closes (an added irritation is the popular pastime of exploding terrifyingly loud firecrackers, although this has been banned in major cities); International Working Women's Day (8 March); International Labour Day (1 May); Youth Day (4 May); Children's Day (1 June); Communist Party Anniversary Day (1 July); People's Liberation Army Day (1 August); National Day (1 October, usually with an additional day).

Other traditional festivals include the Lantern Festival on the 15th day of the 1st lunar month; the Dragon Boat Festival on the 5th day of the 5th lunar month; and the Mid-Autumn Festival on the 15th day of the 8th lunar month.

Time differences
China is 8 hours ahead of GMT and thus 13 hours ahead of New York, and 2 hours behind Melbourne. China adopts summer-time (forward one hour) in mid-April and winter-time (back one hour) in mid-September.

Clocks throughout China are set according to Beijing time which means, given the size of the country, that sunrise and sunset can occur at peculiar hours.

Money matters
Until recently there were two types of money – one for locals, called Renminbi, and another for foreigners which came in the form of Foreign Exchange Certificates or FECs. Thankfully this system has been done away with and everybody now uses the national currency, the *yuan*, divided into 100 *fen*. Ten fen are called a *mao* or *jiao*. Exchange rates vary from day to day but little, if at all, from place to place. When you buy *yuan* keep the receipts in case you need to re-exchange when you leave China (although you are allowed to return no more than 50 per cent of what you have bought). Traveller's cheques and all major currencies are acceptable and many larger shops are happy to accept US dollars directly. Credit cards can be used in all major hotels and in some shops.

Foreigners usually pay more than locals on planes, trains and some buses, and for hospital care and some hotels.

China's police, an ubiquitous presence

Crime and the police

Until recently one would have had little hesitation in pronouncing China one of the safest places in the world from the point of view of the foreign visitor. It remains very safe compared to almost everywhere else but you are advised to take sensible precautions – keep valuables in safe boxes where available in hotels; do not leave money or valuables lying around hotel rooms and conceal them when out on the streets; lock your suitcases. The streets at night are very safe – violent crime against foreigners is almost unknown.

It is difficult to assess the ability of the police but unless the crime is serious enough to reflect badly on China, swift action is unlikely. None the less, report cases of theft to the police or the nearest Foreign Affairs branch of the Public Security Bureau for insurance purposes. If a serious crime is being ignored, contact your embassy or consulate.

Emergency telephone numbers

The emergency travel assistance number of CITS is Beijing (01) 603 1185.
Police 110
Fire 119
Ambulance 120

Embassies and consulates

Most countries have embassies in Beijing and some have consulates in other major cities.

In Beijing

Australia: 15 Dongzhimenwai Dajie (tel: (01) 532 2331)
Canada: 10 Sanlitun Lu (tel: (01) 532 3536)
France: 3, Sanlitun Dongsan Jie (tel: (01) 532 1331)
Germany: 5 Dongzhimenwai Dajie (tel: (01) 532 2161)
Irish Republic: 3 Ritan Dong Lu (tel: (01) 532 2691)
New Zealand: 1 Ritan Donger Jie (tel: (01) 532 2731)
Norway: 1 Sanlitun, Dong Yi Jie (tel: (01) 532 2261)
United Kingdom: 11 Guanghua Lu, Jianguomenwai (tel: (01) 532 1961)
United States: 3 Xiushui Beijie, Jianguomenwai (tel: (01) 532 3831)

In Canton (Guangzhou)

United States: White Swan Hotel, 1 Shamian Nanjie, Shamian Island (tel: 8888911)

In Shanghai

Australia: 17 Fuxingl Xiu (tel: 4374580)
Belgium: Jing'an Guest House, Room 303 (tel: 2538882)
Canada: Union Building, 100 Yan'an Dong Lu (tel: 202822)
France: 1431 Huaihai Zhong Lu (tel: 4377414)
Germany: 181 Yongfu Lu (tel:

4379953)
Italy: 127 Wuyi Lu (tel: 2524373)
United Kingdom: 244 Yongfu Lu (tel: 4374569)
United States: 1469 Huaihai Zhonglu (tel: 4378511)

Lost property (*shiwu zhaolingchu*)
If you lose anything, inform your hotel – there is every chance that it will have been handed to Reception. Then speak to your guide for further advice. If credit cards or traveller's cheques have been stolen, inform the issuer. In serious difficulty, get in touch with your embassy.

Health, vaccinations and pharmacies
Health Considering its comparative poverty and its climatic extremes, China is a remarkably healthy country. The Chinese are fairly punctilious about hygiene, particularly where food and drink are concerned. Tap water is not safe but any water you are offered to drink is sure to have been boiled; mineral water is widely available. Food ingredients are always fresh and cooked or cleaned thoroughly. However, stomach upsets are possible so take a proprietary medicine with you. More common ailments are sore throats and chesty colds which can strike at any time of year. The summer heat can seriously affect your health and a steady supply of liquids is essential to prevent dehydration. Hospital care is, on the whole, reasonable and in major cities foreigners receive special attention (for special prices). Usually payment is made afterwards, but some hospitals may ask for payment in advance; in any case it is sensible to check the cost beforehand. Traditional Chinese medicine can be efficacious but requires patience. For minor ailments, hotels frequently have their own clinics. For Beijing, see page 79.

Vaccinations Currently no vaccinations are required but check with your doctor or clinic for up-to-date information. Tetanus and typhoid injections are essential for travel anywhere and it is advisable to consider vaccinations against rabies and hepatitis. There is a risk of malaria in south China in the remoter areas, and it is recommended that you check this before you go.

Pharmacies Pharmacies in the big cities are well stocked with both Western and Chinese drugs. Without a prescription, however, it will be difficult to explain what you want, so if you are already taking a course of prescribed drugs, bring your own supply. Women are advised to stock up on tampons or sanitary towels if visiting remoter areas.

The British Embassy, Beijing

Car rental
It is possible to hire a self-drive car at Shanghai airport but not from any other location as yet, although foreigners, usually those resident for one reason or another, are permitted to drive in China. Cars with drivers may be hired (at a price) on a daily or weekly basis in major cities – addresses of such companies can be obtained through CITS. In Beijing, telephone 863661 or the Beijing Car Company on 594441.

Traffic tips
Driving in China presents special problems which also affect foreign pedestrians and cyclists. Generally roads and traffic regulations still tend to favour pedestrians and bicycles. Traffic in towns moves very slowly, and learning to negotiate it involves the acquisition of special skills. Patience is vital and so is the ability to feel your way through streams of bicycles, handcarts and donkeys.

On the whole people are law-abiding road-users, although country-dwellers, who now visit cities like Beijing in considerable numbers, are quite unused to cars and busy roads.

Old tramcars still running in Anshan, Liaoning province

Horns are sounded all the time, which, while very annoying, is necessary since absence of the horn is taken by the car in front to mean that the coast is clear. The use of headlamps is curious, too: night drivers often dispense with them altogether, merely using full-beam from time to time to warn on-coming vehicles, a rather unnerving habit but drivers seem to think it is easier on the eyes.

Drive on the right-hand side of the road. In most cities it is permissible to turn right when the traffic lights are at red.

Public transport
Domestic flights China's size and the virtual absence of a motorway system mean that the principal methods of getting from place to place are train and aeroplane. Although it has improved over the last few years, Air China does not enjoy a favourable reputation, despite being broken up into a series of regional carriers, a process supposed to increase efficiency. The main fault is delay, made all the more frustrating because of the absence of explanation or apology. However, delays are much less frequent than in the past, the aircraft fleet is made up of modern planes from the USA, Britain and Russia, and airports in major cities have been modernised.

Tickets for domestic flights are reasonably priced but are beginning to rocket. Main routes are very busy and need to be booked well in advance either through CITS or a similar agent, or direct from Air China offices. Airport tax, variable from place to place, is payable for domestic flights, usually at a special desk before you check in. All flights are non-smoking. Hand-luggage is limited to one item and check-in luggage must be locked. You will be expected to present passport and visa, with boarding-pass, and to go through X-ray checks. Flights are usually announced in English as well as Chinese but surrounding noise often renders things incomprehensible.

Yibin buses, run on natural gas, Sichuan

Trains The train system, on the other hand, is very good. Tickets, obtainable through CITS and other agents, or directly from stations, are reasonably priced (though prices for foreigners are higher than for locals), and the trains generally dependable. There are two classes, so-called 'soft' and 'hard', both of which are manned by attendants. Pullman cars exist (crowded wooden benches in hard class, upholstered seats in soft) but, because of the distances involved, most rolling stock is made up of sleepers. A hard-class sleeper carriage (*yingwoche*) has a series of alcoves filled with triple-tiered wooden-slat bunks with thin mattresses and no bedding. There will be a basic lavatory at one end. A soft-class sleeper (*ruanwoche*) is divided into compartments each containing four bunks with bedding and flasks filled with hot water. There will be a lavatory at each end of the carriage, one Western, one Eastern. A very few carriages on certain routes are air-conditioned; most are cooled in the summer by fans. Long-distance trains have dining-cars, often serving meals of surprisingly high quality.

Trains are graded according to speed: *tekuai* is very fast, *zhikuai* is fast and *kuaike* reasonably fast.

Buses Buses are widely used within towns and cities, and between towns. The cheapest form of travel, they are also the least comfortable. Urban buses, whilst offering a comprehensive service, are frequently impossibly crowded, and long-distance buses are rather old-fashioned, even though there are now non-stop services on some longer routes. However, to

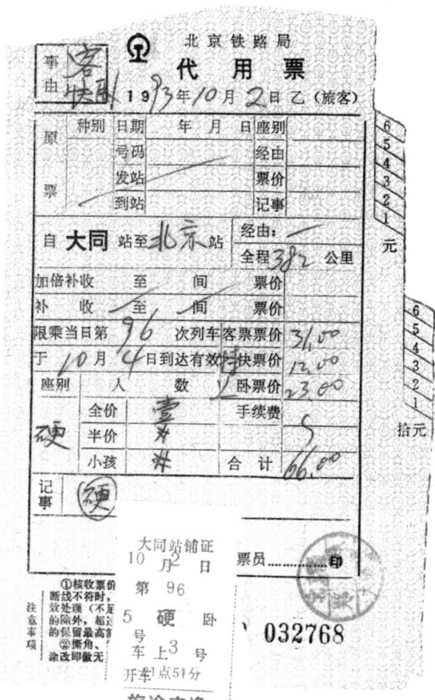

A foreigner's-priced train ticket

travel by bus is to travel as most Chinese do. Buy tickets for urban buses on board; for long-distance buses, buy in advance from the bus-station. Inside, there is little room for luggage – it will often go on the roof.

Taxis Taxis are easy to hire in most cities and can generally be hailed in the street. Most drivers use the meter but sometimes a reminder to use it is greeted with disdain, in which case it is wise to agree a price before you start. There are several categories of taxi, both state-owned and private. Basically, the smaller the taxi the cheaper the fare. See also page 79.

Above: pedicab driver. Below: kiddie transport, Chengdu-style

Bicycles
Bicycles (*zixingche*) are widely used and can be hired at little cost in most cities from hotels or from specialist outlets. Check the brakes and tyres before setting out and observe how the traffic functions in China – joining it unprepared can be an unnerving experience. Wayside repairs can often easily be effected by mechanics who ply their trade on the pavement.

Student and youth travel
The China Youth Travel Service (23-B Dongjiaominxiang, Beijing 100006; fax: 512 0571) is the branch of CITS which specialises in travel arrangements for students. Tour operators which specialise in travel to China can often make arrangements for younger people according to need, especially for groups of children or students; and it is often possible to make arrangements in advance to visit institutions which may be of particular interest. Bear in mind that few concessions are made to youth, particularly when it comes to money.

Camping and self-catering organisations
There are no opportunities for camping in the casual way that is taken for granted in many other countries. Even if the authorities permitted it, bedding down at the side of the road with a small bivouac would prove difficult because there is precious little land which is not cultivated, except in the wide empty provinces in the fringe areas of China. Camping is possible only when organised through CITS or one of its branches, and there are no organised camping sites.

There are no opportunities for self-catering holidays, unless you happen to know a foreign resident who is vacating his house for a while.

Visitors with disabilities
Despite a general improvement in many services and facilities China's provision for dealing with visitors with disabilities is almost non-existent. In general public transport, institutions, and Chinese towns lack facilities for visitors with disabilities, and although modern hotels are well equipped, China is a country of steps, crowded streets and unpleasant lavatories. Airlines and airports, however, have made efforts to improve their facilities and wheelchairs can be found when necessary.

Opening times
Banks, offices, government departments and public security bureaux Monday to Saturday, usually 8–6. Most close for at least one hour at lunch-time, usually from 12noon.

Shops Usually remain open 7 days a week and generally from 9 to 7.

Monuments and museums Apart from the larger ones like the Forbidden City, most often close for lunch and shut finally at 4pm. Many are open seven days a week and those which are not usually close on a Monday.

Restaurants and bars These are beginning to stay open later at night, and although at one time it was impossible to eat after 8pm, now you can find a meal at least as late as 9 or 10pm. Small open-air restaurant stalls often stay open into the small hours.

Places of worship
Buddhists will have no trouble finding places for worship since temples have reopened all over China following the end of the Cultural Revolution, and are open all day, every day.

For Muslims there is usually at least one mosque in every major city.

There are not yet synagogues in China. In theory Christian worship, still subject to persecution, is feasible in most large cities (and in some smaller ones) but churches often open only for services, usually at difficult hours.

Lavatories (*cesuo*)
To be blunt, where they exist, public lavatories in China are usually dreadful beyond belief, even in large cities. You are advised to do your utmost to avoid them but when

there is no help for it enter armed with your own toilet paper at the very least. Be prepared for a hole in the ground, no privacy, and a lack of accuracy by other users. Do not expect any washing facilities, either (except in a few cases where there is an attendant, to whom you will be required to pay a small fee). In restaurants or places which are aimed at foreigners the standard is altogether higher, though toilet paper may be absent here too.

Photography
In many ways China is a photographer's dream. Despite the general absence of brilliant colour, the country is immensely photogenic because there is so much taking place on the streets or in the fields and because the countryside is uniquely beautiful. Furthermore, people are oblivious to cameras on the whole, although the privacy of those who do object should be respected.

Photography is forbidden in most museums and archaeological sites (notably the main pit of the Terracotta Warriors), but some institutions permit it on payment of a fee, in advance, with a stiff fine for those who do not comply.

Colour print film is widely available, black and white or slide film much less so. Video film can be found but not always readily. All security X-ray machines on mainland China and at Hong Kong airport are film-safe.

As the atmosphere in China is often hazy, filters are advisable.

Electricity
Electricity is 220 volts, 50 cycles AC. Plugs are usually two prong, set at an angle to each other. Bulbs are both bayonet and screw type. Travel plugs are useful.

Computing in the 20th century: the abacus is still widely used

Etiquette and local customs

Getting on with the Chinese One of the purposes of a visit to China is to see and try to understand a culture which is, at least superficially, contrary to everything taken for granted at home. The Chinese people are a vital, fascinating part of the experience. The word often used to describe the Chinese is 'inscrutable', and while it is certainly true that the Chinese give few emotional messages this is not to say that they are unfathomable or that foreigners cannot empathise with them.

The Chinese do not display emotion and feelings in public and find plain-speaking unnerving. Often, therefore, decisions which would be made instantly elsewhere are accompanied by long preambles and detailed, if futile, consultations. This demands patience and politeness from those on the outside, for anger is seen as weakness.

The Chinese have an excellent sense of humour but it usually avoids sexual or political subjects. Skimpy clothing, whilst sometimes worn by the more daring among the nation's youth, is frowned upon on the whole.

The lack of information or the thoughtless omission of relevant facts which may be obvious to the Chinese host but not to his visitor can be particularly irritating to the foreigner. It is important, therefore, to check on arrangements as unobtrusively as possible.

People tend to stare, especially in the country, which can be off-putting but is nothing more than harmless curiosity. Privacy, it must be remembered, is an alien notion to the Chinese.

Tipping Despite official disapproval, tipping is no longer an offence; indeed it is now expected by tourist guides who prefer money – preferably American dollars – to any well-intentioned gift. Hotel porters will usually happily accept a tip, and so will taxi drivers although it is not necessarily expected. In most restaurants, tips are not usually expected, except in some of the top establishments.

CONVERSION CHARTS

FROM	TO	MULTIPLY BY
Inches	Centimetres	2.54
Centimetres	Inches	0.3937
Feet	Metres	0.3048
Metres	Feet	3.2810
Yards	Metres	0.9144
Metres	Yards	1.0940
Miles	Kilometres	1.6090
Kilometres	Miles	0.6214
Acres	Hectares	0.4047
Hectares	Acres	2.4710
Gallons	Litres	4.5460
Litres	Gallons	0.2200
Ounces	Grams	28.35
Grams	Ounces	0.0353
Pounds	Grams	453.6
Grams	Pounds	0.0022
Pounds	Kilograms	0.4536
Kilograms	Pounds	2.205

MEN'S SUITS

UK	36	38	40	42	44	46	48
Rest of Europe	46	48	50	52	54	56	58
US	36	38	40	42	44	46	48

DRESS SIZES

UK	8	10	12	14	16	18
Rest of Europe	34	36	38	40	42	44
US	6	8	10	12	14	16

MEN'S SHIRTS

UK	14	14.5	15	15.5	16	16.5	17
Rest of Europe	36	37	38	39/40	41	42	43
US	14	14.5	15	15.5	16	16.5	17

MEN'S SHOES

UK	7	7.5	8.5	9.5	10.5	11
Rest of Europe	41	42	43	44	45	46
US	8	8.5	9.5	10.5	11.5	12

WOMEN'S SHOES

UK	4.5	5	5.5	6	6.5	7
Rest of Europe	38	38	39	39	40	41
US	6	6.5	7	7.5	8	8.5

	CHINESE	METRIC
Length	1 chi	0.3333m
	1 li (1,500 chi)	0.5km
Area	1 mu	115ha
Volume	1 sheng	1lit
Weight	1 liang	50g
	1 jin (catty or 10 liang)	0.5kg

Tourism is now highly developed in some areas

Tourist Offices
China does not yet have tourist information offices. Most people still travel in groups so the main source of information will be local guides; individual travellers have to rely on their own ingenuity. The China International Travel Service (CITS, the state-run travel service and still the main one in China) is becoming more professional in its outlook and will often help even when you are not organising your trip through them.

CITS main offices and other travel services
Beijing, China International Travel Service (CITS), 103 Fuxingmennei Ave., Beijing 100800 (tel: (01) 601 1122; fax: (01) 601 2013)
Beijing, China Travel Service (CTS), 8 Dongjiaominxiang, Beijing 100005 (tel: (01) 512 9933; fax: (01) 601 2013)
Canton (Guangzhou), Guangdong CITS, 179 Huanshi Lu, Canton 510010 (tel: 6 666 271; fax: 6 667 8048)
Canton (Guangzhou), Guangdong CTS, 10 Qiaoguang Lu, Canton 510115, Guangdong (tel: 3 336 888; fax: 3 336 625)
Changchun CITS, 10 Xinming Dajie (tel: 647 052)
Changsha, 9 Wuyi Dong Lu (tel: 24855)
Chengdu,180 Renmin Nan Lu (tel: 679186)
Chongqing, 175 Renmin Lu (tel: 385 0188)
Dalian, Chantong Jie (tel: 363 7956)
Fuzhou, 73 Dongda Lu (tel: 755 5617)
Guilin, 14 Rhonghu Beilu, Guilin 541002, Guangxi (tel: 225 744)
China Guangxi Tourist Corp., 40 Xinmin Lu, Nanning 5300212, Guangxi (tel: 202 042; fax: 204 105)
Guiyang, 11 Yanan Zhong Lu (tel: 524693)
Haikou, Rm 306,3/f, HTSO Bldg, Sanjiaochi (tel: 535 8187)
Hangzhou, 1 Shihan Lu (tel: 515 2888)
Harbin, 95–1 Zhongshan Lu (tel: 262 2534)
Jinan, Shandong International Tourist Corp., 88 Jingshi Lu (tel: 296 5858)
Kunming, 218 Huancheng Nan Lu (tel: 313 2895)
Lanzhou, 361 Tianshui Lu (tel: 26181, ext: 761)
Lhasa, 148 Beijing Xi Lu (tel: 22980)
Nanjing, 202–1 Zhongshan Beilu (tel: 334 6444)
Nanchang, Jiangxi Binguan, Bayi Dadao (tel: 224 396)
Nanning, 40 Xinmin Lu (tel: 204 960)
Shanghai, 2 Jinling Dong Lu Shanghai 200002 (tel: 3 217 200; fax:

3 291 788)
Shanghai Jinjiang Tours Ltd, 27/F Union Bldg, 100 Yanan Dong Lu E., Shanghai 200002 (tel: 329 1025; fax: 3 200 595)
Shenyang, 113 Huanghe Nan Dajie (tel: 684 6501)
Suzhou, 115 Shichuan Jie (tel: 223 175)
Taiyuan, International Travel Bldg, 6 Pingyang Lu (tel: 707 5954)
Tianjin,22 Youyi Lu (tel: 835 8349)
Ürümqi, 51 Xinhua Beilu (tel: 221 427)
Wuhan, 48 Jianghan Yilu (tel: 282 1265)
Wuxi, 7 Xinsheng Lu (tel: 200585)
Xiamen, 15/f Zhenxing Bldg, Hubin Beilu (tel: 505 1822)
Xi'an, 32 North Chang'an Beiduan, Xi'an 710061 (tel: 526 2066; fax: 526 1558)
Xining, 215 Qiyi Lu (tel: 42721)
Yinchuan, 150 Jiefang Xijie (tel: 543 720)
Zhengzhou, 15 Jinshui (tel: 595 1134)

China has a selection of good information offices around the world:
Fremdenverkehrsamt der VR China, Ilkenhansstrasse 6, 6000 **Frankfurt**/M50 (tel: 049-520135; fax: 049-520137)
CITS Hong Kong, 6/F Tower 2, South Seas Centre, 75 Mody Road, Tsim Sha Tsui, **Kowloon** (tel: 7215317; fax: 7217154)
China National Tourist Office, 4 Glentworth Street, **London** NW1, England (tel: 0171 935 9427; fax: 0171 487 5842)
China National Tourist Office, **Los Angeles**, 333 West Broadway, Suite 201, Glendale, CA 91204, USA (tel: 818 545 7504; fax: 818 545 7506)
Oficina Nacional de Turismo de China, Gran Via, 88 Grupo 2, Planta 16, 28013 **Madrid**, Spain (tel: 34 1 5480011; fax: 34 1 5480597)
China National Tourist Office, Lincoln Building 60E, 42nd Street Suite 3126, **New York**, NY 10165, USA (tel: 212 867 0271; fax: 212 599 2892)
Office du Tourisme de Chine, 116 Avenue des Champs-Elysées 75008, **Paris**, France (tel: 44 21 8282; fax: 44 21 8100)
China National Tourist Office, 1 Shenton Way, No.17-05 Robina House, **Singapore** 0106 (tel: 0065-2218681; fax: 2219267)
China National Tourist Office, 19 Frishman Street, POB, 3281, **Tel-Aviv** 61030, Israel (tel: 972 3 5226272; fax: 972 3 5226281)
China National Tourist Office, Hachidai Hamamatsu Cho Bldg, 6F, 1-27-13 Hamamatsu Cho, Minato-Ku, **Tokyo** 105, Japan (tel: 03 433 1461; fax: 03 433 8653)

Chinese travel about China in greater numbers today

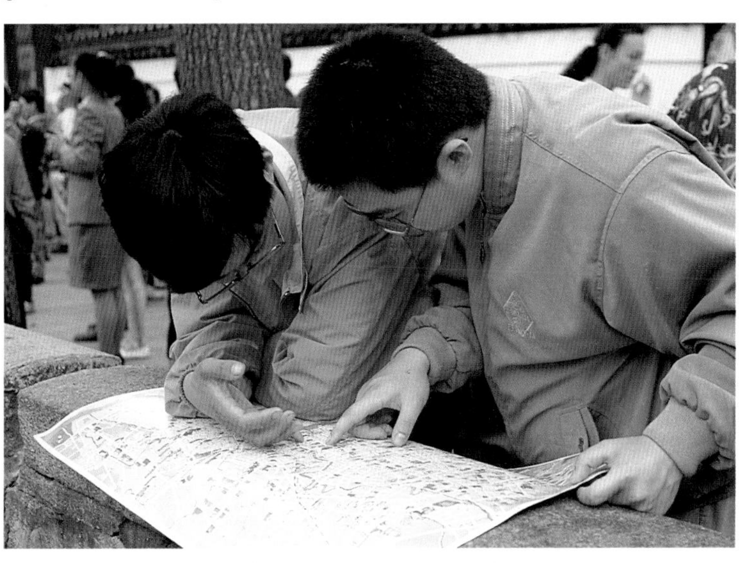

The post and telecommunications office in remote Daju, Yunnan

The media

Freedom of the press does not yet exist in China. Foreign observers trying to establish political trends, notoriously difficult in China, have learnt to read the newspapers for clues, since they tend to act as subtle mouthpieces for the government.

However, the English-language newspaper, *The China Daily*, available from most hotels, reads quite well and is not overtly biased. Although national television is similarly restricted, the CNN world service is received uncensored in hotels in all but the remotest corners of China. The same is true of radio services, although English-language services are sometimes provided locally, for example in Beijing, on Beijing Radio.

Post offices

China's postal service is quite efficient. It is easiest to buy stamps for letters and postcards in hotels. The airmail rate for postcards is slightly less than for letters. For insured postage, express mail and other services you will usually have to go to public post offices, which are open from 8 to 7.

Telephone (*dianhua*) and fax (*chuanzhen*)

The international telephone system is surprisingly good and the national service is improving as the system is gradually updated. Local calls are usually free, although some hotels do make a charge. Two 5-fen coins are needed for public phones. Check the rates for international calls before using the service – there is often a minimum charge and sometimes a small fee is made even when there is no answer. This is also the case with faxes. Many hotels boast 'business centres' featuring fax machines and other services. If you intend receiving incoming telephone calls give the caller your room number in advance since operators and receptionists frequently have difficulty in understanding foreign names.

The Chinese language

The national language is Mandarin (*putonghua*), based on Beijing dialect. Although there are a vast number of other dialects, most people understand *putonghua* and all Chinese speakers share the same written language. A surprisingly large number of people have a smattering of English. However, knowledge of some basic spoken Chinese is useful as well as courteous.

Each Chinese character represents a single-syllable sound, which in turn is converted into the Latin alphabet by the process of 'romanisation'. The official romanisation system is *pinyin*, used throughout China. In addition, syllables are given 'tone' values in order to differentiate between several characters which have the same romanisation but radically different meanings – thus the syllable *ma* can mean 'mother', 'horse', 'hemp', or 'scold' depending on which tone is used.

Putonghua has four tones, indicated by the following symbols:

¯ Ist tone: high, level
ˊ 2nd tone: starting lowish and rising
ˇ 3rd tone: starting low, falling then rising
ˋ 4th tone: starting high and falling.

Pinyin pronunciation guide

a as in car
b as in back
c when an initial consonant is a 'ts' sound as in bits
d as in doll
e as in her
f as in fat
g as in go
h as in house
i is an 'ee' sound as in feet unless preceded by c, ch, r, s, sh, z, zh, when it becomes 'er' as in her
j is like the g in gin
k as in kip
l as in lot
m as in man
n as in ran
o as in ford
p as in pin
q is 'ch' as in chin
r as in rum
s as in simple; sh as in shut
t as in time
u is 'oo' as in cool
w as in wade
x is like the 'sh' in sheep but with more emphasis on the s
y as in yoyo
z is a 'ds' sound as in lids; zh is a 'j' sound as in jam.

Geographic legend

This list of geographical terms may be useful when reading maps.

bandao	peninsula
bei	north
co	lake
da	great, greater
dajie	road, street
dao	island
ding	mountain, peak
dong	east
feng	mount, peak
gang	harbour
gaoyuan	plateau
guan	pass
hai	lake, sea
haixia	strait, channel
he	river
hu	lake
jiang	river
jiao	cape
jie	road, street
kou	estuary, river mouth
la	pass
liedao	archipelago, islands
ling	mountain, range
lu	road, street
nan	south
nur	lake, salt lake
pao	lake
pendi	basin
qu	canal
qundao	archipelago, islands
ringco	lake
shamo	desert
shan	mountain, range
shan kou	pass
shi	municipality
tag	mountains
wan	gulf, bay
xi	west
xiao	lesser, little
yanchi	salt lake
yumco	lake
yunhe	canal
zangbo	river

Numerals

English	Pinyin	Chinese
1	*yī*	一
2	*èr*	二
3	*sān*	三
4	*sì*	四
5	*wǔ*	五
6	*liù*	六
7	*qī*	七
8	*bā*	八
9	*jiǔ*	九
10	*shí*	十
11	*shí yī (10+1)*	十一
12	*shí èr*	十二
13	*shí sān*	十三
20	*èr shí*	二十
21	*èr shí yī (2x10+1)*	二十一
100	*(yī) baǐ*	一百
101	*yī baǐ yī*	一百一
1000	*(yī) qīan*	(一)千
10,000	*(yī) wàn*	(一)万

Useful words and phrases

English / *Pinyin*	Chinese
hello/how are you? *ní haǒ/ní haǒ ma?*	你好?/你好吗?
good bye *zài jiàn*	再见
thank-you *xìe xìe*	谢谢
good/OK *hǎo*	好
very good *hén hǎo*	很好
not good/bad *bù hǎo*	不好
cheers/to your health *gān bēi*	干杯
please *qǐng*	请
yes/have/ there is/are *yǒu*	有
no/have not/ there isn't/aren't (any) *meí yǒu*	没有
I *wǒ*	我
you (you, plural) *nǐ/nǐmen*	你/你们
he/she *tā*	他
we *wǒmen*	我们
be/is *shì*	是
when? *shén mè shí hòu?*	什么时候
today *jīn tīan*	今天
tomorrow *míng tīan*	明天
yesterday *zúo tīan*	作天
morning *shàng wǔ/* or *zǎo shàng*	上午/早上
evening *wǎn shàng*	晚上
afternoon *xìa wǔ*	下午
where?/ where is? *zaì ná lǐ / zài nǎr*	在那里/在那儿

Calligrapher at work

wait a moment 等一下
děng yī xià

please give/bring me..... 请给我
qǐng géi wǒ......

I would like..... 我想要....
wó xiǎng yaò.....

is there anyone who speaks English? 有没有人会说英文?
yǒu méi yǒu rén huì shuō yīng wén?

may I take a photograph? 我可以照相吗?
wǒ kéyi zhào xiàng ma?

I understand 我懂
wǒ dǒng

I don't understand 我不懂
wǒ bu dǒng

please write (it down) 请写
qíng xǐe

At the hotel

hotel/guesthouse 饭店/宾馆
fàndìan/bīngǔan

room 房间
fáng jīan

how much is it? 多少钱
dūo shǎo qían?

cheap/cheaper 便宜/便宜的
pían yì/pían yì de

expensive/too expensive 贵/太贵
guì/taì guì

At the post office/bank/shops

post office 邮局
yoú jú

stamps 邮票
yoú pìao

postcards 明信片
míng xìn pìan

airmail 航空
háng kōng

phone call/telephone 电话
diàn hùa

long-distance phone call 长途电话
cháng tú diàn hùa

bank/Bank of China 银行/中国银行
yín háng/zhōng gúo yín háng

money exchange 换钱处
huàn qián chù

Travelling around

CITS (China International Travel Service) 中国旅行社
zhōng gúo lǚ xíng shè

can you take me to.....? 你可不可以带我去...?
nǐ ké bù ké yǐ daì wǒ qù.....?

(to) buy 买
maǐ

ticket 票
pìao

taxi 出租汽车
chū zū qì chē

airport/CAAC 飞机场/中国民航
feī jī chǎng/zhōng gúo mín háng

train/train station 火车/火车站
hǔo chē/hǔo chē zhàn

bus: public bus 公共汽车
gōng gòng qì chē

long-distance bus 长途汽车
cháng tú qì chē

bus station 汽车站
qì chē zhàn

boat 船
chúan

bicycle 自行车
xì xíng chē

In a restaurant

restaurant:
fàn guǎn 饭馆

fàn diàn 饭店

cān tīng 餐厅

do you have an English menu? 有没有英文菜单?
yǒu méi yǒu yīng wén caī dān?

I am a vegetarian 我是素食者
wǒ shì sù shí zhě

water/boiled water 水/开水
shuǐ/kaī shuǐ

coffee 咖啡
kā fēi

black tea 红茶
hóng chá

jasmine tea 茉莉花茶
mò lì huā chá

beer 啤酒
pí jǐu

soft drink 汽水
qì shuǐ

rice 饭
fàn

glass/cup 玻璃杯/杯子
bō lí beī/beī zi

table knife 餐刀
cān dāo

fork 叉子
chā zi

spoon 勺子
sháo zi

Medical emergencies

I feel ill 我不舒服
wǒ bù shū fu

doctor 医生
yī shēng

pharmacy 药店
yào diàn

Signs you will see in public places

entrance 入口
rù kǒu

exit 出口
chū kǒu

toilet 厕所
cè sǔo

embassy 大使馆
dà shí guǎn

Countries

USA 美国
měi guó

Canada 加拿大
jiā ná dà

Australia 澳大利亚
ào dà lì yà

Great Britain 英国
yīng guó

France 法国
fǎ guó

Germany 德国
dé guó

Japan 日本
rì běn

China 中国
zhōng guó

HOTELS AND RESTAURANTS

ACCOMMODATION

In contrast to the early 1980s, when there were almost no reliably comfortable hotels, China now has a plethora of luxury hotels in all the major cities (and many lesser towns). They are good, but on the whole lack character, and often have service that seems more efficient than it really is. However, foreigners are usually pleasantly surprised at the comparatively high standards.

It should be noted that the telephone system in China is currently being updated and this necessitates changes in telephone and fax numbers.

Hotels have been graded as follows:

- cheapest hotels with private facilities (£)
- good, comfortable hotels in medium range (££)
- the best hotels available (£££)

Beidaihe

Jinshan Hotel (£), 4, Third Road of East Beidaihe (tel: 441338; fax: 442478). Modern resort hotel with facilities for bowling and tennis.

Beijing

Bamboo Garden Hotel (££), 24 Xiao Shi Qiao, Jiugulou Street, Xicheng District (tel: 4032229). Two-star hotel, well located for the northern part of the city.
Beijing Hotel (£££), 33 Dong Chang'an Avenue (tel: 5137766; fax: 5137307). Centrally located, dating back in parts to the beginning of the century. Generally comfortable with wide range of restaurants.
Beijing Peace Hotel (££), 3 Jinyu Hutong, Wangfujing (tel: 5128833; fax: 5126863). Good location in Beijing's busiest shopping district; pool.
Beijing-Toronto (Jinglun) (££), 3 Jianguomenwai Dajie (tel: 5002266; fax: 5002022). Good, central modern hotel with a variety of restaurants.
China World Hotel-Traders Hotel (££), 1 Jianguomenwai Dajie (tel: 505 2266; fax: 505 3167). A large, modern business hotel with 21 restaurants of all types reasonably located just to the east of the central areas.
Desheng (£), 14 Beisanhuangzhong Lu (tel: 2024477). Bargain hotel in the east of the city.
Diaoyutai State Guesthouse (£££), Sanlihe Lu (tel: 868833; fax: 8013362). Offering the peculiar flavour of late 1950s China, built to house visiting heads of state and now is open to deluxe tour groups.
Feixia (£), Building 5, Xili Xibiangmen, Xuanwuqu (tel: 3412470). Dormitory rooms.
Fragrant Hills Hotel (££/£££), Beijing Haidianqu 100093 (tel: 259 1166; fax: 259 1762). Modern hotel of award-winning design located in the Western Hills, beyond the Summer Palace.
Friendship Hotel (£/££), 3 Baishiqiao Lu (tel: 8498888; fax: 8314661). Older Russian/Chinese hotel near the Summer Palace. Good value. Outdoor pool.
Gloria Plaza (££/£££), 2 Jianguomennan Avenue (tel: 515 8855; fax: 515 8533). Modern, located close to the railway station in the downtown area, and among the cheaper of the centrally located comfortable hotels. Rather soulless but with a pool, gym, restaurants.
Grand Hotel (£££), 33 Dong Chang'an Avenue (tel: 5137788; fax: 5130048). Luxury hotel built in a very central location adjoining the Beijing Hotel.
Great Wall Sheraton (£££), Donghuan Beilu (tel: 5005566; fax: 5001919). One of Beijing's first luxury hotels, reasonably well located near the diplomatic corner, it has 10 restaurants, a nightclub, health club, pool, theatre and tennis courts.
Guanghua (£), 38 Dongsanhuanbei Lu (tel: 501 6515). Bargain hotel in the northeast of the city.
Hademen (£), A–2 Chongwenmenwai Dajie (tel: 7012244). Quite well located at good price.
Hilton (£££), I Bei Dong Sanhuan Lu (tel: 4662288; fax: 4653052). New member of the well-known luxury chain located in the northeast of the city.
Holiday Inn (££), 98 Beilishi Lu (tel: 8322288; fax: 8024696). Good-value hotel in a good central location; babysitting, pool, several restaurants including Indian.
Holiday Inn Lido (££/£££), Jichang Lu, Jiangtai Lu (tel: 5006688; fax: 5006237). Good-value hotel but situated on the edge of the city near a diplomatic area, convenient for the airport. Good facilities including pool.
International Hotel (Guoji) (£££), 9 Jianguomennei Dajie (tel: 5126688; fax: 5129972). Good location, 12 restaurants, business centre.
Jianguo (££/£££), 5 Jianguomenwai Dajie (tel: 5002233; fax: 5002871). The first of Beijing's joint-venture hotels, the Jianguo is central and has succeeded in maintaining its standards. Business centre, pool and airport shuttle bus.
Kempinski Hotel (£££), Xiaoliang Maqiao (tel: 4653388; fax: 4653366). New luxury hotel in the northeast of the city, considered one of the best of the newest generation of foreign-managed hotels.
Kunlun (££), 2 Xinyuan Wanlu, Chaoyang (tel: 5003388; fax: 5003228). A Chinese version of the Sheraton; tennis courts, pool, revolving restaurant.
Leyou (£), 13 Dongsanhuan Nanlu (tel: 771 2266). Some dormitory rooms.
Minzu Hotel (£/££), 51 Fuxingmennei Lu (tel: 6014466; fax: 6014849). Pretty good location at very good prices if you can get in. Adequate comfort, good range of facilities.
Beijing Movenpick Airport Hotel (££/£££), Xiaotianzhu Village, Shunyi County, PO Box 6913 (tel: 4565588; fax: 4565678). Best of the airport hotels with business facilities, pool and tennis courts.
Hotel New Otani (££/£££), 26 Jianguomenwai Dajie (tel: 5125555; fax: 5139813). Pretty good location on main central thoroughfare; pool

and several restaurants.
Novotel Songhe (££/£££), 78–88 Dengshikou Lu (tel: 5138822; fax: 513 9088). Modern chain hotel well located for Wangfujing shopping area and the Forbidden City.
Overseas Chinese Hotel (£/££), 5 Santiao Beixinqiao (tel: 4016688; fax: 4012386). Older hotel but in a good fairly downtown location at good prices if you can get a room.
Palace Hotel (££/£££), 8 Jinyu Hutong, Wanfujing (tel: 5128899; fax: 5129050). Well-located new hotel close to main shopping areas. Pool, nightclubs, European and Chinese restaurants.
Qianmen (£/££), 175 Yongan Lu (tel: 3016688). Older 1950s hotel, modernised to a reasonable standard. A bargain for its basic comfort and good location in an interesting area.
Qiaoyuan (£), Dongbinhe Lu, Yongdingmen (tel: 338861). Dormitory accommodation available.
Ritan (£), 1 Ritan Lu, Jianguomenwai (tel: 5125588). Bargain hotel in reasonable location.
Shangri-la (£££), 29 Zizhuyuan Lu (tel: 8412211; fax: 8418002). Luxury hotel with good reputation in the northwest of the city. Pool, business centre, several restaurants and a delicatessen.
Taiwan (££), 5–15 Jinyu Hutong, Wangfujing (tel: 5136688; fax: 5136596). Well located in main shopping area. No pool but most other standard features.
Zhaolong (££), 2 Gongti Beilu, Chaoyang (tel: 5002299; fax: 5003319). In the same area as the Sheraton and the Kunlun but considerably cheaper. Facilities, including a pool, are of reasonable quality.

Canton
see **Guangzhou**

Changchun
Changchun Hotel (£), 10 Xinhua Lu (tel: 22661). Central and good value.

Changsha
Changsha Hotel (£), 116 Wuyi Lu (tel: 25029). Central location and also convenient for railway station.
Xiangjiang Hotel (£/££), 2 Zhongshan Road (tel: 408888; fax: 448285). Dating from the 1950s, central and of a reasonable standard.

Chengdu
Chengdu (£/££), Shudu Dadao (tel: 444112; fax: 441603). Modern hotel; indoor pool, tennis court.
Jinjiang Hotel (££), 180 Renmin Lu (tel: 582222; fax: 581849). A huge monolith, this is the oldest hotel in the city. It has been modernised, has a good location, and a number of facilities but they are of varying quality.
Minshan (££), Renmin Nanlu (tel: 583333). Well-located hotel opposite the Jinjiang, though more modern and smaller.

Chongqing
Holiday Inn Yangtze (££/£££), 15 Nanping Beilu (tel: (811) 2803380; fax: (811) 2800884). International-style hotel with the usual Holiday Inn facilities, something of a bonus in this city.
Renmin Hotel (£), 175 Renmin Road (tel: (811) 3851421; fax: (811) 3852076). The old tourist hotel, modelled on the Temple of Heaven in Beijing with a spectacular exterior, has now been updated.

Datong
Yungang (£), 21 Yingbin Datong Lu (tel: 521601). Basic but reasonable hotel in a central location.

Dunhuang
Dunhuang Binguan (£), 1 Dong Dajie (tel: 09474 224 15). Reasonable quality.

Emeishan
Hongzhushan Hotel (£), Mount Emei, Sichuan (tel: (0833) 33888; fax: 0833 33788). Old simple hotel with pool. A good base for visiting the holy mountain.

Fuzhou
Hot Spring Hotel (££), Wusi Zhonglu (tel: 551818). Modern facilities; pool, piped-in hot spring water.

Guangzhou (Canton)
China Hotel (£££), Liuhua Lu (tel: 6666888; fax: 6677014). Huge, with fine amenities, beautiful outdoor pool and good location for railway station.
Dongfang Hotel (££/£££), 120 Liuhua Road (tel: 6669900; fax: 6662775). Very large, with tennis and squash courts.
Hotel Equatorial (££), 931 Renmin Road (tel: 6672888; fax: 6672583). Standard modern hotel; good location near the Trade Fair. Among its amenities it claims a 'horoscope service'.
Garden Hotel (£££), 368 Huanshi Donglu (tel: 3338989; fax: 3350467). A well-located hotel for Friendship Store, airport and railway station. Excellent facilities, beautiful gardens.
Holiday Inn City Centre (£/££), Huanshi Dong (tel: 7766999; fax: 7753126). Usual Holiday Inn standards at reasonable prices, pool.
Hotel Landmark (£££), Qiaoguang Road, Haizhu Square (tel: 3355988; fax: 3336197). Good downtown location, very comfortable, with fine views from upper rooms, several restaurants and a helipad.
Victory Hotel (£), 54 Shamian Beijie (tel: 8862622; fax: 8862413). A colonial building in an excellent location with reasonable standards of service.
White Swan (£££), Shamian Island (tel: 8886968; fax: 8861188). This stylish hotel has a lovely central location on the riverbank. Still the best hotel in Canton, perhaps in China.

Guilin
Guishan Hotel (£££), Chuanshan Lu (tel: 443388; fax: 444851). Luxury hotel on the riverbank with pool, tennis courts, business centre.
Holiday Inn (££/£££), 14 Ronghu Nanlu (tel: 223950;

fax: 222101). Pleasant location with health club and two restaurants.
Hong Kong Hotel (££), 8 Xihuan Yi Lu (tel: 333889). Pool, tennis courts, revolving roof-top restaurant.
Lijiang (£/££), 1 Shanhu North Road (tel: 222881; fax: 222891). A cheaper alternative to the Sheraton but some way behind in terms of comfort.
Osmanthus Hotel (££), 451 Zhongshan South Road (tel: 334300; fax: 335316). Perhaps the best location in the city, lying alongside a creek off the main street.
Ronghu Hotel (££), 17 North Ronghu Road (tel: 223811; fax: 225390). Just outside the busy part of town, prettily situated by a lake.
Sheraton Guilin Hotel (£££), Bingjiang Nanlu (tel: 225588; fax: 225598). Possibly the best hotel in the city, well located. Architecturally uninspiring, but reliable.

Hangzhou
Dragon Hotel (£££), Shuguang Road (tel: 554488; fax: 558090). Luxurious and modern; excellent amenities.
Hangzhou Huagang Hotel (£), 4 Xishan Road (tel: 771324; fax: 772481). Pleasant, good-value hotel in pretty surroundings and well located for the lake.
Huajiashan (£/££), Xishan Road (tel: 771224; fax: 773980). Tranquil location, good for the West Lake.
Shangri-la Hangzhou (££), 78 Beishan Lu (tel: 777951; fax: 773545). Lakeside hotel; pool and good facilities.

Harbin
Heilongjiang Guest House (£/££), 52 Hongjun Lu (tel: 329509). Old-fashioned establishment with good restaurant and location.
Swan Hotel (££), 73 Zhongshan Lu (tel: 220201). The best hotel in town but some way from the centre.

Hohhot (Inner Mongolia)
Nei Mongol Hotel (£/££), Hulun Nanlu (tel: 25754). Air-conditioned modern hotel.
Zhaojun Hotel (£/££), 11 Xinhua Road (tel: 662211; fax: 668825). Reasonably priced and comfortable hotel in the city centre.

Hong Kong, Hong Kong Island
Caravelle (££/£££), 84 Morrison Hill Road (tel: 25754455). Located near Happy Valley racecourse .
Excelsior (££/£££), 281 Gloucester Road (tel: 28948888). Very good value with an excellent location overlooking the harbour and a popular bar.
Furama Kempinski (£££), 1 Connaught Road (tel: 25255111). Excellent location; revolving restaurant on the top floor.
Harbour Hotel (££), 116-122 Gloucester Road (tel: 25118211). A good-value waterfront hotel located in the old nightclub area.
Hilton (£££), 2 Queen's Road Central (tel: 25233111). Still a good hotel well sited for the business district, Peak Tram and ferry services. One of the few hotels with a pool.
Mandarin Oriental (£££), 5 Connaught Road Central (tel: 25220111). Regularly voted one of the finest hotels in the world, it is indeed excellent but with prices to match its reputation. Pool.
Park Lane (££), 310 Gloucester Road (tel: 28903355). Reasonable position on the edge of the busy Causeway Bay district.

Hong Kong, Kowloon
Eaton Hotel (££), 380 Nathan Road (tel: 27821818). A new reasonably priced hotel with a good location and pool.
Holiday Inn Harbour View (££/£££), 70 Mody Road (tel: 27215161). Good-value comfort with good views in the right rooms and within walking distance of the shopping districts. Pool.
Hong Kong (££/£££), 3 Canton Road (tel: 27360088). Well located next to the Star Ferry terminal; near shops.
Peninsula (£££), Salisbury Road (tel: 23666251). No longer considered the best in Hong Kong but still one of the world's great hotels for the discerning.
Regal Airport Hotel (££/£££), Sa Po Road (tel: 27180333). Airport hotel linked by a walkway to main terminal.
Regent (£££), Salisbury Road (tel: 27211211). A luxurious, well-located establishment.
YMCA (£) 41 Salisbury Road (tel: 23692211). An absolute bargain in a good location if you can get a reservation.

Jinan
Nanjiao Hotel (£/££), 2 Ma'anshan (tel: 2953931). Older, comfortable hotel on the edge of town with pool.
Qilu Hotel (£/££), Qianfoshan Lu (tel: 12966888). Comfortable; tennis courts.

Kaifeng
Dongjing Hotel (££), Yingbin Lu (tel: 555544). New and reasonably comfortable.

Kunming
Cuihu Guesthouse (£/££), Cuihu Nanlu (tel: 5155788). Nice location near lake and interesting old streets. Choice of old or new wings.
Golden Dragon Hotel (££), 575 Beijing Lu (tel: 313015; fax: 313082). Modern comfortable hotel with good facilities; not well located.
Holiday Inn (££/£££), 25 Dong Feng Donglu (tel: 3165888; fax: 3135189). The best hotel in the city with central location, pool, friendly bar and good discothèque.

Lanzhou
Friendship Hotel (£/££), 14 Xijinxi Lu (tel: 30511). The only hotel of any comfort in the city.

Lhasa
Holiday Inn (££), 1 Minzu Lu (tel: 32221). Good hotel with, given the difficult circumstances, good food. Oxygen on tap in the rooms.
Tibet House (£), Minzu Lu (tel: 23738). Good location and reasonable standard.

Luoyang
Friendship Hotel (£/££), Xiyuan Lu (tel: 412780). Comfortable, old-fashioned, with pool but in unexciting location.
International Hotel (£/££), Renmin Lu (tel: 27155). Well located in the old town.

Macao

Bela Vista (£££), Rua Comendador Kou, Ho Neng 8 (tel: 965333; fax: 965588). Macao's first colonial hotel and its most famous. Long history, considerable character. Book well in advance.
East Asia Hotel (££), Rua da Madeira 1 (tel: 922433). In the heart of the old quarter.
Lisboa (££/£££), Avenida da Amizade (tel: 377666; fax: 567193). Waterfront hotel with several casinos and well-known restaurant.
Mandarin Oriental (£££), Avenida de Amizade (tel: 567888; fax: 594589). Waterfront luxury, pool, casino.
New Century Hotel (£/££), Estrada Almirante, Marques Espartaro, Taipa (tel: 831111). Five-star hotel at reasonable prices and with highly recommended Cantonese restaurant.

Nanjing

Jinling Hotel (££), Xinjiekou Square (tel: 4455888). High-rise hotel in the town centre; pool, revolving roof-top bar.
Nanjing Hotel (£), 259 North Zhongshan Road (tel: 66341212; fax: 3306998). Old-fashioned hotel set in pretty gardens; famous for its chocolate soufflé.

Nanning

Xiyuan (£/££), 38 Jiangnan Lu (tel: 229923). Old and comfortable hotel in pretty gardens with pool.

Qingdao

Huiquan Dynasty Hotel (££), 9 Nanhai Lu (tel: 2879279; fax: 2871122). Modern and comfortable hotel opposite one of the main beaches.
Zhanqiao Guest House (£/££), 31 Taiping Lu (tel: 83402). Opposite a beach, tranquil accommodation with good restaurant.

Qufu

Queli Hotel (£/££), 15 Zhonglou Street (tel: 411303; fax: 412022). Charming, traditional hotel, good location; ancient Chinese music performed.

Shanghai

Cypress Hotel (££), 2419 Hongqiao Lu (tel: 2558868; fax: 2423739). Early joint-venture hotel, well located for the airport.
Garden Hotel (£££), 58 Maoming Lu (tel: (021) 4331111; fax: (021) 4338866). A comfortable, well-located hotel built in the grounds of the former 'Cercle Sportif Français' (French Club).
Holiday Inn Yin Xing (££), 338 Panyu Lu (tel: 2528888; fax: 2528545). Pleasant location, pool, sauna.
Jinjiang Hotel (££), 59 Maoming Nanlu (tel: 2582582; fax: 14725588). Stylishly modernised hotel in the old French Concession. Good restaurants and bars.
Jinjiang Tower (£££), 161 Changle Road (tel: 433 4488; fax: (433 3265). Modern skyscraper in the old French Concession with revolving restaurant.
Park Hotel (££), 170 Nanjing Xilu (tel: 3275225; fax: 3276958). Colonial skyscraper in excellent location, renowned for its restaurant.
Peace Hotel (££), 20 Nanjing Road. (tel: 3211244; fax: 3290300). Perhaps the most famous hotel in Shanghai, with art deco features and an excellent location on the harbour front. Noel Coward wrote *Private Lives* here. Famous for its jazz band.
Shanghai Hilton (£££), 250 Huashan Lu (tel: 21480000; fax: 21483848). Skyscraper in good location with excellent facilities; pool.
Shanghai Mansions (£/££), 20 North Suzhou Road (tel: 3246260; fax: 3269778). Dating from the old foreign concession days, a good location at the north end of the Bund.
Sheraton Huating (£££), 1200 Caoxi Beilu (tel: (021) 43910000; fax: (021) 2550830). A taste of luxury, a little cheaper than some. Pool. On outskirts, convenient for Longhua and Ziccawei
Xingguo Guest House (£/££), 72 Xinguo Lu (tel: 4331220). In the heart of the former French concession, consists of some ten villas that used to belong to wealthy foreigners and were favoured by Mao.

Shenyang

Dongbei Hotel (£), 100 Tianjin Beijie (tel: 368120). Cheap, centrally located.
Liaoning Hotel (£), Zhongshan Square. Comfortable old-fashioned hotel with art deco features and well located.
Phoenix Hotel (£/££), 109 South Huanghe Street (tel: 6846501; fax: 6865207). The best hotel in the city but some way from the centre; tennis courts, fitness centre.

Suzhou

Bamboo Grove (££), Zhuihui Lu (tel: 225601; fax: 778778). Comfortable, modern hotel; tennis courts, health centre but not the best location.
Nanlin Hotel (£), 20 Gunxiufang (tel: 222808; fax: 771028). Tolerably comfortable and well located for visiting some of the gardens. Several restaurants in different styles.
Suzhou Hotel (£), 115 Shiquan Jie (tel: 224646; fax: 771015). Reasonably comfortable hotel, well sited for walking around the pretty streets of old Suzhou.

Taiyuan

Shanxi Grand Hotel (£/££), Xinjian Nanlu (tel: 443901; fax: 443525). Recently built hotel of reasonable comfort.

Tianjin

Astor (££), Taierzhuang Lu (tel: 331 1112). Old hotel recently refurbished with good central location.
Crystal Palace (£££), Youyi Lu (tel: 8356666). Suburban location by a small lake, with pool and tennis courts.
Hyatt Tianjin (£££), Jiefang Beilu (tel: 3318888). Luxurious, central hotel, with seven restaurants and business centre.
Sheraton (£££), Zijinshan Lu (tel: 3343388). Suburban location with pool and gym.

Ürümqi

Holiday Inn (££/£££), 168 Xinhua Beilu (tel: 218788; fax: 217422). Variety of restaurants; sauna, tennis courts. Central location.

Wuhan

Shengli (Victory) Hotel (££), 11 Siwei Lu (tel: 283 1241, fax 283 2604). Old colonial hotel in Hankou's former concession area, with a good restaurant.
Yangtze Hotel (££), 361 Jiefang Dadao (tel: 5862828; fax: 5854110). Comfortable if soulless middle-range hotel in reasonable location.

Wuxi

Hubin Hotel (££), Liyuan Road (tel: 601888; fax: 602637). An adequately comfortable hotel on the edge of Lake Tai, with rooms overlooking the lake.
Milido Hotel (£/££), 2 Liangxi Road (tel: 665665; fax: 601668). Reasonably priced, on the edge of central Wuxi.
Pan Pacific Wuxi Grand (££), 1 Liangqing Road (tel: 0510 606789; fax: 0510 200991). Wuxi's most luxurious hotel, on the fringes of the city centre and with a pool.

Xiamen

Gulangyu Guest House (£/££), 25 Huangyan Lu (tel: 2031856). A group of villas on the old concession island close to a beach but a 20-minute walk to the ferry.
Holiday Inn Harbourview (££/£££), (tel: 2023333; fax: 2036666). Very comfortable hotel with pool.
Lujiang (££), 3 Haihou Lu (tel: 2022922). Well located opposite the Gulangyu ferry.

Xi'an

Bell Tower Hotel (£/££), Southwest Corner of Bell Tower (tel: 727 9200; fax: 727 8767). One of the first hotels to be built in Xi'an since the discovery of the Terracotta Warriors, this has the best location of any in the city and is now a bargain.
Golden Flower (£££), 8 Changle Lu (tel: 32981). The first luxury hotel in Xi'an and in some ways still the best; pool, health club.
Holiday Inn (££/£££), 8 South Section, Huancheng East Road (tel: 323 3888; fax: 323 5962). Ideal for those who want comfort and service without huge expense.
Hyatt Regency (£££), 158 Dong Dajie (tel: 723 1234). A standard luxury hotel; several restaurants, entertainment centre and fitness centre.
Jianguo Hotel (££), 20 Jinhua Nanlu (tel: 323 8888; fax: 323 5145). Country cousin of the first joint-venture hotel in Beijing, affordable comfort with pool, sauna and gym.
Sheraton (£££), 12 Fenggao Lu (tel: 426 1888; fax: 426 2188). In the suburbs near the old airport, well-appointed; restaurants, pool.
Xi'an Garden Hotel (£££), 4 Dongyanyin Lu (tel: 526 1111; fax: 526 1998). Built in traditional Chinese style around pools and rockeries within sight of the Big Wild Goose Pagoda.
Xi'an People's Hotel (£), 319 Dongxin Xinjie (tel: 721 5111; fax: 721 6177). Built in the 1950s for 'Russian experts'; excellent location just off the central square. Rather gloomy building, but pleasant gardens and low rates.

Xining

Qinghai Hotel (£/££), 20 Huang He (tel: 23905). New hotel of reasonable quality.

Yinchuan

Ningxia Binguan (£/££), 3 Gongyuan Jie (tel. 545131). Adequately comfortable.

Zhengzhou

International Hotel (£/££), 114 Jinshui Dadao (tel: 5956600). Reasonably comfortable hotel with pool.

RESTAURANTS

It is invidious to give a list of recommended restaurants in China whene the country is still in a state of flux – restaurants come and go – and little that is new seems to have much sense of permanence.
As prices are governed more by what you eat than by the 'standing' or standard of the restaurant, no price grading for the restaurants is given.

However, it is possible to make some generalisations about eating in China. First, you can be reasonably sure of eating well in Chinese restaurants in the major hotels, but you will pay a premium price for the privilege. Secondly, there are certain restaurants which at any given time are used by CITS for tourist groups and in the smaller, poorer cities, where there appears to be less choice, this can be quite reassuring. Thirdly, it is fair to say that you run little risk of eating really badly in a country where good food is so highly appreciated. Fourthly, apart from the CITS-recommended establishments, there is no way of knowing what is exceptionally good and what is not. Sticking to expensive hotels and CITS-approved restaurants will ensure quality at a price. Otherwise you must trust to your nose.

Price and hygiene are the two things you must scrutinise. Foreigners are sometimes seen as fair game for higher prices and although compared with most similar countries China is clean, in the simpler restaurants you need to make judgements about cleanliness. The Chinese themselves will often check chopsticks and bowls.

It is easy to eat cheaply in China. Most streets have stalls selling plates of noodles or bowls of dumplings for next to nothing, where the quality is often high and the food is generally safe to eat. Small restaurants, selling beer and soft drinks, will have more variety and be a little more expensive. Restaurants of this type often have another, costlier section offering more sophisticated food and surroundings.

How to order Eating in China is a group activity. In most of the restaurants listed below tables can be booked in advance. Some restaurants may require prior warning for certain, more complicated dishes.

A Chinese meal is normally

served in sequence according to local specialities. Different dishes are placed in the middle of the table and diners are expected to serve themselves (except at banquets or in Cantonese restaurants where it is customary to be served) either with chopsticks or with serving-spoons if provided. Cold dishes are served first, then hot dishes which will arrive singly or in clusters. Rice usually arrives late in the meal and soup usually appears at the end.

Chopsticks Chopsticks (*kuaizhi)* are provided as a matter of course but forks (*chazi*) are usually available.

Beijing

Alfred's Tex-Mex, Sara Hotel Beijing, Huaqiao Dasha, 2 Wangfujing Dajie (tel: 5136666). Mexican.
Bavaria Bierstube, Palace Hotel, Wangfujing (tel: 5128899 ext: 7410). German.
Beijing Doo San, Hualong Jie, Nanheyan (tel: 5129130). Korean.
Café Kranzler, Kempinski Hotel West Wing, 50 Liangmaqiao Lu (tel: 4653388). Continental.
Chalon Restaurant, 50 Tiantan Donglu (tel: 7012660). Japanese.
Chaojing City, 24 Dong Xuanwumen (tel: 3014499 ext: 2242). Chaozhou school of cooking.
Confucian Heritage Restaurant, 3 Xi Liulichang, Xuanwu (tel: 3030689). Shandong food.
Cuihualou, 60 Wangfujing. Shandong seafood, and toffee apples.
Dasanyuan, 50 Jingshan Xijie (tel: 445378). Cantoneseg.
Donglaishun, 16 Jinyu Hutong (tel: 5139661). Excellent Mongolian hotpot.
Fangshan, Beihai Park (tel: 4011889). Specialising in imperial banquets.
Fengzeyuan, Xingfu Sancun, Chaoyang (tel: 4217508). Shandong cuisine, noted for seafood and soups.
Frank's Place, Gongti Donglu (tel: 5072617). American style cooking.
Gongdenlin, 158 Qianmen Nan Dajie (tel: 5112542). Vegetarian food.
Guangdong, Xijiao Market (tel: 894881). Cantonese.
Hongbinlou, 82 Xi Chang'an Jie (tel: 6014832). Well known for its Mongolian hotpot.
Kaurouji, 14 Qianhai Dongyan (tel: 445921). Specialises in Mongolian.
Kentucky Fried Chicken, Zhengyang Market, Qianmen Xi Dajie (tel: 5241317). Fast food.
Laozhengxing, 46 Qianmen Dajie (tel: 5112145). Specialises in Shanghai and Huaiyang styles.
Le France, Great Wall Sheraton, Donghuan Beilu (tel: 5005566 ext: 2119).
Liyuan, 8 Xi Huangchenggen (tel: 6015234). Thai food.
Macau Grill, Swissotel, Hong Kong Macau Centre, Dongsishitiao Lijiaoqiao (tel: 5012288 ext: 2271). Portuguese food.
McDonald's, A31, Dong Chang'an Jie (tel: 5120499) and 15 Fuwai Lu (tel: 8539185). Fast food.
Minim's, 2 Chongwenmenxi Dajie (tel: 5122211). Little brother to Maxim's of Paris.
Mitsukoshi, Fortune Bldg., 5 Dongsanhuan Beilu (tel: 5010591). Japanese food.
Nobel Grill, Sara Hotel, Huaqiao Dasha, 2 Wangfujing Dajie (tel: 5136666 ext: 2207). Swedish.
Peretti's Bar & Bistro, Level 3, Asia-Pacific Building, 8 Yabao Lu (tel: 5139988 ext: 10328). Italian food.
Pizza Hut, 27 Dong Zhimenwai Dajie (tel: 4082233 ext: 272 and 33) and Zhushikou Xijie, Xuanwuqu (tel: 3031272). Fast food.
The Poacher Inn, Friendship Restaurant, Sanlitun (tel: 5323063). English cooking.
Qianmen Quanjude Roast Duck Restaurant, 32 Qianmen Dajie (tel: 511 2418). One of the older and better duck restaurants, with central location.
Ren Ren, 18 Qianmen Dongdajie. Specialises in *dim sum.*
Ritan Park Restaurant, Ritan Park (tel: 5005939). Beijing style food.
Riverside Palace, Shuizha Beilu, Mentougou (tel: 9843366). Comfortable, if expensive restaurant serving Sichuanese food.
Saigon Inn, Gloria Plaza Hotel, 2 Jianguomennan Dajie (tel: 5158855). Vietnamese.
The Sichuan, 51 Xirongxian Hutong (tel: 6033291). Former Qing palace specialising in Sichuanese food.
Sichuan Douhua, 29 Guangqumenwai (tel: 7712672). Sichuanese.
Spring Restaurant, Shuizha Beilu, Mentougou (tel: 9843366). Swiss.
Tingliguan, Summer Palace (tel: 2582504). Imperial Beijing style food in good atmosphere.
Wangfujing Quanjude, 13 Shuaifuyuan, Wangfujing (tel: 553310). Roast duck restaurant.
Xiangshu, Wangfujing (tel: 558351). Specialises in chicken dishes in the Sichuan and Hunan styles.

Canton
see **Guangzhou**

Changchun

Changbaishan Guest House, 12 Xinmin Dajie (tel: 643551). Good reputation for Shandong cooking.
Chunyi Hotel, 2 Stalin Dajie (tel: 279966). Shandong cooking.

Changsha

The Changsha Restaurant, 116 Wuyi Donglu (tel: 25029). Well known for its regional spicy dishes.
Youyicun, 225 Zhongshan Lu (tel: 2222797). Spicy Hunan cooking closely related to that of Sichuan.

Chengdu

The Chengdu, 642 Shengli Zhong Lu (tel: 27301). Good local-style food.
Furong, 27 Renmin Nanlu (tel: 24004). Near the Jinjiang Hotel and famous for both hot Sichuan cooking and the milder style using herbs and flowers.

Chongqing

The Chongqing, Xinhua Lu (tel: 43996). Centrally located restaurant serving Sichuanese food.
Weiyuan, 37 Zhouyong Lu (tel: 43592). Sichuan-style cooking in reasonably comfortable surroundings.

Datong

Huayan, Da Xijie (tel: 32175). One of the few tolerably good restaurants outside the hotel in a region not noted for fine cooking.

Fuzhou

Banyan City, Bayiqi Lu. Popular restaurant specialising in seafood noodles.
Juchunyuan Restaurant, 130 Bayiqi Beilu (tel: 32338). Old restaurant specialising in Bees' Nest Beancurd and Jade Hatchet Dumplings.
Qingzhen, 342 Bayiqi Beilu (tel: 33517). Specialises in Muslim and vegetarian.

Guangzhou (Canton)

Home of one of the four main schools of Chinese cooking; light sauces and the freshest ingredients are the main characteristics. *Dim sum* are savoury snacks sold from trolleys which trundle among the tables.
The Banxi, 151 Longjin Xilu (tel: 8815718). The biggest restaurant here, noted for *dim sum* (including shark-fin dumplings and monkey brains) and stewed turtle.
The Guangzhou, 2 Wenchang Nanlu (tel: 8888388). Famous old restaurant, built around a central garden courtyard.
The North Garden (Beiyuan), 202 Xiaobei Lu (tel: 3330087). A traditional restaurant in busy but tranquil surroundings. Shark's Fin Soup is a speciality.
The Snake Restaurant (Shecanguan), 43 Jianglan Lu (tel: 8883811). Specialises in snakes – in soup, stewed or any other way.
South Garden (Nanyuan), 142 Qianjin Lu (tel: 4448380). On the south bank of the Pearl River and noted for chicken and pigeon.
Taipingguan, 344 Beijing Lu (tel: 332938). Western food as well as Chinese, but the latter is better.
The Taotaojiu, 20 Dishipu Lu (tel: 8816111). Centrally located, noted for *dim sum*.
The Wild Animals Restaurant (Yeweixiang Fandian), 247 Beijing Lu. Specialises in everything you ever feared about Chinese food – dogs, cats, snakes.

Guilin

Yueyalou, Seven Star Park (tel: 3622). Pleasant location, specialising in game.

Hangzhou

Luwailou, 2 Waixihu (tel: 21654). On Gushan Island and recommended for its seafood and fish dishes.
Tianxianglou, 166 Jiefang Lu (tel: 7063104). Restaurant specialising in giant prawns and Su Dongpo pork.

Harbin

Beilaishun, 127 Shangzhi Dajie (tel: 4619027). Noted for its Muslim dishes.
Futailou, 19 Xi Shisandou (tel: 47598). Good general Chinese food, including Beijing duck.
Huamei, 142 Zhongyang Lu (tel: 47368). Restaurant specialising in Western and Russian dishes.
Regency Gourmet Centre, near International Hotel. Good food but at a price.

Hong Kong

Au Trou Normand, 6 Carnarvon Road, Kowloon (tel: 23668754). Long-established, French-run restaurant with solid cooking and good service.
Café de Paris, 30-32 California Tower, D'Aguilar Street (tel: 25247521). Authentic French cooking in the business district.
Gaddi's, Peninsula Hotel, Kowloon (tel: 23666251). Still an excellent, stylish, if fairly expensive restaurant with good French cooking.
Jade Garden, Star House, 3 Salisbury Road, Kowloon (tel: 27306888) and 1 Hysan Avenue, Causeway Bay (tel: 25779332). Long-standing restaurants with solid reputation for standard Cantonese cooking.
Jimmy's Kitchen, South China Building, 1 Wyndham Street (tel: 25265293) and 1st Floor, Kowloon Centre, 29 Ashley Road, Kowloon (tel: 23684027). Originally in Shanghai, easygoing and serving good, comforting food at reasonable prices.
Luk Yu Tea-House, 26 Stanley Street (tel: 25235464). Old tea-house well known for its *dim sum*.
Stanley's, 86 Main Street, Stanley (tel: 28138873). Provençal cooking and fine views overlooking the bay.
Tai Woo, 15 Wellington Street, Central (tel: 25245618) and 14 Hillwood Road, Kowloon (tel: 3699773). Fine Cantonese food at reasonable prices.
Vegi Food Kitchen, Highland Mansion, 8 Cleveland Street, Causeway Bay (tel: 28906660). Small vegetarian restaurant specialising in beancurd dishes and stuffed mushrooms.
Yung Kee, 32 Wellington Street (tel: 25221624). Restaurant with very good reputation serving excellent seafood and roast goose.

Jinan

Daminghu, Daming Lu (tel: 20584). Located not far from the Daming Lake.
Yanxitang, 292 Quangcheng Lu (tel: 23451). In the older part of town, specialising in lotus and mushrooms.

Kunming

Dongfeng Restaurant, Wucheng Lu (tel: 24808). Very good food, particularly the 'pot-cooked chicken'.
Guoqiao Mixian, Nantong Lu. Noted for Kunming's famous dish, 'Across the Bridge Noodles'.
Yiheyuan, Zhengyi Lu. Noted for its roast duck.

Lanzhou

Lanzhou Canting, Jiuquan Lu. Large restaurant with a good reputation in an area not noted for good food.

Macao

Alfonso III, Rua Central 11 (tel: 586272). Solid and reasonably priced, in the Portuguese/Macanese style

and open from noon to 11.
Bela Vista, Rua Comendador Kou, Ho Neng 8 (tel: 965 333). Macao's most exclusive restaurant with matching prices.
Fat Siu Lau, Rua da Felicidade 64 (tel: 573585). The oldest and most famous restaurant in Macao; food no longer in the first rank, but still good; relaxed atmosphere.

Nanjing

Nanjing food, part of the Huaiyang school, is similar to that of Shanghai, with salted duck a speciality.
Dasanyuan, 40 Zhongshan Lu (tel: 6649027). A good all-round restaurant with cheap and cheerful section.
Jiangsu Restaurant, 26 Jiankang Lu (tel: 623698). A large establishment specialising in the local salt duck.
Maxiangxing, 5 Zhongshan Beilu. Good general restaurant, very popular.

Nanning

Bailong, Renminyuan. Specialises in game dishes.
Nanhu Fish Restaurant, Nanhuyuan (tel: 2477). Fish from nearby lake.

Qingdao

Chunhelou, 146 Zhongshan Lu (tel: 2827371). Seafood dishes with scallops and sea cucumber.

Quanzhou

Mantang, 3 Zhongshan Zhonglu (tel: 2887). Known for the regional specialities of Fujian/Canton.

Shanghai

Fangshan Tang, Dahua Hotel, 914 Yanan Lu (tel: 252 3079). Food is served in Qing imperial style.
The Luyangchun, 763 Nanjing Xilu. Near the People's Park specialising both in snacks and Huaiyang and Sichuan food.
Meilongzhen Jiujia, 22 Nanjing Xilu (tel: 2551157). One of the most famous restaurants in the city specialising in hot and spicy Sichuan cooking.
The Meixin Fandian, 314 Shaanxi Nanlu. In the old French concession; serves Cantonese food and specialises in Meixin crisp chicken and crispy duck.
Old Shanghai Restaurant, 242 Fuyou Lu (tel: 3289850). On the edge of the most picturesque part of Shanghai, the old Chinese town; Shanghai/Huaiyang cuisine.
The Qingzhen Fandian, 457 Nanjing Donglu (tel: 222264). Muslim restaurant specialising in beefsteaks, mutton, lamb, toffee apples.
The Red House, 37 Shaanxi Nanlu (tel: 2565748). Formerly called Chez Louis, this is something of an anachronism, serving Western food in an old-fashioned environment.
Xinghualou, 343 Fuzhou Lu (tel: 3263492). In a central location, dating from the 19th century, and specialising in Cantonese food.
The Yangzhou, 308 Nanjing Donglu. Well located, specialising in Yangzhou or Huaiyang cuisine, and very popular.
Yongjiang Zhuangyuan Lou, 162 Xizang Zhonglu (tel: 225280). Well located, specialising in seafood and other regional dishes.

Shenyang

Laobian Eating House, 6 Zhongyang Lu (tel: 447941). Famous for dumplings, served with warm vodka.
Lumingchun, Zhonghua Lu (tel: 25127). Seafood and chicken restaurant, plus the hotpots famous in the area.

Suzhou

Dongting, Renmin Lu. Good reputation for local dishes.
Songhelou, 141 Guanqian Jie (tel: 777003). Old restaurant (Emperor Qianlong is reputed to have eaten here), well known for crispy duck.
Xinjufeng, 657 Renmin Lu (tel: 7737994). Many duck and chicken dishes.

Tianjin

Dengyinglou, 94 Binjiang Dao (tel: 7302071). Shandong cooking.
Quanjude, 3 Rongji Dajie (tel: 7350046). Noted for the Beijing version of Shandong cooking.
Food Street, in the southern central area, is lined with restaurants and snack bars.

Ürümqi

First Muslim Restaurant, 16 Hongmian Lu (tel: 2177). Local cooking based on lamb and kebabs.

Wuhan

Laotongcheng, 1 Dazhi Lu, Hankou. Specialises in the dumplings which are highly favoured in Hubei province.
Shengli Hotel, 222 Shengli Lu (tel: 21023). Period charm, excellent local specialities.

Wuxi

Wuxi specialises in Wuxi spare ribs and whitebait from Lake Tai.
Hubin Hotel, Liyuan Lu, Lake Tai (tel: 668812). The hotel is short of character, but the food is usually good.
Jiangnan Caiguan, 435 Zhongshan Lu. Restaurant with consistent reputation.

Xiamen

Ludao, 230 Zhongshan Lu (tel: 22264). Good Xiamen food, in the Fujian/Cantonese tradition.
Seafood Restaurant, 1 Fengchaoshan Lu (tel: 25561). Local seafood is the staple here.

Xi'an

Dongya, 45 Luomashi Jie (tel: 28410). Local dishes as well as Shanghai cooking.
Jiaozi Restaurant, 29 Jiefang Lu (tel: 29087). Dumplings of all shapes, sizes, flavours.
The Xi'an, 298 Dong Dajie (tel: 712037). Serves plain food, including noodles and mutton dishes.

Yinchuan

Hanmin Canting, Wenhua Lu. Good, solid fare in an area not noted for its food.

Zhengzhou

Restaurant on the Water, Renmin Yuan (tel: 23317). Pleasant location on the banks of the Jinshui River.
Shaolin, Jinshui Lu (tel: 22441). Specialising in regional dishes.

Index

A

C

D

Picture credits

The Automobile Association wishes to thank the following photographers and libraries for their assistance in the preparation of this book.

INGRID MOREJOHN/BILDBRUKET PICTURE WORKS was commissioned to take all the pictures in this book with the exception of:

AA PHOTO LIBRARY 222a (M Trelawny), 222b (R Holmes), 223a (R Victor). **BRIDGEMAN ART LIBRARY** 249a *Willows and Distant Mountains* by Ma Yuan (*fl.*1190–1225) Song Dynasty (ink and colours on silk) Zhang Shui Cheng/Bridgeman Art Library, London. **MARY EVANS PICTURE LIBRARY** 42b Sun Yatsen, 43b Shanghai, The Club 1926. **FEI CHONG XIAN** 188b Shanghai Peace Hotel. **RONALD GRANT ARCHIVES** 78a *Raise the Red Lantern*, 118/9 *The Last Emperor*. **HULTON DEUTSCH COLLECTION LTD** 119b Pu-Yo Henry. **MAGNUM PHOTOS LTD** 44a Chiang Kaishek, Madam Chiang & General Stilwell, 46/7 People's Army arriving at Yanan (Rene Burri), 111b Mao on Long March (Rene Burri). **NATURE PHOTOGRAPHERS LTD** 158a Père David's deer (E A Janes), 158b Giant panda (R Tidman), 159 Tiger (B Burbidge). **THE MANSELL COLLECTION** 42/3 Port of Shanghai

Contributors

Series adviser: Christopher Catling **Joint series editor**: Susi Bailey
Copy editor: Susan Whimster **Designer**: Design Directions
Verifier: Anna Johnston **Indexer**: Marie Lorimer